Sword and Scalpel

THE LIFE
of
Edward Hand
of
LANCASTER

William W. Betts, Jr.

HERITAGE BOOKS
2014

HERITAGE BOOKS
AN IMPRINT OF HERITAGE BOOKS, INC.

Books, CDs, and more—Worldwide

For our listing of thousands of titles see our website at
www.HeritageBooks.com

Published 2014 by
HERITAGE BOOKS, INC.
Publishing Division
5810 Ruatan Street
Berwyn Heights, Md. 20740

Copyright © 2014 William W. Betts, Jr.

Heritage Books by the author:
Bombardier John Harris and the Rivers of the Revolution
Rank and Gravity, The Life of General John Armstrong of Carlisle
Sword and Scalpel: The Life of Edward Hand of Lancaster

All rights reserved. No part of this book may be reproduced or transmitted in any form or by any means, electronic or mechanical, including photocopying, recording or by any information storage and retrieval system without written permission from the author, except for the inclusion of brief quotations in a review.

International Standard Book Numbers
Paperbound: 978-0-7884-5571-1
Clothbound: 978-0-7884-9046-0

for Maddie, Stephanie, and Will

Where he once stood, to-day we gladly stand,
Like him, we view the gracious landscape o'er,
And calling up "the days that are no more,"
We think upon the men who served our land,
A noble, brave and patriotic band.
O Conestoga! stream of ancient lore,
We would thy memories of old restore
And carve in stone the name of Edward Hand!
Our country claims him as her patriot son –
The friend, the counselor of Washington!
All fresh and verdant, bright and undecayed
The laurels he has won shall never fade.
And, clearly written on the rolls of Fame,
A hero's meed shall ever crown his name.

— Mary N. Robinson

Contents

A Prefatory Note................................... ix
Chronology....................................... xi
Chapter I: The New World.......................... 1
Chapter II: The Gathering Storm.................... 15
Chapter III: Cambridge and Boston.................. 23
Chapter IV: New York City......................... 39
Chapter V: The New Jersey Campaign................ 67
Chapter VI: Fort Pitt............................... 83
Chapter VII: Wyoming............................. 141
Chapter VIII: The Sullivan Expedition............... 151
Chapter IX: Yorktown.............................. 197
Chapter X: Newburgh and New Windsor.............. 235
Chapter XI: Lancaster.............................. 245
Chapter XII: Rock Ford............................ 277
Afterword.. 291
Appendix A...................................... 297
Appendix B...................................... 301
Image Credits.................................... 303
Works Consulted.................................. 309
Notes.. 323
Index.. 353

A Prefatory Note

Some years ago, as I was rummaging around in the chambers of the Cumberland County Historical Society, in Carlisle, Pennsylvania, I happened to run into an old friend, who had been a college classmate and a history major. After some catching-up chatter, aware that I was a casual student of the American Revolution, he inquired into whether I had ever heard of Edward Hand. I was certainly happy to be able to reply in the affirmative, ever how shakily. I said, "Well, yes, I know that he was one of Washington's generals, that he was big at the battle of Assunpink and on the Sullivan Expedition. And wasn't he a physician?" Acknowledging all of this, my friend reported that in his research he was running into Hand's name all the time. "But, did you know," he said, "that there has never appeared a real biography of him. You ought to look into it."

Well at that time I was busy with projects. But I never forgot what my friend had mentioned, and ever so many years later, I did look into it. And the more I pored over the resources the more interested I became in what I could see was a most important and consequential figure of colonial times. Moreover, partly because I have always been quite fond of the Irish, he steadily spiraled in my esteem. And now here I am with the story of General Hand of Lancaster. I very much hope that this account is a faithful one.

Naturally I am much indebted to a great many very helpful people. I should mention first the very generous and gracious staff at the Rock Ford Plantation home of Edward Hand (Melinda Weber, Director Sam Slaymaker, Brian Mclaughlin, et al.). Very accommodating also have been Heather Tennies, and the very kind and obliging staff of the Lancaster County Historical Society; and Cary Hutto, Assistant Director of Archives, Hillary Kativa, and the good people at the Historical Society of Pennsylvania, custodians of the Papers of General Hand. The always resourceful Harrison Wick, Special Collections Librarian, and University Archivist, Indiana University of Pennsylvania, certainly deserves gratitude. Very helpful, too, has been historian Professor Sean Heuvel of the American Studies program at Christopher Newport University, who for a long time has been urging research on General Edward Hand. I am grateful for the help of my Ottawa, Kansas, friends, Woody and Barbara Dew, as well as for that of Aaron McWilliams, Reference Archivist at the Pennsylvania State Archives. Nor could any work of this kind proceed nowadays with much confidence without *The Papers of George Washington*, ed by W. W. Abbott, et al.

Of course by the time I was ready to tackle Dr. Hand, one of his descendants, Michel Williams Craig of Connecticut, had produced his *Winter's Doctor*, a reverent study of the general. This first biography provides a very helpful map of the regions in which Edward Hand was active.

Finally there should be acknowledged the historians of the 18th century America, especially those who have been occupied with the Revolution, who have provided essential data and relevant information. And certainly there would be no book at all without the industry and abilities of my graphics and formatting lieutenant Thomas Betts.

Bill Betts

Chronology

Lancaster County formed	May 10, 1729
Edward Hand born, at Clydruff, King's County, province of Leinster, Ireland	December 31, 1744
Katherine Ewing born	March 25, 1751
Edward Hand earns medical degree	1767
Hand made surgeon's mate in 18th Royal Irish Regiment of Foot	spring, 1767
Hand arrives in Philadelphia	July 11, 1767
Hand departs Philadelphia for Fort Pitt	August, 26, 1767
Hand commissioned ensign	1772
Hand settles in Lancaster	1773-1774
Lancaster Committee of Correspondence formed	June 15, 1774
Hand marries Katharine Ewing	March 13, 1775
Continental Congress authorizes six companies of expert riflemen for Pennsylvania	June 14, 1775

Hand commissioned Lieutenant Colonel of Pennsylvania's First Battalion of Riflemen	June 25, 1775
Hand commissioned Colonel	March 7, 1776
Battle of New York	August 22, 1776–November 20, 1776
Battle of Trenton	December 26, 1776
Battle of Assunpink	January 1-2, 1777
Battle of Princeton	January 3, 1777
First Middlebrook encampment	winter of 1776-77
Hand commissioned brigadier general	April 1, 1777
Hand appointed Head of the Western Department	April 1, 1777
Hand at Fort Pitt	June 1, 1777-May 26, 1778
Massacre at Wyoming	July 3, 1778
Hand receives field commission to Brigadier General	September 17, 1778, to rank from April 1, 1777
Hand made Head of the Northern Department	November 8, 1778
Second Middlebrook encampment	November 25, 1778 - June 3, 1779

Sullivan Campaign	July 31, 1779-October 7, 1779
Battle of Newtown	August 28, 1779
Hand made brigade commander	March 25, 1780
Battle of Springfield	June 23, 1780
Hand made Adjutant General	January 8, 1781
Siege of Yorktown	October, 6-19, 1781
Hand made Major General of Pennsylvania State troops	May 10, 1783
Hand elected to the Continental (Confederation) Congress	November 12, 1783
Hand elected to Pennsylvania State General Assembly	1785
Hand, a Presidential elector from Pennsylvania, votes for George Washington as President	February 4, 1789
Hand a delegate to the Pennsylvania Constitutional Convention	1789-90
Hand commands troops to suppress the Whiskey Rebellion	April, 1794
George Washington appointed Commander-in-Chief of United States armies	July 3, 1798

Hand appointed Major General in the United States Provisional Army	1798
Edward Hand dies at Rock Ford	Sept. 3, 1802
Katherine Hand dies at Rock Ford	June 21, 1805
John Hand commits suicide at Rock Ford	November 13, 1807

I

The New World

The whole country is one continuous wood.

Not long after the conclusion of the Pontiac wars in colonial America, there arrived in the Quaker City of Brotherly Love a seemingly ordinary soldier who was in fact a most extraordinary Irish lad. He would one day play a huge role in the birth of a new nation.

When the young Irish army soldier known as Edward Hand stepped onto the docks at Philadelphia on July 11, 1767, he was astounded by what he saw. Before him was a huge town,[1] teeming with strange people going hither and yon.

It was a port city of course, and active in immigration, but it was also a trading center, with everything hustle and bustle. It was nothing like his native Ireland village, not even much like Dublin, nor any other town he had ever seen.

A little tour of the streets, which were not wandering avenues, like those of the Irish villages, but straight, and intersecting at right angles, provided a sense of the great difference. The streets were ugly with refuse and the excrement of horses and dogs. The people he strolled among were largely German (Many signs were in the German language only!), or Dutch, or English. Although he knew that there were many of his countrymen here in what was known as Pennsylvania, it was in vain that for a long time he listened closely to the speech, longing for the brogue of an Irishman.

The talk, as well as he could make it out, was all of land, of land that could be had at an attractive price, and perhaps for no fee at all. He heard talk of land to the west. He heard names like Lancaster and Carlisle and York and Shippensburg. He got the impression that many of the people he was observing would not be long in Philadelphia.

It was a new world and a strange one for the young Edward Hand. He was a wide-eyed youngster, not yet twenty-three years old. He was Irish through and through. He had been born to John and Dorothy Hand in a beautiful, almost idyllic, pastoral nook of the Emerald Isle, on the last day of the year 1744, so it was. It was a tiny parish that he was reared in, Clydruff (sometimes Clyduff), of King's County, [2] a little west of Dublin. He drifted back in his mind's eye to the River Shannon, to the tall peaks, like Stillbrook Hill and Wolftrap Mountain, from which, on a clear day, he could enjoy a breathtaking, panoramic view of nearly the entire county. He was remembering the great peatlands and the many bogs, and the lovely little lakes. Images of old castles and beautiful gardens floated through his mind. He was thinking that his Ireland had charm. This Philadelphia, well, maybe it had a lot going for it, but nothing close to charm.

He was wondering, as he had done many times during the past year, whether he had done the right thing when he elected not to complete the fifth year of medical training that was required to be certified a full-fledged physician. He had very much enjoyed his studies at Trinity College in Dublin, [3] but he longed for excitement, and when he saw the opportunity, with the training that he so far had, to become a Surgeon's Mate in the famous 18th Royal Irish Regiment of Foot he seized it. It was in the spring of 1766.

The regiment that he had joined, an infantry regiment of course, enjoyed a long and storied history. Young Edward knew all about the 18th Royal Irish Regiment of Foot, that it dated all the way back to 1684, when it was organized by the Earl of Granard from a few small companies of soldiers in Ireland. It could, he very well knew, boast some notable military achievements, enough in fact that it had won the right to display the Arms of the King on its colors. [4] Young Hand was proud of his commission, awarded by King George III. And so here he was, in this strange land, with no family to support him, and, indeed, not even any welcoming friends. As an element of the British Army, the Regiment, which had been stationed in Dublin Castle, had been ordered to America on the first day of the year, 1767, one day after

Arms of the King

Surgeon's Mate Edward Hand had enjoyed his twenty-third birthday. The transport ships, carrying wives and children as well as the soldiers, had finally sailed out into the Atlantic from Cobh, on the south side of Great Island, in the harbor at Cork, on May 20. The sailing was duly noted next day by *The Dublin Journal*: "Yesterday the Transports with the 16th, 18th, and 26th Regiments of Foot on board, sailed from the Cove, with a fair wind for North America." [5]

The passage required fifty-two days, young Hand finally setting foot in Philadelphia in the evening of July 11. The regiment was promptly quartered in the Second Street

Barracks.

And now young Edward was musing. He had abandoned a truly beautiful homeland for the totally unknown. And he was committed to a service which he did not perfectly understand. But he now determined to leave off the nostalgia and to stop thinking, "What if . . .?" He was in America now, and he would make the most of it.

As it happened, the 18th Regiment of Foot, under the command of Lt. Colonel John Wilkins, which had arrived in Philadelphia July 11, would, except for a small detachment scheduled to remain at Fort Pitt, be marching by way of Pittsburgh to the Ohio and down that river to the Illinois country.

In the days that followed the arrival of his ship, during the time he was allowed on his own, Hand wandered through the city. He had been reared an Anglican, and he was easily and much impressed by the stunning beauty of the Christ Episcopal Church on 2nd Street between Arch and Market Streets. But he marveled at the absence of any church steeple with a clock. There was no striking of the hours in this town. He was jostled a good bit by the swarms of strange people he moved among. He had been alerted by his fellow soldiers to beware of pickpockets and swindlers. And, though he knew from the presence of the gaslights that the streets had some illumination at night, he was not about to do any exploring after hours.

According to the reliable memoirs of the regiment's quartermaster, George Buttricks, the officers were enjoying their Philadelphia evenings in the lively company of Madeira and the American ladies. But Hand was not an officer, and not inclined that way anyway.

Edward did enjoy a meeting with the forty-nine year-old celebrated fur trader George Croghan. [6] Croghan was Irish, too, and had emigrated to Philadelphia from Dublin twenty-six years ago. This meeting later events would make most memorable.

And his time in Philadelphia was to be short. When late in the summer of the arrival year of 1767, a small detachment of the 18th Regiment of Foot was ordered to Fort Pitt, Surgeon's Mate Edward Hand found himself in that body. It was a company of officers and some non-coms, who had in their care some new recruits intended to relieve the 34th Regiment of Foot, which was stationed at Fort Pitt, one of the British garrisons in the far west. It was hoped that the recruits could be at Fort Pitt by May 21, 1768. The company was commanded by Captain Charles Edmonstone. [7] Amply provisioned and sufficiently equipped, it departed Philadelphia in plenty of time to reach Fort Pitt by the middle of May, for the departure date was August 26.

Young Edward Hand was ready to go. He was a fairly tall man, easily a good six feet, and slender, physically strong and mentally most uncommonly alert and curious. But there was more to him than that. There was something about him – what was it? – there was *something* about him.

For now, he was just wondering about Fort Pitt. Just where in the world was it? How long would they be on the march? What about Indians? Are there villages along the way? These questions were not long in receiving answers.

From the time the march began, Hand and his fellow soldiers were hearing about Fort Pitt and its exciting history. He learned the location right off, and was made most eager to see firsthand the beautiful junction of the rivers Monongahela and Allegheny. He learned right off, too, just what a distance the regiment would be marching, and he was not all that happy with the figure, which was 300 miles! What does this mean? A wilderness march of twenty-five days? A month? Two months? Three?

But he knew by now that along the way he would be taking in a beautiful, forested region. Indeed, someone had informed the soldiers that "The whole country is one continuous wood," so unlike his native Irish home, where there could be found almost no forest at all. They would be camping in the wild of course, but they would be from time to time accommodated also in the homes of gracious people in the interesting villages, like Lancaster and Carlisle and Bedford.

The route they would follow was known at that time as the Forbes Road. From Philadelphia they would march to Lancaster, and on to Carlisle, the jumping off place. Here at Carlisle their first guide, who had proved quite competent, was replaced by a second, a man provided by "the first citizen of Carlisle," Colonel John Armstrong, who was well acquainted with the frontier and with the route they would be following.

This guide turned out to be every bit as Irish as the soldiers themselves. He was a frontiersman, no question. He wore moccasins, deerskin leggings, and a very loose ash-colored hunting shirt. At his side the soldiers could make out a broad-bladed knife, a hatchet and a wooden canteen. He carried a rifle. His attire was capped off by an almost comical round hat trailing the tail of a raccoon. Armstrong had advised the party that this guide "is a very good man. Has been to Fort Pitt many times. Has only one fault that I would mention, and you'll soon discover it."

And so they did. To put a polite term on it, the guide was garrulous. Unlike their previous guide, whom the soldiers could hardly get to speak, this man rarely ceased his talk. But the soldiers never learned his name. He insisted on being addressed as "Cooch" only. "That'll do for me," he said. One soldier suggested that his actual name was probably something like Patrick O'Leary.

As the column, moving generally in the Indian fashion, single file, set out from Carlisle, Cooch of course could hardly have an audience of more than two or three, and so found himself expounding only to the air a good bit. But when the company paused to rest, he would promptly launch into a narration about the country to the west. What they were hearing about the recent siege of Fort Pitt was most impressive to them, how the garrison of 150 men, with settlers who had fled their homes, had resisted the assault of a huge Indian war party for four months, and how the siege had finally been lifted by the British forces under Colonel Henri Bouquet, in late August of just four years ago, with the miraculous defeat of the warriors at some defile called Bushy Run.

But it did not lift their spirits a whole lot to hear about the atrocities that had occurred at just about that time, like those of the Paxton Boys and the brutal murders of the helpless and innocent Conestoga Indians, near Lancaster, or of the ruthless murder of schoolmaster Enoch Brown and his pupils, or of the Frederick Stump barbarities.

What they needed most to learn was about Fort Pitt itself. There was lots out there to hear about. Bit by bit Hand and his fellow soldiers came to understand, mostly from Cooch, who seemed to know everything they longed to hear, how the French a long time ago had turned away a party of Virginians who were building a fort on the spit of land that brought the rivers together. They discovered that the French then proceeded to erect a fort which they named Duquesne. They were horrified to hear from Cooch that at the site of this fort a British army, under General Edward Braddock, determined on the capture of the fort, was instead almost totally destroyed.

"But why is it called Fort Pitt?" asked one. And then the very touching account of the heroic Scotsman, General John Forbes, who though very ill and close to death, commanded an army just a few years ago (marching along this very road) to capture the fort without a battle. He had it named for the British Prime Minister William Pitt.

The general had promptly ordered the construction of a large and "impregnable" stronghold, and he gave its first command to Colonel Hugh Mercer (whom Edward Hand, by and by, would get to know very, very well).

And General Forbes, who had died in the March

following the November capture of the fort, was buried in Philadelphia, in the chancel of the Christ Church, by which Edward Hand had been so much impressed.

The soldiers were happy to have that history of course. But they wondered, too, about the town of Pittsburgh. They were not much taken by what they were told by people who had been there. It was apparently a rough town, made unwholesome by lechery and drunkenness and riotous, destructive behavior. Pittsburgh of course lay at the heart of the Indian country, and "incidents," which could be blamed on both whites and Indians, regularly occurred.

The little caravan was well into its march by the time Cooch wandered out of his educating. Now, some 100 miles beyond Carlisle, the detachment came to Bedford, where General John Forbes had built a fort on that long march of 1758 to the French Fort Duquesne. As there were but a few scattered houses here, Bedford could hardly be called a village even.

Ligonier, at which site Forbes had constructed another fort, was next. It was on the Loyalhanna, a strikingly beautiful spot. As at Bedford, there were to be seen here but a few log cabins, and some small clearings. And then nothing but the rude forest road wandering through the vast woods and climbing the ridges of the Appalachians.

From Cooch and from interested parties whom the soldiers met along the march and at the various settlements the members of the tiny company heard a lot about Indians. They had never seen Indians. There were no Indians in Ireland, there were no Indians in Philadelphia. There were a lot of Indians to their west. Even though they were assured that the frontier was much more quiet now since the end of a rebellion that was led by some chief whose name they were told was Pontiac, they remained a bit anxious. They were British soldiers. The Indians had been warring against the British, and with great success. Hadn't Pontiac laid waste to all of the British forts, except

~ *The New World* ~

Detroit and Niagara, and Fort Pitt of course.

So, as they marched along, they remained wary and nervous. From the time they had left the flat country of Carlisle, they had found the terrain increasingly difficult. The road or, more properly, the trail, was rough beyond description, here and there swampy, and much of the time rocky and mountainous.

The party had been able in just two days from Carlisle to reach Fort Bedford. Captain Edmonstone allowed two days of rest here, but, considering that sufficient, he soon had the company on the march again. Difficult marshes were occurring now here and there, and great clouds of gnats and deer flies and greenheads and mosquitoes swarmed over the caravan. These took some getting used to.

But the springs! What a joy it was for the company to come upon a mountain spring, a tiny pool of clear, cold water, with clean sand at its bottom, and sometimes embraced by a structure of stones fashioned by some wayfarer, with a large flat one provided for kneeling. More precious than his musket, or his tent, or even his boots, was the soldier's leather or wooden canteen; and at such a spring he would fill it gratefully.

From time to time they sensed the presence of Indians, and from time to time they had their suspicions confirmed. Wraith-like, half-naked figures would float among the shadows, vanishing so abruptly and completely as to make their appearance seem unreal. Still, no run-ins did occur; no assault was ever made upon the column. The Indians seemed more curious than hostile. Cooch did not even remark upon them. "Uneventful" was the tag that Edmonstone would finally place upon the trip.

But the night sounds. Although wearied as they always were at the end of a day's march, and though they knew sentries were posted, sleep did not come easily. From the forest darkness emerged an unsettling symphony of sound: the "hoohoohoo-hoohoo" of the great horned owl, the mournful howling of wolves, and the haunting call of the spectral whippoorwill. Sometimes so close would sound the "whip-poor-will-ll" that the soldiers could make out the little cluck at the end of the call. And often this call, as well as the hooting of the owl, would produce in them the chilling wonder whether it might not be a signal sounded by some cunning warrior. Cooch had assured them all that the Indians never attack at night. Nevertheless on the nights when the soldiers were camping out, it would be a most fitful sleep they would fall into, with the musket close.

By and by the column arrived at the site of Colonel Bouquet's miraculous defeat of the Indian war party. As they approached what was now being called Edge Hill, Cooch remarked that "it was right here, on this very spot, that I lost my brother. A good man so he was. Left his missus and two wee ones." And then to the soldiers eager to hear details, he told the story, how Bouquet after the first day's fighting felt little hope, and how on the second day, just at daybreak, with a clever ruse, he had "invited" the warriors into the midst of his troops and panicked them.

Twenty-five days into the march the company arrived at the site of the settlement established by the pioneer Christopher Gist, with eleven other families, some fourteen years ago. For those close enough to hear, Cooch had a lot to tell about Christopher Gist.

Now Edmonstone has his Irish foot soldiers close to Fort Pitt. The next place of rest, a little north and west of the Gist plantation, was the stagecoach stop known as Widow Meyers'. It was sometimes known as Widow Meyers' Wayside Inn or Tavern.

On the next day the troops, definitely feeling some fatigue, managed only five miles, coming to rest at Bullock Pens, about which Cooch pleased them all with the announcement that there remained only ten miles to Fort Pitt. Bullock Pens was a tiny settlement, but it had acquired a bit of fame because of the vibrant preaching of the pioneer Presbyterian minister the Reverend Charles Clinton Beatty, whom, Cooch, as he was quick to report, had heard many times.

Beatty had been with the General John Forbes after the fall of Fort Duquesne. The church here and the settlement were called Bullock Pens because the community had developed in the area where General Forbes penned his beef cattle during the French and Indian Wars. [8]

Captain Edmonstone did not feel that any rest would be in order here, they were so close. The troops were much fatigued of course, but they were near the welcome end of their march and eager to close it out. Still, it certainly would have taken a spectacle much more ravishing than what finally appeared before the weary soldiers to lift their spirits. They felt much as did a later soldier, who had just completed the march from Carlisle: "We finally arrived at Pittsburgh, a poor place then, — not even a frame house in it. There was a line of soldiers' barracks, frame-work. There were several log houses, with a quarter of an acre of ground attached, which formed the city at that time. There was no real road across the mountain, and from Gettysburg [very near Carlisle] everything was carried by pack-mules. Not much there [in Pittsburgh] but whisky, and it would take a month's wages to buy a gill with the money we were paid with! About eighty dollars good money would buy a quarter of an acre of ground with a log house on it then, but I would not have had one even for a gift if I had to stay there; it was such a poor place and I thought always would be." [9]

Nevertheless, Captain Edmonstone had the company pause at the first view of the fort, which had for so long been their object. Edmonstone was not much for pretty speeches. He never adorned his instructions with any kind of inspiriting phrase or commendation. Here he said only, "Boys, there she is. We've made it." Then, after a moment, he issued his last order of the journey: "We're not going to march in at quick-step, but we are going to march in smartly. Everybody straighten up. We're here."

So on a day in the early winter of 1768, and long before they were due, the little company, footsore and fatigued, heavily bearded and weathered in the face, marched boldly into Fort Pitt. The enthusiastic welcome which they received from the garrison, and especially from the company they were relieving, or augmenting, made them all feel pretty good about what they had accomplished, despite their heavy weariness.[10]

Young Edward Hand had no idea how long he would be stationed here. It turned out to be more than four years!

But it was a quiet time, with no big battles to be fought. The soldiers did entertain the seven companies of the 18th Regiment which had been ordered in May of 1768 to the Illinois country by way of Fort Pitt. Young Hand was particularly happy to see the regiment's surgeon Thomas Thomasson, whom of course he knew very well. And he was very happy when it was decided to leave Thomasson at the fort, along with two companies, when the other five companies set out for the Illinois country. For some time Hand and the recruits who had been at the fort were kept very busy in helping to prepare these troops for their journey down the Ohio and their long trip west. The five companies destined for Illinois, under the command of Lt. Colonel John Wilkins, departed Fort Pitt at the beginning of August; two remained at the fort.

During his time at Fort Pitt Edward Hand entered into the first of what would be many land speculation transactions. In 1769 occurred his first acquisition of land in North America. It was a tract totaling 1,423 acres, which he secured in two separate purchases.[11]

General John Forbes at the close of 1758 had ordered the building of an "English" fort at the site of Fort Duquesne. For thirteen years the British retained command of the structure, and kept it garrisoned. But in 1772, the fort, together with all of its properties, was sold by Major Charles Edmonstone to two speculators, Alexander Ross, a fur trader, and an Irishman known as William Thompson. The date of the bill of sale was October 10, 1772. The sales price was fifty pounds New York currency. [12]

The detachment of the Irish 18th Regiment, according to information supplied by Edward Hand, "surgeon of the said Regiment," in withdrawing was leaving behind only a corporal and three men "to take care of the boats, batteaus, etc."

Edward Hand was a witness to the sale and was empowered "to receive from the said Alexander Ross one-third of the sales of the ruins of the fort, by virtue of a contract subsisting between the said Edward Hand and the Petitioners." As the transaction appeared to many to be "irregular," protest was lodged by the settlers of the area (who naturally feared loss of protection) against the whole deal. But the sale was allowed, and thus jurisdiction over the region passed from the English Crown to the colony known as Pennsylvania (which was, not surprisingly, challenged by the colony known as Virginia). [13]

And not long after, as Edmonstone had been ordered to abandon the post, the Irish Regiment pulled out. For the return trip to Philadelphia, some of the Irish regiment that had gone beyond Fort Pitt to Illinois traversed the same road back. Others went all directions, to Fort Detroit, to Michilimackinac, to Niagara, to Oswego, to Vincennes. To judge from a letter that he wrote at a much later date (see below) it seems definite that the Irish soldier Edward Hand, through all of these deployments, had stayed on at Fort Pitt.

In any case, the Fort Pitt detachment, two companies apparently, which had been ordered in the summer of 1772 to return to Philadelphia, finally set out for the east. It was very late in the fall of that year. Hand, more than four years older than he was when he first set eyes on Fort Pitt, was now an officer, having purchased (with profits realized through his buying and selling of land parcels) his commission as an ensign bearing the date February 1772. [14] His new rank had made possible the office of supply officer in the regiment, but now, as he marched east, he was troubled some. He was not sure that service in the 18th Irish Regiment of Foot was his best option. As the company marched into Philadelphia, in December of 1772, he found himself still musing about his future in this new land.

II

The Gathering Storm

I am certain that you will be both surprised and troubled when I inform you that I last night received orders to join the Continental Army as Lt. Colonel to the rifle battalion, without any application from me.

— Edward Hand to Jasper Yeates

Somehow on the way west Hand had become enamored of the Lancaster area, one day to be known as "The Garden Spot of America." [1] On this return trip, with his original favorable impression reinforced, he perceived, too, that the region wanted a physician or two. He could appreciate that he could be a big help to the farm families, and he was now eager to get into a very different kind of professional life, the one he had prepared for so earnestly so many years ago, back there in Dublin. So on returning to Philadelphia, he promptly resigned the ensign's commission he had received two years ago (actually selling it to Charles Hoar for 400 pounds). The transaction date was June 24, 1774. [2] All in all he had devoted a good six years to the regiment. It was time to begin a new chapter.

He had learned about the Reverend Thomas Barton,

Rector of the Saint James Episcopal Church, one of Lancaster's most distinguished and popular citizens, and an Irishman like himself. He fortified himself with letters of introduction.

The popular minister was much taken with the young army surgeon, and even though Hand had discovered that the Lancaster physicians actually numbered ten (!), it all seemed like a good fit.

So, even before the year 1774 had expired, Dr. Edward Hand found himself comfortably at home in the settlement that had so much impressed him on the way west. It was Lancaster, in the region of the state that was so congenial to the Irish and the Scotch-Irish. At this time the settlement could boast some 2500 residents. He put out his shingle and embarked on the private practice of medicine. He did not want for patients. Indeed, he had his hands full, and as many of those who came to him (or whom he attended at their homes), were of the poorest, struggling farm families, he was providing diagnosis and treatment much of the time for no fee.

It was not long (Indeed he had been in Lancaster less than a year.) before he was struck by the charm of a young lady named Katherine Ewing. And it was not long after that that the two were married. The date was Monday, March 13, 1775. Katherine, the daughter of the prosperous Captain John Ewing and Sarah Yeates, a sister of Judge Jasper Yeates of Lancaster, would not be twenty-four for two weeks yet; Edward was thirty.

But it was not a good time. For some months now the people of the several colonies, most notably Massachusetts, had been protesting the taxes the King of England was levying upon them. As subjects of the King they had in fact quite an array of problems to address. Real trouble seemed not all that far away.

As the sense of injustice grew closer and closer to the unbearable, and the storm clouds roiled over Boston, support in the form of funds, pronouncements of sympathy, and militant expression came pouring into New England from other communities, like Salem, New Jersey, where on October 3, 1774, the citizens held a meeting to declare their outrage at the treatment their fellow colonials were suffering. Salem went on to raise $700, which was promptly dispatched to Boston.

In Carlisle, Pennsylvania, as early as the 12th of July of this year,1774, the vigilant Scotch-Irish convened a most enthusiastic public meeting. Nine resolutions were agreed to. They determined to place an embargo on British merchandise, including tea. They agreed to support the people of Boston with relief. They appointed a Committee of Correspondence, as urged by Philadelphia.

Even earlier than that, on June 15, citizens of the borough of Lancaster, Carlisle's neighbor, in response to a communication from the Committee of Correspondence in Philadelphia, had convened a public meeting at the courthouse. Just as the people of Carlisle were to do, the citizens of the community adopted a number of resolutions. For one thing, they agreed to a censure of the British Parliament. At the same time the people of Lancaster framed a resolution in which genuine sympathy was conveyed to the people of Boston.

The Boston Port Bill, which the British Parliament, angered by the Boston Tea Party, had just passed, March 31, 1774, was particularly obnoxious, for it shut down the Boston harbor until such time as restoration was made for the tea that had been destroyed. The Lancasterites here declared that until that bill was repealed they would not be importing or exporting anything. And, as so many communities in Pennsylvania were doing, the citizens vitalized the Committee of Correspondence they had elected.

This committee held its first meeting on July 2, and its members attended a more general meeting exactly one week later. Three actions were especially noteworthy: (1) the people of Lancaster declared that the King had no right to tax the colonies without the consent of the colonies; (2) they agreed to dispatch their Committee of Correspondence to the convention scheduled for Philadelphia July 15-21; and (3), noting that expressions of sympathy count for little if they are nothing more than high sounding words, the people came through with a subscription of 153 pounds, which was relayed to Boston by way of Philadelphia.

Meetings continued to be called as conditions failed to improve. Again, as other counties were doing, Lancaster elected, at a public meeting held December 15, a Committee of Observation, composed of fifty-five (!) members, twelve from the borough of Lancaster and forty-three from the twenty-three townships of the county. And on January 14 the Committee of Observation met at the courthouse to determine on their delegates to attend the big meeting to be convened in Philadelphia January 23.[4]

Dr. Hand was only on the fringes of all this. He was busy, busy in his medical practice. But he was a highly respected and very influential member of the community. Besides, he was Irish of course, and before long he was naturally drawn into the stream of anti-English sentiment for which the Irish were notorious. His support for the Cause had been much sought for, and before much longer he became extremely active. And when the people of the Lancaster region resolved to organize into a number of military companies,[5] he was summoned into the action. More and more of his precious physician time was devoted to the organizing of a colonial militia.

In many communities these militia companies were called Associators (founded by Benjamin Franklin in 1747), and so it was in Lancaster.

On the 14th of June, 1775, even before it had named a Commander-in-Chief, the Continental Congress began to build the army that would support the revolution. It passed a resolution to raise six companies of expert riflemen in

Pennsylvania, two companies in Maryland, and two in Virginia. These companies were to march north, to join the patriot army at Cambridge.

And just a week later the Congress called upon Pennsylvania for two more companies. These twelve companies, totaling, at quota, some 972 men (many of them very young), were to be formed into a battalion. And on July 11th still another Pennsylvania company was added to the regiment, now known as the Pennsylvania Rifle Regiment. In late June the Pennsylvania Assembly by resolution had made nominations to the Congress for field officers. Dr. Edward Hand on June 23, addressed a letter to his favored correspondent, Jasper Yeates. It opens with astonishing news: "I am certain that you will be both surprised and troubled when I inform you that I last night received Orders to join the Continental Army as Lt. Colonel to the Rifle Battalion, without any application from me."

Hand of course knew Jasper Yeates well enough to be confident of his approval: "Last Tuesday I consented to Mr. [George] Ross's [6] mentioning my name on condition that it did not interfere with any application or promise that had been made by, or given to, any other person. I am too well acquainted with your sentiments of the service, and your tender sense of your own, or a friend's Honour, to doubt your hesitating a moment to pronounce that I should obey the Glorious summons."

He is happy, too, to inform Yeates that he has the much desired approval of others who much matter to him: "My dear Kitty behaves heroically and worthy of herself on the occasion." And he has had a "very obliging letter" from his close Carlisle friend, Colonel William Thompson. The rest of his letter is affectionate small talk: "I am glad that your circuit brings you here the end of the week, as I shall have many things to say to you — Jessy [7] has been at Reading and is returned, as Mrs. Yeates writes by this opportunity I have nothing to add but Kitty's respects and my own to yourself and all our acquaintances at York — " [8]

On June 25 the recommendations of the Assembly were announced: For Colonel Commandant of the battalion, William Thompson of Carlisle; for second in command at the rank of Lieutenant Colonel, Edward Hand of Lancaster borough; for the rank of major, Robert Magaw of Carlisle.

This command, composed of nine companies of highly skilled frontiersmen, was to be recognized as Colonel Thompson's Battalion of Riflemen. When the army was reorganized (Jan. 1, 1776), the Battalion was named the First Continental Regiment of Foot; another reorganization (July 1, 1776), changed the name again, this time to the First Pennsylvania Regiment of the Continental Line.

Each of the nine companies was to be commanded by a captain, who would have as his staff three lieutenants, four sergeants, and four corporals. A drummer (or trumpeter), and sixty-eight privates completed the roster. Most of the soldiers were Irish or Scotch-Irish; those in companies six and seven were largely German.

These men, volunteers all, were enlisting for a term of one year. Each soldier would be paid by the Continental Congress. Captain of the company would receive twenty dollars per month; each of the three lieutenants would be receiving thirteen and one-third dollars, the sergeants eight dollars, the corporals, as well as the drummer (or trumpeter), each seven and one-third dollars. Privates were not treated so handsomely. Each private was to be paid six and two-thirds dollars, and was required to secure his own rifle and whatever other arms he preferred to carry — and his clothes. [9]

Congress was much pleased to hear that Lancaster County, which was expected to contribute one of the nine companies, instead came up with two.

The battalion of riflemen to be commanded by Carlisle's William Thompson, included three officers whose homes were within the borough of Lancaster: Dr. Hand would serve the battalion as a lieutenant colonel; and David Zeigler and Frederick Hubley accepted commissions at the rank of lieutenant. [10] Hubley was made the quartermaster in James Ross's company.[11] Hand's fellow physician, Dr. Robert Boyd of Lancaster, was named surgeon of the Rifle Battalion.

After organization, a lot of training in rifle fire, and some experience in military discipline, the battalion, under Colonel Thompson, was ready to go. It reported to the Commander-in-Chief, George Washington, in August of 1775, at Cambridge, Massachusetts, four months after Lexington/Concord.

III

Cambridge and Boston

They are remarkably stout and hardy, many of them exceeding six feet in height. They are dressed in white frocks or rifle shirts and round hats.

— Dr. James Thacher

General Edward Hand served George Washington and the Continental Army for the entire eight and one-half years of the Revolution. Not many of Washington's officers could make that claim, nor many of the common soldiers either. Moreover, Hand, except for short leaves of absence, was constantly active. He played a major role in bringing the Revolution to a successful close.

He was at Cambridge for the evacuation of the British army from Boston. He fought in the five-stage battle defense of New York City, at Long Island, during the siege of Manhattan, the watch-and-wait period of the Harlem Heights, the battle of White Plains, and the surrender of Forts Washington and Lee. He marched with Washington on the retreat through New Jersey. With Washington he crossed the Delaware. He was a prominent figure in the taking of Trenton and a *most important* officer for the second battle of Trenton and for the success at Princeton. He served fourteen months as Head of the Western

Department, stationed at Fort Pitt. And he had the command of the Northern Department, too, and was headquartered in Albany. As second in command, he marched with General John Sullivan in the 1779 anti-Indian expedition into the Seneca country of New York State. He was Adjutant General during the siege of Yorktown.

Throughout the war he conducted himself admirably and was an officer upon whom the Commander-in-Chief could rely without concern. In grateful recognition of his long and most distinguished career, the Continental Congress in September of 1783 promoted him by brevet to the rank of Major General. He did not resign from the Continental Army until November of that year, *after* the final signing of the Treaty of Paris.

And it all began in Cambridge, Massachusetts.

By the end of July, having been organized and drilled by their officers, some of the companies of Washington's infant army were already on their way to the Hudson River and on to Cambridge. By August 18 all were assembled at the encampment, regarded as light infantry, and ready to take on the British yet in Boston.

For their appearance and their condition and their spirit, the riflemen received high praise from those who studied them. One observed that "They are remarkably stout and hardy, many of them exceeding six feet in height. They are dressed in white frocks or rifle shirts and round hats." [1]

And another noted that "each man bore a rifle-barreled gun, a tomahawk or small axe, and a long knife, usually called a 'scalping knife,' which served for all purposes in the woods. His under-dress, by no means in a military style, was covered by a deep ash-colored hunting shirt, leggin[g]s and moccasins, if the latter could be procured. It was the silly fashion of those times for riflemen to ape the manners of savages." [2]

Awesome was their skill with the rifle. Those who were able to observe the riflemen at drill were very much impressed.

One observer reported: "These men are remarkable for the accuracy of their aim, striking a mark with great certainty at two hundred yards distance. At a review, a company of them, while on a quick advance, fired their balls into objects of seven inches diameter at the distance of two hundred and fifty yards. They are now stationed in our lines, and their shot have frequently proved fatal to British officers and soldiers who expose themselves to view, even at more than double the distance of common musket-shot."[3]

Of course the rifle, not only because it could reach a much greater distance, was much superior to the muskets used by most of the British, as well as by most of the recruits in Washington's army. Although it required more time to fire and reload than did the musket, and was not always designed for a bayonet, in the hands of a skilled rifleman it was much more dependable and accurate than the rather cumbersome musket.

Throughout the long war of the Revolution Edward Hand wrote regularly to his wife, addressing her as "Dearest Kitty," "My dear Kitty," "My dear girl," "Dear Angel," "My Dearest Life," and "My Love." As Katherine Hand, for the entire eight and one-half years, as well as for the time after the war when her husband served the country as a delegate to the Continental Congress, remained keenly interested in his activity, the exchange of letters totaled

Edward Burd

probably close to 300. But much as Hand heard from his dearest Kitty, it was not enough. He was impatient for letters, and was constantly scolding her for her unaccountable silence. He desired to know of his children and of Kitty's situation. Happily, Hand was granted leave from time to time, and, besides, there did occur occasions when his assignment put him near enough to Lancaster that the young couple could get together.

On August 20 of the first year of the war, 1775, Lieutenant Colonel Edward Hand, in the first letter of their correspondence which is extant, reported to his wife that his company had arrived at Cambridge with Colonel Thompson on the 17th, that the unit was originally delivered to General Charles Lee's immediate command but would soon be marching "four and a half miles" into the division commanded by General Israel Putnam. Carlisle's Major Magaw he noted would command a detachment dispatched to Cape Anne. [4]

Yeates home

He reported that Mr. [Edward] Burd [5] "is my Bedfellow and Messmate," and closed with "Let me once more entreat you to keep up your Spirits and remove every Anxiety for the Safety of My Dearest Kitty." [6]

Edward Burd, five (seven ?) years younger than Dr. Hand (Edward Burd's birthdate is sometimes recorded as 1749, sometimes 1751.), was the son of Colonel James Burd and Sarah Shippen Burd. He had studied law with Pennsylvania Chief Justice Edward Shippen, and in the third year of the Revolution would marry the judge's daughter Elizabeth. He was a close friend of Judge Jasper Yeates, and corresponded much with him. In one letter he urged his compliments to "your sociable Neighbour" (Edward Hand), who "is so intimate that he may almost be reckoned one of the family." [7] Indeed, these residents of the Lancaster region, the Yeateses, the Shippens, the Burds, and the Hands, were like one big happy family, very much interrelated, and constantly in close touch.

In one letter to Judge Yeates, sent from his law offices in Reading, Edward Burd, having just heard of the big event, urged Yeates, "I beg my best Compliments to the Bride and Bridegroom (Mrs. and Dr. Edward Hand)."

In the early going, after the Pennsylvania companies had reached the Cambridge-Boston region, some skirmishing occurring near Bunker Hill and Winter Hill and Prospect Hill [8] marked the first action of the regiment. And it was not long before the battalion saw real action. Hand reported in a letter of the 29th that his men on the 26th had taken possession of Ploughed Hill, in order to provide a picket guard for the provincial forces, and had thrown together some entrenchments there. The firing that ensued Hand described for Jasper Yeates three days later: ". . . the enemy . . . did not fire a shot — until between 8 & 9. From that time they kept up a pretty warm cannonade from Bunkers Hill and the floating batteries — The new Englanders in general are brave soldiers. The little boys follow the cannon balls as they bound on the ground like young squirrels learning to fetch and carry." [9]

That very evening of the 26th there occurred the loss of the first Pennsylvania soldier to become a casualty in the war of the Revolution.

Major James Wilkinson, [10] a volunteer in Colonel Thompson's battalion, and later a brigadier general, has the

James Wilkinson

very sad story: "The provincials broke ground at Ploughed Hill, August 26, about one mile north-west, and in front of the British post at Bunker Hill, on the peninsula of Charlestown. A detachment of riflemen ordered to cover the working party took post in an orchard, and under cover of stone fences in advance. As soon as the enemy discovered the workmen, they ordered a battery upon them, and kept up a brisk cannonade by which volunteer [William] Simpson, of Pennsylvania, had one of his heels and ankles so much shattered that mortification ensued, and he died in a few days. The young man was visited and consoled during his illness by General Washington in person, and by most of the officers of rank belonging to the army. Every exertion of the faculty was made to serve him, and his death became a theme of common sorrow in an army of twelve or fourteen thousand men." [11]

Hand, in that same letter of the 29th to his wife, reported, with great pain, the same, describing how "Poor Simpson . . . had one of his legs shattered by a cannon ball. The director general took it off, but the poor lad was buried this evening." [12] Hand was much touched, perhaps the more so because the young Simpson was a Lancasterite, from nearby Paxton.

He was happy to inform Kitty that her dear friend

Edward Burd, with all other officers, was "well and hearty." But the night before last had been a bad one, with "dreadfull Thunder & Lightning & very heavy Rain." Happily, "our little Duck-House kept Mr. Burd and Myself Snug & warm . . . ."

Thompson and Hand, with their Pennsylvania riflemen remained on Prospect Hill through the autumn months. As they were regarded an "elite battalion," the riflemen at first were not assigned to the customary pickets and encampment duties, but by and by, as their behavior caused them to appear rather ordinary, they were obliged to "take their share of all duty, of guard and fatigue, with the brigade they camp with." And for the most part they turned in a commendable service. Some disorder did occur from time to time. There were, for example, altercations in which one soldier would rough up another (and get thirty-nine lashes on his bare back for it).

The indiscriminate firing of rifles was regularly a problem, as of course not only was it a dangerous practice, it also produced the impression, accurate as a rule, of disorder. Orders for Hand's regiment eventually read: "The constant firing in the camp, not withstanding the repeated orders to the contrary, is very scandalous and seldom a day passes but some persons are shot by their friends."

Historian Gregory Knouff, quoting from the Orderly Books of Thompson's Fifth Rifle Regiment and Hand's Rifle Regiment, speaks in concern to the problem: "Even as the Continental army continued to professionalize, the disorder continued. [As late as 1778] the exasperated officers of the First Pennsylvania Regiment excoriated their men for how 'the camp is continually disordered both within its own limits and its vicinity, by a disorderly firing.'" [13]

On one occasion a most severe discipline was called for. Thirty-three riflemen of Thompson's battalion were ordered to general court martial for "disobedient and mutinous behavior." Washington himself had been called upon to put an end to the riot that had resulted. These men were fined twenty shillings each, but, according to Thompson, "seem exceedingly sorry for their misbehavior and promise amendment." While faulting the officers a little, Thompson had good things to say of his soldiers. Praising them for their readiness and their attendance to duty, he observed, "It is only in camp that we cut a poor figure." [14]

And their were "disappearances." On October 3rd Hand had informed his wife that Captain [James] Ross, [15] who was in command of one of the Lancaster companies of the battalion, "goes for Lancaster to-morrow." Doubtless Hand's messmate Edward Burd would have liked to have accompanied Ross to Lancaster at this time, but the best he could do was to get off a letter of affection to his bride-to-be, Elizabeth Shippen.

In a letter of October 23-24, Hand reported to his good Lancaster friend, the uncle of his wife, attorney Jasper Yeates, [16] that Ross was not yet returned, and that Washington is much irritated by the unaccountable absence of the First Pennsylvania Regiment's Captain Ross, "without his knowledge." According to Hand, Washington declared to Colonel Thompson that "any officer who went home from his regiment must resign his commission." [17]

At mid-summer, Washington and the Congress, apparently persuaded that the people of Canada, given a chance, would rise up to support the rebellion, had approved a plan to invade Quebec. Washington was particularly insistent, and felt the conquest of Canada should be accorded top priority. He ordered General Richard Montgomery to capture Canada.

Although three companies from the battalion were delivered to the ill-fated expedition into Canada, Lt. Colonel Edward Hand and most of the Pennsylvania riflemen missed out. Hand even supposes that two of the companies which were drafted were drawn upon because of a reputation for misconduct. Upon the departure of the expedition Hand reported (September 23) to Jasper Yeates: "[Daniel] Morgan,

[William] Hendricks, and [Matthew] Smith [captains] have left with their companies for Canada. Seven hundred musqueteers from here are on the same expedition . . . had Smith's company and Hendricks' [18] been better behaved, they might probably saved themselves a disagreeable jaunt."

And it was found that many of the soldiers who at this time had disappeared from their companies and who, it was supposed, had gone home, instead had joined the Canada expedition. Hand, in a letter to his "Dearest Kitty," dated October 3,1775, wrote that "Mr. Henry, Junior, has followed the troops to Canada without leave. Nothing but a perfect loose to his feelings will tame his rambling drive." [19]

It was early this October that Washington, hearing that there was about to be a vacancy in the medical staff of the army hospital, wrote to John Hancock, the President of the Congress, to make recommendations. Hand, obviously interested, in a letter of the 4th noted for his wife that "The office of Director of the Hospital is now vacant." Washington felt obliged to make two recommendations. He suggested Lt. Colonel Hand, "formerly a Surgeon in the 18th Regt. Of Royal Irish," and "Dr. [Isaac] Foster, late of Charles Town." And he urged that the appointment "be made as soon as possible." But Edward Hand was left to his brigade of riflemen.

On the 10th of October, Hand noted for Kitty that he would be requesting a leave for "the middle of next month." He was very much counting on it: "Believe me my dear Kitty the Prospect of soon seeing you conveys a pleasure I did not feel since I left you. May God Protect & restore you safe to your Very affectionate Edw Hand." [20]

As for the activity at Boston, it is sporadic. Hand and his troops are not greatly involved in the siege. But in a letter of October 23-24 to Yeates, the colonel does report from Prospect Hill what he has been regularly hearing: "One of our armed boats fell down to the mouth of the Cambridge River, and sent a few shots into Boston. One of her guns bursted.

Your old friend Worthington was on board, and had his shins broken . . . . Heard last night that Falmouth [present Portland, Maine] under orders was in ashes." [21]

An officer, James Parr, from Northumberland, "with thirty men from us, marched for Portsmouth. They marched at dawn this morning."

Hand wrote on this same day to his "Dearest Kitty." Said he, "Let me assure you that your desire of seeing me is not exceeded by that of your ever affectionate Edw Hand." [22]

On the 9th of November the riflemen saw some real action. This was at Lechmere's Point, in view of Prospect Hill. The British, under a withering cover of fire from their batteries on Bunker, Breed's and Copp's Hills, as well as from a frigate which lay 300 yards off the point, were able to manage a landing at the point of land which at high tide is an island. They were intent on stealing the sheep and the cattle which were feeding in the marsh.

From Frank Moore's *Diary of the American Revolution* come the details. These regulars, numbering four to five hundred men, "seized a sentinel who was drunk and asleep upon his post." Other sentinels sounded the alarm. Although it was an ugly day, with rain and rough wind, Colonel Thompson, together with Colonel Thomas Mifflin, and Lieutenant Colonel Hand, on orders from Washington, made an instant response. Without waiting for boats, the officers ordered their men into the water, which was up to their shoulders, and marched them to the island. When all had got over, and now protected by a hill, they began to march forward. The British were protected by walls and some good cover and were firing volleys relentlessly. But the Pennsylvania riflemen continued to advance. "Colonel Thompson gave the Indian yell, which was re-echoed back from the whole regiment, who immediately rushed out from their ambuscade, and poured in whole volleys upon the regulars." The British, now in great confusion, "retreated with the greatest precipitation," while all the while a "constant blaze" emerged from the man-of war, the floating battery and the boats. When the British perceived that there was no chance they could secure the cattle, they "with a villainous malice, characteristic of the tools of despotism, stabbed the poor dumb animals."

The affair came to an end as the riflemen of Thomson and Hand drove the redcoats to their boats. Moore's contempt for the British regulars is apparent from his summary, composed the next day: "This day three dead bodies have floated along [the] shore, supposed to be drowned by the sinking of a barge, which our field-pieces stove. The enemy had cannon placed at the water's edge, along Charlestown Point, which, together with the large artillery from Bunker Hill, made an incessant roar, with grape-shot, chain-shot, &c., but to no purpose. The riflemen drove them like a herd of swine down a steep place, where some of them were killed, drowned, or scared to death, in sight of their brethren in iniquity, who covered the tops of Fort Beacon and Bunker Hill to view the noble exploit of cow-stealing." [23]

To his wife back in Lancaster, Hand, from the encampment on Prospect Hill, himself got off a long account of the action the day after the battle: "I give you the particulars of the fun our regiment had yesterday. About one p. m., a number of [British] regulars, taking advantage of a high tide, landed from twenty boats on Lechmere Point, to carry off some cattle. Six men of our regiment were on the point to take care of our horses; they did their utmost, and partly effected it. One poor fellow was taken; he was of Captain Ross' company. I think his name was Burke. I had gone to Watertown to receive the regiment's pay, but thanks to good horses, we arrived in time to march our regiment, which was the first ready, though the most distant of our brigade. Col. Thompson, who arrived before we had crossed the water, with thirteen men only of [James] Ross' company, but not being supported by the musqueteers, before I could get up with the remainder of our regiment off duty, returned, and met Major Magaw and myself on the causeway; the whole then passed with the utmost diligence, up to our middles in water. David Zeigler, who acts as adjutant, tumbled over the bridge, into ten or twelve feet [of] water; he got out safe, with the damage of his rifle only. As soon as the battalion had passed the defile, we divided them into two parties, part of Captain [James] Chambers', Capt. [Henry] Miller's, and Lawdon's, [John Loudon's?] with Major Magaw and Col. Thompson, marched to the right of the hill, with part of [Robert] Cluggage's, [George] Nagel's and [James] Ross'. I took the left, as the enemy had the superiority of numbers, and the advantage of rising ground, with a stone wall in front, and a large barn on their right and flank, aided by a heavy fire of large grape-shot from their shipping and batteries. We had reason to expect a warm reception; but to the disgrace of British arms, be it spoken, by the time we had gained the top of the hill, they had gained their boats, and rowed off. We had but one man wounded, I believe mortally, by a swivel ball, Alexander Creighton, of Ross' company."

Then Hand names some Lancaster riflemen, whom his wife must know: "Wm. Hamilton need not grudge the money his son cost him. His coolness and resolution surpassed his years. Billy Burd had his eyes closed, by the dirt knocked off by a cannon-ball." [24]

In the battle, as best it could be determined, the Pennsylvania riflemen had one man killed and three wounded; the British had seventeen killed and one wounded.

Happily, not all that long after this engagement, Lt. Colonel Hand was able to secure a leave of absence (the first of many) in time to be present with his wife in Lancaster for the birth of their first child (Dec. 8), Sarah, whom he would forever after call "Sally."

On New Year's Day, 1776, a new reorganization of the army commenced, and the rifle battalion became the First Regiment of the Continental Army. Its total strength, including officers was reported at 693. On the 6th of January, Major Magaw was commissioned Colonel of the Fifth Pennsylvania. On the 2nd of February, Hand reported to his wife that he had "just arrived here [Prospect Hill] safe last night." As both Colonels Thompson and Magaw were now setting out for Carlisle, Pennsylvania, Hand, who had just returned from the furlough he had received in November, assumed command of the rifle battalion. [25]

Hand of course, ever since the birth of little Sarah, has been much concerned about both mother and child, but he has not heard from Kitty since his return to Prospect Hill, some three weeks ago. To "My Dearest Life," he writes out of great impatience, "I have been almost three weeks here and have not yet had the Happiness of hearing from you! For gods sake my dear let me not have that to say again." And next day (February 22) he writes again, to repeat the hope of hearing from her, and also to report that Col^l. Thompson left [this place] the morning after my arrival with Col^l. Magaw and I don't expect to see either of them here again. He sends his respects to "all my acquaintances" and "my love to my two little Sallys." [26]

In the succeeding March, during the reorganization of the army, Washington informed the Congress that inasmuch as Colonel William Thompson was being promoted to Brigadier General, "there is a Vacancy for a Colonel in the Regiment he commanded, to which I beg leave to recommend the Lieut. Col. Hand." [27]

Accordingly, Colonel William Thompson having been promoted to brigadier general, Congress, ever respectful of Washington's wishes, commissioned Hand (March 7) Colonel and placed him in command of the regiment, with Captain James Chambers as Lieutenant Colonel, second in command.

On the 8th of March Hand had got off an up-date letter to his wife, who has been, and continues to be, very much interested in his activity: "I am stationed . . . with four companies of our regiment. Two companies, Cluggage's and Chambers', were ordered to Dorchester on Monday; Ross and [John] Loudon relieved them yesterday. Every regiment is to have a standard and colors. Our standard is to be a deep green ground, the device a tiger partly enclosed by toils [trapping nets], attempting the pass, defended by a hunter armed with a spear (in white), on crimson field the motto *Domari nolo.*" The motto, "I refuse to be subjugated," turned out to be quite apt for the regiment. [28]

He reports that the enemy is preparing to depart Boston: "Our regiment is ordered to be ready to march at an hour's warning. New York is at present our destination."

Hand had by this time (March 8) still not heard from Kitty. "It is now almost 7 weeks since I left home & have not in that time had the satisfaction of hearing from you, for Gods Sake Contrive to write Oftener or find better conveyances." But by the middle of March he has had two letters from his wife, one reporting the shocking news that little Sarah has been dangerously ill (" I find that we had nearly lost our poor little

Standard of First Pennsylvania Regiment

Sally, God help you!"). Dr. Hand is of course very grateful for the care she has so far been given: "I am infinitely obliged to Doct^r. [?] for his attention. If he has no reason to contradict it, I think that Castor Oil . . . might be of service to her, a small spoonful once or twice a Day . . ." [29]

On the 13th of March, on orders from Washington, and under the command of Major General John Sullivan, Hand's riflemen (together with five other regiments) prepared to march, and next day set out for New York City.

As his unit is now (March 21) in Hartford, Connecticut, Colonel Hand reports that "our Regiment are so far on their March to New York, the Enemy have evacuated Boston. Expect to be in New York in a week." He notes his promotion to Colonel, sends his regards to Mrs. Ewing (Kitty's mother) and to the Jasper Yeates family, and prays "that God may please to preserve your health" and restore that of "our dear infant." [30]

Little Sarah's father, Colonel Edward Hand, with his Pennsylvania troops was moving to a new theater of the war. The Revolution was about to heat up.

IV

New York City

Never was a greater feat of generalship shown than in this retreat....

— Lt. Colonel James Chambers

General George Washington and General William Howe, who with Thomas Gage had commanded the British forces at Breed's Hill, and who had in October succeeded Gage as Commander-in-Chief, were now locked-in adversaries. Both appreciated that the war, which had so far been fought in Boston, and in Canada, would be moving south. Both understood that New York City, strategically, and for a host of other reasons as well, was critical, was absolutely vital. John Adams had referred to the city as "the key to the continent." And clearly both Washington and Howe felt the same way. Both knew how *very* crucial was control of the city. And certainly both could appreciate the urgency.

And neither was shy about the mission. Howe actually welcomed the prospect of a battle for the city. After all, he was in a superior position in terms of numbers of troops; and, besides, maybe even more important, he commanded the water. The British navy, with a huge number of frigates and gunboats, could bring a devastating artillery to the battle.

But Washington, though without this confidence and certainly a very, very long way from arrogance, simply knew that he *must* control the city. Consequently, shortly after the British exodus from Boston, he moved his army south. The British had evacuated Boston on March 17; Washington removed from his headquarters at Cambridge on April 4, headed for Providence, Rhode Island. By the middle of April he was fortifying the city of New York.

The troops which included the soldiers under the command of Colonel Edward Hand reached the city on the 28th, with the commander of the First Pennsylvania very happy in being so near to "My Dearest Life." He very much hopes their child is recovered. He expects that "in a few days . . . we will be able to learn the Destination of the Enemy." [1]

On this very day, the 28th of March, the up-date to his wife that the colonel had begun on March 8 is continued. The Pennsylvania First Regiment, which had at first been assigned to General John Sullivan's division, had been early on its way: "I left on the 15th. Hartford, 21st of March, our regiment so far on the march to New York. New York, March 28, arrived here with the regiment this day. I received your letter by Capt. [James] Ross. . . Day before yesterday received a letter from the president of Congress [John Hancock] appointing me to the command of the rifle regiment. . . . Howe abandoned Boston on the 17th. Two of my officers were in the town; it is little damaged. Mr. Hancock's house is left in perfect repair." [2]

Four days after the troops reached New York, Hand got off a letter to "My Dearest Kitty." He expressed, first, the hope that the approaching good season would improve the state of "our little girl," and reported that he was "looking out for a Nurse for her." As was his habit, a not so subtle complaint came next: "I expect to hear from you on every post, but will not long content myself with that." He reports that he is "at present in a fine large house but want a House keeper & furniture."

As for the military situation, "It has been hinted to me that we are to be encamped on Long Island as soon as the . . . ground will admit of it with safety to the health of the Troops. All accounts agree in describing it a most lovely situation." He notes that the first troops are daily arriving from the East, and that they are promptly making their fortifications "more formidable."

The really good news is that he has lately purchased for her "a young & gentle Pacing Horse, that holds his head as high as you Please." [3]

One week after the regiment reached the city, on the 5th of April, General Israel Putnam detached three companies from Hand's command to scour the shores of Long Island. This force promptly captured a midshipman with his boat and ten sailors.

Israel Putnam

Hand had reported on April 12th that "I was moved to Long Island last Tuesday (April 5)." His troops were stationed at New Utrecht, eight miles from the Staten Island ferry. New Utrecht would continue as his headquarters through the rest of April and all of May and June, and the Pennsylvania First Regiment continued to picket the shores of Long Island until some time in August, when the unit was moved to Delancey's Mills.[4]

As nothing much was happening, or was even imminent, Hand by the middle of April (by which time

Washington had 19,000 soldiers on York Island) was impatient to get home again for a spell. On the 18th, while suffering from an inflammation in his right eye, he expressed to "My Dearest Life," the hope that he might set out for home "soon as I can with safety travel." He was yet much concerned about "our dear little girl" and was very hopeful that she was continuing to mend. And on May 11, from Philadelphia, he reported that his eye was much improved and that he was "on my way to see you & our dear little one." [5]

Hand, back on Long Island by June 22, reported dutifully to Kitty his safe arrival "on Saturday evening." However, "in my absence a most shocking discovery has been made of a most Horrid plot formed by a Hellish crew of Yorkers to Blow up our Magazine & Murder or Captivate our Generals on the arrival of the [British] Fleet. The Mayor of the City & Several others are already taken, & in Prison. This is all I can tell you, this morning intend to go to York [now Manhattan] & hear the particulars." [6]

It was from this post, New Utrecht, that Colonel Hand recommended to Washington some reorganization of the First Pennsylvania. He had very specific suggestions for the officers: "Sir: I take the liberty to request, that when you next write to Congress, you may be pleased to recommend the appointment of a major to my regiment. As I learn that Congress have an objection to the advancement of my oldest captain, I can't think myself at liberty to recommend any. The annexed gives your excellency the names and ranks of the captains; one of them I hope will be promoted: Robert Cluggage, Matthew Smith, James Ross, Henry Miller, Charles Craig, James Grier, David Harris, James Parr, James Hamilton. I beg your Excellency may please to appoint Lieutenant John Dick to be second lieutenant, vice Jacob Zanck [of Lancaster], resigned since the last promotion, and Robert Cunningham to be third lieutenant, vice John Dick." And then he suggests names for promotions that will be necessary in the event that a major for the regiment is promoted from the captains.[7]

As it happened, Captain James Ross received the promotion to major (Sept. 20), which induced the resignations of offended captains Robert Cluggage and Matthew Smith. Both Henry Miller (September 28) and James Ross (September 25) were promoted to major shortly thereafter, and James Parr would be promoted to major August 9, 1778.

Washington, naturally in much anxiety about numbers for his troops, at the middle of the month of April expressed to Congress his concern about the Pennsylvania riflemen, for whom he had a very high regard: "The time for which the riflemen enlisted will expire on the first of July next, and as the loss of such a valuable and brave body of men will be of great injury to the service, I would submit it to the consideration of Congress whether it would not be best to adopt some method to induce them to continue. They are indeed a very useful corps; but I need not mention this, as their importance is already well known to the Congress." [8]

Happily, Washington's fears were dissolved by Colonel Hand's report to him at the end of June about the number of men in Sullivan's First Regiment of the Third Brigade. On May 5, Hand had reported the total strength at 507. On June 30 the time of those who did not re-enlist expired. But, Hand was happy to advise, "Almost all the men discharged to-day declare that they will stay to know what the fleet will do." [9]

And on the first day of July the brigade of riflemen, now attired in the style of hunting shirts urged by Washington, entered upon another term of service, as the First Regiment of the Pennsylvania Line in the Continental Service. And early in August, though Washington did not like at critical times to shift regiments around, he felt compelled, because of some late promotions, to do some rearranging. Accordingly, Hand's regiment of riflemen was joined with those of William Prescott, James Varnum, Moses Little, and John Nixon to form a brigade under the command of Nixon. And on July 17, Hand was in Philadelphia purchasing regimentals for his much enlarged battalion.

  War came to the new re-enlistments long before their first paycheck. Howe, sailing south from Halifax, arrived at Sandy Hook near the end of June. Hand from New Utrecht on June 30 reported to Kitty: "A Fleet of upwards of 100 sail . . . arrived at the Hook yesterday." Noting that we cannot make a stand here, "we have prepared every thing for a retreat to the main Body." Then, while complaining once more that "I have not yet heard from you" [since his return to Long Island last Saturday], he has good news for her: "The Day before Yesterday [I] Bought a Negroe Boy eleven years old last month [.] his name is Robert, he is a fine smart boy and may be of use to you until you can get a Girl, therefore send him to Princeton by the stage waggon, he is almost Naked but carries with him a Suit of Cloathes (of [at] least the outside) ready cut out — which you will please to have made up for him for State Days & Holy Days." [10]

  And in this letter Hand reported the execution of one of the Loyalist conspirators mentioned in his letter of a week ago.

  His letter of July 20 was chiefly of our "poor little Sally." While much appreciative of the attentions she has been getting, he remains apprehensive. He urges Kitty to use a gargle composed of a fusion of rose leaves and dry sage and a little honey, and a "very few drops of the oil of Vitriol." And he fears the dreaded smallpox: "If it pleases God to spare us till the Beginning of October I wish then to have her & the Blacks Inoculated, you need not now be afraid of infection from Sally Yeates."

  He adds that "I hope you are now Convinced that had I thus long remained inactive that the Present Battle would necessarily Bring me forth, how much more honorable and advantageous my present situation than that of a Militia man tho he is exposed to equal Toil and Dangers." [11]

  On the 28th, first expressing the hope that Robert, who

has been ill, "will mend," he makes arrangements for Kitty to come to Philadelphia. She is to be attended by Captain David Harris, and is to see the very Irish Mr. Milligan, "who lives on Front Street near Walnut Street."

Unfortunately, the "toil and dangers" Hand has spoken of were close upon him by the end of July.

Howe, sailing south from Halifax, and arriving at Sandy Hook near the end of June, had landed troops on Staten Island in July, and steadily over a period of six weeks reinforced them to the number of 22-32,000, and perhaps many more. On August 20, from Eastchester, Hand, conscious of Kitty's concern, assured her that he was "alive & well." He reported then the recent movements of the British and continued with his great concern for their dear daughter: "In my last letter I told you that the enemy had landed on Frogs Neck the 12th. The 18th they moved a little eastward. Our Parties had a few skirmishes with them. The loss on either side was trifling. They have advanced along the shores as far as New Rochelle — we are in Constant Motion. How does our dear little Sally?" [12]

Colonel Hand had been ever vigilant. He had had his riflemen scouring the shores of Long Island through all of April and May and well into August.

On the 22nd of August the British (including a large number of Hessians) arrived unopposed on the northwest shores of Brooklyn, at Gravesend Bay. The outpost established by Colonel Hand had recognized what was happening and had promptly sent word to Washington, who was at his headquarters on York Island (now Manhattan) that it was plain the British were preparing to cross from Staten Island, probably at dawn "tomorrow," the 22nd. "At least fourteen sail of transports, some of them crowded with men," Hand reported on the afternoon of the 21st, "are now under sail; and more, from the noise, are hoisting anchor." [13] And with a huge force of Hessians and Regulars Howe did indeed reach the shores of Long Island, landing on the beaches of Gravesend

Bay. The first major battle ever fought by the new United States was fought not long after, on August 27, 1776. It was the Battle of Long Island (sometimes called the Battle of Brooklyn or of Brooklyn Heights).

    The British arrival on the beaches (8,000 Hessians and Redcoats) was described by Colonel Hand in an up-date letter of the 27th to his wife. Hand had assembled his Pennsylvania riflemen (some 200-300 of them) on the beaches near the landing site, but wisely perceived that any assault, or even resistance, would be a fatal move. He ordered his officers to remove the troops to the stands of trees thick on the heights to their west (present-day Prospect Park). He ordered also the destruction of all grain and forage, and anything that the British might make use of. "Dear Kitty," he reported: "Part of the enemy landed on the Island on the 22nd. They did not advance farther than Flatbush, until last night — I have had a fatiguing time of it ever since — A number of our troops have been hemmed in, but behaved well. Many have got clear and many are yet missing. Our Pennsylvanians were chiefly of the party. I escaped my part only by being relieved at 2 o'clock this morning — Major Burd and Col. [Samuel John] Atlee were out and are yet missing. Jessy and Jacky are yet with me." [14]

    Of the fighting on the 23rd Washington reported to Major General William Heath, noting particularly the effective withdrawal of Hand's riflemen: "Sir: Yesterday morning the enemy landed at Gravesend Bay upon Long Island, from the best information I can obtain, to the number of about Eight Thousand. Colonel Hand retreated before them, burning as he came along several parcels of Wheat, and such other matters, as he judged would fall into the Enemy's Hands. . . ." [15] Later, the Commander-in-Chief, finding Hand just a little too zealous in his destructions, mildly rebuked the colonel.

    About a week later, Hand's fears for Burd and Atlee were confirmed. Judge Jasper Yeates had a letter from Edward Burd himself, now a prisoner of the British on Long Island.

The letter is dated September 3, 1776. "Dear Sir," it opens: "I was taken prisoner at an advanced Post [on the Gowanus Road, near the Red Lion Inn] on the morning of the 27th ult° after a skirmish, on the same day Captain Herbert and Heister [Joseph Hiester?] were both made prisoners. I was used with great Civility by General [James] Grant & admitted to my Parole, Brigadier General [James] Agnew and Major [Brigadier General Alexander] Leslie and Major Batt also treated me with great Politeness." And then he added, "I can not learn the fate of poor Col° Hand or Jesse Ewing but believe they are not prisoners." [16] And in a letter to Jasper Yeates from Philadelphia, December 12, he reports his parole. [17] Because of very poor health, Burd never did return to the Continental Army. Following his release by the British, he resumed his law practice in Reading, Pennsylvania.

James Grant

Burd had had the command of a company of American picquets which had been stationed at the Red Lion Inn. It was just at daybreak that advancing troops of British were able to surround the Americans and compel a surrender. Major Burd and sixteen of the soldiers under his command were captured.

What followed, in what is considered the first major engagement of the Long Island battle, proved to be a disastrous defeat of the rebel forces of John Sullivan, who was commanding in the absence of the very ill Nathanael Greene. Partly because of some nasty weather, but chiefly because of a very skillful flanking maneuver pulled off by Howe, the Continental Army was routed. Losses were heavy, including that of General John Sullivan, who, though heroic with a pistol in either hand, was captured by the Hessians. [18]

As this battle was the first general action in which the First Pennsylvania Regiment was engaged, and thus the first significant military action for Edward Hand, we are fortunate to have a firsthand account from the pen of Hand's Lt. Colonel James Chambers.

The American outpost of Colonel Hand, on August 21 had sent word to Washington that all signs pointed to a British landing at dawn the next day. And so it did occur.

To his wife back in Pennsylvania, in a letter dated Camp at Delancey's Mills, in Westchester County, three miles above King's Bridge, Sept. 3, 1776, Chambers described the action in great detail:

"On the morning of the 22d of August there were nine thousand British troops on New Utrecht plains. [In all, Howe had put 15,000 on the island; and there were more to come.] The guard alarmed our small camp, and we assembled at the flagstaff. We marched our forces, about two hundred in number, to New Utrecht to watch the movements of the enemy. When we came on the hill, we discovered a party of them advancing towards us. We prepared to give them a warm reception when an imprudent fellow fired, and they immediately halted and turned toward Flatbush. The main body also moved along the great road toward the same place. We proceeded alongside of them in the edge of the woods, as far as the turn of the lane, where the cherry-trees were, if you remember. We then found it impracticable for so small a force to attack them on the plain, and sent Capt. [James] Hamilton [of Lancaster], with twenty men, before them, to burn all the grain, which he did very cleverly and killed a great many cattle. It was then thought most proper to return to camp and secure our baggage, which we did, and left it in Fort Brown. Near twelve o'clock the same day we returned down the great road to Flatbush, with only our small regiment and one New England regiment sent to support us, though at a mile's distance."

The account continues with a description of the first exchange of gunfire: "When in sight of Flatbush we discovered the enemy, but not the main body. On perceiving us they retreated down the road perhaps a mile. A party of our people, commanded by Capt. [Henry] Miller [of Lancaster], followed them close with a design to decoy a portion of them to follow him, whilst the rest kept in the edge of the woods alongside of Capt. M. But they thought better of the matter, and would not come after him, though he went within two hundred yards. There they stood for a long time, and then Capt. Miller turned off to us, and we proceeded along their flank. Some of our men fired upon and killed several Hessians, as we ascertained two days afterward. Strong guards were maintained all day on the flank of the enemy, and our regiment and the Hessian jagers kept up a severe firing, with a loss of but two wounded on our side. We laid a few Hessians low, and made them retreat out of Flatbush. Our people went into the town and brought the goods out of the burning houses."

There was little rest for the rifleman, the action continuing until the wee hours of the next day, and resumed at daybreak: "The enemy liked to have lost their field-pieces. Capt. [John] Steel, of your vicinity acted bravely. We would certainly have had the cannon had it not been for some foolish person calling retreat. The main body of the foe returned to the town, and when our lads came back they told of their exploits. This was doubted by some, which enraged our

William Alexander, Lord Stirling

men so much that a few of them ran and brought away several Hessians on their backs. This kind of firing by our riflemen and theirs continued until two o'clock in the morning of the 26th, when our regiment was relieved by a portion of the Flying Camp [militia], and we started for Fort Greene [19] to get refreshment, not having lain down the whole of this time, and almost dead with fatigue. We had just got to the fort, and I had only laid [sic] down, when the alarm guns were fired. We were compelled to turn out to the lines, and as soon as it was light saw our men and theirs engaged with field-pieces." [20]

Though terrific losses occurred, Chambers is amazed that they were not a great deal heavier. He is very high on his troops, for their courage and for their endurance: "At last the enemy found means to surround our men there upon guard, and then a heavy firing continued for several hours. The main body that surrounded our men marched up within thirty yards of Forts Brown and Greene; but when we fired they retreated with loss. From all I can learn we numbered about twenty-five hundred, and the attacking party not less than twenty-five thousand, as they had been landing for days before. Our men behaved as bravely as ever men did, but it is surprising that with the superiority of numbers they were not cut to pieces. They behaved gallantly, and there are but five or six hundred missing."

Among those missing or known to be captured, as best Chambers knew at the time, were General Lord Stirling, who " fought like a wolf, and is taken prisoner." Other officers who, Chambers knew, were made prisoners by the Hessians were the Colonels [Samuel] Miles and Samuel John Atlee, [21] Major [Edward] Burd, [22] Captain [John] Peebles, Lieutenant Frederick Watts; and he knew that there were a great number more. He noted that Colonel James Piper was among the missing.

"From deserters," he reported, "we learn that the enemy lost Maj.-Gen. [James] Grant, [23] [not true] and two brigadiers and many others, and five hundred killed. Our loss is chiefly in prisoners."

Chambers has high praise for those responsible for the great success of the withdrawal: "It was thought advisable to retreat off Long Island, and on the night of the 30th it was done with great secrecy. Very few of the officers knew it until they were on the boats, supposing that an attack was intended. A discovery of our intention would have been fatal to us. The Pennsylvania troops were done great honor by being chosen the *corps de reserve* to cover the retreat. The regiments of Colonels Hand, Magaw, John Shee [of Lancaster], and John Hazlett [Haslet] were detailed for that purpose. We kept up fires with outposts stationed until all the rest were over. We left the lines after it was fair day, and then came off. Never was a greater feat of generalship shown than in this retreat, to bring off an army of twelve thousand men within sight of a strong enemy, possessed of as strong a fleet as ever floated on our seas, without any loss and saving all the baggage. General Washington saw the last over himself." [24]

John Ewing, a decade younger than Edward Hand, was a brother to Jasper Ewing. He was a jeweler, residing in Lancaster. In a letter to his uncle Jasper Yeates, who was at the time in Pittsburgh, he provided another vivid and dependable eye-witness account of the action: "As it has pleased Divine providence to spare my life, I think it my duty to send you as good an Ac't of the engagement . . . as lays [sic] in my power."

He proceeds then to describe what he actually saw: "As I had gone from Elizabeth Point, New Jersey, to Long Island, to see my brothers, I had an opportunity of seeing every thing that occurred from the time the enemy landed on the Island until a day or two before we retreated from thence. Col. Hand's Reg^{mt} had been on duty 2 days, & the second night were relieved between 12 and 1 o'clock in the morning, and about Two, it is thought, the Enemy began their movements from Flat Bush to the Right, and Left, and at between 7 & 8 o'clock in the morning, we had the mortification from our Lines to see our men, commanded by Lord Stirling, almost surrounded by the Regulars, as they kept their stand on a Hill without flinching an inch. The Regulars were firing at them like Fury[;] they at last descended; then there was a continued peal of Small arms for an Hour or better. Our men at last partly got off by the marsh . . . ."

The Grand Retreat he declares "will ever reflect honour to our Generals." He laments the loss of Major Edward Burd, but believes that General Howe is treating the prisoners with "great politeness."

John Ewing has, however, been quite ill, struck down by a fever, "which I got by being cloathed too thin." After two days at York, he was removed to King's Bridge, and after recovering his health, "the Col° was good enough to send me Home in a Carriage." [25]

Washington had the army in retreat to Brooklyn Heights, and as Howe waited to secure the victory next day, the American Commander-in-Chief pulled off the first of what would be many clever military moves. On the very dark night of August 29-30, miraculously the entire army that had been engaged at Brooklyn, was able to negotiate the twelve miles to the East River and cross over the mile-wide stretch of water into York Island without the loss of any cannon, or any material whatsoever, and without the loss of a single man!

Washington had accorded great honor to the Pennsylvania troops, whom he had chosen to serve as the *corps de reserve* to cover the retreat. Lt. Colonel Chambers, as noted, was proud of the First Pennsylvania for, first, being chosen for the assignment, and, second, for the extraordinary success. In fact, for the achievement managed in the Grand Retreat, Chambers, like many, was inclined to give a lot of the credit to these Pennsylvania troops.[26]

From the account provided by Colonel Hand himself it

is clear that smooth and trouble-free as the East River crossing may have seemed (because of its total success), it was actually a rather touchy and danger-ridden experience, fraught with some perilous confusion. Among the papers he has left appears this narrative: "In the evening of the 29th of August, 1776, along with several other commanding officers of corps, I received orders to attend Major General [Thomas] Mifflin," [27] who was a Philadelphia Quaker, and well known to Hand.

Once assembled, the officers of the First Pennsylvania heard what the troops were not hearing, that it had been determined to evacuate Long Island, and that it was to be accomplished this very night!

Hand and the others learned that the First Pennsylvania, under command of Mifflin would have the "honor" to provide cover for the movement. "He [Washington] then assigned us our several stations, which we were to occupy as soon as it was dark, and pointed out Brooklyn Church as an alarm-post to which the whole were to repair, and unitedly oppose the enemy in case they discovered our movements, and made an attack in consequence."

Hand's regiment was to be posted in a redoubt (commanded by Captain Henry Miller, who was from Lancaster) "on the great road below Brooklyn Church." Hand reports that "Part of a regiment of the flying camp of the State of New York were, in the beginning of the night, posted near me," but "they showed so much uneasiness at their situation, that I petitioned General Mifflin to suffer them to march off, lest they might communicate the panic with

Alexander Scammell

which they were seized, to my people." When Mifflin acceded to the request, Hand urged the nervous New Yorkers to withdraw from the station.

The time was probably 8:30 p.m. Nothing happened from that time on until two o'clock in the morning, when Alexander Scammell, acting as aide-de-camp to Washington, appeared at the post to inquire the whereabouts of General Mifflin. As Mifflin was with Hand at the time, Scammell promptly made his report. Scammell told Mifflin and Hand that the boats were in readiness and that Washington was eager to have the troops at the ferry. When General Mifflin insisted that there must be some mistake, that he did "not imagine the General could mean the troops he immediately commanded," Scammell declared that he was not mistaken, and explained, as proof, that he had just ordered all the troops he had come upon to get to the river, and that they were doing just that. Still uneasy, but partly satisfied by this explanation, Mifflin ordered Hand to call in his pickets and sentinels, "to collect and form my regiment, and to march as soon as possible, and quitted me."

What follows in Hand's narrative is of great interest: "Having marched into the great road leading to the church, I fell in with the troops returning from the left of the lines. Having arrived at the church, I halted to take up my camp equipage, which in the course of the night, I had carried there by a small party. General Mifflin came up at the instant, and asked the reason of the halt. I told him, and he seemed very much displeased, and exclaimed 'D-----n your pots and kettles! I wish the devil had them! March on.' I obeyed, but had not gone far before I perceived the front had halted, and, hastening to inquire the cause, I met the commander-in-chief, who perceived me, and said: 'Is not that Colonel Hand?' I answered in the affirmative. His Excellency said he was surprised at me in particular; that he did not expect I would have abandoned my post. I answered that I had not abandoned it; that I had marched by order of my immediate commanding officer. He said it was impossible. I told him I hoped, if I could satisfy him I had the orders of General Mifflin he would not think me particularly to blame. He said he would undoubtedly not. General Mifflin just then coming up, and asking what the matter was, His Excellency said: 'Good God! General Mifflin, I am afraid you have ruined us by so unseasonably withdrawing the troops from the lines.' General Mifflin replied, with some warmth: 'I did it by your order.' His Excellency declared it could not be. General Mifflin swore 'By God, I did,' and asked: 'Did Scammell act as an aide-de-camp for the day, or did he not?' His Excellency acknowledged he did. 'Then,' said Mifflin, 'I had the orders through him.' The General replied it was a dreadful mistake, and informed him that matters were in much confusion at the ferry, and, unless we could resume our posts before the enemy discovered we had left them, in all probability the most disagreeable consequences would follow. We immediately returned, and had the good fortune to recover our former stations, and keep them for some hours longer, without the enemy perceiving what was going forward." [28]

Did not this evacuation come at the most critical moment of the entire revolution? Many would say so. For them the destruction of the army that Washington had assembled and organized at Cambridge would mean the end of the rebellion. Period. Credit for its survival of course goes first to Washington himself, for the decision that he made, for the strategy, and for the timing. Lots of credit, too, must go to John Glover and his Massachusetts boatmen, who were able to ferry the entire army across the river through an impenetrable fog. Those who have attempted to row a boat through dense fog to a destination a mile away could only marvel.

Then there were the Pennsylvania riflemen, who by Washington had been given a suicidal mission. It was up to the troops of Colonel Hand to delay any movement of the British toward the crossing point, in the very possible event that some

Hessian or some Redcoat would discover what was happening. James Chambers and Edward Hand had every right to be proud of their riflemen.

Colonel Hand of course could not know that he here played the role that he would play throughout the war. For Washington he would regularly command the light corps and through harassment and skirmishing he would buy his commander some time. He became very good at it. He could provide the time that the rebel troops needed, whether to go forward or backward.

Here in Brooklyn, Hand's riflemen were glad finally to hear the order to withdraw from their buffer post. They were the last of Washington's army to abandon the sinking ship.

Hand's brother-in-law Jasper Ewing, [29] serving as the Colonel's aide, on August 30 had advised his uncle, The Honorable Jasper Yeates, back in Lancaster, of the escape. He reported that Generals Sullivan and Lord Stirling are taken prisoners, and that the situation in New York "is very critical." He fears the enemy may reduce the whole of Long Island to a heap of ashes. [30]

On September 3, as noted above, Major Edward Burd, a prisoner of war, had lamented that "I can not learn the fate of poor Col. Hand or Jesse [Jasper] Ewing." But Colonel Hand, who had not been in touch with Kitty in quite a while, was able to report, September 7, from King's Bridge that Jacky Ewing sets out for Lancaster this day. Still uneasy about the smallpox, in this letter he expressed the hope, "Next month please God we shall be inoculated." [31]

Howe was shocked when he discovered that the Continental Army had totally disappeared. But he promptly assembled his forces and organized a siege of York Island (Manhattan). By September 16 Washington had formed a new line at Harlem Heights and here resolved to rest his troops and to determine just what Howe might be planning next.

During this time both Colonel George Weedon [32] of

Virginia and Hand, much concerned about numbers and way below quota, appealed to Washington for permission to recruit from the militia forces. Washington, feeling that he could not authorize it, relayed the request to Congress. But shortly thereafter he had recruiting instructions delivered to Colonel Hand. Here is what you might do, he said: "You are immediately to Inlist such of your Regiment or any other troops raised in the province of Pennsylvania, as are able of Body and Willing to enter into the Service of the United States of America, upon the following Terms."

The terms he catalogued did not make it easy: "1st. You are not to inlist any but Freemen, able of Body and under the age of 50. Carefully avoiding all persons Labouring under any Lameness or other Defect of Body prejudicial to the service. 2dly. You are not to inlist any Deserters from the Army of the King of Great Britain, or persons of Disaffected and suspicious Character, the American Service having already Suffered greatly by the Desertion of such persons."

Noting the change in the enlistment term, he reminded Hand, "$3^{dly.}$ You are to inlist Men to serve during the Continuance of the present War . . . unless sooner Discharged by proper Authority." The fourth restriction required the enlistee to sign the articles of rules published by Congress September 20, 1776.

Washington adds, then, some suggestions for encouraging enlistments: Soldiers are to be paid twenty dollars bounty money, and each soldier shall be "entitled to 100 acres of land at the expiration of his inlistment, this to go to a representative, in the case of death in the service." [33]

During September and October, in a number of letters, Washington expressed to Congress his concern about vacancies in Hand's regiment, enclosed Hand's letter about promotions he would like to make, and noted a reorganization which has the brigades of General Gurdon Saltonstall, General Paul Dudley Sargent, and Colonel Edward Hand into a division commanded by Sullivan.[34]

Hand, with his regiment, is in Westchester in September, and all has been quiet for a while ("Nothing has happened here worth mentioning."). He is much thrilled to be able to get a gift off to Kitty: "I have this Day sent to Easton in Captn [Charles] Craigs name a Very Beautyful Bay mare just fit for your Ladyship to ride . . . ."[35] And shortly there occurred events that indeed were very much worth mentioning.

In a most disappointing but happily brief action, at Kips Bay, between present East 32nd and 38th Streets (September 15), the Continentals were routed in a shameful panic. At Harlem Heights on the very next day only one real battle occurred, and in this, with the heroic Washington in the middle of it, the rebels did enjoy something of a victory over the Redcoats. But the Commander-in-Chief did not make much of the engagement, calling it a "sharp skirmish."

By the bearer Adam Hubley, Hand, who was now at Delancey's Mill, on the 26th had a packet containing 1221 Dollars delivered to Kitty. In this letter he lamented the news that the northern 1/3 of New York "is in Ruins. What a pitty!" He noted that the only movement by the enemy since his last letter was the landing of a few men at Powles Hook.[36]

There is much talk of the French fleet he reports, and he is hopeful on the Indian troubles: "I expect the Apprehension of an Indian War will blow over." He closes, as always, with "God help and preserve you & our little Daughter," and urges "Write soon and give me something jocular."[37]

It was not a big problem with Hand's regiment, but General Orders did on September 20 address the unseemly flight of the riflemen during battle. The admonition declared that those who fled the enemy would be most severely punished so that "the brave and gallant part of the army may not fall a sacrifice to the base and cowardly part or share their disgrace in a cowardly and unmanly retreat."[38]

Ever since the astonishing escape from Long Island, Howe had been searching for a way to engage Washington's army, and hopefully entrap the rebels this time. Now, suffering many disappointments, he ordered the Royal Navy up the Hudson, and effectively shut off that escape hatch. That was October 8. Three days later there occurred for Hand's riflemen some dramatic action on the East River. The colonel's assignment was to prevent a British crossing of the river at the popular Throg's Neck (Throng's Neck, Frog's Point, Frog's Neck) Ford. [39]

The peninsula called Frog's Neck, or, more often, Throg's Neck, reached out into the Long Island Sound, and, except at high tide, made possible a connection to the mainland. For some unaccountable reason Howe had chosen this avenue ("the worst place," according to one analyst) [40] rather than one farther east, which would have been comparatively easy.

General William Heath had had intimations of this intention and had so advised Washington. With Washington's approval Heath had ordered Hand's riflemen to so damage the bridge as to make it impassable. This they had done with dispatch; and now, ten days later, having even removed the planks from the bridge, they lay in wait for the expected appearance of the Redcoats.

As recognized by General Heath, it was imperative to prevent the crossing of Howe's troops. In his *Memoirs*, he notes the presence of a mill and a huge pile of wood near the bridge and recalls the orders given to Hand to take advantage of this "naturally defensible spot." [41] Here, with the kind of cover Colonel Hand relished, the riflemen, twenty-five or thirty only, lay in wait.

The British did not disappoint. Four thousand troops marching out of the early morning fog of October 11, had shown up pretty much as expected.

The Redcoats and Hessians, as they came to the Pelham

Road, divided into two parties. The larger body approached the bridge, intent on a crossing. The British officers could perceive that though the bridge appeared to be defended, it was by a very modest force, perhaps as few as twenty-five riflemen. But the officers were startled to discover that the planks had been removed. [42] And at the moment of that surprise, they got another, for Hand's riflemen delivered a withering fire from their very secure cover. The fire was lethal, and as Hand had given orders to shoot the officers' horses [43] confusion and panic took over. In great disarray, the British fell back.

And the smaller detachment, which had made its way to the ford, was also turned away, by the outpost Heath had stationed there.

During the time the British were milling around and considering what strategy to employ, General Heath sent a runner to Washington, who was at the Morris House, with a report on the British attempt to cross. The Commander-in-Chief, as he explained very precisely to the Congress, insisted on a continued defense: "The grounds leading from Frogs Point to [Kings Bridge] are strong and defensible, being full of Stone fences, both along the road and across the adjacent Fields, which will render it difficult for artillery, or . . . [for a] large body of foot to advance in any regular order except through the main road." [44]

By the time darkness had begun to descend upon the battle site, very welcome reinforcements for Colonel Hand had arrived. Now, instead of twenty-five or thirty riflemen, the American force consisted of a very formidable 1500 infantrymen.

History does not provide a large place in the Revolution for the battle at Frog's Point, but in fact it was a *most* significant engagement. Had the British effected a crossing here, it very well might have cost Washington the time that he needed to save his army.

Twenty-five or thirty Pennsylvania riflemen had held the bridge. The sharp-shooting troops of Colonel Hand, firing in the style they preferred, from secure cover, were able to hold back the British (4000 Redcoats and Hessians!) for some time, in fact until their Continental Army support arrived. Howe's troops were totally isolated for six days! By that time they had had enough. They vanished just as abruptly as they had appeared.[45] No longer was there any hope to cross over here to the Westchester mainland. Hand had bought Washington the time that he needed for the trek to White Plains.

Colonel Hand throughout the fighting on Long Island and in every engagement since had proved a most inspiring figure, "a natural leader." He was in able command of "tough and undisciplined back-country riflemen." [46] By this time his regiment knew him well, and the soldiers were devoted to him. Hand knew that he could count upon them for courage under fire and for strict allegiance to orders. And the riflemen very well knew that they could count upon their commander to order the proper action, and to take advantage of every opportunity.

On the 14th of October, Hand, from the encampment at Valentine's Tavern, near Kingsbridge, got off a letter to Kitty, back in Lancaster. He rejoices in the news that "my dear little Sally" is likely to recover, and he urges again inoculation for the child, "& the Blacks at the same time." Of the British landing at Throgs Neck, he said, "I suppose they think that movement will induce our Army to move farther back, but I think they will find themselves much disappointed. Our late retreats were dictated by prudence not by a dread of their arms." [47]

Now Washington, grateful for time that he needed, made his decision, after almost a month on York Island, to withdraw altogether from the city. On the 18th he began moving the many elements of the Continental Army to White

Plains, a site most of the soldiers had never even heard of.

Hand could not know at this early time that the war was fated to be a very long endurance contest. He certainly still had no notion that his role, in engagement after engagement, would be to buy his general precious time. His was the light infantry responsibility for harassment, for skirmishing, for delaying the advance of the enemy.

But the Continental Army had been beefed up a good bit by this time. It was very happy to have back at the head both General Stirling (via a prompt prisoner exchange) and General Nathanael Greene, who had finally recovered from his debilitating illness. As it marched off to White Plains, Washington and his officers were confident that Fort Washington, garrisoned as it was by more than 2000 men, under the command of Colonel Robert Magaw, the very feisty Carlisle attorney, would be okay. But he left 1400 men at Mount Washington and another 600 at King's Bridge.

It had been a most trying two months, with skillful retreats the only thing in his favor. Yet, the morale of the foot soldiers, as he could readily perceive, was remarkably high. And a good thing too, for the march from Harlem Heights to White Plains was to be a most difficult one. Probably most painful was the paucity of horses. This meant that foot soldiers would be toting supplies, and it clearly meant, too, that the field guns would have to be transported by the artillerymen heaving at drag ropes.

Washington's force had departed York Island (Manhattan) on October 18. With Howe inexplicably remaining at New Rochelle, the army (13,000 troops) moved slowly along the Albany Road north toward the tiny hamlet of White Plains. It arrived at nine o'clock in the morning of October 21. Washington promptly began to establish fortifications. He took advantage of a series of rises in the ground, the hills known as Purdy, Hatfield, Miller, Chatterton, and Merritt.

Meanwhile, Howe, with all of his trouble from Colonel

Hand at Throg's Neck and the routing of Colonel Robert Rogers' Queen's Rangers at Mamaroneck ("the place where the sweet waters fall into the sea") by the spirited companies of Colonel John Haslet and his Delaware Blues and the Virginia troops of Major John Green, *finally* arrived at White Plains.

He engaged the Continental Army on October 26. The early fighting included a surprise assault on the British by Colonel John Haslet (fresh from his success at Mamaroneck) [48] which was only partially successful. That was a Delaware regiment. The First Pennsylvania riflemen of Colonel Edward Hand not long after enjoyed more success. In an assault on a Hessian force of equal numbers Hand's regiment routed the enemy with the loss of but a single man. [49]

The most significant fighting occurred on Chatterton's Hill on October 28. When the patriot forces were at length dislodged from their entrenchments, Howe in organized pursuit may have won a decisive victory here, but he chose instead to wait for reinforcements. By the time he was ready to renew the assault against Washington's troops, which had regrouped near North Castle, torrential rains made attack unthinkable. An astounded Washington awoke November 4 to find that the Redcoats had thrown in the bag and had marched back to York Island. Hand reported to Kitty that "The Enemy have this Day Disappeared." Without claiming victory Washington withdrew his forces from the region five days later.

Meanwhile, Fort Washington, a five-sided earthenworks fortification at the crest of Mount Washington overlooking the Hudson River in northern Manhattan, has been under siege. Colonel Robert Magaw, never short on spunk, had spurned British invitations to surrender, and for some time continued to feel confident he could hold the fort. But by early November, having suffered many casualties, it became plain to him that he could not. On a very cold and blustery afternoon, with a light snow contributing to the gloom, the defiant and feisty Magaw turned over Fort Washington, with all of his troops, nearly 3000 men and 161 cannon, to the British General Charles Cornwallis and the Hessians. General Wilhelm Knyphausen accepted his sword. The fort was promptly re-named, by the Hessian captors, Fort Knyphausen. The date was November 16.

Washington, who had been following closely the fortunes of Fort Washington, now had to consider Fort Lee, which was on the opposite side of the Hudson River from Fort Washington, on the Palisades on the New Jersey shore. Fort Lee, which had been built expressly to command the Hudson River, had, like Fort Washington a certain symbolic value. It had been known first as Fort Constitution and was now named in honor of Washington's top lieutenant, the British-trained General Charles Lee. But by now it had become very clear to the Commander-in-Chief that it would be futile to continue the defense of Fort Lee. On November 20, four days after the fall of Fort Washington, with the fort threatened by the approaching Redcoats, he ordered General Greene, who had

Capture of General Nathaniel Woodhull

been inclined to continue the defense, to abandon it. Greene promptly withdrew the garrison and with that action brought an end to the Battle of New York. [50]

Victory was clearly and totally to the British. The defending Continental Army had been forced to surrender New York City (including Forts Lee and Washington), lost an inestimable quantity of munitions and supplies, suffered more than 1500 casualties (captured, wounded, missing, and killed), saw three high-ranking officers captured (General Nathaniel Woodhull,[51] besides Stirling and Sullivan) as well as a number of other important officers, like Colonel Robert Magaw, and experienced such a terrible blow to morale that new volunteers could hardly be expected. In fact, desertions began immediately to occur wholesale, complete companies abandoning the army en masse.

The British, with their Hessians, lost probably no more than 377, including five officers.

Some insist that if General Howe had more promptly followed up his victory in pursuit of Washington's withdrawing forces that the war would have ended in the fall of that year, just five or six months after the new nation had declared its independence. But Howe in fact apparently believed the war already to be at an end. And he could hardly be blamed for that. From every means of measurement it must have seemed so.

Except for Yorktown, the four months-long Battle of New York was the most critical and militarily significant battle of the entire revolution. In no other battle was the final outcome of the war so close to being determined. The King's men here came within a hair's breadth of bringing the rebellion to a very early conclusion.

For this magnificent victory, which had apparently squelched the rebellion, General Howe, who was a cousin to King George III, was made a baronet. From this time forward he would be known as Sir William Howe, and although he would not be present in the city, or even in the country, after the spring of 1778, New York would continue to be occupied by the British until 1784!

And though the war had not ended, for the Continental Army it was certainly a dark hour. The much reduced force of 5000 men fit for duty (perhaps even fewer) trudged south through New Jersey at the lowest point of its fortunes — with Lord Cornwallis in leisurely pursuit. The pitiful remnants of the army were in disarray. Desertions were occurring, and enlistments were running out, and new enlistments certainly were not numerous. Many felt that all hope was extinguished, that there could be no recovery for the patriots; many thought that success would be possible only if the Commander-in-Chief were replaced. Everybody was experiencing dire forebodings.

Washington was discouraged. He knew how grave a loss was New York City. He knew that he had made mistakes. It was a pathetic remnant that he had for an army now.

He was so disconsolate that he got off a letter to John Hancock, President of Congress, in which he wrote: "Unless some speedy, and effectual measures are adopted by Congress, our cause will be lost." He understood, of course, that one possibility for Congress was a change in the Commander-in-Chief, and he knew that Charles Lee was waiting in the wings. And, indeed, in communications to friends and family he confessed to doubts about his abilities as Commander-in-Chief. He questioned his capacity to command.

But Washington was still Washington. He was not about to surrender the Continental Army. He knew what had to be done, and he knew that it must be done quickly. As he marched south through New Jersey he was thinking.

V

The New Jersey Campaign

Here Freedom stood by slaughtered friend and foe,
And, ere the wrath paled or that sunset died,
Looked through the ages; then, with eyes aglow,
Laid them to wait that future, side by side.

> "Lines for a monument to the American and British soldiers of the Revolutionary War who fell on the Princeton battlefield and were buried in one grave."
>
> – Alfred Noyes

Because of his greatly diminished numbers, Washington moved through New Jersey in constant concern about Cornwallis. On November 19, from Hackensack, he expressed this anxiety to the President of the Congress, John Hancock: "If the Enemy should make a good push in this Quarter, the only Troops that there will be to oppose them, will be Hand's, Hazlet's [Haslet's]; [and] the [five] Regiments from Va . . . ." He reminded the Congress that all elements of the army have been "greatly reduced by losses sustained on Long Island." [1] Indeed, even Hand's regiment was very thin, decimated as it was by battle losses, by sickness and fatigue. Washington was depending a lot on militia.

As it happened, the Advance Guards of the Cornwallis force, some 400 Hessian troops, did catch up, in the region of Trenton Falls. The engagement was with the riflemen of Captain Henry Miller of Colonel Hand's regiment. Far outnumbered, Miller was able to manage an escape by boat, as Washington was pleased to report to Congress.

With the winter season on its relentless way, Washington's army moved steadily south toward the Delaware River. December 11 found the portion including Colonel Hand's command at Kirkbride's Ferry opposite Bordentown.[2] Here Hand found the time to get some instruction through to Kitty. After a prayer that "little Sally continues to mend," he requested that Robert be sent "with 2 or 3 shirts, my Regiment Coat, shaving apparatus, powder bag, etc." As the colonel has acquired new boots, Robert is welcome to his old ones. The horses, he reminds Kitty, may be wintered in the country.[3]

Five days later, farther along the Delaware, he suggests to Kitty that she find winter quarters. "I long had an inclination," he says, "for the little House M^r. Michaels occupied, perhaps you may get that . . . or any other you like. [I] can send you cash."[4]

By the middle of December, the Commander-in-Chief had settled on a plan. He would need of course the approval of his major officers. But he was confident of that. He had in mind the Hessian-held city of Trenton. He was in command now of a force, including officers, of 3966.

Colonel Edward Hand crossed the Delaware with Washington on that terribly cold and miserable Christmas night of a typically rough December. He had the command of the 1st Pennsylvania Regiment, some 254 riflemen, a large portion of the total force. Washington's orders had him responsible for the road to Princeton. That was to be so well covered that no Hessians might escape that way.[5]

It is not known, of course, in which of the many boats

Colonel Hand was a passenger. Emanuel Leutze's famous painting has him, with eighteen-year-old Lieutenant James Monroe also, in the lead boat with the Commander-in-Chief.[6] Colonel Edward Hand is supposed by many to be the officer at the rear of the boat, who is, apparently, trying to hold onto his hat.

Washington Crossing the Delaware

    Washington was anxious now, because he feared the delays in crossing the river had cost him the very desirable element of surprise. But he knew that there could be no turning back. As it happened, he had managed surprise enough.

    As his troops poured into Trenton, the main force attacked right at the intersection of King and Queen Streets. The artillerymen of twenty-nine-year-old Captain Thomas Forrest [7] had found a great spot for their cannon, which his fifty-two gunners had seen ferried across the river. It was a knoll, fairly high ground, which commanded a lovely view of the intersection of King and Queen Streets. From here Forrest with his six-pounders and lighter guns raked the streets.

    Washington, alerted by a stranger to the fact that the east side of town was quite unprotected and at the same time

Thomas Forrest

to the determination of Colonel Johann Gottlieb Rall (sometimes Rahl), commander of the Hessian forces, to escape to Princeton, ordered Colonel Hand with his 1st Continental regiment of "very able" riflemen and the German battalion under Colonel Nicholas Hausegger of Brigadier General Matthias Alexis Roche de Formoy's [8] brigade, which was made up of Pennsylvanians and soldiers from Maryland, to cut off the escape route.

Actually the force called upon by Washington was quite large. Major Wilkinson in his *Memoirs* later vividly recalled the scene. He had noted that in the troops dispatched by Washington, besides the riflemen of Hand and the German soldiers of Hausegger (a 374-man battalion), there were a brigade of Virginia infantry commanded by Colonel Charles Scott, [9] and a battery of six guns attended by the artillerymen of Captain Thomas Forrest, altogether perhaps as many as 1000 patriots! [10]

These men raced through the fields on their left to take possession of the Princeton Road. The order that Washington had given these troops, that is to cut off the Hessians' exit route, was one of the most important orders that he ever gave. There was now no escape for the panicked Hessians.

For the Congress, Washington supplied some detail of the first moments. Noting that as the assault was launched the main body of Hessians had got assembled into a battle formation, the Commander-in-Chief perceived that they "seemed not to know how to act." He had the confusion he had been counting on. "They first moved towards their left, but being briskly charged by Genl. Sullivans division, they were drove into the town again; they filed off to their Right and I suspected were attempting to gain a Road leading to Princeton, upon which I ordered Col. Hand's and the German battalion to throw themselves before them, this they did with Spirit and Rapidity and immediately checked them." [11]

Charles Cornwallis

When Rall perceived that escape to the east was not possible, he ordered his troops to head north. The German brigade promptly moved even farther east, and effectively sealed off completely the road to Princeton. As the situation for the Hessians became ever more hopeless, Hausegger's men called out in German (which they very well could do) to "lay down your weapons and surrender." [12] With other troops convening on the Hessians (notably Lord Stirling's brigade) from every quarter, they readily agreed to "lay down" their arms.

Hand received the surrendering Hessians. Killed or captured were 1000. The entire battle had required but forty-five minutes! It was a glorious victory for Washington. And of course it was just what was needed, if the Revolution were to go forward. But there was trouble yet for the troops of the

Surrender of the Hessians

Commander-in-Chief.

Cornwallis had arrived at Princeton on January 1. He left Princeton with 5500 troops (Some historians report 8000!) at daybreak the very next day. Leaving a detachment behind, perhaps as many as 1200 men, under the command of Lt. Colonel Charles Mawhood, he set out for Trenton, some eleven miles away. He was transporting twenty-eight cannon. [13] He saw a chance to trap Washington, and perhaps to destroy the Continental Army.

Meanwhile Washington who had crossed back over the Delaware, and was now returned again to Trenton, was made aware (as early as December 31) that Cornwallis was assembling a large force at Princeton, presumably to march to Trenton. Electing to intercept him (not with a main army action but with harassing light troops), he determined to place a force at a point about midway between Princeton and Trenton. He was hoping at least to buy some time. The command of these troops he turned over to a French soldier of fortune, the aforementioned Brigadier General de Fermoy. Fermoy's brigade, composed of course of Hand's First Pennsylvania and

Hausegger's German unit, was ordered to establish a "defensive line" at a distance some five or six miles south of Princeton, not to engage the enemy, but simply in order to delay its advance.

General Fermoy's conduct in leading his brigade in the initial assault on Trenton had been certainly a responsible one, but he was not ready for this. At the very critical moment that the British approached the point at which Washington had scheduled the resistance, Fermoy appeared six miles away, in Trenton, four sheets to the wind. [14] Major Wilkinson, who knew him "a little," later described him as a "worthless coward." And he certainly had produced an accurate estimate of his character, for on July 6 of 1777, when Fort Ticonderoga, under the command of General Arthur St. Clair, was lost back to the British, Fermoy was in large measure responsible. According to trustworthy reports, Fermoy, in order to disclose the American defenses to the approaching Redcoats, had treacherously set fire to his quarters. In consequence he was cashiered from the Continental Army.[15] Washington here, at the second battle of Trenton, was quick to relieve him of command, and in his place installed the resourceful Colonel Edward Hand.

One of Hand's most able and most courageous officers was Major Henry Miller of Baltimore, "distinguished for his cool bravery wherever he served." Employing the Indian-style of fighting, Hand and Miller had the riflemen secret themselves "under whatever cover you can find." [16] Happily there was plenty of that, in the form of hollows, dense thickets, and scraggly rock formations. From this protective cover, the riflemen waited patiently as the Redcoats advanced down the Princeton road. When the British column was *very* close, on orders from Miller, the riflemen unleashed "a deadly fire from ambush." So surprised was this vanguard of Cornwallis' troops, and so withering the volleys, that the British broke ranks and were forced back to the main body of the army "in great confusion."[17]

And with the contribution of frightful artillery fire from the guns of Thomas Forrest, the whole column was abruptly stopped. But Colonel Hand was satisfied to harass the Hessians and the light corps, which Cornwallis had out front; he did not expect, nor did he attempt, to halt the advance. He was buying time, as he had been asked, precious time. Washington had given him a big order, explaining to the colonel that he was hoping that he could hold the British back through the rest of the day.

Hand's method was to honor the success of this first engagement by assuming a new position (which provided the very essential cover), to fall back when necessary, to occupy a new position (which provided cover), and to fire in volleys after an advance by the British. Having withdrawn from his positions along the Eight-Mile Run (now Shipetaukin Creek), he had his riflemen fall back to a stream known then as Little Shabbakunk Creek,[18] which the Redcoats would have to cross. History has applauded Hand's decision to so secret his men in the heavily forested area near the bridge that the Hessians had the impression that the rebels had withdrawn. The withering fire that greeted them upon their approach to the bridge caused panic. Now the Hessians Von Lingsingen and Von Block assumed they had come up to Washington's main army. By the time the officers recognized the truth and had restored order and had begun a search for the American location, Hand was long gone.

Washington's army had formed on the south side of Assunpink Creek, a small stream which runs through Trenton in a number of different places before reaching the Delaware. It was imperative that the stream be defended. Darkness would help. By mid-afternoon Hand had retreated, firing and falling back, nearly the entire distance to Trenton. He established another line at a ravine called Stockton Hollow, just one-half mile from the community of Trenton, but, chiefly because of the artillery which the British had brought up, he was compelled now to withdraw into the town itself. [19]

It was now just a little after three o'clock. He had held up the Hessian advance guard, and indeed the whole Cornwallis army, for two hours. But, as General Henry Knox later described the action to wife Lucy, the Hessians pushed the patriots through the town, "with vigor." [20]

As the Pennsylvania riflemen arrived at the creek, still with all of their equipment, and with the guns of Captain Forrest, the Hessians, who had drawn close, on Queen Street, now determined on a bayonet charge. At this point Colonel Hausegger, together with some of the German men of his battalion, surrendered. According to historian William Stryker, "The capture was made in so suspicious a manner that Col. Hausegger's devotion to the cause of liberty has ever since been doubted." [21]

In his *Memoirs* Alexander Graydon, [22] who had been captain of a company in Colonel John Shee's battalion of Pennsylvania militia, and who had become a prisoner of war at the fall of Fort Washington (some say Harlem Heights) in New York City, had this to say of Hausegger: "He was a German, or rather a man of no country or any country; a citizen of the world, a soldier of fortune, and a true mercenary. Thinking that our cause was going down rapidly, he saw no reason for adhering any longer to it; but came over to the enemy in the season of our extreme adversity, though he did not reach us until after the affairs at Trenton and Princeton. Not liking the name of a deserter, he called himself a prisoner, but certainly, if he was one, he had much better terms than we had." [23]

And historian Mark Boatner was not kind, remarking that Hausegger's unit "disgraced itself." As still another historian, Edward Lengel, reports, the ensuing chaos was arrested by nobody less than the Commander-in-Chief himself. Washington had earlier asked the Hand detachment to make as "obstinate a stand as could be made on the ground, without hazarding the pieces [Forrest's guns]." He had explained, speaking directly to the foot soldiers, just how important it was to slow the army until nightfall. Now, together with Generals Greene and Knox, he had ridden out across the bridge, through the soldiers who were crossing, and ordered Hand's rear guard to "pull back and regroup under the cover of the American artillery."[24] And this of course they were quick to do.

So far it had been skirmishing, chiefly between the riflemen of Hand and the light corps of Hessians and British infantry Cornwallis had placed at the head of his army of 5500. Casualties had been light, the British losing only one soldier at Five-Mile Run, and ten killed, twenty wounded, and twenty-five captured at Stockton Hollow, one-half mile from the community of Trenton.[25]

All that was about to change.

Washington was much pleased with Hand's delaying action, for now it was about five o'clock in the afternoon. The early darkness of the wintertime was not far off. He elected to make a stand at the bridge over Assunpink Creek. He had his troops drawn up on the south side. Astride a beautiful stallion the Commander-in-Chief made an imposing figure at the bridge, on that side of the creek.

Washington had stationed his troops most strategically, covering as best he could the popular fords. He had General Hugh Mercer with his brigade at one of the crossing points, known as Phillips Ford, which was about two miles above the bridge at Trenton. That put Mercer at the extreme right of the army. John Cadwalader's troops were occupying an expansive field about one mile from the bridge. And Washington had the artillery of Captain-Lieutenant Winthrop Sargent (who had fought for Henry Knox at Boston, Long Island, and White Plains with great courage, and here at Trenton was still only twenty-four years old) stationed at a good height on a commanding hill.[26]

At the bridge itself, he posted the Virginia foot soldiers

of Colonel Charles Scott. The riflemen of Colonel Hand and the German soldiers of Hausegger who had not been captured backed up Scott.

Three times the British assaulted the bridge, and three times they were turned back. One American soldier, who had been in the thick of it, was heard to observe, "The bridge looked red as blood with their killed and wounded and their red coats." [27]

Many historians regard the repulsing of the British at Assunpink Creek as more important to the revolution than the initial battle of Trenton. They point to one telling statistic, that the number of British slain at Assunpink Creek was much greater than the number slain on the streets of Trenton. Indeed the British lost here perhaps even five times as many.

Cornwallis was given pause. It was still not really dark, but light was fading fast. It was decision time. He called a Council of War. The question that he put out before his officers was, "Do we continue the attack?" According to the reports that have come down, the general's quartermaster general, and aide-de-camp to the King, Sir William Erskine, promptly answered in a very strong affirmative. Said he, "If Washington is the General I take him to be, his army will not be found there in the morning." [28] Had not the Washington army of 12,000 men simply vanished from Brooklyn not so very long ago?

Cornwallis was, apparently, inclined to the same view. But, persuaded by other voices that since "there was no way for Washington to retreat from that position" it was better to rest the army and attack in the morning, he decided to let it all go till the morrow. He was confident. "We've got the old fox safe now. We'll go over and bag him in the morning." [29]

Washington, too, called a Council of War. He knew what he wanted to do. He was hoping he would hear the same from his officers. The officers met at the headquarters of General Arthur St. Clair, which was the home of Alexander

Douglass. John Cadwalader and Arthur St. Clair did not disappoint the Commander-in-Chief. It was their opinion that an attack on the troops Cornwallis had left at Princeton had not only the promise of success, but would be recognized as another aggressive action, like Trenton, and therefore great for the morale of Congress and the country.

By two o'clock in the morning the troops, some 6000 Continental Army soldiers (Washington's forces had been augmented by the arrival of the troops of Cadwalader and Thomas Mifflin.), were on their way, skirting the Cornwallis army by marching off to the East and then to the North. Washington had left 500 men behind. They had a job to do. The general wanted Cornwallis to have the feeling that the Americans were in camp for the night. These 500 soldiers were to keep the fires alive and to make whatever noise they could to suggest the construction of fortifications. They even had pickets patrolling the lines. They did a good job, and before daybreak were on their way to catch up with the main army.

Washington had been well on his way to Princeton not long after real darkness descended. He was hoping to arrive before dawn. Because of the general's concern for secrecy and because he was beginning to appreciate the great value of surprise, none of the common soldiers, in fact no one below the rank of brigadier general, had been given any idea where they were going or just what their mission was. It was Brooklyn and the East River all over again.

He was behind schedule, but as the army approached Princeton, a wee bit before daybreak, it found itself at a small grove of trees, not far from the Quaker Meeting House and very near to Stony Brook. Here Washington did some organizing. He divided the troops into three separate forces. The division commanded by John Sullivan was ordered to "wheel to the right" at Saw Mill Road, and then to follow this road back to Princeton, and attack from the east. The brigade commanded by Colonel Thomas Mifflin was ordered to "wheel to the left." These soldiers were to march to the Post Road by following Stony Brook. After that, with Sullivan coming from the east, Mifflin could assault the British from the west.

Washington's third division, composed of the troops of Generals Mercer [30] and Cadwalader,[31] had the big assignment. Orders required these men to follow Sullivan's troops at a short distance and attack the British from the south and east, "straight on."[32] But Mercer's troops were spotted by Mawhood, who had set out that morning for the troops of Cornwallis which had been left at Maidenhead on the Princeton-Trenton route.

The battle which followed took place largely in the orchards of the Quaker farmer Thomas Clarke, which were embraced by 200 acres of farm fields. The engagement took the form of a stand-off for a time, but then Mawhood, taking advantage of the fact that most of the Americans carried rifles which were not designed for bayonets, and well aware that more time is required to load and fire a rifle than a musket, ordered a bayonet charge. That proved to be devastating. Mercer himself, who was mistaken by some of the British for Washington, was bayoneted at least seven times (Some reports had the number at "three times," and others were of "more than a dozen."), and died of his wounds nine days later at the Clarke House, to which he had been carried. His second in command, the Irish Colonel John Haslet,

Death of Hugh Mercer

who had accompanied Mercer on the Forbes Expedition to capture Fort Duquesne (almost nineteen years ago) was shot through the head and died instantly.

In the panic that ensued Mawhood was beginning to overrun Mercer's troops. At this moment the soldiers of John Cadwalader's unit appeared, and shortly thereafter Washington himself arrived on the scene. The Commander-in-Chief, however, was not at first enjoying great success in rallying the remnants of Mercer's troops and turning the battle around. It was only when the riflemen of Colonel Hand's brigade, as well as the Virginia and Rhode Island Continentals from Sullivan's division, appeared on the scene that the Americans began to rout the Redcoats.

These forces Washington ordered to take position on the hill which overlooked the orchard.[33] As the battle continued, Hand's riflemen enjoyed steadily increasing success in picking off Redcoats. Mawhood ordered a retreat, and the British made for the bridge on the nearby Post Road. This action was intercepted by the Americans, who swarmed to block their passage across the bridge. But again Mawhood ordered a bayonet charge, and in the melee the British were able to break through and escape over the bridge.[34]

Their flight, however, continued to be costly, as Hand's riflemen, whom historian David Fischer (thinking back to Trenton and Assunpink) declared were "ubiquitous," and some other units were quick to follow. The relentless pursuit actually continued until nightfall, and when the reports came in they were to the effect that the Americans had killed some and had taken a number of prisoners.[35]

With Sullivan and Alexander Hamilton doing their damage in another quarter of the Princeton scene, notably at Nassau Hall, the battle at Princeton drew to a close.

Relishing the victory, Washington now determined on New Brunswick, where, he understood, there lay a British pay chest of 70,000 pounds. That he felt would make a nice reward

for this valiant army. His generals, however, were not of the same mind. Henry Knox and Nathanael Greene both strongly insisted that he forget about that. In the end their arguments prevailed, and
Washington marched the army off to Somerset Court House, and then on to the safety of the Morristown encampment grounds. The army arrived there on January 6. Princeton would prove to be the last major action of the New Jersey Campaign.

Washington Rallies Rebel Troops at Princeton

It had been a frenzied two weeks. But Washington and his officers were very proud of the Continental Army and of the militiamen. Their feelings of course were tempered much by the loss of so many good men and a number of officers, including Mercer and Colonel Haslet. There is almost always a cost to a battle won.

The Commander-in-Chief was very conscious of the great significance of these victories, and there were three. He understood just how important the New Jersey Campaign, with its two battles at Trenton and the climactic battle of Princeton, would be to the Continental Congress, to the morale of the army which had been so decimated by New York, and, indeed, to the spirit of all who were counting on the liberties promised by the revolution.

Of these battles and these two weeks Sir George Otto Trevelyan, in his beautiful classic study of the American Revolution, had this to observe: "It may be doubted whether so small a number of men ever employed so short a space of time with greater and more lasting effects upon the history of the world." [35]

No question the New Jersey Campaign was immensely important to the Congress, to Washington, and to the morale of the rebel population of the whole country.

VI

Fort Pitt

I am sorry your force is not more adequate to the uses you have for it.

— General George Washington

The Pennsylvania First Regiment, with its Colonel Edward Hand and the most of the army, now moved into winter quarters at Morristown. For the opening of the spring campaign the regiment would operate in General Anthony Wayne's Division.

Hand with his regiment was to be at the Morristown encampment only a short while. But while he was there his command was a matter of concern. Washington had informed the Congress on January 19 that a number of regiments, including Colonel Hand's, have been reduced to "a handful of men." As this was still the case three weeks later, he ordered Lt. Colonel James Chambers to augment Hand: "The service, rendering your presence with Col. Hand's Battalion indispensably necessary, you will prepare to join it immediately, bringing on with you all the Soldiers belonging to it . . ." [1]

But Hand is still trying to get his regiment up to quota. Actually, he has disappeared for a while. Under date of March 14, a somewhat exasperated Washington from the encampment at Morristown dispatched a letter of rebuke: "Sir: You left this place many weeks ago to collect, as I understood, the remains of your Regiment together. No good, that I have yet seen, has resulted from it; by your last returns, just handed in, you have 263 Sick, absent; Strange this! After such a length of time spent in assembling your Regiment. The season of the year and the exigency of our affairs, will admit of no more delays; I have therefore, in express terms, to desire that you will immediately join your Regiment, that you will order all your Straglers to be brought forward, and that you will use your utmost endeavours (by employing the best qualified and most diligent of your Officers) to compleat your regiment to its Establishment. What is to become of your Lieut. Colo. [Chambers] If there is not some urgent reason to assign, his long absence from Camp will stand in a very unfavorable point of view. As your Regiment is deficient in point of numbers and wanting of Officers, I think you had better reduce the number of Companies to the proper establishment of eight." [2]

A week later Washington is *still* searching for General Hand. In a letter to General Greene, after noting the reception of twelve British deserters by Hand's regiment, he laments the unaccountable absence of Colonel Hand at this critical time. Greene does not need any more assignments just now, but Washington urges him to locate the recalcitrant officer: "I . . . beg that you will Order Colo. Hand, immediately to join his Regiment, and to bring with him such of his Sick as are recovered and what recruits have been lately inlisted. He left the Army some time ago for this purpose, but tho' I have wrote to him expressly, to come forward, I have never heard of him or from him, which I can not account for, unless my Letters have miscarried. [3]

But Hand was not going to be any longer at the Morristown encampment.

For the military acumen, his great skill and courage, as well as for the inspiration he clearly meant to his troops, at New York and in New Jersey, Colonel Edward Hand, on April

1, 1777, was promoted by Congress to the rank of Brigadier General and given a totally new assignment. And it was huge. He was being asked by Washington and the Congress to assume command of the Western Department, which would mean headquarters at Fort Pitt, and the enormous responsibility for peace on the always turbulent frontier.

His orders, as Washington reported to Horatio Gates on the 28th, were to repair to Fort Pitt immediately, to relieve Major John Neville, and "to take measures for the defence of the western frontiers."[4] Whether Congress knew it or not, its new general had already been at Fort Pitt, of course, with the 8th Regiment of Royal Irish, for more than four years! He had some understanding of the situation there.

So Edward Hand, who had for so long been with the Pennsylvania First Regiment, would never serve it again, although without him it would continue to enjoy a most distinguished career for the rest of the Revolution.

The command of the First Pennsylvania Regiment was now turned over to Lt. Colonel (now Colonel) James Chambers, a *very* loyal and able officer, and devoted to General Hand.[5] He would have the command for the duration of the war.

During the Revolution Fort Pitt served as the Headquarters for the Commander of the Western Department, and though constantly under threat from the British fort at Detroit, it was never really assaulted, not after the siege by the Indian war party during the Pontiac wars. It played a most prominent role in the colonial-Indian affairs of the west. It was at this post that Brigadier General Edward Hand would make another contribution to the ultimate success of the patriots of the Revolution.

The end of February, when Washington began his search for the absent Colonel, had found Hand in Baltimore on business. He is not impressed by the city. "There is no wine & little company in the house" where he has his lodgings. People are disagreeable and "the town has been robbed of all society." But he is able to get to Lancaster in March, and he is on his way to Philadelphia early in April. Kitty has a letter from him dated Philadelphia, April 8. He reports his safe arrival in the City of Brotherly Love "on Thursday morning and found that I had been appointed to a new office [command of the Western Department] before my arrival which serves more to embarrass than give me satisfaction." And, still in Philadelphia on the 11th, he writes, "I hope to see you very soon." [6]

    The spring of 1777 was most momentous for Edward Hand. Not only was he advanced to the rank of Brigadier General and delivered a real challenge with the command of the troubled Western Department, but he was the father of a bouncing baby girl, now sixteen months old. And he was fast becoming an enterprising landholder. He had long ago acquired nearly 1500 acres of land in Pittsburgh, which he was now being given the opportunity to enjoy. And now, on March 15 and on April 10 of this spring, 1777, conscious of his impending promotion and confident of success in the Revolution, he purchased two adjoining parcels totaling 271 acres of land in Fawn Township, York County. Fawn Township, near the Maryland-Pennsylvania border, at this time was largely Irish. The settlers had named the region for Fahen County, Donegal, Ireland. Edward Hand's tract, to be known as "Reliance," was made available to Dr. Hand at a cost of 1180 pounds, ten shillings. [7]

    That Kitty Hand has visited the property and knows it well is quite obvious from the letter Hand addresses to her from Carlisle on May 22. He is on his way to Pittsburgh from his Lancaster home, but has gone east first and out of his way, to York County to take a good look at the farm, which he has put into the care of a manager.

    "My Dearest Kitty, " he writes, "I had great satisfaction in the receipt of your kind letter by Jefry [Jasper Ewing], I don't find that the ride has hurt me in the least, I was amply paid for the trouble of the round by the farm, by the pleasure of Seeing every thing in a more promising state than I expected. Heron [?] has been very industrious, he has Sowed a field of Oats and better than 2 Bushells of Flax Seed, & Planted two large fields of Corn, the apples have not been the least hurt by the Frost, therefore the Cyder will be worth attending to. I have there one Hogshead & 3 Barrels the remainder of the [illegible] are to be provided — what Peaches were Kild by the Frost will be of Service to the trees as they are yet as heavy loaded as they can Bair [bear] there are also a great many Cherries — there are 85 [?] Sheep & six [?] Lambs at the place, one Sheep remains yet at M^r. Whirters. it was sick when the others were delivered — one of the Sows died. The other is [illegible] and all the Pigs I fitted all the males for the Stage for which reason the Pigs Mr. Hough Promised me must be sent when Convenient — the Horned Cattle look very well, the Pasture will be very good Soon — today I am to arrive at Genl. Thompsons [General William Thompson, near Carlisle] — tomorrow I proceed — I have just been to breakfast with M^{rs}. Montgomery [wife to John Montgomery of Carlisle]. She is well & desires Compl^{ts}. to her Lancaster acquaintances.

I beg my Duty [respects] Love & Compl^{ts}. To all — Adieu! My love God Bless you & our Little Daughter Dearest Kitty

most affectionately Yrs
Edw. Hand"

In a postscript he laments "I lost poor Sancho at York — " [8]

The winter of 1776-1777 had been restless, with a number of blood-curdling "incidents" occurring in the relations between the settlers and the Delaware Indians. Major John Neville, with a garrison of some 100 men, had had the command of the Western Department, with headquarters at Fort Pitt, during this time. For the new Head of the Western

Department, conditions had only steadily worsened.

As General Edward Hand traveled west, pretty much on the route he had followed a decade ago (the old Forbes Road, cut in 1758), concerned about provisions he had ordered up, he tested his authority over the militia forces of the region. As he neared Pittsburgh, from Hannastown, near present Greensburg, he got off a dispatch to Colonel Archibald Lochry, County Lieutenant for Westmoreland County since March 21. The date was May 30. Hand was ordering Lochry to Pittsburgh: "I did myself the Honour of writing to you by Capt. [Jeremiah] Lochry (who had been commissioned Captain of the 6th Pennsylvania on February 15 of this year, 1777) from Bedford a few days ago informing you that I expected 50 men properly Officered and Armed to assist in escorting the stores to Pittsburgh. The waggons will march in two divisions, 25 men will Escort each division from Bedford. I hope that 25 men with their officers from this county will be ready to meet them at the East side of Laurel-Hill, the first division of waggons left Bedford yesterday, therefore the 25 men for that Party must march so as to meet them as above directed, from the first party you will learn when your other 25 men will be wanted. Please to direct your officers to pay the utmost attention to the safety of the stores — if you can provide the troops provisions I believe it will be very necessary." [9]

It was on a Sunday, the very first day of June in the year 1777, that Brigadier General Edward Hand arrived at the fort, having accepted (in April) his promotion to rank of brigadier general, which carried with it this new assignment from the Continental Army. As he was arriving with no troops at all, only a handful of officers and his wife's brother, Jasper Ewing,[10] who was attending him as brigade major, he was escorted into the fort by a troop of Westmoreland County lighthorse militiamen, who were very happy to see him.

In a letter addressed to his uncle Jasper Yeates, under date of June 3, 1777, Ewing writes: "On Saturday last we arrived here not a little fatigued with the Journey. But, notwithstanding the Badness of the roads and still worse accommodations, I think myself amply Compensated for all my Fatigues by being stationed at this delightful Place." Delightful place? Well . . . .

General Hand's first Fort Pitt letter to Kitty was composed on the 4th: "My Dearest Kitty, I have been so much hurried since I arrived here that I can only find time to tell you that Jefry & I arrived here safely on Sunday last, Escorted by a Troop of Westmoreland Light Horse.

"I have the Happiness to inform you that from every Appearance we shall escape the Dreadfull Calamity of an Indian War, so much Apprehended some time ago —

"I now Occupy Col. [George] Morgans house his very kind & polite treatment makes me much his debtor — "

He hopes to see Judge Yeates at Fort Pitt when Colonel Morgan returns, and urges her to send all the news at first opportunity. [11]

Hand wrote dutifully to Kitty from Pittsburgh over the next few months, posting letters, besides that on June 4th, on June 10, 19, 30, July 12 and 24, and August 11, 15, 25, and 30. He reported his activities, sometimes noting that "nothing of any Material Consequence has happened here since my last."

As Commandant of the Western Department, Hand was assuming a huge responsibility. He understood very well what the Congress and General Washington were expecting of him. He appreciated that, first, he was to bring peace to the turbulent western frontier. This of course he knew could mean a campaign into the Indian country. Clear in his mind was the second big problem. As the boundaries of the two states Pennsylvania and Virginia were not yet fixed (Even Pittsburgh was up for grabs.), he knew he would have a role to play in that matter. He was directly responsible for the counties of Westmoreland and Washington in the region that seemed to belong to Pennsylvania and for Monongahela and Ohio in the more southern territory. It became his job for two states to establish an effective defense of the western frontier from the Shawnee and those Delaware Indians who were hostile. The relations between the Indians and the frontier settlers was the big thing. He had to remember also that his adopted country was at war with Great Britain. There continued the threat from the British menacing from Detroit. And of course he was tackling all of this at age thirty-three.

What he understood his mission to be is plain from a letter he promptly (June 3) got off to Colonel David Shepherd, County-Lieutenant for the newly erected Ohio County in what promised to become Virginia: "Whereas the Honourable the Continental Congress have thought proper to appoint me to take the Command on the Frontiers of Virginia and Pennsylvania & to embody such of the Militia as I shall think adequate to the Defence of the Country. And whereas the late Murders committed by the Savages, encouraged & supported by our cruel Enemies evidently point out the absolute Necessity of a perfect union and Harmony amongst the Frontier Inhabitants in Defence of their Lives, Liberties & Properties I do hereby declare, that in Execution of the Trust reposed in me, I shall consider those persons as dangerous & disaffected to the American Cause, who abet or in any wise foment the present unhappy [boundary] disputes between the states of Virginia & Pennsylvania to the public injury."

Then, with a little naiveté evident, he reports his feeling about the situation, his impression of the "savages" and of the state militia: "The Love of our Country will I trust, teach us to forget all Invidious distinctions & to pay the proper attention to merit, unconfined to Party. We shall do the most essential Service to the Common weal by Carefully avoiding the giving any just cause of offence to the Indians. Should a General war with the savages be inevitable, I have the highest Confidence in the fortitude of the Militia & their Zeal for the public Service, which Comprehends their dearest Interests. The knowledge I have formed of the Country & its Inhabitants by a long residence at Fort Pitt [1767-1772] renders my present Command highly pleasing to me. Happy should I be if I can Conduce by my Labours to the Safety of the Frontier."

He closes with some specific instructions: "Congress hath directed the removal of the Continental Troops from this Quarter except the 300 Men to be stationed at Forts Pitt, Randolph [which was at the mouth of the Kanawha] & the Kittanning as these Companies are not yet Compleated; I expect you will be pleased to take the most effectual methods in your Power to have the posts directed to be occupied on the Frontiers by the late Board of officers, kept up untill some more advantageous regulation can take place. If in the mean Time any pressing Occasion should demand an additional number of the Militia I hope they will be in readiness to march on the shortest Notice."

His introduction to Shepherd closes with "I rely greatly on your activity & public Zeal & have the Honour to be Y^r. Most obed^t. & most Hble. Servt." [12]

As is clear from this letter, one of General Hand's big concerns was the availability and readiness of the various county militia forces. Another was the forts of the region. If he was to make the frontier safe for settlers, he had to be confident of the forts. These had to be sufficient in size and number and adequately garrisoned. And clearly there was a paucity of forts. Besides Fort Pitt the only structures that Hand could consider forts were those at Wheeling (Fort Henry) and at Point Pleasant (Fort Randolph). Some private forts in which the frontier folk could find protection existed, and some crude and hastily erected stockades were actually garrisoned by small detachments from Pennsylvania's troops and from the 13th Regiment of Virginia. But all in all, their number was far from sufficient.

One of the "private" forts was simply the very large log house of one John McKibben. It was in present-day

Washington Township, not far from the nearest structure that could be called a fort, Carnahan's Blockhouse. As well as they could, a very modest company of sixty men patrolled this region, alert to the Indian presence.

During Hand's first autumn at Fort Pitt, with the farmers in the fields to harvest the oats, an Indian raiding party was discovered. There was time for warning, but Carnahan's Blockhouse, in which the frontier people had taken shelter, was furiously attacked. General Hand, much distressed, by the inadequate protection he could provide the settlers, ordered the building of a real fort for that area. It was erected promptly, but was yet only a very small stockade structure. And of course it was named for General Hand.

Although today nothing much remains, it may have been located not far from the McKibben house, according to some, on White Pine Run, some six miles from the Allegheny River and perhaps four from the Kiskiminetas. There is great confusion. The *Pennsylvania Archives* has it located in Westmoreland County, "about fourteen miles North of Hanna's Town, near the junction of Loyalhannon and Conemaugh." And a letter from a later commander of the Western Department, Colonel Daniel Brodhead, under date of June 15, 1779, suggests that it was located probably very close to Fort Crawford, "as it is there said the Indians killed a soldier between Forts Crawford and Hand, and proceeded towards the Sewickly settlement, where they killed a woman and four children, and took two children prisoners." [13]

Besides the accounts of incidents mentioned above there survives a report of Captain Samuel Miller of the 8th Pennsylvania Regiment, who was in charge of a detachment of Continental Army soldiers (nine in all) conveying grain to Fort Hand, when on July 7, 1778, they were "surprised by a party of Indians who lay in wait for them on their return and killed the Captain and seven others." [14] There is the report of another assault also, this report made in 1778 by militia Captain John

McClellan, who lived on Big Sewickly Creek, and who had been at the time providing an escort for provisions being delivered to Fort Hand.[15]

According to the Massy Harbison - Fort Hand Chapter of the Daughters of the American Revolution, "The most serious attack on Fort Hand . . .came on April 26, 1779," long after General Hand's leaving of Fort Pitt. The account which has come down has two men plowing near the fort and fired upon by a large party of Indians. Somehow the men managed an escape to the fort, but the Indians "killed horses and oxen used for plowing, as well as all cows and sheep."At this time the stockade was under the command of a Captain William Moorhead, and he had but seventeen soldiers with whom to defend it against a force thought to have numbered no fewer than one hundred. The Indians kept the fort under siege from one o'clock in that afternoon until "about noon the next day." According to the report that was made, the Indians, out of disgust apparently, set fire to an empty building which stood nearby. And on the next day abruptly and unaccountably the raiding party withdrew. [16]

As for Fort Pitt, General Hand found himself with a garrison probably sufficient to defend the fort, but certainly far from adequate for any offensive operation against the Indian country. It was composed of two companies of the Thirteenth Virginia, which Hand readily perceived were extremely short on discipline and likely to be "difficult." But at least, he reasoned, they were Continental Army regulars. He would have more authority over them than over the militiamen. Besides, there was a handful of men whom he knew could be thought of only as come-and-go independents.

During his term at Fort Pitt General Hand wrote letters constantly. He had of course to address the Supreme Executive Council of Pennsylvania and the Governor of Virginia regularly. He dispatched communications naturally to the Congress. He was, with every prospect of an "expedition," and there were many, also soliciting the lieutenants of the many counties for troops of militia. He addressed the friendly Delaware Indians on a number of occasions. But his most favored correspondent, excepting only his wife, was his wife's uncle, Jasper Yeates of Lancaster.

Shortly after his arrival at Fort Pitt, June 10, to Yeates he got off a letter of information on his situation and activity. "Dear Yeates," he addressed his friend, "Since I wrote to Kitty by Col: [George] Morgan [who had traveled to Philadelphia to consult with Congress on the Indian situation] nothing has happened in this part of the World worth notice except the murder of One man on the evening of the 7th. Instant at wheeling, I suppose by a part of the Pluggys town Gang [a hostile band of Indians noted for cruel barbarities]. The Chiefs of the wianddots & Mingoes are expect[ed] to Assemble here [Fort Pitt] towards the end of next month. . . . I have seen an Address from some of the Principle [sic] Inhabitants of Philad^a to the Inhabitants of Westmoreland, inclosing a Coppy of one to the Board of War & Assembly of Pennsylvania, & the Boards Ans^r when I saw it there was but two Signers. I am tomorrow to Attend a Genl Meeting of Militia Officers at Catfish's Camp [a white settlement at the site of present-day Washington, Pa.]. It is not improbable that the Congress will send Commissioners to meet the Indians at the Approaching Treaty." [17]

On this same day Hand wrote to Kitty. He reported that "nothing bad" has happened lately, and that "Fruitful mediation" has occurred with the Chippewas and Ottawa Indians. [18]

And as he continued to feel his way, it was not long before Hand realized (1) that some of the western Pennsylvania Delawares, and even more certainly the brazenly hostile Indians of the Ohio country, were under the influence of the British, and (2) that the threat from Detroit was real. Consequently, he came to feel that it might be best for him to organize and launch an expedition against the Indians in their nest. The reports which came steadily into him were of Indian ravages of the frontier homes along the Allegheny River and along the Ohio River as far downstream as the mouth of the Great Kanawha. Figures which came to him indicated that responsible for the incursions were some fifteen Indian war parties composed of a total of almost 300 warriors with a handful of British Rangers.

In the time before the general's arrival, many murders, Indians of whites and whites of Indians, had troubled the frontier. But after his relief of Neville such incursions became steadily more frequent. It was well known that Colonel Henry Hamilton, in command at Detroit, was dispatching war parties to attack the settlements. Toward the end of July, not without some pride, the Commandant described for his superiors at Quebec just what he was doing. He reported that he was sending out fifteen war parties, each made up of nineteen warriors (Wyandots and Miamis mostly) and two rangers.

Happily for General Edward Hand, the thirty-three-year-old Colonel George Morgan had been appointed by Congress, in April of 1776, the Indian Agent for the Middle Department, with headquarters at Fort Pitt. One of his duties, and certainly the chief one, was to oversee diplomatic relations between the settlers and the Delaware Indians, and he was very good at it. He was a close friend to the Lenape Chief White Eyes (Koquethagechton). [19]

Historians credit Morgan's highly skilled mediation with preventing any full-scale, organized Indian uprising. And he was yet in harness when General Hand showed up.

Hand was also very lucky to find at Fort Pitt Colonel John Gibson, [20] who in 1775 had been made the Indian Agent for the Pittsburgh territory to represent the interests of Virginia. He had also been elected Colonel and given command over the 6th Virginia Regiment. Like Morgan, Gibson was on very good terms with Chief White Eyes, and with many of the influential native Americans of the region. Although born in Lancaster, which fact he promptly made known to the new commander at Fort Pitt, Gibson had been active mostly in the west, a trader and a military man all his life. Regarded as a leader on the frontier, he was accorded great respect by the settlers and by the Indians alike.

General Hand was not so lucky in some of the others he discovered in Pittsburgh. He had in Simon Girty, Alexander McKee, and Matthew Eliot three notorious renegades. And from the beginning he misread the infamous Girty, actually employing him as an interpreter and a courier, even as a guide for his expeditions into the wilderness. All three of these had strong ties to the British, and at just about the end of Hand's tenure at Fort Pitt, all, with four or five others of the like mind, fled from the vicinity of Fort Pitt to the enemy.

And then there was George Croghan, whom Hand had met a decade ago. General Hand had a big problem here. Croghan was a *very* important figure on the frontier. And *very* controversial. Was he a patriot tried and true, or a Tory, sympathetic to the British? Or simply a scoundrel playing both sides against the middle? Ireland-born, like Hand (but twenty-six years older than the general), he was very early a fur trader par excellence, establishing trading posts and speaking the language of the Indians with whom he had dealings. He was much involved in land speculation and acquisition (purchasing, as early as 1749, from the Indians thousands of acres), and even something of a schemer apparently. He served as president judge in Pittsburgh, and he headed up the city's Committee of Safety.

It was during the summer of 1777 that Croghan journeyed to Williamsburg in order to clear up some confusion about rights to land that he had sold the Gratz brothers, Barnard and Michael, immigrants from Silesia, Germany and successful merchants. [21] In Croghan's absence there was uncovered a somewhat awkward suggestion of a Loyalist plot.

Already under arrest were Indian Agent Colonel George Morgan (who "had absolutely no use for George Croghan"), Simon Girty and his cohort Alexander McKee, and some others. In the course of the investigation Hand consulted the documents provided by Justice Thomas Smallman (who had been much involved in the boundary disputes), but turned up nothing much to incriminate Croghan. Still he remained suspicious, and when Croghan returned from Williamsburg, Hand accused him of treason and ordered him to Philadelphia to establish his innocence. Shortly after his arrival in the City of Brotherly Love, Philadelphia was captured and occupied by the British. General Howe, who apparently did not buy into Hand's suspicion that Croghan was motivated by Loyalist sympathies, and noting that Croghan in fact had been presiding over Pittsburgh's Committee of Safety, had him placed under house arrest.

    When the British marched out of Philadelphia in the spring of 1778, now under the command of Henry Clinton, Croghan was left behind, on parole. Patriot officials on returning to the city were just as unhappy with Croghan as Hand had been, and in fact similarly accused Croghan of treason, of collaborating with the British. In a trial, November 12, Croghan presented a most effective defense and was exonerated. Because General Hand *still* did not permit him to return to Croghan Hall in western Pennsylvania, Croghan's home for the succeeding two winters became, ironically, the home town of General Hand, Lancaster, Pa. In the spring following the second winter, May, 1780, he returned to Philadelphia, and lived out his life in Passyunk Township, dying August 21,1782, before the Treaty of Paris. [22]

    Edward Hand was a soldier, an officer in command of soldiers. But he was, first of all, a physician. He had not been at Fort Pitt long before he was made much concerned by the number of sick in the garrison. As smallpox was the big thing and terribly contagious, he elected, with the authority of

Congress, to build a quarantine hospital in which could be isolated soldiers who had been felled by a contagious disease. Accordingly, he ordered the construction of a hospital "across the river." By "across the river" he meant a portion of his own land, a very active, horse-breeding farm.

At some time, while west of the Appalachians (most likely near the end of his long stint at Fort Pitt), Edward Hand had patented some 1482 acres of land on Chartiers Creek. That he managed a farm on these acres is evident from letters that he wrote to Kitty on June 4 and June 10, 1777 (above cited). Obviously most impatient to see his property, he complains, only three days after his arrival at Fort Pitt, about how very hurried he is. He reports (as noted earlier) that he is lodging in the home of Colonel Morgan, whose "very kind & polite treatment makes me much his debtor." And then in a postscript He adds: "I have not yet been at my farm but have Seen my Steward & five of his Breeding mares."

And a week later, having noted that "nothing material has happened here Since my last [letter]" (except the murder of one man at Wheeling), he then reports his first visit to his property: "Since my last [carried] by C: Morgan, Jefry & myself have been to the farm. I could Scarcely keep him from Diving for fish in my pond — I am farming away & have no doubt of reaping the fruits of my labour —" [23]

That he got to the farm more and more often is plain from a letter he wrote to Kitty in the fall of this year, on September 27: "Jefry & myself are well and hearty. I parade two or three times a week between this place [Fort Pitt] & my Farm where I have established a Small Pox Hospital with 12 Expert Riflemen. The Exercise is good & wholesome." [24]

Upon the general's orders, the hospital had been promptly erected. It was not a large building, but it was a two-story structure, and at least 100 feet long. Of course, across the river, it was at a safe distance from Fort Pitt and protected by blockhouses. As most of the hospitalized soldiers were smallpox victims, many of them felled by a recent outbreak of the disease, it became known as the "smallpox hospital." It may have been located on that portion of Hand's property known as the Mount Pleasant Tract (present-day Ingram). Although an historical marker has been installed on West Steuben Street in the community of Ingram, in Pittsburgh's West End, the exact location of the hospital is not definitely known. At the Crafton High School athletic field a possible location is marked by a well and a tablet. It is fairly certain that the site is close to the generally muddy Chartiers Creek, and some have it precisely at the fording between the Thornsburg Bridge and the Brodhead-Fording Road. [25]

It is known that Edward Hand rented his Pittsburgh property, or portions of it. One of his tenants was James Stoops, who, perhaps with his wife Jane, may have come from Ireland with Edward Hand. Stoops was a sergeant in the Irish regiment which garrisoned Fort Pitt in the time before the Revolution. It was at some time after his discharge from the army that Stoops settled as a tenant on the land of then Ensign Edward Hand, described as two miles above the mouth of Chartiers Creek.

More information comes from a long letter from Alexander Fowler to General Edward Hand. It is dated Pittsburgh, July 22, 1780. Fowler had come to America in 1768 as a lieutenant in the British infantry. During 1769 he was a member of the Fort Pitt garrison, and in 1771-72 he was at Fort Chartres in Illinois. By 1780 he had become a permanent resident of Pittsburgh, and may have been a tenant on Hand's property. [26]

In his assignment as Head of the Western Department, Hand had arrived at Fort Pitt the first of June. He early was made to sense the situation. The frightening thing was the strong possibility that the atrocities which were occurring would escalate into an all-out war. And one of the most troubling of the conditions was that the inhabitants of the region would not, or could not, distinguish between the friendly Delaware Indians (and there were many) and the hostile Delawares. That was the fear that Indian Agent George Morgan had. As early as March of this year, 1777, Morgan expressed this concern. He declared to all who would listen that the settlers would "massacre our known friends at their hunting camps." [27] The consequences of that, he warned, were frightening to contemplate.

On the first day of August Colonel John Gibson informed the new commander that among the Delaware Indians their greatest friend was Chief White Eyes, and that, because of recent altercations, he was in real "danger of being killed." He reported that "it was with the utmost difficulty [that] I prevented one of the men who escaped [from a recent battle] from killing the [friendly] Delawares." [28]

And Gibson, shortly thereafter, following an assault by the hostile Indians which resulted in the death of a militiaman, repeated for Hand his abiding great concern. He insisted that it is "not safe for the [friendly] Delaware to pass unless you send a party down to escort them to Fort Pitt to treat." [29]

Hand, speaking to an assembly he had brought together, was quick to alert White Eyes and the friendly Delaware Indians: "Brothers the Delaware — I lately told you it would be dangerous for any Indian to come near this place [Fort Pitt] owing to the foolish conduct of the Mingos and Wyandots." [30]

By the time he had got his feet wet at Fort Pitt, and had come to understand the situation, General Edward Hand suffered the same anxiety that Morgan and Gibson had expressed. He had absolutely no doubt now that the Indian raids were inspired by Detroit. Six weeks after his arrival, in a letter to Jasper Yeates, he informed his friend that "you will see how busy the British are to engage the savages to depopulate the frontiers." [31]

It was clear to the Quakers who came west to assist the

Indians (as later at the Cornplanter tract on the upper Allegheny), as well as to the officers of the Continental Army units, that the frontiersmen were "scarcely more civilized than the Indians, redeemed only by their 'whiteness'."[32]

Benjamin Franklin, on hearing of the brutal murder of the innocent Conestoga Indian women and children in the sanctuary jail in Lancaster, in mid-December of 1763, had declared the same. And Timothy Pickering in a letter to Washington, delivered the next year, had come to a like conviction. He urged the Commander-in-Chief to recognize that "savagery was a commonality among Indians and frontier inhabitants." The only difference he could note was in skin color.[33]

But all in, all, as Hand was soon to discover, it was next to impossible to provide the kind of protection the frontier peoples of the Western Department needed and deserved. The incursions and grisly murders of the settler families continued; and reprisals in the form of militia parties were becoming better organized and more frequent.

Disappointed by his recognition of how difficult it would be to get off with an expedition into the Indian country, Hand attempted to bring peace to the frontier through councils with the Indians and overtures of friendship. He had very early called a council for June 17 at Fort Pitt. He simply wanted to address Indians who he had reason to believe would be receptive. Present were the influential Captain White Eyes and Captain John Killbuck, as well as "the wise Delawares and Shawanese at Cochocken." He first thanked them for coming and, pausing throughout for the interpreter, declared he was "much rejoiced" by the good words relayed to him by his messengers, John Jones and Thomas Nicholas. The address which followed was in the most sincere and feelingful tone that Hand could manage.

"Brothers," he begins, "As you see that what I told you when we first spoke to you, comes to pass; and as you are wise Men [you] can perceive that the Lies told you by the Governor of Detroit are likely to fall heavy on his own Head."

His chief concern seems to be the Wyandot Indians of the Ohio Valley. "You tell me that you imagine that if I spoke in a friendly manner to the Wiandots, they would now listen to me. Brothers, Tho' they have been long astray and listened only to the evil Spirit, the United States are more willing to forgive an Injury than to avenge it; therefore if the Wiandots will immediately call in their foolish young Men, and send some of their Chiefs with you to the Treaty to be held here next Month [I] will be ready to take them by the Hand and enter into friendship with them."

In a more plaintive tone, with a warning attached, he appeals to the chiefs to "tell this to the Wiandots and assure them that if they refuse it they will never have another opportunity," and he predicts, "you may depend, that before the waters are again frozen, there will not be an English Soldier at Detroit or Niagara, unless they are Prisoners."

He has bad news for those who ally with the British: "Every person who comes up says, that the English are making ready to go on board their Vessels at Philad'a; and that the French have taken two of their West India Islands from them, but I can't tell you this is true." He has a specific favor to ask: "I desire you may watch the Motions of Mr [Robert?] Lemot, and the Canadians under his Command, and give me timely notice of his Movements, the Number he has with him, & where he intends to Strike; if you will appoint ten or twelve of your active young men to do this Business, they shall have two Dollars per Day each, for the time you employ them, provided they give me good & timely Intelligence."

All of this General Hand asked "as a Mark of your Friendship." He closed with "Farewell, and be assured of the good Intentions of the United States towards you & all friendly Nations." [34]

But General Hand through this first summer was

experiencing a very rough time as Commander of the Western Department. Almost every day brought a new report of an Indian raid or of some horrible barbarity practiced on the frontier families. These he reported in a steady stream of letters to the Supreme Executive Council of Pennsylvania. More than ever before he felt the very real need to dispatch a punitive expedition into the Indian country. With this in mind, and having enclosed documents providing details of recent murders, on July 24, 1777, he continues to appeal to President Thomas Wharton, who is a close Lancaster friend: "From the inclosed papers your Exc^y will be able to inform a tolerable idea of the disposition of the Indians [.] To what may be learned from these acc'ts I must add the murder of two men on the Allegany River about 20 miles from this place on the 21st ultimo, Pluggy's Town gang with two Tribes of the Shawanese, & some of the Delawares, refuse to listen to the advice of our few Friends.

"In short, every days experience teaches me that nothing but penetrating their Country & destroying the settlements of these perfidious miscreants, can prevent the depopulation of the frontiers. This I have determined on, as soon as I can procure a sufficiency of Provisions, and raise enough men to ensure success."

He knows the Indians; he knows what he is talking about: "Sad experience has taught us that little dependance can be put on the promises or professions of the savages, & I am well assured that the tribes making the greatest show of Friendship, will not sit still whilst we chastise the Banditti that infests our settlements, unless we have a force sufficient to intimidate them."

With the expedition in mind, he has an urgent request of President Wharton: "As I shall be under the necessity of applying to the County of Westmoreland and probably to that of Bedford for aid, I beg that your Exc^y may be pleased to give orders to the Militia Officers of these Counties to furnish me with what men they can spare for that purpose." And then, out of the instinct he was famous for, and which Washington had many occasions to applaud, General Hand reported to Wharton that the "Indians are now going to a treaty at Oswego [Fort Ontario]" and he infers from his knowledge that "some men and Stores have lately been sent to Oswego," that "something may be attempted by the way of the Susquehanna, or towards Albany."[35] This letter was written from Fort Pitt on July 24. On the very next day General Barrimore ("Barry") St. Leger landed with his troops at Fort Ontario, in a prepared invasion towards Albany, the first leg of the Saratoga Campaign.

Confident that Wharton will come through with the necessary pressure, Hand plunged forward with organization. During the first two weeks of August he dispatched alerts to his officers, to Captain Samuel Moorhead, Major Henry Taylor, Colonels David Shepherd and Zackwell Morgan, to Thomas Brown, David Mclure, and John Bowyer. On August 12, from Redstone, he appealed to Colonel William Fleming,[36] the County Lieutenant of Bottetourt, in the Virginia territory. In all of these letters General Hand first noted that he had determined on a punitive campaign against the hostile Indians, and, second, urged the officers to posthaste strengthen the forts for which they were responsible, and, third, alerted all to his need for militia men in big numbers.

The month of July had been rife with atrocities; for August it was more of the same. Indian raids upon the settlements, with the murder of frontier families continued. Hand had a steady stream of anguished reports coming in from all corners of his department. He had letters not only from Gibson (who was much of the time at Logstown), but from Colonel David Shepherd, Captain Samuel Moorhead, Samuel Mason, James Booth, Archibald Lochry, and James Chambers. On July 27, a troubled Patrick Henry, Governor of Virginia, from Williamsburg, pledged to General Hand, "every possible Aid & Furtherance." He declared that he would advise the

~ Fort Pitt ~

county lieutenants of this promise and would urge them to be prepared to provide the provisions necessary for a punitive campaign.[37][

But despite the frequency of raids and the "orders" laid down by Governors Henry and Wharton and the entreatments of the Head of the Western Department, response was not enthusiastic. It could almost be considered indifferent. General Edward Hand, not surprisingly, was brought close to despair. He is certainly much discouraged by the failure of those most in need of protection to supply the men he requires. But he does not give up; he does not abandon hope. He continues, *constantly*, to report the barbarities and to complain to the Supreme Executive Council.

The Council, Thomas Wharton still President, is responding. On August 5, it advises Colonel Archibald Lochry, who insists he has been wanting instruction, rather curtly: "Council have understood that you have been called upon by General Hand for detachments & parties of the Militia of Westmoreland to defend the frontier, that you have granted them from time to time, but were anxious to be instructed on this subject . . . ." The council's instruction is simple: "Do it." [38]

But still Hand was getting little satisfaction, from Lochry or anybody else, and when Pennsylvania's Supreme Executive Council met on Thursday, August 7, 1777, it had another and even more impatient letter from the general at Fort Pitt. President Thomas Wharton read it to the Board. It repeated the earlier request. What Hand wanted was the issuing of *orders* to the militia officers of Westmoreland and Bedford County, these orders to *require* them to provide him "what Men they can spare, for the purpose of penetrating the Indian Country and destroying their settlements." If we are to put a stop to the cruelties these Indians have been engaged in, it is absolutely necessary, Hand insisted, that we mount an expedition.

Council ordered the request be sent to Congress,"for

their consideration and direction thereon." [39] And the Continental Congress does get in on it. It had passed, on August 16, a plain enough position statement: "That the president & supreme executive council of Pennsylvania be requested to give Brigadier Hand such assistance from the militia of the counties of Westmoreland, Northumberland & Bedford, as General Hand may think necessary." [40]

To the increasingly impatient General Hand, on August 22, President Wharton reported on what so far has been done: "I communicated to Council your Letter, & the inclosed accounts of the late inroads & cruelties of the savages. You may be assured that Council without loss of time, took the same into consideration, and I take this opportunity to inform you, that the most full and explicit Instructions had been already forwarded to Archibald Laughrie [Lochry], Esqr, of Westmoreland. He is commanded to fulfill your order for detachments & parties of Militia to the utmost of his power. These dispatches are dated the 5th of this month."

But there was more: "The like injunctions are now forwarded to John Piper, Esquire, Lieutenant of Bedford County, & to Samuel Hunter, Esqr, Lieu^t of Northumberland. We hope that you will be able to derive the necessary advantage from the Militia of these Counties." [41]

On August 25, from Fort Pitt, Hand advised Jasper Yeates that "Indian affairs remain as when I last wrote to you," that is, requiring action. "I have demanded 2000 men from the Several frontier Counties of Virginia and Pennsylvania if I get them [I] cant have a doubt of reducing the Wyandots & Pluggys Town Confederacy, at present our most Troublesome Neighbours." He laments that "This County is in great confusion & Distress at present. The prospect of fixing a permanent boundary between Virginia and Pennsylvania, gives the people much satisfaction, next to Chastising the Indians, they desire that may take place." [42]

On the very same day, out of the same anxiety, he

reported to Kitty on the situation: "The safety of the country depends on our being able to penetrate the Indian country; but whether I can accomplish it, I don't yet know. Certain it is, that with a proper force (without which it will not be attempted), a measure of that nature be executed without greater danger than this garrison [Fort Pitt] is exposed to."

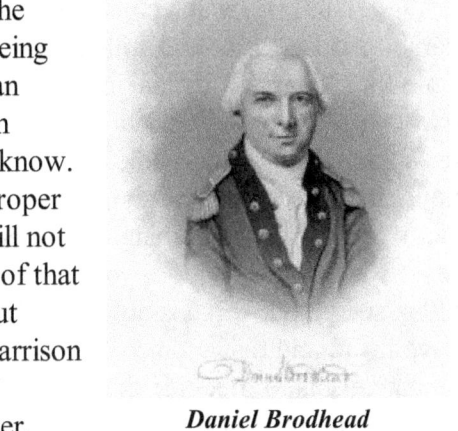

Daniel Brodhead

He describes for her, then, two recent incursions, one on August 16 at Beaver Run in Westmoreland County, and another the next day from a party of Chippewas.[43]

During September, Fort Henry, which had been built in the summer of 1774 by William Crawford and Angus McDonald, came under siege on three different occasions. These assaults General Hand learned about from Colonels John Gibson and David Shepherd, and from Devereux Smith.

As if the general did not have enough trouble he had at about this time an unsettling letter from the Commander-in-Chief. Washington, now in Wilmington, Delaware, on September 4, is very much hoping that what he has heard is not true, but if it is . . . : "Sir: Colonel [Daniel] Brodhead of the 8th Pennsylvania Regiment has represented to me, that several of his Officers [Captain Samuel Miller, Lt. Richard Richardson, Lt. John Hughes] sent to Westmoreland with large sums of Public Money, for the purposes of recruiting men for his Corps and recovering others who had deserted from it, were detained by your influence and countenance from their Regiment. I know not what foundation he may have for this assertion, but if the fact be true, it is a piece of conduct of a very unwarrantable and injurious nature . . . ."[44] As apparently nothing ever came of this, it should probably be charged up to confusion.

Hand, still much concerned about the size of his garrison at Fort Pitt, and still not getting sufficient satisfaction from the Congress, and anxious about the assignments that may be given the Continental soldiers he has in garrison, wrote to Washington in the middle of September. He expressed the hope that he would be retaining the men who belonged to the Continental Army. Washington promptly responded with regrets about the "state of your garrison," but with good news: "I am sorry your force is not more adequate to the uses you have for it, and that such coldness appears in the neighboring inhabitants as to preclude the assistance you had a right to expect from them. I have no objection to you detaining any of the Continental troops now with you: except which belong to the 8th Regiment . . . ." [45]

Hand, having suffered discouragement and triumphed over it, became steadily more and more determined to get his expedition launched. To Colonel William Fleming, September 7, he repeats his earlier appeal for militiamen: "Sir — on the 12th Ultimo I did myself the Honour of writing to you and requesting you to furnish 200 men properly Officered and equipped for an Expedition into the Indian Country. For Six months from the 1st. Inst. If so long wanted, and to order them to march to Fort Randolph on the Great Kanawha as soon as possible, I can Assure you that what has Since happened encreases rather than lessens the necessity for Accelerating their March. I beg you may therefore Use every possible means to Accomplish my desire, and Inform me by express when your men March & the time you expect them to Arrive at Fort Randolph. The Inclosed you will please to forward to the Officer Commanding at the Kanawha by the Troops that march from your County." [46]

On September 17, General Hand, in an address enthusiastically applauded by David Zeisberger, reached out to the friendly Delawares; and on this day and the next so did

John Page, Lieutenant Governor of Virginia, and so did Colonel George Morgan. For these expressions of friendship Chief White Eyes expressed his gratitude, September 22 and 23.

It was about a week later that General Hand's campaign, only in its forming stages, suffered its first tragedy. Captain William Foreman, of Hampshire County, Virginia, with forty-six militiamen, on a march to "take part in Hand's projected expedition," were ambushed by a party of twenty to twenty-five warriors, and largely wiped out, nearly half the party murdered by the marauding Indians. The dead, including two of Foreman's sons, were all buried in a common grave, and a monument was installed at the site. The inscription is very touching: "This humble stone is erected to the memory of Captain Foreman and twenty [twenty-one?] of his brave men, who were slain by a band of ruthless savages — the allies of a civilized nation of Europe — on the 28th [27th] of September, 1777. So sleep the brave who sink to rest by all their country's wishes blest." [47]

General Hand followed up his address to the friendly Delawares with a continued reassurance delivered October 1; and that was supported by George Morgan, over a period of two days, who was after that again on his way to Philadelphia and the Continental Congress. [48]

From the letter Hand dispatched to Jasper Yeates on October 2, it is clear that the expedition is now in big trouble: "Dear Yeates — from Intelligence rec^d Yesterday from the Delawar[e] at Coochachunk, I find that the Tweetees [Twigtwee (Miami)], Wyachtanas [Ouiatanon, a sub-tribe of the Miami], & Kickapoo, have returned the Tomahawk, and that the tribe of Delawares headed by Wendaughaland are Wiavering [wavering]. The Regular troops at Detroit, am^t. to no more than 70, & the Militia to 300, so that we need not dread a Visit from that Quarter, tho the People here are well disposed, savage like, to Murder a defenceless unsuspecting

Indian. I do not find them Much inclined to enter the Indian Country, and believe that no great matter will be achieved in the West this Season. . . . Jessy is well." [49]

That same day he dispatched a thank-you letter to Kitty: I have tried your Smok'd Beef, Tongues & think all are Exquisitely good. In return I intend Sending you Some [?] preserved with Grapes when I have an Opertunity." [50]

And it was the very next day on which General Hand had detailed reports from both Colonel David Shepherd and Major James Chew (who are both at Fort Henry) on the Captain Foreman disaster. And one week later Major Chew produced for the general a *very* long letter on the conditions at Fort Henry, information which could only distress Hand the more.

But the impression that his campaign plans have not been completely laid aside emerges from a letter from Captain William Linn, from Catfish Camp, October 11, about troops for the expedition. He is, obviously, hopeful; and Hand's letter (October 13) to Colonel John Piper, now head of the Bedford County militia, is still about raising troops for a late fall-winter march into the region producing the Indian raiding parties. In this letter to Piper, the general notes that he "has ordered 150 men from Bedford and 250 from Westmoreland for an expedition into the Indian country." Moreover, in a letter (October 14) to Colonel William Russell, [51] while acknowledging that he has been plagued "with many difficulties," General Hand declares that he has yet the "hope to drink your health in pure element at Sandusky before Christmas." [52]

But then the discouragements began to appear. While General Hand was on his way to Fort Henry (October 21) an urgent letter from Archibald Steel back at Fort Pitt caught up with him: "Dear General Hand — I Need Not inform you how the Militia Behaved after you Set out for Wheeling . . . . they Left this [Fort Pitt] at 10 of the Clock on Sunday Evening.

Yesterday they Stoptd at Logs town in the morning where the[y] met with two or three indians. Which By all accounts Defeated the whole Party killd one and wounded one. Magor [Major James] Chue [Chew] hapned to Com to them Just after the indians fired and fled. He found the whole Party So alarmd that he Could Not get one Man to assist him to Surround a Cornfield where the[y] thought the indians were. But I Beleve they Proceeded on their Jorney." . . . I have just Convers^d with Capt. Wm. Loughry [brother of Archibald] about the Militia of westmoreland. He Cannot Give any acount whether one man from that Place will come to your assistance or Not." [53]

    Hand heard that same day from Major James Chew and again just two days later. The major was continuing hopeful that the expedition would go. And Colonel John Gibson, who had had the discouraging report from William Loughry, was remaining optimistic.

    On the subject of whether to proceed at this time with an expedition General Hand called for a meeting of his officers November 1. Because of the approaching winter and the limited number of militiamen available, the officers' decision was negative on the campaign for this time. Hand's letter to Kitty, November 2, reports the outcome: "I am just returned from a visit to Fort Henry on the Ohio, and am sorry to inform you that I despair of being able to do anything effectual this season." [54] Three days later, a "mortified" General Edward Hand, unable "to collect a sufficient body of men," countermands the orders to assemble the militia. From Fort Pitt on November 9, he reported to the Commander-in-Chief, General Washington, that the expedition had been abandoned. He also on this day notified Governor Patrick Henry of Virginia, and Richard Peters, Secretary to the Board of War. [55]

    On this same day General Hand got off a letter to Kitty: "I believe I informed you in my last that I could not accomplish an expedition into the Indian country. I was much deceived in the real Strength & Spirit of this part of the county; but hope that the prosperity of our affairs to the Northward [the defeat of Burgoyne at Saratoga, October 17, with the surrender of his entire army, 5800 soldiers] will have a happy influence on the Western Indians."

He hopes to get to Lancaster soon: "Jesse [Ewing] & myself intend a voyage to the Great Kenahawa & are to set out to-morrow; on our return which will be by Staunton, in Virginia, I will apply for leave to go down the country." [56]

It had been a very rough summer for the new Commander of the Western Department; and it had been an anguished and most disappointing fall season. But for General Edward Hand by far the worst was yet to come.

On November 10, 1777, one of the closest of the settlers' Indian friends, the Shawnee Chief Cornstalk (Hokoleskwa, Colesqua) was brutally murdered at Fort Randolph. Cornstalk, the influential head of the Shawnee in the Virginia territory had commanded the Shawnee and Mingo Indians at the battle of Point Pleasant (where the great Kanahwa joins the Ohio) on October 10, 1774. His defeat put an end to Lord Dunmore's War, and made Cornstalk an agent for peaceful relations between the Shawnee and the frontier settlers.

During the first two years of the American Revolution, Cornstalk worked tirelessly to keep the Shawnee neutral. At the treaty councils, including two at Fort Pitt, Cornstalk spoke eloquently for his people. He signed the first Indian treaties ever negotiated with the new nation, called the United States.

The chief, so far successful in keeping his Shawnee people out of the Revolution, and determined on peace, was, in November of 1777, on a diplomatic mission to Fort Randolph (at the very site of the Point Pleasant battle), when he was detained, without any greater authority, by the commander of the fort. When an American militiaman was slain by unidentified Indians in the immediate neighborhood of Fort Randolph, his enraged fellows rushed to the fort and brutally executed Chief Cornstalk, his son Elinipsico, and two other Shawnee. It was an unconscionable act, and for it, though he was not in any way responsible, General Edward Hand from some quarters received blame.

Perhaps Hand should have countermanded the order for the detention of Cornstalk, but he could have had no intimation of what was to occur. He certainly was appalled by the assassination. And Patrick Henry, Governor of Virginia, and responsible for Fort Randolph, was outraged. He declared the murderers "vile assassins," and he insisted vehemently that those responsible for the murder be brought immediately to trial. And so they were. And they were acquitted — simply because not a single soldier of the Fort Randolph garrison, nor any militiaman, "could be moved to testify against them." The date of the murder was November 10, 1777. The noble Chief Cornstalk was probably sixty years old.[57]

But the Indians, too, were guilty of atrocities of this kind, and as more and more reports of murdered frontier families came to him, General Hand became ever more determined on an expedition of his own. It would be composed of whatever militiamen he could round up from Bedford and Westmoreland counties, and all of the frontier counties of western Virginia. He would descend the Ohio with this force, assembled in Pittsburgh and at Forts Henry and Randolph, and at the mouth of the Big Kanawha proceed to march overland to destroy the Shawnee towns on the Sciota River.

Letters were dispatched to the militia commanders of all these counties. The response was disappointing, almost no men from Bedford County and only 100 from Colonel Lochry's Westmoreland. Hand set out to recruit anyway, hoping for sufficient numbers from Virginia. In Wheeling (site of Fort Henry) only a few squads appeared, and these were most inadequately equipped. After one week of waiting for more militiamen, Hand threw in the bag and returned to Fort Pitt. The largest body of volunteers had assembled at Fort

Randolph. In vain they waited for their commander. After two weeks, they returned to their homes.

General Hand of course was keenly disappointed. He could never understand why the settlers, with their homes constantly in great danger, could not mount an organized resistance. It was what bothered him most — the great difficulty he had in securing cooperation from the settlers themselves. A letter from General Daniel Roberdeau to Lancaster's Thomas Wharton, is interesting in this respect. From York, November 19, 1777, Roberdeau reports that General Hand has been "sent westward authorised by this State to call the Militia together for the very purpose now solicited by the back Inhabitants." Unfortunately, as Hand, to his astonishment, has discovered, it seems that the settlers "were not in a humour to turn out, for this, that and a Thousand reasons which probably could not be obviated without violating the Militia Law and Discarding many Officers the Gen' perhaps not excepted." [58]

On November 20, Congress, in response to Hand's declaration of needs (His letter was read to the Congress.), resolved to appoint three commissioners to repair to Fort Pitt "without delay" to investigate Hand's litany of troubles. They were to apprise the Shawanese Indians and the Delaware of the genuine friendship and services of the United States. They were empowered to carry the war to Detroit if thought desirable. It was hoped also that Colonel William Crawford (with whom Hand had already had association) could be of help to the general. [59]

During this November General Hand had very little to feel good about. But one event of great good news came to him just at the close of the month. It was the happy report from Kitty of the birth of their second child. Arriving on the 26th and named Dorothy, as they had agreed a female child would be, she was doing fine. Naturally her father was most eager to see her. He began to think about how that might be managed. He was overwhelmed with problems.

Some idea of the gravity of the situation and of the difficulty General Hand was having with the frontier settlers and with the numbers of militia may be gleaned from a letter dispatched from the above mentioned Archibald Lochry, County Lieutenant for Westmoreland County.[60]

To President Wharton he reports on December 6 to verify the "unspeakable ravages of the Indians," and to lament again that General Hand required "more than I could Possibly furnish from two Batallions . . . I sent One Hundred Men for the Expedition, some of them reached the General at Fort Pitt, the Remainder was Stopt by His Order." [61]

All the while General Hand was trying to put together an army barbarities and "unspeakable atrocities were occurring" in his department. Raids in Ligonier Valley, and at Fort Wallace, near present Blairsville, Pa., not to mention a number on the Ohio and the Allegheny, resulted in the indiscriminate murder of women and children, the firing of homes, the destruction of livestock and grain fields, and the theft of horses.[62]

While Hand was visiting Fort Henry at Wheeling, on the 5th of December, Colonel John Gibson got off a letter to the Commander-in-Chief, which alludes to anxiety on the frontier and the likelihood of war in the spring. He encloses for Washington an account of the size of the garrison at Fort Pitt, reporting three companies of the 13th Virginia Regiment and two companies of independent Virginia troops, including fifteen commissioned officers, twenty-eight non-commissioned officers, and 213 rank and file. In view of the increasing likelihood of an assault, he does not regard the garrison as sufficient: "By the inclosed Return Your Excellency will be made Acquainted with the strength of the Garrison of this place. Genl Hand ordered me to send the Deserters from the Different Corps at Camp down by Capt. Saml Miller of the 8th Pensl. Regt, which I Accordingly have done, Excepting those of the 13th Virga Regt and some who were sick. I shoud have sent the whole of them But at the time of Capt. Millers March, from the number of men who were on Commands, at the Smallpox Hospital, & Employed as Artificers, we cou'd hardly mount a Serjts Guard. I make no doubt Genl. Hand has already Acquainted your Excellency of the Situation of Affairs in this Country and of his having gone down to Regulate the Garrisons on the Ohio. [Hand had done this, Nov. 9.] Since he left this place nothing Material has happened. Simon Girty a Messenger dispatched by General Hand to the Seneca towns on the Heads of the Allegheny, Returned here a few days a goe, he in forms us Guasota [Guyasuta, Cornplanter's uncle] a Chief of them had Returned from War, that he had killed four people near Legonier, that another party Returned and Brought in a white Woman and three Scalps whilst he was in the towns, that they told him all the Nations Excepting White Eyes and a few Delawares would strike us in the spring . . . . " [63]

The coming of the snows toward the end of November had quieted the frontier a good bit. But Hand had very bad news at Christmastime. It was reported to him that the British had established a magazine at the mouth of the Cuyahoga River (present Cleveland), and were day by day storing arms and ammunition, provisions and miscellaneous supplies, presumably to equip the Ohio Indians for their raids on the settlements in the spring. Even though it was mid-winter, Hand was quick to respond. The destruction of the magazine, which was precisely located, he regarded as an "easy" mission for a company of militiamen. And it would do wonders for morale. As is known from the letters exchanged by Washington and Colonel William Crawford,[64] he dispatched all over Bedford and Westmoreland Counties urgent calls for "brave, active lads" to come to Fort Pitt in order to organize for a short campaign.

One of the letters he addressed to Colonel William Crawford, dated February 5, 1778, read, in part: "As I am credibly informed that the English have lodged a quantity of arms, ammunition, provision and clothing at a small Indian town about 100 miles from Fort Pitt to support the savages in their excursions against the inhabitants of this and adjacent counties, I ardently wish to collect as many brave active lads as are willing to turn out, to destroy the magazine. Every man must be provided with a horse, and every article necessary to equip them [him] for the expedition, except ammunition which, with some arms, I can furnish."

He very much hopes that Crawford can round up a sufficient militia force: ". . . it may not be necessary to assure them, that everything they are able to bring away shall be sold at public venue for the sole benefit of the captors, & the money equally distributed, tho' I am certain that a sense of the service they will render to their country will operate more strongly than the expectation of gain. I therefore expect you will use your influence on this occasion, & bring all the volunteers you can raise to Fort Pitt by the 15th of this month [February]." [65]

It had required more than a month to assemble the party, but eventually Hand had the men he felt he needed, 357 (perhaps 362) horsemen, organized into four battalions under

William Crawford Cabin

the command of Colonel Alexander Barr. Many of the militiamen had been rounded up by Colonel Crawford from all along the Braddock Road, near the Youghiogheny and the Monongahela. General Hand was pleased. He was ready to go.

The weather was mean for the early stages of the trip (snow followed by a "miserable" rain), but the company proceeded at a fair pace, down the Ohio by way of a familiar Indian path, then upstream on Beaver Creek to the Mahoning River, and north toward Cuyahoga. They were headed for Sandusky.

The streams, of course, were much swollen from the ceaseless rains, and swamps had appeared everywhere. As the going became more and more difficult, the men, soaked through and very cold, turned sour on the campaign. Persuaded by these ugly conditions, Hand elected to give up on the expedition. But just as he was about to issue a command, the footprints of Indians were perceived in the mud. The tracks led the militiamen to a small village on the Shenango River, near present New Castle. An attack was ordered. No warriors appeared. The natives who were in the huts were all old men, women and children. Upon the appearance of the horsemen, all fled into the surrounding forest. And all escaped into the welcoming gloom — except three. Two were shot down, an old [man and a woman]. One woman was taken prisoner. When the militiamen made as if to kill her, General Hand and his officers interfered.

Apparently the woman who had been spared was grateful, so much so that she reported the location of a salt lick some ten miles up the Mahoning, at which they would find ten young men at work.

As it turned out, the ten men, whom she had identified as Wolf Clan or Muncy warriors, proved to be five. And these were four Indian women and one small boy!

What happened next goes down as one of those senseless, cowardly murders that were so tragically common on the western frontier. Three of the four women were ruthlessly murdered, and so was the boy. The remaining woman was made a prisoner, and was spared, presumably by the appearance of the officers. *Much* distressed by what had happened, and noting that any advance in weather conditions like these would border on the ridiculous, Hand ordered an end to the expedition.

For the details we have an eye-witness account. It makes vivid an impression of the extreme cruelty and the shameful cowardice of the militiamen. It is provided by Samuel Murphy, who was a member of the expedition: "General Hand's expedition. This was in the winter 1777-78 with a slight fall of fresh snow. About 400 men . . . [Lt.] Col. Providence Mounts, of Mounts Creek, which empties in Youghiogheny, was out. Col. William Crawford, Major Brenton, Capt. John Stevenson, captain Scott, etc. William Brady, a blacksmith of Pittsburgh, was chosen pilot. Simon Girty was out, and wanted the appointment.

"On the way out, Major Brenton lost his horse, and he got Simon Girty to remain with him, they found the horse, and rejoined the army just at the close of the fight, or rather firing [!], on the Indian town, in the forks of Neshanek and Shenango and on the eastern bank of the latter. Orders had been given as they approached the town to surround it, but [Lt.] Colonel Mounts did not fully accomplish his part, and left a gap, and Pipe's wife and children got off, a little fall of snow on the ground. This Pipe was a brother of Captain Pipe, who was a most influential Lenape chief of the Wolf Clan. The Mother of the Pipes, an old squaw, was pursued and shot at repeatedly, when [Lieutenant] Thomas Ravenscroft ran up to the old squaw and tried to pull her away, but the bullets [were] still flying, and [he] had a ball through his legging; when a Major came up and put a stop to [the] firing, when it was ascertained that the only injury she had received was the loss of an end of the little finger. An old squaw was shot by Lieut. [John]

Hamilton and wounded in the leg, mistaking her for a warrior [!]; and a soldier ran up and tomahawked her, and a second ran up and shot her. Pipe shot and wounded Captain Scott and disabled his arm, and when nearly ready to shoot again, some one shot Pipe, and Reason Virgin passing sunk the tomahawk in his head. There commenced a wild yelling and shooting, without giving the least heed to the officers. A few cabins only were there, a little plunder obtained. This was about midday in February or March.

"That afternoon a party started off for a small settlement several miles up the Mahoning at a place called the Salt Lick. Simon Girty went as pilot. They did not reach the place until in the night, found the warriors all absent hunting, found a few squaws there, and took [one] prisoner and brought her off, the others were left. A small Indian boy out with a gun shooting birds was discovered and killed, and several claimed the honor; and it was left to Girty to decide, and his decision was that one Zach Connell killed the lad."

Upon reaching the first town, the militia determined to leave the mother of Pipe there. "An old Dutchman scalped the squaw that had been killed, and put the scalp in his wallet with his provisions and in swimming a stream on return the Dutchman lost off his wallet, and exclaimed pathetically 'O, I loss my prosoc and my sculpt'."[66]

When the people of the Pittsburgh region had the details, they referred to the expedition derisively as the "Squaw Campaign," a term that carried with it both the sense of shame and contempt.

How much to blame was General Edward Hand, not only for the failure of the mission, but, most especially for the senseless murder of women, old men, and children?

When the first village of friendly Delawares was attacked, Hand, as he explained to Jasper Yeates in a letter of March 7, was "mortified" by the murders. He could not believe what was happening. "The men were so impetuous that I could not prevent their killing the man & one of the women. Another woman was taken & with difficulty saved." This woman, apparently grateful for her life, "told us that ten miles higher [on the river], ten Moncy [Muncy] men were making salt. I detached a party to secure them, they turned out to be 4 women & a boy." For this second assault General Hand again pleaded helplessness. He insisted that the efforts he made to dissuade the militiamen from their determination to kill every Indian, regardless of age or sex were tardy or in vain. To Yeates he described how the troops attacked "four women with a boy, of these, one woman only was saved." [67]

When writing to Kitty on this same day he reports merely that "Since I last wrote to you Jefry & Myself have had a Disagreeable tour into the Indian country." He is a most unhappy officer. He complains about the failure of the Indian Commissioners to appear, and says that I "expect every week to be the last of my stay here — what shall I complain of next?" [68]

General Hand of course, as organizer and commander of the expedition has to be held responsible. And he accepted the blame. In no way could he excuse himself. He may, indeed, have felt helpless. But it was his mission. He had organized it and commanded it. But he was woefully discouraged. This "expedition into the Indian country" was a far cry from what he had been envisioning since his arrival at Fort Pitt. He was most unhappy with frontier militiamen. He found himself longing for the professional army. He promptly got off a letter to the Commander-in-Chief, not to resign from the army, but to request a new command. Washington had the request put before the Continental Congress.

While the Squaw Campaign failed in its mission, it did have some noteworthy effects, many of them negative for the frontier Americans. It was certainly not without consequence. For one thing, it reinforced the impression that General Hand and regular army officers had had for a long time, that in

Captain Pipe

dealing with Indians regular army soldiers and officers are better (that is, more humane) than are the militia, most of whom were remembering the murder by Indians of members of their families or neighbors.

In the second place, it produced the likely effect of bringing over to hostility the heretofore friendly Delawares (Chief Pipe's brother of course was a casualty of the campaign.). And indeed it was not long before the increased hostility among the Delawares became evident. Clearly very strong anti-American feelings were being voiced in the Indian councils. In May hostile bands of Delawares (some of whom had been previously friendly) joined a huge force of Wyandots and Mingos to lay siege to Fort Laurens. According to a communication delivered to Congress by Colonel George Morgan, among the Delawares were John Montour and his brother Che,cheas, who had fled from Kuskuski when General Hand's men murdered the Delaware women and children. Poo,ques,an,geech,ca, a nephew of Captain Pipe was also among them. According to Morgan, Poo,ques,an,geech,ca had always been friendly, "a man well-disposed toward the United States." He had never fought against the Americans or had been involved in any of the frontier barbarities. Even for a while after the Squaw Campaign murders he remained quiet, but was finally made hostile to the Americans and joined the

Wyandots.[69]

Thirdly, it provided the British with another argument for the friendship of the native Americans.

Fourthly it inspired a review of the frontier conditions and Indian-white relationships and an assessment of the chances for peace, which certainly were much imperiled by the campaign.

Fortunately, most of what might have happened did not, as explained by Daniel Sullivan. In a letter to Colonel John Cannon, from Fort Pitt, March 20, he advised that the Delawares "have always been and still are well-disposed for peace, unless the late unfortunate affair at Beaver Creek and the other murders committed at Fort Pitt has soured their mind." And George Morgan immediately wrote to his friend Chief White Eyes: "I hope you will use your interest to bring Captain Pipe and other wisemen here that we may renew and strengthen our ancient friendship."[70]

As it happened Captain Pipe had not been totally alienated by the Squaw Campaign. On December 21 in a letter to Captain John Killbuck [71] he indicated that he had nearly forgotten the whole thing: "I am greatly rejoiced to hear the message you sent me. You make mention in your speech to me of the loss of my relations who were killed last spring at the Salt Licks. I now inform you that I never thought of it until your mentioning it put me in mind of it." He insists on a continuing friendship: "I now acquaint that my heart is good and that I never meant to quit the hold I have of the friendship subsisting between us. If you are desirous of speaking of the loss of my friends who were killed at the Salt Licks, there is a great many of my relatives at Cooshackung [Coshocton]. Your speaking to them will answer the same as speaking to me. As the weather is very cold, I cannot tell you in how many nights I shall come to see you. But you may depend on it shall be soon."[72]

It is worth noting, however, that the torture-death of

Colonel William Crawford at the hands of Captain Pipe's warriors, in June of 1782, was carried out with the permission of Captain Pipe, who, in fact was presiding. It is also worth noting that after the war and during President Washington's difficulties with the hostile Indian tribes of the Ohio Valley, Chief Pipe counseled the Miami and Shawnee and the Wyandots to establish and maintain friendly relations with the new United States.[73]

But in the fifth place, because of the atrocities that were now being paraded, the campaign pointed up the need for more forts for refuge for the settlers.

And what did it mean to General Hand? He had come to Fort Pitt with a very clear view of his responsibility. What the Congress wanted was peace on the frontier, which could come only through friendship with the people whose land the settlers were trespassing on. With a limited understanding of how very difficult it would be for the Head of the Western Department to achieve and preserve such a friendship, General Hand earnestly and most intensely himself desired the same.

But in just a years's time he had been reduced to disappointment and a sense of futility. This last campaign had given him great pain. He was made most sad by what had happened, and ashamed of the entire mission. He was a soldier, not determined on the murder of innocent and helpless women and children. He now felt next to helpless to accomplish what he had hoped for.[74] What he could not know at this time was that by his abbreviated command at Fort Pitt, painful and disappointing as it was, he had been provided mighty preparation for his next big assignment.

Way back in December, in a long letter of the 9th General Hand, who was then in Staunton, Virginia, had described for the Governor the most regrettable murder of Cornstalk; and from Fort Pitt he wrote the same to the Secretary of War.[75]

On the day before Christmas, while addressing Jasper

Yeates, he was yet on this subject: "Jessy can give you the Particulars of Our late Ramble, & of the Murder of Cornstalk, his son & two other Shawanese Indians at Fort Randolph. If we had anything to expect from that Nation it is now Vanished." And he has a bombshell to drop: "I am so heartily tired of this place that I have [this day] petitioned Congress to be recall'd. I hope it may be granted me." [76]

Apparently Hand expects that he could be replaced by Colonel William Crawford. His request for reassignment was dispatched to Richard Peters, Secretary of the Board of War: "I think that as it is now winter, & Col. Crawford present, my absence for some time would not be attended with inconvenience. If Congress have no particular objection, [I] would esteem it as a most singular indulgence to be recalled & suffered to join the grand army, with them to share the honors & fatigues of the field. Indeed, unless our affairs will admit of the assistance of a regular force, I had rather resign my office than continue here in command of militia." [77]

Hand's lieutenant, his brother-in-law Major Jasper Ewing, had an easier time of it. Just after Christmas he began preparations for his departure for Lancaster.

But as the new year broke, new plans were laid down, and they included expeditions. One was to be headed up by Virginia's George Rogers Clark. General Hand had a letter from

George Rogers Clark

Governor Henry which appealed for cooperation. On January 2, he requested Hand "to furnish Major [now Lieutenant Colonel] G. R. Clark with boats sufficient for conveying seven companys of militia on an expedition of great consequence. . . . And I must entreat you, Sir, to give Major Clark every assistance [including powder and lead] which he may want. The boats I hope will not long be wanted . . . it is needless to inform you how necessary it is that the whole affair should be kept impenetrably secret." [78] And Governor Henry asked pretty much the same of Hand for the planned expedition of Colonel David Rogers (a native of Virginia, or perhaps Maryland) to New Orleans. Hand, with boats and provisions was able to accommodate David Rogers, too, though the expedition was destined for disaster.[79]

It was just at this time (January 6) that the first of the three commissioners whom Congress had authorized way back on November 20 showed up at Fort Pitt. General Hand was glad to see him. This was Pennsylvania's delegate to Congress, George Clymer. As he informed Yeates, Hand entertained Clymer that evening, but of the other two knew only that all had been dispatched December 7. Actually the other two appointed by Congress, the Virginian Sampson Mathews, and Samuel McDowell, who had been born in Pennsylvania, but was now a member of the

George Clymer

Virginia State Senate,[80] were fairly long in coming. Indeed, it was March 15 (though they had shown up in February) that Hand reported to his wife that the Virginia commissioners had arrived. In this letter, as always, he asked about his "dear little Sally," hoping that she is perfectly recovered, "& that I shall have the Happiness of seeing you & her Soon." But there is Dorothy now too. "How comes it you never mention her Sister. I promise myself much Satisfaction in being introduced to her." [81]

    Careful appraisals of the sessions that the commissioners had early in the year with the headmen of the friendly Delawares reveal that "the negotiations they had with the chiefs were eminently successful." Still, the commissioners' report to Congress allowed that Indian attacks on the forts and upon settlements along the frontier were likely. For Congress, Clymer, Mathews and McDowell had very specific recommendations to make about the number of militia from Virginia and Pennsylvania which would make the frontier "safe." In response to this warning Congress ordered 3000 militiamen to the western frontier. [82]

    Amazingly, Hand, who had not yet been recalled by the Congress, was *still* determined on an expedition of his own. This is very clear from a letter addressed to Colonel David Shepherd, March 7, in which he urges Shepherd to promote "so laudable an enterprise." [83]

    Exactly three weeks later Hand had his response. On March 28, Colonel Shepherd reported from Wheeling's Fort Henry with some rare good news "I have Engaged some Volunteers to go on the Expedition you formerly mentioned to me against the first of Aprill and have ordered them to be at Fort Pitt against that time." [84]

    News not so good came to him from Captain William McKee at Fort Randolph. From his descriptions of conditions at the fort, it was plain enough that there was little at Fort Randolph which would support an expedition. He lamented the many desertions and the declarations by soldiers which indicated they were content to serve out their enlistment terms. None of that seemed too consistent with what he reported last, which was "I have learned from good Authority that the Indians Intend striking a severe Blow at this place [Fort Randolph] some time in May next." [85]

Conditions at Fort Pitt and in the neighborhood of Forts Henry and Randolph remained fairly quiet through February and most of March. General Hand's big concern was the building of the boats required by Colonel Rogers, and the provisioning of the expedition into the Illinois country. But Fort Pitt never went very long without some crisis appearing. This time it had to do with the renegades.

General Hand had, off and on, for a long time been plagued by desertions and escaping prisoners. Numerous flights, many including large numbers, had been reported during the late winter and early spring. Loyalists were making big inroads on Pittsburgh and its environs, and Detroit was doing the wooing. The flight that excited most consternation occurred while the commissioners from Congress were still present. On March 30, General Hand filed a report with General Horatio Gates: "Sir — I have the mortification to inform you that last Saturday night, Alex^r. McKee made his escape from this place, as also Matthew Eliot [born in Ireland], a person lately from Quebec on parole, Simon Girty, Robt. Surplus [Robin Surphlitt, cousin to McKee] and one [John] Higgions [Higgins, servant of McKee]." Of course Girty had not only served Fort Pitt as an interpreter for many of the treaty sessions, but as a guide and scout.

And on the same day he reported the same to Jasper Yeates: "Dr. Yeates — I am in such Distress on being Satisfied that M^r. M^c.Kee has made his escape from here the night before last, Accompanied by Mat: Elliott, Simon Girty, two others I am not Acquainted with & two negroes [McKee's slaves]. Yeates was also informed on all of this by his nephew Jasper

Ewing, in a letter of the same date. [86]

Alexander McKee, whom the British regarded as "a man of great character," was congratulated on his escape and made welcome in Detroit by Governor Henry Hamilton. Simon Girty the British were also much pleased to have on board. He was promptly made an official in the Indian Department.

In a letter to General Horatio Gates from Pittsburgh, General Hand complained that this kind of thing had been going on since the preceding January. According to his tally, some forty men had abandoned his too-small garrison. Fourteen of these had vanished on the night before this letter (April 23), "taking with them a part of the country people." To Gates Hand reported that he had promptly dispatched four officers with a company of forty men to arrest their flight. One of the deserters Hand identified as Henry Butler; another he knew to be James Girty, brother to the infamous Simon Girty. Both of these presumably wound up in Detroit. [87]

For a number of reasons this escape of the villains jinxed the expedition that the general had had in mind, as he was quick (this same day) to make plain to Colonel William Crawford. Having noted the escape, Hand adds for Crawford, "This will make it improper to proceed with the intended expedition to French creek, which I beg you may give proper notice to the gentlemen who are preparing for it . . . ." [88] At this time there was still much concern being felt at Fort Pitt about the murder of Cornstalk. On the third day of April an appeasement address was delivered to the Shawnee people by Colonels William Preston and William Fleming. For the time being, at least it appeared there would be no hostile activity in consequence of that heinous deed.

Meanwhile the George Rogers Clark expedition was about to go into motion. From Redstone in April, Lt. Colonel Clark advised General Hand on the 17th, "Sir — As I found by express from Maj. [William Bailey] Smith that my recruiters on Holston River [89] had been more successful that [than] I expected, in raising four companies, and receiving intelligence of two companies more now on their March from Winchester, I shall not attempt to recruit any more men in this department, as I believe I shall have my full quota, but shall prepare to set out on the intended expedition as soon as possible. I shall order what recruits I have west of the Monongahela to repair to Wheeling immediately, where they may probably be of service and shall stay here [Redstone] myself until the arrival of the troops I expect [from] across the Mt^n. I should be glad to know by an answer to this letter whether I am to receive any provisions at this place [Redstone] or at Pittsburgh, if at Redstone, I hope, Sir, that you will send an order for the receipt of it. I suppose it would at any rate, be of service to take the boats that I have loaded to Pittsburgh."

One can sense from his language that Colonel Clark is both impatient to get going and full of confidence. "I should be glad," he notes for Hand, "to receive my powder, &c., at this post. The provision boats that you were to send down, I expect may be ready at any time. [In fact they were ready, and extremely well provisioned, at just this time, Hand having had George Morgan build thirty vessels.] If you will send them under my convoy, I shall take pleasure in doing that or any other service that lays [sic] in my power. Be pleased to send me a few lines by the bearer, M^r [William] Linn, who will wait on you with this letter."[90]

On May 2, 1778, the Continental Congress honored General Hand's request that he be relieved of his command, and ordered his recall. Happily, just before his leaving Fort Pitt, the Head of the Western Department was able to satisfy fully the request of Lt. Colonel George Rogers Clark for the provisions and boats he needed to launch his Western Operation. Clark's army, numbering 175 frontiersmen, had been assembled at Redstone Old Fort on the Monongahela and was ready to go. About General Hand a gratified commander Clark, on his setting out for Kaskaskia and Cahokia, had this to report: "He supplied me with every necessity I wanted." [91]

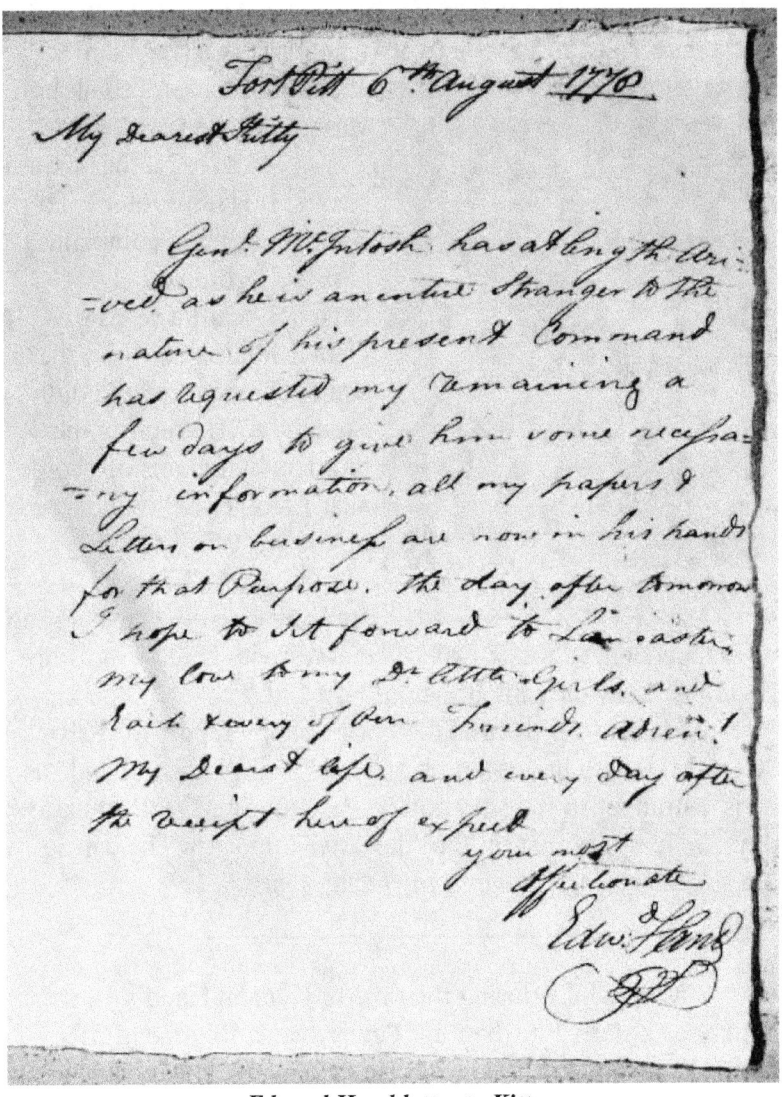

Edward Hand letter to Kitty

But Clark is getting away long before General Hand. On May 15 all General Hand can do is to send his love to "my Dear little girls." Five weeks later [!] he is still at Fort Pitt: "I did not apprehend [I should write] you from this place at so late a date, but can't move from here until Gen. [Lachlan] McIntosh arrives. I think him very slow in his motions." [92]

Lachlan McIntosh

Almost another month passes. It is now July 7! To Kitty the general complains: "Since I wrote you last [I] have not heard a word of Genl. McIntosh . . . So that I can only repeat the old dull Story . . ." He reports the murders by Indians of people near Ligonier & "two or three on the west fork of Monongahela." The anniversary of the Declaration of Independence "was a Day of Genl festivity here." And Jefre Ewing is "busy drawing a Plan of Fort Pitt." [93]

Finally — Edward Hand has a happy report for Kitty: "Genl. McIntosh has at length arrived." It is August 6, and "as he is a stranger to the situation he has requested I stay on a few days." He hopes that on the "day after tomorrow" he can set out for Lancaster. "Love to my D^r little girls." [94]

Meanwhile, during the time of General Hand's command at Fort Pitt the First Pennsylvania Regiment, of which Hand had been the head for so long, had been playing a very big role in Washington's main army. After wintering with the Continental Army at Morristown, still under Colonel Hand, the regiment opened the spring campaign of 1777 in the First

Pennsylvania Brigade of General Anthony Wayne's division. As it was regarded by the senior officers as an elite regiment, it was regularly assigned to the post of honor, the right side of the line.

During the summer, the regiment was divided, a portion of it, under Captain James Parr, being dispatched to the north to augment the force of General Gates for the battle of Saratoga; the balance, under Chambers, now mostly battalion soldiers armed with the sleek new muskets they had received during the past winter, sent south to fight with the main army under Washington.

Through the summer months of 1777, Hand's old regiment, as one of its captains, David Harris, reported, had "traversed all the Jerseys, and a part of Pennsylvania."

Colonel Hand has been hearing regularly from the officers he knows so well, and most notably from the present commander, James Chambers. Their devotion and their high regard for their former commander is everywhere evident.

They are keeping him apprised of the regiment's activities. Of the movements in the area of Trenton and Middlebrook, halfway between Somerset and Brunswick, Colonel James Chambers, now head of the regiment, having described some skirmishes, reports from Mount Prospect camp on June 18: "General Washington long undisturbed. Has left the way Clear for Men to advance to Trenton if they Chuse; but it seems to me they [the British] see his Scheme, and Will not go that Way, for if they do, their Ruin, to all appearances, is inevitable. We have always three days' Provisions Ready Cooked, and kept in Readiness to March at a Minute's warning." He closes with "My best Compliments to Major Ewing. Look out for Good Mill Seats, and Remember old friends." [95]

It was shortly after this letter, on June 26, that the battle of Short Hills (or the battle of Metuchen Meetinghouse) occurred. Washington had been resting his army in the

Middlebrook encampment, in a defensive position in a part of the ridge of the First Watchung Mountains, with General Howe awaiting a chance to get at him. When Washington did venture out, in an effort to shadow Howe, the British general found him sufficiently vulnerable and determined to attack. He marched two columns forward in an effort to cut Washington off from high ground. The result was a skirmish with the troops of Lord Stirling that developed into a full-blown battle. This was at what was called the Scotch Plains. Stirling was forced to retreat, and Washington returned to the safety of the hills.

And still from the Prospect Camp, a little later in this month of June, Hand has good news: "This day . . . we drove the enemy from Brunswick, and I [Chambers] was one of the first officers that entered the town. The advanced party took two prisoners, one a Hessian officer. We cannonaded them smartly; and they ran, and left the work as we approached, without firing a gun, though we were within shot of small arms." And then, just two days later, he files with Hand a long report of the regiment's action over the summer. Much fatigued with constant and very long marches, he narrates the history of the regiment: "After leaving Delancey's Mills, the regiment was ordered to Sufferance at the mouth of the Clove, then on to New Windsor, Chester, Howell's Ferry on the Delaware, the Sussex Courthouse, Hackett's & Pitts."

Washington at this time is still complaining about the paucity of brigadier generals in the Pennsylvania Regiment, noting for Congress that "as General Hand is not here, [the regiment] has but one [!] with the Army."

After some recuperation at Morristown, the regiment marched to Carrell's Ferry and Howell's Ferry, crossed the Delaware and marched through Germantown to Schuylkill Falls, and back to the Mount Prospect encampment.

Chambers is pleased to report that "I am quite well, and fleshy as ever you seen me. It would give me great pleasure to hear from you . . . I have given you a small history of our manuvers, though a very irregular one." [96]

In his August 13 letter to General Hand, his former commander, Captain David Harris, now senior captain in the Pennsylvania Line, does some speculating about Howe's plans and Washington's winter quarters, and then writes, mentioning names of officers and men whom Hand knows well, "Now for a little Regimental News. In the first place, we have often wished to be under your command, had it not interfered with your interest. Coll. [Richard] Butler, Captain [James] Parr, with two subalterns, and ab^t 50 privates, are detached in Morgan's Partizan Corps. Captain Parr has killed three or four men himself this Summer. His expressions at the Death of one I shall ever Remember. Major [Henry] Miller had the Command of a Detachment, and had a skirmish at very close shot with a party of Highlanders. One of them being quite open, he motioned to Capt. Parr to kill him, which he did in a trice, and, as he was falling, Parr said: 'I say, by God, Sawny, I am in you.' I assure you Parr's bravery on every occasion does him great Honour."

Harris concludes his letter: "Dr General, you must be convinced from some little matters when we had the Pleasure of being commanded by you that the Regiment is not very Happy in their present Commander; but, greatly to the credit of the officers, they have done their duty in every respect to the satisfaction of everybody.

I must beg a line from you informing the news of the Western Department, as we have had so many different acc'ts from that Quarter that we can't place any confidence in them, they are so very contradictory. . . . You may rely on it you shall hear from me every opportunity. My kind Comp^{ts} to Major Ewing." [97]

From his old comrades General Hand heard through the fall of 1777 and through the summer of 1778 about the battles of the Brandywine, the unfortunate affair at Paoli, the battle of

Germantown, the skirmishing at Whitemarsh (when Howe ventured out of Philadelphia), the Valley Forge winter encampment, Clinton's exit from Philadelphia, and the battle of Monmouth.

Chambers, with much detail, reported to Hand on the September 11, 1777, battle of the Brandywine, in which the regiment lost "six or seven" killed and probably the same number wounded. General Hand was much grieved to hear of the deaths of Lieutenants John Holliday and Jacob Wise. Among the wounded, besides Chambers himself, were Captains James Grier and Captain Robert Craig of Lancaster.

He heard also about how the regiment had been called on to cover the retreat of Wayne's remaining soldiers from the midnight massacre at Paoli. And he was made proud by the news that the regiment had been forefront in the assault on Germantown.

The First Pennsylvania played a limited role in the battle of Monmouth, but a commendable one. Chambers, from the camp at Englishtown on June 30, two days after the battle, reported to his former commander General Edward Hand, who is now returned to the army (Lafayette's division), from Fort Pitt: "I have the pleasure to inform you that on the 28th ult., we gave the enemy a fine drubbing at Freehold Church, about four miles from this place. The attack commenced at eleven o'clock, and a most violent cannonade continued for nearly five hours, in which time both armies were maneuvering on the right and left. Our Division was drawn in front of our artillery, in a small hollow; while the enemy's artillery was placed on an eminence in front of our brigade."

The regiment, pinned down as it was, found itself in a most perilous position. Chambers, very proud of his riflemen, continues: "Of course, we were in a right line of their fire, both parties playing their cannon over our heads, and yet only killed two of our men, and wounded four of my regiment with splinters of rails. Our army out-generaled them, and at the same time, advanced some artillery across a swamp, and drove them before us. They fled in all quarters, and, at sunset, we had driven them near to Monmouth town. We encamped on the field that night. They left on the ground several officers of distinction, amongst them Colonel [Robert] Monckton; [98] and, yesterday, we buried upwards of two hundred and fifty of the bold Britons who were to conquer the world!"

    Although history, as Chambers would never know, looks upon the battle as a stalemate, the captain, who was there, has another impression: "I rode over the whole ground, and saw two hundred of their dead. It is surprising that we lost not more than thirty. However, of this I can assure you that for every ten of them, I did not see one of ours killed. During yesterday, our fatigue parties were collecting the dead in piles, and burying them. The enemy is flying with precipitation to the Hook [Sandy Hook], and we are now on our march to Brunswick. They desert very fast, so watch for news." [99]

    A detachment of Hand's old regiment was with General Wayne's light infantry in the storming of Stony Point, July 15, 1779; and the First Pennsylvania fought very hard at Bergen Neck, July 21. As noted above, a detachment would catch up with its old commander later that summer, serving as it did with Sullivan in the campaign against the Iroquois in New York. In June of 1780 it joined other Pennsylvania regiments in a mutiny at Morristown that did not amount to much. Some companies of the regiment saw action at Yorktown and in South Carolina. The regiment of Pennsylvania riflemen closed the book on a most distinguished career in November of 1783, when it was officially mustered out in Philadelphia.

    Because of his assignment to the Western Department, Colonel Edward Hand of course missed out on some of the big battles of the Revolution, but he had had excitement enough at Fort Pitt, and though he could not know now, as he gave up his command in the west, there lay ahead of him still a lot of the American Revolution. What the general of course would by and by appreciate was that what he had learned about Indians and their warfare, and about expeditions, in his time at Fort Pitt would prove of *great* benefit to him. He had not got launched a major anti-Indian expedition as he had hoped, but he felt that in his thirteen months he had done all he could. He hungered now for *real* military service. and was happy to hear that his request for reassignment had been honored by Congress.

The Continental Congress, with the report of the Commissioners sent west, as noted above, had plans for the Western Department: "Resolved — That two Regiments be raised in Virginia & Pennsylvania to serve for one Year unless sooner discharg'd by Congress, for the Protection & operation on the Western Frontier . . . . That Brigadier General Hand be recalled from his Command on the Western frontier, agreeable to his request."

And of course a replacement is needed: "That a proper Officer be immediately sent to take the Command on the Western frontier . . .. that General Washington be desired to appoint the officer to take the Command at Fort Pitt . . . ." [100]

On May 16, George Morgan, who had traveled to Yorktown, Virginia, from Lancaster, Pennsylvania, sent to Hand the good news about the alliance with France, and noted that "The Appointment of an Officer to succeed you was referred by Congress to his Excellency General Washington who has named General McIntosh who is expected to arrive here [Yorktown] tomorrow on his way to Fort Pitt." Morgan had visited with Kitty Hand in Lancaster, and was very happy to report to the general that Mrs. Hand was well at Lancaster last Monday. I did not know then of this Opportunity or I would have informed her of it." [101]

General Edward Hand was being returned to the Continental Army. Washington was giving him the command of a brigade of light infantry in General Lafayette's division. On

May 26, 1778, upon the recommendation of the Commander-in-Chief, Hand was relieved of his command as Head of the Western Department. He was succeeded by Brigadier General Lachlan McIntosh, who promptly had a fort built and named in his own honor.

General Hand's term of duty as Head of the Western Department had come to an end just as Washington's army was preparing to withdraw from the winter quarters at Valley Forge. From his headquarters there Washington advised General Lachlan McIntosh: "Sir: the Congress having been pleased to direct me to appoint an officer to command at Fort Pitt and in the Western Frontier, in the room [place] of Brigadier General Hand I . . . nominate you." [102]

So Edward Hand was returned to the main army under the Commander-in-Chief. By the time he caught up with the army he was too late for the battle of Monmouth, but the war had yet five years to go. Of course he did not know, nor could he possibly guess, what role he would play.

He did get in on the Council of War that Washington had called for Fredericksburg, October 16. Besides Hand, the officers present were Major Generals Horatio Gates, Baron Johann de Kalb, Alexander McDougall, and Baron Von Steuben; Brigadier Generals John Nixon, Samuel Holden Parsons, William Smallwood, Henry Knox, John Paterson, and Anthony Wayne.

The question posed for these officers was whether it would be "prudent and advisable" to send a detachment of troops toward Boston, and of what force. Although Washington did not know the winter encampment plans of the British, he could, and did, provide good information on the present disposition of the troops and their apparent design. Not surprisingly the vote on this proposal was negative.[103]

What Washington did not know, although he had had warnings enough, was that a new and very dangerous enemy would have to be dealt with. And what General Edward Hand did not know was that the General Edward Hand who as Head of the Western Department failed miserably in his determination to organize and launch an expedition into the Indian country would be provided a second chance.

VII

Wyoming

On Susquehanna's side, fair Wyoming!
Although the wild-flower on thy ruin'd wall,
And roofless homes, a sad remembrance bring,
Of what thy gentle people did befall;
Yet thou wert once the loveliest land of all
That see the Atlantic wave their morn restore.
Sweet land! may I thy lost delights recall.
And paint thy Gertrude in her bowers of yore,
Whose beauty was the love of Pennsylvania's shore.

"Gertrude of Wyoming: A Pennsylvania Tale"

— Thomas Campbell

In the days preceding the outbreak of hostilities between King George and the colonials, long before the battles of Lexington and Concord, both the British and the steadily more rebellious colonists were wooing the Indian tribes of the Iroquois League.

As tensions built, overtures to the Indians were stepped up. The American colonists seemed not to be interested in the Indians as allies, but they certainly did not want them allied with the British. The American Commissioners urged a neutral

Cornplanter

course for them. In council after council they hammered home their point: "You Indians are not concerned in it. We desire you to remain at home." They insisted to them that "You have nothing to do with our father-children quarrels." The message to the Iroquois was simple: "Stay out of it."

But the British were determined to have their actual support, and they most aggressively courted them. They were particularly eager to secure the friendship of the Senecas, who were not only the most populous of the six, but also were known to be the most warlike and fierce. Besides, located as they were, at the western end of the "longhouse," as the Federation was called, they exercised an influence over the tribes of the Ohio Valley and the Northwest Territory.

Consequently, during the period 1770-77 there occurred a steady succession of councils to which the Indians were invited. The Senecas found themselves scurrying from their homes in the Allegheny region and the Valley of the Genesee in western New York back and forth to Fort Pitt, to Albany, to Oswego, and to German Flats in the Mohawk Valley.

In these early councils, and most particularly at German Flats, Cornplanter, war-chief of the Senecas, and his uncle Kayahsotha regularly pledged to the American Commissioners that the Senecas would remain neutral, and for some time they were able to keep their warriors on the sidelines. But most influential in the jousting for Indian favor were the Mohawk Chief Joseph Brant, his brother-in-law (and perhaps father) Sir William Johnson, who for a long time had been serving the Crown as Commissioner of Indian Affairs, and who was to die before the War of the Revolution began, and John Butler, destined to be a Tory.

The conflict between the Indian factions became steadily more intense, finally reaching the crisis point in mid-summer of 1777, two years into the Revolution. The difference was fully resolved in July, at the council of Oswego, when the commitment to the British, including that of the Senecas, became "official." But the agreement did not come easily, and in fact only after a great deal of drama.

Some 2000 (!) Senecas had made their way to the council site at the fort and trading post on the southeastern shore of Lake Oswego.

Butler, in his ferocious desire to persuade the Indians to the British cause, was lavish in the distribution of gifts, which of course included ample rum. It was merrymaking and "getting to know you" that characterized the early going.

But after almost three days, the frivolity was swallowed up in very bitter arguments. Opposed to Brant and Butler were Cornplanter, Old Smoke and Kayahsotha. The debate featured a most heated exchange of angry words, that very nearly brought Cornplanter and Brant to blows. When the much older Mohawk screamed at Cornplanter to "shut up" and then proceeded to declare him a coward, consternation ensued. The Indians repaired to mini-councils. In the end, the Senecas were won over. And what had begun in rum now ended in rum. The die was cast. Butler next day reported the good news to the British commissioners.

It was one of the most critical moments of the revolution. What it would mean to the frontier settlements, to Washington, to Generals Edward Hand, John Sullivan, James Clinton, Enoch Poor, and countless Continental officers and foot soldiers, it was frightful to think.

It was not long before it had been made painfully clear to the Commander-in-Chief, that four of the six nations of the Iroquois had come into the war on the side of the British. The most dramatic announcement of that most unwelcome fact would come in the form of an unspeakable massacre destined to occur in the beautiful Susquehanna River valley known as Wyoming.

The Susquehanna River is one of the principal waterways of the Indian country now known as Pennsylvania. The West Branch of the wandering river flows east from its source at Cherry Tree some 150 miles to Williamsport, then abruptly turns south. The North (or East) Branch flows west a little on its way out of New York State, then south and east to meet her sister at Northumberland before striking out for the Chesapeake. One of the names given by the Indians to the North Branch is M'chewamisipu, "the river on which lie extensive clear flats."

Joseph Brant

These broad, clear flats, fertile and lush, are beautiful, spread out as they are on either side of the river. Perhaps the most lovely region of all is the valley known as Wyoming. No one has looked upon it but what he or she has sought in vain to account for the rapture of the scene.

A noble effort was delivered in 1786 by Colonel Timothy Pickering, [1] who had moved to the Wyoming Valley and in five years would be named Postmaster General of the United States and after that become Secretary of State in the Cabinet of George Washington. When for the first time he came into view of the valley he declared it "the most beautiful tract of land my eyes ever beheld!" He insisted that industrious farmers could make "the whole a garden." [2]

Some years later, Reverend Edmund D. Griffin of Columbia University reported: "A scene more lovely than imagination ever painted presented itself to my sight — so beautiful, so exquisitely beautiful . . . ." [3] So it has been for thousands of years, and so is it still.

Perhaps it was inevitable that in this garden spot of the world, one of Nature's choicest bowers, the wrangling that leads to violence and bloodshed should occur. For it is a "fatal beauty" that is presented by the Valley of Wyoming.

During the first week of July, 1778, when Washington was recovering from the fighting at Monmouth, one of the most awful and ugly events of the Revolutionary War occurred at Wyoming. What happened here has fascinated historians for 200 years, and the accounts of what happened here are legion. Not all are accurate; in fact, none can be strictly accurate. Some, especially those which appeared early, were composed out of such strong feeling and out of such confusion that they cannot be trusted in their details. Nevertheless, it would be difficult to exaggerate by much the terror of that day and night. The most faithful account, even the most restrained report, would chill the blood. If ever the term *massacre* was apt, it was most fitting for Wyoming on July 3 of 1778.

Butler's Rangers and their Indian allies, who were from the beginning intent on Wyoming, warmed up for their assault with a fierce battle at Oriskany just a month after the council at Oswego, August 6, 1777. In a bloody ambush of colonial militia, the Iroquois, led by Brant, conducted a devastating raid on a poorly protected white settlement and made plain the kind of warfare in which they would be indulging.

In the succeeding spring, these same Iroquois, led by Brant in league with Butler and his Rangers, assaulted the helpless village of Cobleskill, and produced a massacre that is now thought of as a practice session for the blood-bath that was to occur at Wyoming. On May 30 the tiny settlement in the Schoharie Valley was approached by a large war party of Senecas and Mohawks. The settlement was defended by patriot forces numbering 30-50 men, under the command of Captains William Patrick and Christian Brown. Despite Brown's warning to Patrick that the seeming flight of but a handful of Indians might be a ruse, Patrick pursued for about a mile, and right into an ambush prepared by Joseph Brant. It was an old Indian trick.

Twenty-two of the defenders were killed outright, six were wounded and two were captured. And the Indians destroyed ten to twenty buildings, burning families in the fires. It was on to Wyoming.

The British force proceeding to Wyoming was composed of two divisions. One body was made up of 464 warriors, mostly Senecas. It was complemented by Butler's Rangers. The war party, and especially the Indians, became somewhat unsettled when upon coming into the valley that was their object they discovered before them a number of forts. But they recovered in time to present a fearsome and formidable force. Butler made overtures to all three forts. On July 1, both Wintermoot's Fort, under the command of Lt. Elisha Scovell, and Jenkins' Fort capitulated. Forty Fort, named for the forty pioneers who had built it, defied the ultimatum.

The defenders, under the command of Colonels Zebulon Butler and Nathan Denison, fearing a long and possibly fatal siege, resolved to meet the enemy in the field. When they marched out of the fort at two o'clock in the afternoon, as historian Barbara Graymont puts it, ". . . they must have presented to the Indians a most gratifying sight." According to the Graymont account, when Butler perceived that the advancing soldiers "were within a mile of them," he instructed his Indians to put afire the two captured forts, this to give the Americans the impression that he was in retreat. He then secreted his Indians and Rangers in a swampy, open wood, where "all lay flat upon the ground, quietly awaiting the approach of the Americans."

    Colonel Zebulon Butler, as his party, now in battle formation, neared the woods, ordered his men to "stand firm the first shock." When some 200 yards distant from the woods, he ordered the first volley. There was no response. By the time of the third volley, the colonials were now within 100 yards of the woods. Now Sayenqueraghta, "from his perch on horseback," gave the signal. The withering fire which followed dropped a great many of the Americans and threw all into disarray. As the Indians closed their net around them, the militiamen who had composed the left wing moved in a body for a more advantageous position. By the rest, this move was totally mistaken for retreat, "and the result was a rout." In the panic, with rifles cast aside, only a very few, "a pathetic remnant," reached the safety of the fort. Many who were forced into the river were there promptly tomahawked.

    Survivors were those few who hid under the bushes which hung out over the water, or who were able to swim down the river out of gunfire. All who were arrested in flight "were murdered without mercy."[4] Still the worst was to come! As evening settled over the bloody ground, the Indians, now completely out of the control of Butler, and whether inspired or simply unrestrained by their own chiefs, entered into an orgy of cruelty and torture that violates every sense of the human.

    Fierce assaults were made upon the individual homes scattered throughout the valley and frightful atrocities perpetrated. And then the savage celebration, about which so much has been written. One early historian, noting the horror, declared he would not turn the picture with its face to the wall. "It is indelibly engraved on the minds of the civilized world and will remain." [5]

Near Tioga Point (present-day Athens), up the river from the battle scene, lay the village of Queen Esther, called Queen Esther's Flats. It was a substantial village of some seventy houses. From her home here came the "fiend of the night," to avenge, history infers, the death of her only son, who apparently had been slain on the day just before the assault on the forts. Queen Esther, for many, is the central figure of Wyoming's most awful moment. At a spot where an enormous boulder emerged from the ground she presided, and herself carried out the executions. The scene has been described a thousand times, and doubtless in many cases some distortions of the truth appear, but, as has been wisely noted, no account could ever possibly "convey to our mind an adequate conception of what occurred." [6]

To the rock were brought the prisoners captured from the river or the swamp, some of whom had given up their persons to the promise that they would not be harmed. There were at least twelve, perhaps as many as sixteen. Reigning over the hideous scene was Queen Esther, inspired by an enraged grief for her only son.

Most accounts have the fire on a level, open place. The prisoners were brought to the center of the circle formed by the warriors. Scalps were waved and grotesque dances, complete with the most hideous contortions, further uglied up the scene. As one account has it, "They shouted, whooped and grinned, the scene becoming a wild carnival that filled the hearts of the savages with delight. They knew that on the morrow they could turn themselves loose and plunder and burn without restraint. They came to the valley for revenge and plunder, and their day had come. They were wild men and this was their reward." This historian has no stomach for the gory details of the slaughter, noting only that "Queen Esther had presided and the death maul had done its work." [7]

Similar is the account provided in another version. Here we have the prisoners placed in a circle with a warrior behind each, and Queen Esther going round the circle and braining each one with a tomahawk, "except for one or two who somehow broke away and escaped." [8]

But no matter the version, the descriptions of the murders are so blood curdling that some historians are tempted to regard the whole episode as a myth too awful to have happened. And Cornplanter's erstwhile companion Blacksnake absolutely denies Queen Esther's tomahawking. [9]

But the Queen Esther episode is perfectly consistent with all that had gone before. Colonel John Franklin, for instance, writing in 1828 for the Towanda *Republican*, declares that a large number of soldiers surrendered on the battlefield and that these afterwards were most inhumanely murdered." [10]

Few survived the massacre, but Colonel Zebulon Butler, who had made his way safely back to the fort from the battlefield, at some time in the night was able with his wife to steal out of the fort and under the blanket of darkness escape from the valley. [11] But all in all, the Indian brutalities through the year 1778 proved to be too much for the American colonials. Pennsylvania had had enough. New York State had had enough, the settlers along the frontier had had enough. Certainly Washington had had enough. It was time to punish the Indians for Wyoming and Oriskany and Cobleskill and for countless other atrocities. The Commander-in-Chief was now compelled to acknowledge a new and formidable enemy. A new chapter had begun. General Edward Hand would help to write it.

VIII

The Sullivan Expedition

Sir: The expedition you are appointed to command is to be directed against the hostile tribes of the six nations of Indians, with their associates and adherents. The immediate subjects are the total destruction of the crops and devastation of their settlements and the capture of as many prisoners of every age and sex as possible.

— Washington to General John Sullivan

Through the fall and winter of 1778 and the spring of 1779, Washington had the main army encamped again at Middlebrook. The army was housed in cabins. Washington had his headquarters at the Wallace House in Somerville. The army would remain here until June 3.

General Henry Clinton, with an army of 22,000 (!) British and Hessian troops at New York City, did not disturb the Continental Army. Clinton apparently had the impression that Washington was simply too well fortified, too strong. But Washington had another problem, and it was this problem that occasioned the flurry of correspondence which passed between him and one of his chief lieutenants and resource officers, General Edward Hand. What these letters show is that General George Washington very much respected the judgment of Edward Hand and would be depending upon him greatly.

The subjects of this flurry of letters were primarily the Wyoming Valley, Cherry Valley and other Indian incursions, the results of conferences with General James Clinton, and the anti-Indian expedition of Colonel Thomas Hartley up the North Branch of the Susquehanna. But by far the matter that dominated the correspondence was the organization of a massive campaign against the Seneca and Cayuga Indian villages of the finger lakes region of New York, from which the border troubles were emanating.

In September it was learned from some Tory prisoners who had been taken that the Mohawk Joseph Brant was putting together a massive force of Indians and Rangers at Unadilla ("Meeting Place"), an Iroquois village at the confluence of the Susquehanna and Unadilla Rivers. The information suggested that this force would be unleashed to "lay waste" to the frontiers of New York. Accordingly, William Butler, who, immediately after the destruction of Wyoming had been made Lieutenant Colonel and given the command of the 4th Pennsylvania Regiment, was detached from the Pennsylvania Line, and with a force of Continental soldiers and some militia was ordered by General John Stark to stave off the threat.

Not only did Butler, early in October, erase the village of Unadilla, he destroyed also the neighboring Oneida village of Onaquaga (headquarters of Brant), which was located on both sides of the east branch of the Susquehanna River, near present Windsor, New York. General Stark for General Washington provided an account of Butler's great success. It is a little too optimistic: "Dear Sir — I have just returned from Schoharie, and find that the enemy have been driven too far from the frontier for me to overtake them this season, as it is so far advanced. Too much honor can not be given to Colonel Butler and his brave officers and soldiers, for their spirited exertions in this expedition against the Indians. They have put it entirely out of the power of the enemy to do our frontier any serious injury for the remainder of the campaign. I beg your excellency that they may be relieved, as soon as the nature of the service will admit it, as both officers and men are much fatigued."

In more detail General Stark explained to Washington that Colonel Butler had marched from Schoharie to penetrate the Indian country only with great difficulty. The force experienced great hardship in negotiating high mountains and deep waters, and in crossing the river where it is "two hundred and fifty yards wide." His tally of the destruction reveals "Many farm houses and about four thousand bushels of grain were destroyed." [1]

General Washington had just begun to receive hints of the Butler expedition at the time he responded (October 22-23) to a query from President of Congress Henry Laurens: "Previous to the receipt of your Letter, inclosing a Copy of Colo. Hartley's [2] I had determined and ordered another Regiment to march and cooperate with those under Colo. [Ichabod] Alden and Lieutt Colo. Butler, which have been employed on the frontiers of this state for some time. [3] It was intended that the whole should go against the settlement of Anaquaga, with such Militia as might join; but from the accounts received this morning, I have reason to hope — that Colo. Butler has already destroyed the Town? I am now consulting Governor [George] Clinton & General [Philip] Schuyler, who are much better acquainted with the frontiers in this Quarter than I am, upon the practicability of an expedition upon a larger scale against Chemung. I don't know what will be the result; but I am apprehensive from the advanced season of the year and the daily increase of the Rivers and Creeks — it will be found impracticable or at least extremely difficult in the execution." [4] Washington could not know, of course, that the events of the succeeding month would deliver a greater urgency to the plan.

Naturally, with the huge success of the assault on the forts at Wyoming, the Indians were inspired to countless barbarities along the frontier. One of these was the raid on German Flats in September; the most notable was the brutal ravage in November of the sleepy village of Cherry Valley, close to the source of the North Branch of the Susquehanna.

As early as November 8, Colonel Ichabod Alden [5] had been warned that an Indian-Ranger expedition was intent on the village of Cherry Valley. But apparently he did not take the warning seriously. In any case he made almost no preparation. Thus the tiny settlement, during a terrific sleet storm, was taken by a fatal surprise by the savage horde which, led by Brant and by Walter Butler, son of John Butler, fell upon the village in the November after Wyoming.

Butler's force, numbering 200 British Rangers and 442 Indians, under the skillful command of Joseph Brant, had camped, undetected, the night of November 10, not far from the village. Early in the morning of the next day the village, defended by at best 250 armed men, was brutally assaulted. Because of the total surprise there was offered little resistance. The terrible toll showed thirty-two civilians, many of them women and children,

Philip Schuyler

murdered, sixteen soldiers killed, seventy-one residents of the settlement taken prisoner. Colonel Alden himself was a casualty. When his pistol mis-fired, he was struck down by a thrown tomahawk. Some say that the massacre, and it was that, was even more horrible than what had happened at Wyoming!

Some accounts of the horror have Brant attempting to restrain Butler in his cruelties, but what happened here was indeed so terrible that both the names Brant and Butler were blackened beyond recall. They were forever anathema to frontier people.

The news of course horrified those who heard it. New York State's Governor George Clinton pledged to do everything within his power to provide protection and comfort for the frontier people. And, naturally, the massacre made even more necessary and urgent the expedition into the Indian country already so much talked about. With Generals Philip Schuyler and Edward Hand, Clinton promptly advised a winter attack on the Indian stronghold. But not four days later both Schuyler and Hand reconsidered. Noting the many difficulties, but not altogether fixed in an opinion, they reported to Washington that "a winter campaign seemed impracticable." [6]

Even as much as a month before the awful events of Cherry Valley, the Continental Congress, chiefly because of Wyoming, had resolved to take action against Chemung. President Henry Laurens in a letter to Washington, October 13, had reported the determination Congress had taken. Now irrevocably fixed on a punitive expedition into the Indian villages of the Chemung-Tioga region, there remained the question of when. Is this winter season a proper time?

Before that question could be answered Edward Hand was given a new and very formidable assignment. A letter from Washington, dated October 19, 1778, had contained his orders: "Sir: You are forthwith to proceed to Albany and take the command of that place and its dependencies. The forts on the frontier, and all the troops employed there will be comprehended under your general command and direction. Besides the garrisons, there are at this time Seth Warner's Regiment, [Ichabod] Alden's, the fourth Pennsylvania Regiment under Lt. Colo. [William] Butler and the rifle corps, late [Daniel] Morgan's, now commanded by Major [Thomas] Posey. The principal objects of your attention will be the defence of the frontiers, from the depredations of the Enemy, and the annoyance of their settlements, as much as circumstances will permit; in which you will be aided by the Militia of the County." [7]

Hand would be relieving Brigadier General John Stark, the hero of Breed's and Bunker Hill. [8] And of course he was vividly remembering his time as Head of the Western Department, and how he had not been particularly happy with the cooperation he was requesting from the militia forces. Now he would be, in effect, Head of the Northern Department, responsible for another frontier much threatened by Indians. He did not expect to enjoy this assignment any more than he had the Fort Pitt situation. But he accepted it as he always did, if not gratefully, at least graciously. The effective date was November 8, 1778.

The big question to be decided was that of the campaign into the Indian country, when it should be undertaken and how it was to be organized.

By Washington, besides Hand, Generals James Clinton and Philip Schuyler were promptly brought into the discussion. Washington, in response to an October 20 letter from Hand, noted that he had provided General Schuyler with a copy of the Resolve of Congress to direct an expedition against Chemung. He is now urging Schuyler, Hand and Clinton "to take the matter fully into consideration." [9]

On November 10, from Coughnawaga, a settlement on the Mohawk River, General Hand had advised Washington that an Indian-Ranger attack on Cherry Valley was imminent, and

~ *The Sullivan Expedition* ~

defined the steps he had taken to thwart it. But, apparently, this important letter never did reach the Commander-in-Chief. On the 13th Hand had to lament the failure of the village to ready itself, and for Washington he enclosed letters from officers who had provided him the sorry details of the assault. And again on the 18th he reported to Washington what he had learned about the fate of the village.[10] The Cherry Valley tragedy could only intensify the feeling that an anti-Indian invasion of the Seneca territory was not only desirable, but absolutely imperative.

From his headquarters at Fredericksburg, New York, Washington on November 16 in effect authorized Hand to make the big decisions on the anti-Indian campaign. He reported that he has ordered General Clinton "to march immediately to Albany," so that his regiments "may be ready to act as circumstances may require."

He is of course much troubled by the Indian barbarities and growing ever more impatient to do *something*: ". . . it is in the highest degree distressing to have our Frontier so continually harrassed by this collection of Banditti under Brant and Butler. I would have you without loss of time consult Genl Schuyler and some of the Gentlemen and others in that part of the country where you now are [Albany], upon the propriety or practicability of some offensive operation at this season of the year, with the number of Men which the addition of the two Regiments [Clinton's] will make, against these people; by the means of which they may be removed to such a distance as to make it inconvenient for them to make such frequent incursions. If any thing is to be undertaken, let me know upon what Quarter it is to be, as soon as it is determined. If it shall not be judged expedient to carry on an expedition at this time, you will then consult with the Gentlemen above mentioned, upon the most proper disposition of the troops to support each other in case of an attack upon the separate posts, and at the same time afford cover and protection to the Country."[11]

On November 20, Washington, writing from his

headquarters at Middlebrook, informed Hand that he is ordering up the New York Brigade, which means that General Clinton, already in Albany, will supersede Hand. General Edward Hand is to "repair as speedily as possible to the northern New Jersey post at Minisink," and is urged to brief Clinton and to assist him in every possible way. Moreover, Washington has placed Colonel Thomas Hartley's regiment, which is on the Susquehanna and preparing to march into the Indian country, under General Hand's "general direction." [12]

At Minisink he will be relieving Count Casimir Pulaski, [13] who has had the command and whose legion has been ordered to repair to South Carolina.

Washington is impatient to get Hand to his new post, and on November 26 nudges him a little: "When you arrive at Minisink you will dispose of these [Count Pulaski's force] and all the other troops, under your command . . . . You will then inform me where the troops are posted." [14]

By the end of the month Hand, who has been back and forth between Minisink and Albany, complains to Washington: " I am heartily tired of the Frontier Commands." He expresses a desire to join the Pennsylvania Troops, and wishes he had leave to go home to Lancaster for the winter. As for the Indian campaign he thinks that assembling at Wyoming is quite possible. [15]

At this same time (Nov. 28) Washington has a letter from Clinton, in which the general reports that Hand has been to Saratoga to consult with General Schuyler, and that as soon as Hand returned from Albany he (Clinton) went with Hand to consult Brigadier General Abraham Ten Broeck and a few of the principal inhabitants of Albany about the praticability of an operation against the Indians at this time of year. He reports to Washington a unanimous decision against the measure, and notes that Hand's report is on its way to the Commander-in-Chief. All have agreed that a wintertime campaign is out of the question. Both Hand and Clinton list for Washington the many reasons (number of available troops, weather, distances, provisions, etc.).

But apparently the door on a winter campaign has not been entirely closed, for as late as January 1, Washington, while for many reasons he is against a winter expedition, is still allowing it. It would take a lot of doing but apparently he could still be persuaded. His letter to Hand (from Philadelphia) on that date reads in part, "With respect to an expedition against the Indian and Tory settlements, which you mention, their reduction is to be wished; yet it appears to me, that great difficulties and expence must attend it; and, that nothing will justify it's [its] being undertaken, but the fairest prospects — indeed a certainty of success. These, from the idea I have of the Country — from the sentiments of Others — from the precarious supplies of provender necessary for the Horses to be employed — which would consequently place the support of the troops on a very doubtful & hazardous footing — do not present themselves — and without taking any consideration of the opposition on the part of the Enemy — of the harrassing of Your Men — and of many other difficulties which occur always in Winter enterprizes — more especially where the common benefits of shelter cannot be received, induce me for the present to be against the measure; You may nevertheless inform yourself by the best inquiries as to the facility and the means of attempting it — and transmit me your advices upon the subject." [16]

Hand wrote to Washington on the subject on January 9, 10, and 15. The letters of the 9th and 10th have not been discovered. His letter of the 15th, from his headquarters at Minisink (a little to the southeast of present-day Port Jervis), suggests that Washington is misinformed about the strength of Chemung, for it has been much exaggerated. He argues that the warriors who populated the region last summer and fall did not belong there and have now "generally return'd to their different Castles."

Finally, the question of whether to undertake a winter expedition is answered. It will not be done this winter. Washington, still writing from his headquarters at Middlebrook (February 7) informs Hand, " . . . all thoughts of an Indian expedition are laid aside for the Winter." He does allow for its possibility in the spring, "should circumstances demand it." He therefore advises Hand to discover from "those who are best informed" what he can about the best routes into the Indian country, and the distances from village to village, and the terrain to be negotiated. This investigation, he insists, is to be conducted in secret.

The letter closes with more considered and thoughtful suggestion: "Upon a supposition that an Expedition will be carried into the Indian Country from Susquehannah, I should be glad to be informed where you think would be the most proper place to establish a Magazine for the supply of the troops destined for that service . . . . After having satisfied yourself as to the most probable Route, it will be well to have some place reconnoitered upon that Route to which we may advance a post for the security of the main Body, while they are assembling and preparing for their march." [17]

As spring comes on, naturally the decisions on the campaign become more urgent. One of the many big matters to be addressed was the providing of provisions. For the kind of army that Washington had in mind, a *lot* of grain would be needed, a *lot* of horses, a *lot* of cattle. Hand would be the man. To General Hand, on February 28, Washington provided instructions, and then appended a list of very specific questions which would have to be answered. He advised Hand to "take the opportunity of putting them [these questions] occasionally without any seeming design to persons acquainted with parts of the Country which they respect, and mark down the answers, in the Margin opposite each question. When you have obtained answers to all or as many as you can, be pleased to return them to me." [18]

~ The Sullivan Expedition ~

In a letter of March 20, from Minisink, Hand responded to the great many questions Washington has asked about distances, terrain, boats and water travel. Much of the information he supplies can be credited to his own experience, but much of it is the product of diligent research. He has even detailed the particular needs for firelocks and bayonets, kettles and canteens. He has been tireless in his preparation for the campaign. But by now he is just a bit fatigued. Even though Washington has ordered him (March 16) to "hold troops in readiness to march" he does not think it improper to ask for a leave: "Mrs. Paid me a visit here [Minisink] in the Winter [January 11] & is still with me. [I] will be particularly obliged to your Excy to permit me to Conduct her to Lancaster the beginning of next Month. I would not wish to be Absent more than 15 or 20 days." [19]

Washington, though he was not happy to lose Hand, even for just a few days, at this critical time in the preparation for the campaign, granted the request. He was careful to attach a condition: "Should you accompany Mrs. Hand to Lancaster, I must insist upon your punctual Return within the time you mention, as the season will be considerably advanced by that time. I shall be glad, indeed it is expedient that I should see you at Head Quarters [Middlebrook] in your way to Lancaster, as from thence it will be found necessary for you to proceed to Wyoming. The sooner you set out the better . . . as the Season will render it very inconvenient for an Officer who is to bear a principal share in the intended expedition to be absent." [20]

Washington, with the site for the launching of the expedition still not settled on, had two concerns that he wanted addressed. One anxiety concerned the starting point and the mode of travel: "I wish to reduce the following as near to a certainty as possible. Whether the principal settlements of the Indians of the Six Nations (particularly the Senecas) are most accessible by the Waters of the Susquehanna or by the Mohawk River." He asks Hand please to ascertain this.

His other concern derives from his impression that the ground beyond Chemung is so swampy as to make the march difficult if not impossible. Hand responds to the first by explaining that it will be the river route for the boats transporting the supplies and the artillery, and he much prefers the Susquehanna. To Washington's expressed concern about difficult swampy ground beyond Chemung he replies that he can add nothing to the information he has already supplied, but he can and does provide in letters of the 29th and 31st of March, lots of vital information, very precise, on distances to be traversed. Much of this information he has had from Lt. John Jenkins, whom he later credits for the providing of "superior intelligence."

Through the month of March and most of April, a time when Wyoming was assaulted again, preparations were stepped up for the launching of the campaign. The matter of provisions was one of the top concerns, but at some time in March Washington addressed the biggest decision of them all, a commander for the expedition. He began to search among his generals. Did he consider General Edward Hand? Most likely he did, for Hand enjoyed a big reputation as an Indian fighter and as an Indian-style fighter. Besides he had done most of the necessary research for the campaign and had made most of the arrangements for boats, provisions, routes and assembly points. He had had the command of the Western Department, headquartered at Fort Pitt. But Hand was only thirty-five years old and as yet only a brigadier general. There were officers out there with a great deal more military experience, and an available number held the rank of major general.

But Washington did consult Hand on the choice to be made. And he consulted also Colonel Zebulon Butler, who had had the command at Wyoming on that fateful night; and he sought also the advice of the above-mentioned Lieutenant John Jenkins, a surveyor and one-time captive of the Indians, who knew very well the country the expedition would be traversing, and would actually serve the expedition as a scout.

For one good reason or another he could not seriously consider the major-generals Philip Schuyler, Charles Lee or Israel Putnam. After his consultations Washington seemed to fix on Horatio Gates. This, declares Washington's biographer John Fitzpatrick, was a rather remarkable choice, inasmuch as Gates was already known to Washington as vain and ambitious and the kind of general who conducts the battle from his tent. [21] But the Commander-in-Chief must have sensed, or hoped, that Gates would not accept the commission. An artful Washington so worded his letter as to make plain just what would be required and just what would be expected; and then he was careful to include in the dispatch to the general another letter addressed to his real choice, Major General John Sullivan. This letter he directed Gates to relay to Sullivan if he did not himself care for the command. And it worked beautifully. Gates promptly responded: "Last night I had the honor of your Excellency's letter. The man who undertakes the Indian service should enjoy youth and strength; requisites I do not possess. It therefore grieves me that your Excellency should offer me the only command to which I am entirely unequal. In obedience to your command I have forwarded your letter to General Sullivan." [22]

Sullivan was a good choice. Though he was not in the best of health, he was capable of great energy (as he had demonstrated many times) and he was courageous almost to a

John Sullivan

fault; he had proved himself most impressively through the first four years of the war. He had served at the patriot siege of Boston, had been captured by the British at Long Island (Congressman John Adams was not happy with Sullivan's presenting to Congress the British surrender terms!), and had been exchanged in time to fight valiantly at Princeton, at the Brandywine, and at Germantown. He had been freed of blame for the failure at Staten Island, and those members of Congress who had urged his removal from the army had been obliged (though it was still felt that he could have done much better at both the Brandywine and Germantown) to revise their estimates of the general upward. Washington, though not always on the best of terms with him, knew that he could depend upon him, first to accept a big job, and, second, to do it. But even Sullivan had his misgivings. First, he was not all that excited about the prospect of burning Indian villages through the summer; and, second, he was not confident that there was a value to it. But after turning it over in his mind for a week he finally agreed at least to meet with Washington at Middlebrook to discuss the enterprise.

As Washington explained it to Sullivan, the campaign was not just for show. It was to be punitive, of course; it was to put the Indians "in their place." But he was hoping that the villages and fields could be so completely destroyed as to render Indian aid to the British negligible. To disable the British war machine, that was the primary mission.

He informed the general that the expedition would be two-pronged in its organization, for Brigadier General James Clinton, father of one colonial governor and brother to another, would lead a force along the Mohawk River west while Sullivan was marching from the south up the Susquehanna. It could even be considered a three-pronged operation, for Colonel Daniel Brodhead would at the same time command a force that would operate in the West, moving up the Allegheny River north from Pittsburgh and into the

Seneca country. If all went as planned, these three armies would come together at some convenient point, "advance against the stronghold of the enemy [Chemung and Tioga and the villages in the region of the finger lakes] in such a force as could not be resisted and then overrun the whole Iroquois country west of the Oneida villages." [23]

The plan called for a junction of Clinton's forces with Sullivan's wherever Sullivan would suggest. Brodhead's campaign for the time would be considered a separate operation.

Sullivan was persuaded to the efficacy of the expedition and made happy, perhaps even eager, to accept responsibility for it.

It had been a long time since Wyoming and Cherry Valley. But *finally*, after ten months of decision making and working out details, the campaign, first proposed by Hand and Clinton and Schuyler, was now ready to go. It might be said that it lumbered into motion. General Hand and the other officers were notified by the end of April that "In future all arrangements coming from Major General Sullivan, is to be obeyed and executed, he being appointed to the command of the Indian Expedition — He will also receive such applications as you may judge expedient for the better prosecution of our operations." [24]

Meanwhile Indian raids along the border continued. Typical of the reports both Hand and Pennsylvania's Executive Council were receiving is a letter from Captain George Bush addressed to General Hand, "commanding in Susquehanna." He is reporting, at 11:00 a. m. May 17, 1779, a border outrage in the Wyoming Valley: "Just this moment a party of Indians on the opposite side of the River from us killed a family of people who lived about one mile from this [Fort Jenkins], but unknown to me & burned the House. I immediately sent a party after them, they found the dead lying scalped, two men, one woman and 7 children." It is his impression, deduced from the tracks of the raiding party, that the band numbered "Better than 30." He closes with the oft-expressed desire of the border officers, "I wish we were strong enough to send out a strong party."[25]

The President of Pennsylvania's Executive Council, Joseph Reed, has ever since Wyoming been most fearful about the Pennsylvania communities lower on the Susquehanna, notably Northumberland and Sunbury. He had been hopeful of engaging General Hand for their protection. But Hand is yet at home in Lancaster, and in fact has had an impatient letter from the Commander-in-Chief: "After having spent the necessary time with your family at Lancaster, you are to proceed from thence to Wyoming and take command of the troops there and in that neighbourhood." After some instruction, then, on disposition of units, Washington orders, "You will make yourself as well acquainted as possible with the Route from Wyoming towards Chemung, to gain intelligence whether the Enemy are making any offensive preparations or whether they expect an attack from us and in short to keep me regularly advised of any occurrences that you may think material."[26] Hand was back to headquarters at Minisink by April 5, for on that date he issued marching orders to Major Daniel Burchardt in command of the 550-man German Regiment (four companies, raised in Pennsylvania): "Sir: Agreeable to the orders you yesterday rec^d, you will proceed to Wyoming [to provide relief to Colonel Zebulon Butler], on the Susquehanna River, with the Regiment under your Immediate Command. . . . It will take you four days from Col. [Jacob] Stroub's [Stroud's] to Wyoming."

Hand then provides very specific directions and instructions on provisions (Burchardt is to leave the baggage at Fort Penn, under guard.), and urges the major to beware of surprise. "Relying Much on your Steddyness, Industry, Zeal and Activity, I wish you a Good march. . . ."[27]

On April 16 of '79 President Reed had from General

Hand, who much regrets that he cannot respond to Pennsylvania's request for protection, the following: "Sir, I think it my duty to inform your Excel^y that on consequence of his Excellency, General Washington's orders, I am thus far on my way to Wyoming, on the Susquehannah, to take the command of the Troops on that River. As their number is but small, and the principal object of my Command lies above Wyoming, I am apprehensive that I can't pay much attention to Sunbury or the contiguous settlements, should the Enemy [attempt] anything in that Neighborhood. Your Excellency will therefore be pleased to take such Measures for their particular security as you think necessary."

He is much concerned of course, and very sorry not to be able to help out, but he remains ready for service when he can supply it: "It is needless, I hope, to mention how happy I Should deem myself could I render any services to the distressed Inhabitants of that part of the State, and that I shall be ever ready to direct in their favour, as far as the nature of my instructions will admit of, if your Exc'y will please to Honour me by any Commands, direct them to be forwarded by Col. Geo. Ross." [28]

Besides this letter of April 16 to Reed, Hand was in touch with Washington by letters of the 23rd and 26th. He was advised (again) by the Commander-in-Chief that in future all orders coming from Major General Sullivan are to be obeyed, as he has command of the Expedition.

About a week later, Executive Council President Joseph Reed in a long letter to George Washington noted, among other interests, that he had had the letter of concern from Hand. He expressed the opinion that if Sullivan's movements took place on schedule, concern for Northumberland would be removed. "Otherwise, I fully understood that his [Hand's] Detachment would be so stationed as to cover Wyoming & that County, until an offensive Movement should take Place." [29]

On the 26th of the month Hand wrote again to Reed to make certain that the governor fully understands the situation with respect to the Wyoming area. He knows that the distance from Sunbury to Fort Jenkins and Wyoming is bound to make the settlers uneasy, but he refers to the new fort at Muncy, and the possibility that another post may be erected on the river. Reassuringly, he declares that "there can be no doubt that the Commander in Chief wishes to afford every degree of Security to the Frontiers consistent with his ultimate views." He promised to report to Reed any change in his situation. [30]

From a letter addressed to Sullivan May 4, from his headquarters at Middlebrook, it is clear that Washington regards Edward Hand as second in command to the Major General. It is also plain that the Commander-in-Chief is keenly interested, as he seems always to be, in the smallest detail: "It is expected that the Road from Easton to Wyoming be opened without delay that the troops and supplies passing that way meet with no obstruction. You will open a correspondence with General Hand at Wyoming and instruct him to give all the aid he can with the troops under his command to accelerate the transportation of provisions and stores up the River. You will also direct him to put every engine in motion to obtain the most precise intelligence of the enemy's situation and views. And in short you will make every expedient to complete the preparations for penetrating into the Indian Country by way of Tioga, on the Susquehannah on the plan which has been already explained, and may be finally adopted." [31]

Sullivan was in harness. The general arrived at Easton on May 7, and there promptly assembled some 3500 men in three brigades under Generals William Maxwell, Enoch Poor [32] and Edward Hand. Proctor's artillery, to be under the command of Hand, arrived May 20. But not for a month more was Sullivan provisioned and ready to set out. At last, at 5:00 in the morning of June 18, the General broke camp at Easton and began the trek to Wyoming.

In the meanwhile the Commander-in-Chief was obliged to take time out from the war and from Sullivan's Expedition to deal with a nasty distraction. It was a question of seniority in rank. It happened that Brigadier General William Irvine [33] of Carlisle (a physician like Hand but three years older) had filed a claim challenging the superior rank of Brigadier General Edward Hand (Irvine had been promoted to Brigadier General, May 12, 1779.). It seemed to Irvine that he should not be considered inferior to Hand.

Somehow Hand heard of the complaint. From Wyoming to Washington, on May 12, he reported, "It has been hinted to me that some Gentn have propagated a report of my being removed

William Irvine

from the Pennsylvania Line & that it was to prevent my giving opposition to Col. Irwines in supporting that argument . . . [which] however I beg leave to Assure your Excy I do not give the least credit to." He makes a good point: "I don't conceive that any set of men have a Power of Proscription, where there is no crime laid against the Party to be Banished — I therefore claim my Rank in the Pennsylvania Line next after genl Wayne agreeable to the Commission I have the Honour to hold from Congress — Perhaps those Gentn who wish to support the propriety of taking Rank from former Commissions do not recollect that Adhering to that rule Invariably, would give me the Rank of every other Officer now doing duty in the Pennsylvania Line — but this I wish not to have Occasion to mention a Second time." He looks up reverently "to your

Excy as my Military Father . . . for Protection & justice." [34]

The matter of course was taken up by the Board of War. It found itself helpless to render an opinion. On May 17, it solicited advice from Washington. The Commander-in-Chief, becoming impatient, responded on the 22nd. In a *very long* letter he debated in his mind the issue, and closed with the conviction that he is likewise helpless to render a judgment. He suggests that the matter be turned over to Congress. [35]

On the 31st Washington wrote to Hand, and after reporting that he has transmitted Hand's concerns about provisions for the expedition to Sullivan, he refers to the seniority question: "With respect to your relative rank, in the line of Brigadiers. It is a subject on which I have never given an opinion. Should it be found to interfere with that of others, when you join this army that mode will be adopted for its determination which may appear free-est from exception. To do justice and preserve harmony is my principal care. Be assured therefore no advantage whatsoever shall be taken from remoteness of situation [Hand of course is in Albany], so far as I am concerned."

Not until July 3 of the next year (!) was the matter broached again. On that date, in camp at Pracaness [Preakness], the officers had this in the General Orders: "A Board to be composed of all the General Officers in Camp [Greene, Lord Stirling, La Fayette, Maxwell, Knox, and Wayne] except the parties will meet tomorrow morning nine o'clock at Major General Greene's quarters and will hear a dispute of rank between Brigadiers General Hand and Irvine and will report their Claims and their opinion of the right of Precedence. The General will lay before the Board such Papers and resolutions in his Possession as regard the subject."

Four days later Washington had the report: "It is the unanimous opinion of this Board that they have not powers to alter the standing of any General officers different from their appointment and therefore cannot determine upon the Claim of

General Irvine of precedence to General Hand." [36] And there the matter rested.

On May 31, Washington, from Middlebrook, spelled out to Sullivan his mission: "Sir: The expedition you are appointed to command is to be directed against the hostile tribes of the six nations of Indians, with their associates and adherents. The immediate subjects are the total destruction of the crops and devastation of their settlements and the capture of as many prisoners of every age and sex as possible."

As for the structure of the army, "The troops to be employed under your command are: Clinton's, Maxwell's, Poor's and Hand's brigade, I comprehend all the detached corps of Continental troops now on the Susquehanna and [Joseph] Spencer's brigade." [37]

No problem was too small for the Commander-in Chief. On the first of June he appealed to the Board of War to address the matter of shoes for soldiers who will be marching for a long time. Noting that General Hand has reported the shoes with which the men are now equipped to be "worthless after one week of wear," he suggested that "a set of shoe-makers tools and spare pieces of leather for soles to be sent to each regiment." As this proposition appeared to Washington to be "very good," he recommended it to the attention of the Board and urged that "A proportion of sets of tools, and spare bits of leather & c. should be forwarded as soon as possible, put to Gen: Hand and the rest to Easton . . . ." [38]

From Easton, with all the pack horses and some of the necessary stores (more to be picked up along the way), the army made twelve miles on this first day, encamping at the foot of the Blue Mountains. According to the Reverend William Rogers, [39] who, though still not twenty-six years old, would be serving as chaplain for Hand's brigade, "On the road from Easton . . . nothing is to be seen [for the first twenty miles] but hills, stones, trees and brush, except here and there a scattered house and a lake near the mountain. And the remainder on the way to Wyoming he found almost completely uninhabited, "except by wild beasts and roving animals." But from a mountaintop in the Poconos "we had a fine prospect of nature's works. We discovered the water gap of the Blue Mountains and hill upon hill surrounding us." [40]

The army on its march from Easton to Wyoming proceeded in an order which had General Maxwell's brigade in the van, followed by Colonel Thomas Proctor's regiment of artillery, then Poor's brigade, and, last, the baggage train, General Hand having been dispatched to round up provisions.

The third day out proved a difficult march, the soldiers passing through thick stands of pine, poplar, oak, and chestnut, as well as some very dense mountain laurel. The artillery horses suffered most, and by early afternoon had gone as far as they could. The Reverend Rogers noted in his journal that he had done "no preaching to-day on account of the fatigue of the troops." [41]

The next day, if anything, was worse. The road which they followed was a recent but hardly adequate enlargement of the very narrow path that led through the Great Swamp and a different kind of timber — ash, locust, maple and hemlock. Because the trees reached so high, no sunlight penetrated the forest, and the constant gloom had inspired for their maps the appellation "Shades of Death." The troops somehow made twenty miles on this day, but by the time they were setting up tents they were so exhausted that Sullivan named the place Camp Fatigue. And because they had marched so far, and because some of the supply wagons did not reach the encampment until midnight, he declared a day of rest.

One of the sentinels who were posted at the camp reported the sighting of a bear and a wolf, but no Indians. This day was Tuesday, June 22.

Only a few miles remained to Wyoming, and the soldiers marched briskly when the march was resumed. Three miles along the road, however, they suffered a bad moment.

They had come to the place "where Captain Davis and Lieutenant Jones, with a corporal and four privates, were scalped, tomahawked and speared by the savages, fifteen or twenty in number." The site had been marked by two boards fixed in the ground where Davis and Jones had fallen, with their names upon them, and that of Jones besmeared with his own blood. Reverend Rogers later confided to his journal his recollection of the scene: "In passing this melancholy vale, an universal gloom appeared on the countenances of both officers and men without distinction, and from the eyes of many, as by a sudden impulse, dropt the sympathizing tear. Colonel Proctor, out of respect to the deceased, ordered the music to play the tune of Roslin Castle, the soft and moving notes of which, together with what so forcibly struck the eye, tended greatly to fill our breasts with pity, and to renew our grief for our worthy departed friends and brethren." [42]

When, after five days of laborious marching, at last the army reached Wyoming, on Wednesday, June 23, all were afforded from "a fine eminence" a most thrilling view of the settlement on the river. "There it is," exclaimed an officer. "That is Wyoming." And some of the soldiers murmured to themselves, "So this is where it happened." What they were remembering the Reverend Rogers turned slowly over in his own mind: "At the battle . . . about two hundred and twenty were massacred within the space of an hour and a half, more than one hundred of whom were married men; their widows afterwards had all their property taken from them and several of them with their children were made prisoners. It is said that Queen Esther, of the Six Nations, who was with the enemy, scalped and tomahawked with her own hands in cool blood eight or ten persons. The Indian women in general were guilty of the greatest barbarities. Since this dreadful stroke they have visited the settlement several times, each time killing, or rather torturing to death, more or less. Many of their bones continue yet unburied where the main action happened." [43]

Sullivan was disappointed to discover that the stores and provisions he required were *still* not here in Wyoming. He was impatient to get the mission underway, but he would have to wait. He would have to wait, perhaps, a long time. Happily, he had General Edward Hand.

He now delivered to his brigadier a huge assignment. Hand was to acquire all provisions, including pack horses, and the watercraft, that would convey everything up the river, just as soon as he possibly could. Hand of course was very sensitive to the general's impatience, and he knew at the same time that he could not have everything up the river from Sunbury in anywhere near the time that would satisfy the commanding officer. He would do the best he could.

During the last week of June Sullivan stocked up as provisions came upriver from Sunbury. On the 29t^h , courtesy of Edward Hand, upwards of thirty fully loaded boats arrived from downriver. As these provisions continued to arrive, some of the officers (General Maxwell, Colonels Proctor, Butler, and Israel Shreve among them) [44] were given a tour of the region, visiting the remains of Forty Fort and discovering skulls and bones on the field of battle, now twelve months old. Particularly gruesome was the "place of skulls" near Wintermoote's Fort (up the river four miles from Forty Fort), where Colonel Zebulon Butler's routed soldiers were horribly butchered. They came to a grave where seventy-five skeletons were buried; and farther on they discovered a plot where the grass was distinctly different from the grass everywhere else. Here, it was tearfully explained to them, "Fourteen wretched creatures, who having surrendered upon being promised mercy, were nevertheless made to sit down in a ring, and after the savages had worked themselves up to the extreme of fury in their usual manner, by dancing, singing, halloaing, etc., they proceeded deliberately to tomahawk the poor fellows one after another." [45]

For these barbarities which they were hearing about,

and for which there was ample evidence, Reverend Rogers blamed King George. "Good God!" said he, "Who, after such repeated instances of cruelty, can ever be totally reconciled to that government which divesting itself of the feelings of humanity, has influenced the savage tribes to kill and wretchedly torture to death, persons of each sex and of every age — the prattling infant, the blooming maid and persons of venerable years, have alike fallen victims to its vindictive rage." [46]

On the 9th of July, more boats, fifty of them, loaded with supplies, arrived from Sunbury. These boats were guarded by Hand's Eleventh Pennsylvania Regiment, under the command of the general's ever reliable Colonel Adam Hubley, who was also a Lancasterite and a good friend to the general.

Once the boats were unloaded they whipped back out into the river, and headed downstream to secure even more provisions.

On Saturday, July 10, very early in the morning General Hand himself set out for Harris's Ferry. He was accompanied by his aide-de-camp, Lt. Jonathan Snowden, [47] and escorted by a company of light horse. He had 130 miles to go. But he meant to hurry on the provisions which, "owing to the unaccountable neglect of those who have the superintendence of the same, has occasioned the army to continue at this post [Wyoming] for such a length of time." Hand appreciated that the campaign had been imperiled before it had even begun. He knew that what was required was "the spirited exertion of some superior officer." [48]

And when, a fortnight later, on that Saturday, the 24th, General Hand himself showed up with 112 loaded boats, General Sullivan sent word throughout the army, "Get ready to march."

It had required more than a month for Sullivan to acquire all that he needed, including 1200 pack horses and more than 700 cattle. It was not until the last day of July that the Sullivan expedition was completely assembled and equipped and pronounced ready. The Commander had been delayed, but he was not unhappy. He was ready to march. He knew whom he had to thank. He conveyed sincere congratulations and his gratitude to Brigadier General Hand, and to Captains Samuel Rice and Thomas Porter, who had come through for him.

At precisely 1:00 in the afternoon, on this last day of July, the expedition got underway. The signal for the boats to weigh anchor was sounded from one of the guns aboard the *Adventure,* which was Proctor's "flagboat." As the flotilla passed the fort at Wyoming, it was saluted by the firing of thirteen cannon; and Proctor ordered a proper response. By the time the army on shore had all moved forward, it occupied a distance of some two miles. The parade of vessels on the waters of the Susquehanna was probably also two miles long. The pack horses, about 2000 in number, it has been estimated, extended the column another six miles! [49]

All in all, it made quite a show, with drums and fife, and flags aloft, "and Colonel Proctor's regimental band playing a lively air." It doubtless dazzled whatever Indians were able to view it, or to hear it. General Edward Hand was certainly impressed. He was thinking, "Now this is the kind of expedition I would have liked to have launched from Fort Pitt!"

Hand was the youngest of the brigadiers, but though he was only thirty-five years old, he would serve as second in command to Sullivan throughout the campaign. Sullivan's order of march had General Hand's brigade, considered the light corps, in the van in three columns. It was to keep ahead of the main body by something like a mile. Maxwell's brigade marched a mile behind and to the left, while Poor was to the right.

As commander of the light troops, Hand had a single function. That was to provide protection to the main body, to harass and delay any frontal attack on the army. The light corps traveled light, the soldiers carrying only rifles. It could be counted on for any pursuit of the enemy that might be desirable. It could be expected to experience a lot of skirmishing.

Hand's brigade of light troops, the third brigade of the Eleventh Pennsylvania Regiment, was staffed by the following officers: Jonathan Snowden, Aide-de-Camp and lieutenant; Captain William Sprout, Aide-de-Camp and Brigade Major; the Reverend William Rogers, chaplain of the brigade; John Van Anglen, Commissary; William Kennedy, Surgeon; Lieutenant Colonel William Butler, a transfer from the 4th Brigade; Lieutenant Colonel Adam Hubley, Eleventh Pennsylvania Regiment; Major Daniel Burchardt, Pennsylvania German Regiment; Major James Parr, a transfer from the 4th Brigade; Captain Anthony Selin, Schott's Rifle Corps; Captain John Franklin, with his Wyoming Military; and Captain Simon Spalding, with his Independent Wyoming Company. Colonel Thomas Proctor's 4th Continental Artillery was also continued under Hand's command.

The first night of the march was a tough one, rainy and cold, the men sleeping, as best they could, on the ground. In the morning of Sunday, August 1, General Hand, reaching back for his experience with Indians in the Fort Pitt region, instructed his soldiers. Aware that an unexpected attack could fall upon the advanced light corps at almost any time, he issued his advice in his most persuasive manner: "The Brigadier begs leave to assure the light troops that experience has taught him that maintaining a good countenance and a little perseverance, which from their known valor he has every reason to expect will ensure success against the kind of enemy they have to oppose [is most desirable], and that turning their backs, let them be pressed ever so closely, will end in their ruin." [50]

The best way to appreciate just exactly what happened during the months of the Sullivan Campaign, from July 31 through October is to march with the soldiers who formed the various companies. Happily, anyone who wants to can do exactly that, for the journal accounts of twenty-seven officers who served the expedition are available. Besides, there are the recollections of some of the common soldiers made later on. Taken together, these provide *vivid* day-by-day impressions of the marches and the engagements, of the burning of the Indian houses, the destruction of the fields of corn and squash and cucumbers, of peach trees and other fruits. Of course for the reader there will occur a great deal of repetition, as the soldiers are observing the same thing, but in these diaries the campaign comes alive.

What strikes one as he or she pores over these pages is the awe by which the soldiers are overcome. They revel in the beauty of the forests, the white pine and the spruce, and in the sparkle of the mountain streams. They are impressed by the size of the Indian buildings, and even more by the vast fields of corn (some extending 200 acres), with the stalks reaching to seventeen feet!

Lancaster's Adam Hubley sets down a striking impression of the valley of Chemung. He has his view from a mountain height: "The summit was gained with the greatest difficulty; on top of the mountain the lands, which are level and extensive, are exceedingly rich with large timber, chiefly and excellent grass. The prospect from this mountain is most beautiful; we had a view of the country, of at least twenty miles round; the fine, extensive plains, interspersed with streams of water, made the prospect pleasing and elegant from this mountain." [51]

But it rains every day, or it seems to. Sometimes the rains are heavy; sometimes the days are simply dismally damp, shrouded in fog. The officers describe in their diaries the picking of huckleberries, the sighting of rattlesnakes and blacksnakes, fishing parties, corn roasts, the execution of deserters and traitors, the monotonous hours of sentinel duty.

~ *The Sullivan Expedition* ~ 179

And the rain!

General Edward Hand kept up a modest journal. And, happily, his chaplain, the Reverend William Rogers, religiously maintained a very full and most revealing diary. Its pages reflect his great regard for his general and provide very sensitive readings of incidents. But the journal terminates early, as the Reverend withdrew from the army during the night of August 28, to return to Philadelphia.

The army, because it had to accept the pace established by the boats on the river, moved slowly, four to sixteen miles a day. Sullivan had a program that was followed religiously. It called for Proctor's artillery to announce each day, both morning and evening, just exactly where the army was. Apparently it was Sullivan's intent, first to let the Indians know that this army was on the march, that it was moving so many miles per day, and that its march was unrelenting. This army is coming on! Second, it seemed to suit General Sullivan to avoid actual battles. His mission was to destroy the corn and the habitation, livestock and fruit trees, to do all he could to make life for the Indian difficult if not impossible. If the warriors chose to make a stand, so be it. If they preferred simply to withdraw and leave the army to its work, well, maybe all the better. He would make it easy for them. Besides that, the general seemed to understand that the sound of cannon, which the Indians called "thunder trees" or "thunder sticks," was an unsettling disturbance to them.

On Tuesday, August 3, the army, breaking camp at 5:00 a. m., as would be its custom, marched twelve miles through beautiful country, which featured the lovely Buttermilk Run and the sparkling waters of Tunkhannock Creek. The next day brought the troops to the necessity to ford the Susquehanna. Although fording sites are generally shallow and present little problem, here the waters were waist deep and frightfully swift. Sullivan had ordered the men to remove their overalls and to tie them round their necks, and to support each other. General Hand here amazed his troops. Apparently to animate his riflemen, or perhaps simply to show that he was with them, "he dismounted and marched through on foot at the head of his soldiers." [52]

The sixth day out, the army having encamped at the abandoned farm of Frederick Vanderlip on its way to Wyalusing, finds General Hand *very* impatient for an engagement. He noted for his diary — yes, he was still recording from time to time in a journal the progress of the expedition — the discouragement he was experiencing: "From this place I wished to be permitted to march across the country with a party to surprise the Indian & Tory settlement at Chemung while the fleet and army [traveled] by the common route persuaded that the enterprise would be attended with success & put a number of prisoners into our power. This I communicated to the General, but found him adverse to it."

And not only was his request denied, but the ever sensitive Hand sensed some petty jealousies among the officers: "A council of the General officers indeed was cold but the General's sentiments on the subject were previously known. It is no wonder my proposition was unanimously [!] rejected."

He is made a little bitter: "This was the first time I found that my having command of the advance corps had given jealousy — or that it was possible that men engaged in their countries cause would approve arbitrary measures because the honor of a military action could not be immediately attributed to themselves or favourites who had perhaps no great desire to leave the beaten path but this was not the only conviction I had during the Campaign that I knew better of mankind." [53]

By August 6 the army had reached Wyalusing, which the soldiers found to consist "of about one thousand acres of clear land amazingly fertile and containing beds of extraordinarily fine English grass." Here the army made camp, and just in time, for here came the rains again. After waiting

~ The Sullivan Expedition ~

out the rain, the army moved on to Standing Stone Flats and beyond, to Rush Meadow Creek. But on the ninth day out, General Sullivan was taken so ill that he could not proceed any farther on his own. When the fleet of boats caught up to the main army at Standing Stone, he was taken aboard, and for the time of his illness (which fortunately turned out to be less than two days) was transported up the river, a royal member of the fleet. One of the chief functions of the boats was the transport of the sick, of whom there were regularly many.

At last they found themselves at Tioga (present-day Athens, Pa.). Here, on August 11, Sullivan had a fort constructed, and did not complain when it was named for him. It was built at the "carrying place," a shallow water canoe portage linking the Susquehanna and Chemung Rivers. The troops were now in Indian country.

The Indian town of Chemung had been all along their first target. Now here, early in the morning, the work of devastation commences. Finding the town abandoned on the very foggy morning of August 13, the soldiers promptly set fire to the thirty log houses, totally erasing any sign of an Indian village.

Supposing that the Chemuing Indians had fled in the direction of Newtown, some seven or eight miles away, Hand, with Sullivan's permission, elected to pursue them. After about a mile the riflemen came upon a hastily abandoned campsite, with fires still burning, blankets cast aside, and dogs sleeping. Assuming that the Indians had spent the night here and could not be far away, Hand, by way of his courier Major Edwards, requested of General Sullivan the authority to pursue the Indians even farther. Sullivan allowed it, but insisted that Hand be back to Tioga on the next morning.

General Hand then "determined instantly to push forward." He had put out flankers, but within a mile he ran into trouble. The party found itself approaching a high hill or ridge, "which ran along on their right." A pretty place for an ambush it was, and so it was. The advance party received a very sharp volley from the secreted Indians. The Reverend William Rogers had all the details from returning riflemen. He reported to his journal that "the 11th Pennsylvania regiment hereupon pushed up the hill with an astonishing rapidity. The savages as they were advancing gave them another well directed fire, but seeing the determined spirit of our troops, suddenly fled." [54]

The soldiers of the light corps pursued the warriors some little way toward Newtown, but General Sullivan, arriving at the scene of the skirmish, thought it best to return to the destruction of the Chemung cornfields.

The 11th Pennsylvania did not fare well in the skirmish. Reverend Rogers reported six killed, two officers gravely wounded, and six privates slightly wounded. Next day the young Baptist minister at the burial site conducted services for the dead.

On Sunday, after his preaching in the forenoon, Rogers was sitting with General Hand and some other gentlemen, when "we heard the discharge of several guns across the Tioga, and immediately afterwards the Indian warhoop." A hurried investigation of the riverbanks ended in the discovery of several warriors absconding with four or five horses. Pursuit was instant and furious, but in vain, Rogers noting that it was like "looking for needles in a haystack." [55]

The next day was a big day. With 900 carefully selected men, and an appropriate number of officers Generals Poor and Hand marched off the encampment grounds in order to reach the main branch of the river and thus eventually to meet the boats of General James Clinton. Sullivan had had word from Clinton that the general would be leaving Lake Otsego on the 9th. And Sunday, August 22, was a *really* big day. For here arrived the army of General Clinton, escorted by the Poor-Hand detachment. The most of Clinton's army came downriver in bateaux, 207 of them. When the boats floated into view of the Sullivan troops, "there went up such a shout as never before shook the wilderness." [56]

As the boats passed by the encampment of the light troops of Hand, they were saluted by thirteen rounds from two six-pounders. And on top of that, Colonel Proctor had his drummers and fifers provide a celebratory music that made it all a grand occasion.

Now the army, with Clinton's regiments, boasts probably 5000 men. Sullivan has laid waste the village of Chemung, which had been abandoned by the Indians; Clinton has destroyed a settlement of the Onondagas. Butler and the Indians under Cornplanter, Old Smoke and Brant, have yet to make a stand. On August 26 the expedition proceeds up the Chemung Valley toward the Indian village of Newtown. Hand's brigade of light troops, as was normal, marched at the left in six columns and formed the advance, with a captain and thirty men from the line on each flank. Hand's Major James Parr (a rifleman officer, who had just transferred from the 4th Brigade on August 6) with 100 expert riflemen marched out in front of Hand. There was a different spirit to the march. The campaign was about to heat up.

General Hand was thinking. Scouts had reported that they had "good information" that the Indians ahead were led by Chiefs Cornplanter and Brant. He knew the reputation of Joseph Brant. He knew that Brant and many of his Mohawks had been very early in the war allied with the British. He had even heard that this Joseph Brant had powwowed with King George the III in London. This was the Mohawk who had so brutally destroyed Cherry Valley. And this Cornplanter. Was this not the Seneca war-chief who was responsible for the terrors of Wyoming! Some kind of reckoning was surely in order.

With the strong impression that resistance would be encountered on the next day, the Sullivan army made camp at a distance beyond the ruins of Chemung. The customary patrols were sent out, and they were not long in reporting evidence to confirm the feeling that the Indians were preparing an ambush of some kind. Major Jeremiah Fogg recalled for his journal that in the region patrolled by Jason Wait smoke had been perceived from a number of fires that evening, and that just six miles up the trail (north), on the left bank of the Chemung River, some six miles southeast of present-day Elmira, fortifications were recognizable. [57]

As one historian has put it, "as morning dawned on 29 August, every soldier in Sullivan's army expected he would find himself in a fight before the end of the day." [58]

With a rosy red sun climbing the sky behind them, the troops moved out. Warily the army marched forward through the Chemung Valley, General Hand's brigade in the lead. It was just at 11:00 that the advance guard discovered the location of the warriors. With this report, General Hand instructed his riflemen "to form about a thousand feet from the enemy." The soldiers were to hold their fire until the remainder of the light corps could be brought forward. This was not an easy order to respect, as the Tory Rangers and the Seneca warriors were resorting to their old ruse (so successful at Oriskany and at Wyoming and at Cherry Valley), whereby they would rush out from their fortifications, firing as in a panic, suggest that their numbers were few and retreat to the ambuscade. General Hand would not fall for this; he had seen it many times. And as these sorties failed even to excite a response the Indians disappeared. In the meanwhile Hand had successfully brought forward his entire brigade; and he so notified General Sullivan.

Now that the situation was clear, it became time to work out a battle plan. Sullivan assembled his generals, Poor, Clinton, Hand, and Maxwell. After some discussion, each contributing his impression of the enemy position and numbers, Sullivan defined the plan of attack: "(1) the artillery to be placed on a ridge 300 yards from the angle of the enemy's fortified line so as to enfilade his lines and to command the space behind; (2) General Hand to support the artillery with part of his troops and to threaten the breastworks with the rest; (3) a movement up the river to flank the enemy, cut off his retreat in that direction, and pursue him when he retreated; [General Hand's detachment] (4) General Poor supported by General Clinton to form the right flanking division in a movement along the hills; (5) General Maxwell's brigade to act as a reserve." [59]

It was a good plan, and if executed properly, should result in a resounding defeat of any resistance to the campaign of village destruction. Timing, of course, would be critical. Noting that the terrain through which Poor and Clinton would be passing was extremely difficult, Sullivan would give them one hour.

Hand's deployment was described by Sullivan in his official report to Washington of the battle: "General Hand formed the light corps of the army in the wood within four hundred yards of their works. The riflemen in his front kept skirmishing with the enemy, who frequently sallied out and suddenly retired, apparently with a view of drawing our men into the works, which they supposed had not been discovered. The growth upon the hill being pine, interspersed with very low shrub oaks, they had cut off shrubs and stuck them in the ground in front of their works and had some reason to suppose that we should not distinguish them from those growing in the eminence. General Hand remained at his post until I arrived with the main army. . . .When sufficient space of time had been given to General Poor to gain the hill in their rear, our artillery was to announce our attack in front, which was to be made by General Hand's corps." [60]

One unforeseen big problem concerned the artillery. Sullivan wanted it mounted on a ridge. After about two hours of some sporadic musketry exchange, Hand ordered Proctor to bring his artillery forward to some high ground about 300-400 yards from the ambuscade the Indians had thrown up. That turned out to be much easier ordered than accomplished. The extreme difficulties were later recalled by Samuel McNeill, who had been serving as Quartermaster in Hand's brigade: "General Hand would, after Putting himself in a proper Position, have attacked their works, sword in hand, had not General Sullivan Sent orders to the contrary. General Hand Continued Transmitting his Discoveries to General Sullivan from time to time, while the Artillery was Crossing an Exceeding bad Defile, and the men had to hitch wagons, and with the help of Horses, it took one hundred and Twenty men to each waggon to draw it up the Hill. At 12 o'clock the artillery was brought before the enemy's works. The Riflemen kept up a slow fire, amusing the Enemy, and in order to keep them from Turning out of their works to make Discoveries, the artillery was planted in the most advantageous Place at about 400 yards Distant." [61]

  It was Sullivan's hope that the artillery could produce enough of a barrage to keep the Indians pinned down and buy enough time for Poor to outflank them. At just about 3:00 in the afternoon he ordered the cannon to fire. McNeill reported that "once the gun crews found their mark, they proceeded to pour a combination of solid shot, iron spikes, grape, and exploding shells into the ambuscade which proved so intense that the Indians chose to abandon their positions long before Gen. Enoch Poor could reasonably be expected to be in position." [62]

  Because Poor had run into extreme difficulty with swampy ground and very dense bushy growth, he had not quite completed his assigned flanking movement before the Indians, terrified by the thunder-sticks, "retreated from their works with the greatest precipitation." [63]

  Colonel John Butler, who had commanded the Indian defense at Newtown had afterwards great praise for Sullivan's artillery. He attributed the general consternation of the Indians to the effect of Proctor's six-pounders. He noted that the Americans had "six pieces of Cannon & Cohorns," which

~ *The Sullivan Expedition* ~ 187

began "discharging shells, round & grape shot, Iron Spikes &c. Incessantly which soon obliged us to leave . . . ." He describes the flight: "The shells bursting beyond us, made the Indians imagine the Enemy had got their Artillery all round us, & so startled & confounded them that [a] great part of them run off." In fact, Butler notes, they abruptly panicked and were pell-mell in their flight: "Many of the Indians made no halt, but proceeded immediately to their respective Villages . . . ." [64] No wonder General Sullivan had the cannon fired morning and night, all through the expedition.

But the great irony here is that Sullivan did not want the Indians to flee. In a way, the artillery was *too* effective, perhaps too zealous. While it was actually the element that won the battle, Proctor's artillery could be blamed for the failure of the army to achieve the kind of victory that was desired.

It has been suggested that General Sullivan ordered the artillery fire too early, for General Poor had not yet out-flanked the Indians, and they were able to retire, albeit in confusion. But Sullivan, had given Poor, he thought, plenty of time; and of course, besides that, he could hardly have expected the Indians to flee so early in the cannonading. Explained the general: "Fear had given them too great speed to be overtaken."

And the August 29 journal entry made by Lieutenant Robert Parker, far from finding fault with Sullivan, blamed bad roads for Poor's delay and the unfortunate timing: "It must be allowed that our plan of attack was judiciously laid, well executed and must reflect great Honor on those that conducted it — but the badness of the road with some other circumstances, prevented the right wing [Poor] from gaining their post as soon as could be wished for & thereby part of the plan proved unsuccessful." [65]

Most amusing is Parker's description of the effect of the artillery. Having described the guns and the shot they were launching, which he called a most pleasing piece of music, he remarked on the warriors: "But the Indians I believe did not admire the sound so much, nor could they be prevailed upon to listen to its music, although we made use of all the eloquence we were masters of for that purpose, but they were deaf to our entreaties and turned their backs upon us in token of their detestation for us." [66]

Of the battle of Newtown, Blacksnake, Cornplanter's companion here as ever, and a participant in the action, many years later reported, in his characteristically artful understatement, that "the Indians did not manage well."

Although at Newtown it might have gone much better for Sullivan, it was a victory, and, if nothing else it put an end to any kind of organized resistance and opened the way for an almost undisturbed destruction of houses and cornfields.

On August 30, Sullivan fired a full official report of Newtown to the Commander-in-Chief. It was closely detailed, and closed with Sullivan's commendation for his troops: "Indeed, the conduct of the whole army was truly pleasing and gave the most striking evidence that no equal number of troops can oppose their progress." [67]

Washington, much gratified of course, responded, from his headquarters at West Point, with warm congratulations on the success enjoyed in the engagement at Newtown. He proceeds then to encourage a follow-up: "The advantages we have already gained over the Indians, in the destruction of so many of their settlements, is very flattering to the expedition. But to make it as conclusive as the state of your provisions and the safety of your army will countenance, I would mention two points which I may not have sufficiently expressed in my general instructions, or if I have, which I wish to repeat. The one is the necessity of pushing the Indians to the greatest practicable distance from their own settlements and our frontiers; to the throwing them wholly on the British enemy. The other is the making the destruction of their settlements so final and complete as to put it out of their power to derive the smallest succor from them in case they should attempt to return." [68]

On the next day after Newtown, there were no Indians to be seen. After General Sullivan commended the army for its performance in yesterday's action, thanking the troops for their fine execution of the battle plan, almost all of the soldiers were employed in cutting down the corn in the neighborhood, several hundred acres. And with the dawn of a new day, the men of the expedition, much animated with their success, moved forward with great confidence and high morale. In fact the soldiers were feeling so good that, without complaint, they agreed to half rations for the time being.

Intent now on the villages located on both sides of the finger lake called Seneca, the army arrived at Catherine's Town on the first day of September. The town had taken its name from Catherine Montour, the wife of a noted Seneca chief, Telenemut (Thomas Hudson), and sister of the "fiend of Wyoming," Queen Esther. Like that at Chemung, this village had been earlier (autumn of 1778) wiped out by Colonel Thomas Hartley. [69] It was promptly destroyed again.

As the army moved up the eastern shore of the beautiful lake, it came to Kendaia (Appletown), Blacksnake's birthplace, a small village about a half mile from the lake itself and on both banks of a small stream. After erasing this community, abandoned, like the rest, the army moved on along the shores of Seneca Lake, coming on September 7 to the capital of the Seneca nation, the home of the chief sachem. It was composed of nearly sixty solidly built houses and stood on both sides of Kanadaseaga Creek. Called Kanadaseaga ("the grand village"), it reposed about a mile and a half to the east of the site of present-day Geneva. [70]

Cornplanter had actually persuaded the Indians to make a stand on the beaches of the lake at this castle, but as Hand's light corps approached, the warriors grew skittish. Cornplanter tried to rally them. Leaping in front of the infamous Red Jacket, not celebrated for courage, he insisted that the warrior stand and fight. When Red Jacket indicated that he certainly did not mean to do so, the enraged chief turned to the very young wife of the timid warrior and exclaimed in great heat, "Leave that man — he is a coward!" [71]

No battle occurred here. It required Sullivan only two days to put an end to the chief city of the Senecas.

Sullivan continued to keep Hand's light corps in advance of the main body of the army, and, although there occurred some occasional firing, hardly anything like a skirmish, and nothing approaching an actual engagement, had so far ensued.

Next to be destroyed were the villages of Kanandaigua, Hanneyaye, Kanaghsaws (Great Tree's town), and Gathsegwarohare. [72] But while the army was still in the region of Kanaghsaws, delayed because of the necessity to build a bridge over a large sunken place, so that the troops might cross the swamp, the Indians, under the leadership of Old Smoke, Cornplanter, Brant, Sagwarithra, Little Beard, Fish Carrier, and Blacksnake, with some 500 warriors, prepared an ambush. Only because Lieutenant Thomas Boyd and Michael Parker, who had been sent out on a scout with twenty-six men, stumbled into this ambush, was the plan of the Indians frustrated. Nine soldiers of Boyd's party escaped, but others, including Lieutenant Thaosagwat, whose brother was fighting on the side of the British, were killed, scalped, and mutilated. Boyd and Parker, having been captured and questioned by Butler and Brant, were dispatched under guard of Butler's Rangers to Genesee Castle, the village of Little Beard. [73]

On the next day, Tuesday, September 14, the advance troops of Sullivan's army came upon the most grisly sight of the entire expedition. Many are the accounts of how it all happened. All make the blood run cold. One must have a *very strong* stomach to endure the details.

~ The Sullivan Expedition ~

One of the many records of the torture and murder of Boyd and Parker is that by Mary Jemison. Jemison, who as a youngster had been taken from her eastern Pennsylvania home by a raiding party of French and Shawnee and at Pittsburgh turned over to Seneca women, had been living among the Senecas for almost twenty years at the time of the Sullivan expedition. She tells how Boyd and Parker were brought to Little Beard's town, "where they were soon after put to death in the most shocking and cruel manner." In describing such scenes, particularly when her ruthless husband Hiokatoo is the agent of the cruelty, she rarely registers much feeling. Here she is moved to pity: "Little Beard, in this, as in all other scenes of cruelty that happened at his town, was master of ceremonies, and principal actor. Poor Boyd was stripped of his clothing, and then tied to a sapling, where the Indians menaced his life by throwing their tomahawks at the tree, directly over his head, brandishing their scalping knives around him in the most frightful manner, and accompanying their ceremonies with terrific shouts of joy. Having punished him sufficiently in this way, they made a small opening in his abdomen, took out an intestine, which they tied to the sapling, and then unbound him from the tree, and drove him round it till he had drawn out the whole of his intestines. He was then beheaded, his head was stuck upon a pole, and his body left on the ground unburied. Thus ended the life of poor William [Thomas] Boyd, who it was said, had every appearance of being an active and enterprizing officer, of the first talents. The other prisoner was (if I remember distinctly) only beheaded and left near Boyd." [74]

Skeptics are many ("too horrible to be true"), but the story is preserved by the locals, and to this day one may stand next to the tree (the sapling) to which Boyd was bound. It is a huge tree now, a white oak, said to be 270 years old, and called "the torture tree." It is designated by an historical marker at the old site of Little Beard's town.

Doubtless the sight of this scene of torture and

mutilation and murder impelled the soldiers to a greater zeal as they went about their business. It required the army only until the middle of the afternoon of the next day to destroy totally the very expansive fields of corn and the enormous town of the infamous Little Beard, called Genishau (Genesee Castle). An incredible number of very sturdy houses were flattened or burned. Lt. Erkuries Beatty of the 4th Pennsylvania Regiment, the keeper of a richly detailed diary, and not yet twenty years old, counted seventy; and Lt. Thomas Blake of Colonel Henry Dearborn's 1st New Hampshire Regiment counted 180!

    At the close of this day of destruction, satisfied that they had reached the end of the trail of villages, and heedless of Washington's injunction to take Fort Niagara "if possible," the army of Generals Sullivan and Clinton marched only about four miles farther. It never did reach the village of Cornplanter's birth, which lay just a few miles beyond the town of Little Beard, and a number of other villages escaped their attention altogether, but it seemed enough. The soldiers had been burning cornfields and firing villages for six long weeks, all of August and well into September. Next day, September 16, they set out on the return trip.

    General Hand has been in touch from time to time with Joseph Reed, President of Pennsylvania's Executive Council. From the army's encampment at Kanawaluhaly (twenty-one miles from the mouth of the Tioga), on the 25th of September, he ventured one of the very first evaluations of the expedition. He is much pleased with what has been accomplished: "I have the satisfaction to inform your Excellency that the Body of the Army under Major General Sullivans Command has arrived at this place on its return from the Indian Country, having compleated the desolation of all the principal Settlements within its reach."

    But he knows Indians, and his instincts require him to register concern: "The loss of their Crops and Houses must render the subsistence of the Savages very difficult in this part of the World, so much so, that I think they cant bring any considerable Parties into ours — and as no terms have been sought by them, I am apprehensive that the spirit of revenge so natural to Savages, which their good allies the English will not fail to foment, a desire to persuade other nations that they are not Conquered, or even hunger may bring straggling parties on our Frontiers this fall."

He closes by alerting Reed to the possibility of continued raids upon the settlements: "I take the liberty of mentioning these [and] my suggestion to your Excellency [is] that you may make timely provision for the security of the frontiers, should you think them in any danger." [75]

Reed in fact through September and the first three weeks of October received a number of letters from General Hand. These provided updates on Wyoming and other settlements and included suggestions for improving the safety of the frontier. On October 19, at the meeting of the Supreme Executive Council in Philadelphia, Reed had these letters read to the Council. Having resolved to honor Hand's suggestion for the augmentation of troops at Sunbury, the Board dutifully transmitted the whole to the Board of War. [76]

The expedition, in regardless formation and order, by water and along the river shores, by the same route it had followed into and through the Indian country, moved fast. It set out from Genesee on September 15, reached Tioga on the 30th, promptly destroying Fort Sullivan, and, picking up the soldiers who had been left there, arrived at Wyoming on the afternoon of Thursday, October 7. Wyoming was ready for the army. A big celebration, including the firing of cannon for every toast, lasted almost two days. On Saturday, the 9th, at 6: a. m., the army set out on the last leg, the march to Easton.

Lt. Robert Parker's journal entry for the date of September 16 provides a short summary of the expedition and a vision for the future of the beautiful Susquehanna River Valley:

Thus had we advanced 140 miles in the Enemy's country from Tioga and carried fire, sword and destruction in every part, that we could possibly find out or approach, in the prosecution of which, we had to encounter many and almost insurmountable difficulties, such as forcing a march all the way, cutting a Road for the Artillery, in many places a continued swamp for several miles, want of provisions, hard marches, and fatigue.

But here let us leave the busy army for a moment and suffer our imaginations to Run at large through these delightful wilds, & figure to ourselves the opening prospects of future greatness which we may reasonably suppose is not far distant, & that we may yet behold with a pleasing admiration those deserts that have so long been the habitation of beasts of prey & a safe asylum for our savage enemies, converted into fruitful fields, covered with all the richest productions of agriculture, amply rewarding the industrious husbandman by a golden harvest; the spacious plains abounding with flocks & herds to supply his necessary wants. These Lakes & Rivers that have for ages past rolled in sacred silence along their wonted course, unknown to Christian nations, produce spacious cities & guilded spires, rising on their banks, affording a safe retreat for the virtuous few that disdains to live in affluence at the expense of their liberties. [77]

It is difficult to assess the effect, the value, of the Sullivan-Clinton-Brodhead campaign. Some historians insist that the invasion of the Indian country did little more than to exacerbate the Indians, that it was in fact a failure. More than a decade later, it has been noted, ". . . the Seneca chief Cornplanter reminded Washington of the legacy of the general's decision [to invade the Indian country]." In 1790, Cornplanter declared to the President at their meeting in Philadelphia: "When your army entered the country of the Six Nations, we called you Town Destroyer and to this day when that name [Sullivan] is heard our women look behind them and turn pale, and our children cling close to the necks of their mothers. Our counsellors and warriors are men, and cannot be afraid, but their hearts are grieved with the fears of our women and children, and desire that it [the pain inflicted by the campaign] may be buried so deep as to be heard no more." [78] To the very end of his very long life the venerable Iroquois chieftain inveighed against the inhumanities of the Sullivan expedition.

But the campaign did more than simply anger the Indians. They clearly suffered an almost total devastation of buildings and grain fields, and vegetable plots and fruit trees. Before the battle of Lexington/Concord, the Seneca Indians of the Six Nations lived in thirty-some widely scattered villages. By the spring of 1780 most of these had been reduced to ashes, had simply disappeared. Sullivan alone claimed to have destroyed forty (!) villages, and thirty is the total, with villages named, in another report. And this count is without reference to the damage done by Brodhead in his march up the river Allegheny. One tally declares that only two of all the many Indian villages known to the frontier people survived undamaged. [79]

Besides the destruction of 30-40 villages, one of which contained 128 (!) houses the expedition could claim 160 thousand bushels of corn, and all the fruit trees. [80]

Sullivan's General Orders for September 15, 1778, just as the expedition started home from Genesee, included a summary of what the expedition had accomplished: ". . . the total ruin of the Indian settlements and the destruction of their crops, which were designed for the support of these inhuman barbarians while they were desolating the American frontier."

Homeless Seneca families were clamoring at the gates of Fort Niagara, and Chief Cornplanter, after a little of that, soon removed his family to the Allegheny River in Pennsylvania. He was out of business.

And when it is considered what the casualty figures might have been, the official tally of forty soldiers lost is most remarkable.

When the object of the campaign, as defined by Washington to Sullivan, "to put the Indians in their place," and to render the Indian aid to the British negligible, is brought to mind, it would seem that the Expedition was a success.

And the campaign can be considered a success, too, for what it did not do. It did not do what it might have done, that is to unite the Indians generally, and to bring closer together the fragments of the Six Nations.

But there did occur response. The major campaign of the year following the Sullivan campaign, one that includes the Indians, was that led by Sir John Johnson himself into the Schoharie Valley of New York. Historians regard it as "comparable in size and destructiveness to the Sullivan Expedition of the year before." And clearly it was by way of answer to Sullivan. The Indians were ruthless in their burning and ravaging. Some say that it "virtually wiped out all the white settlements in the Mohawk Valley west of the environs of Schenectady."[81]

And there were other raids upon the frontier in the wake of the Sullivan Expedition. But, devastating as they were, they are best viewed as the last gasp of the warriors allied with the British. And one has to ask, what would be the character of the Indian alliance with the British had *not* the Sullivan Expedition taken place?

In any case, General Edward Hand had done, as always, the job that was asked of him.

IX

Yorktown

The play, sir, is over.

— Marquis de Lafayette

As the fifth summer of the Revolution began to wane, Washington, whether he had firmly calculated it in his strategy, or simply slid into it, elected to play a waiting game. With Clinton somewhat idle in New York City, with the Hessians under Wilhelm Knyphausen, Washington seemed to sense that the Cause would profit from the failure of the British to embark on any aggressive campaign or to register a significant victory anywhere. He understood, perhaps better than did Cornwallis and Henry Clinton, that King George and the British Parliament would be most impatient for some sign that the rebellion was being squelched.

In November of 1779, a month after the return of the Sullivan army from the Indian country, he began to move the main army into winter quarters at Morristown, Hand's brigades marching from Pompton Lakes to the encampment grounds, where each unit had been assigned a very specific location.

After the battles of Trenton and Princeton, for the time January-May, 1777, Washington's army had camped at Morristown. Washington considered it an ideal location for many reasons, not the least of which were the Watchung Mountains, which provided a natural defense. Besides, while seemingly safe from attack, he was but a two-days' march (some thirty miles) from New York City, which Henry Clinton continued to occupy. For that winter he established his headquarters at Jacob Arnold's Tavern, near the center of town.

Now here he was again, for the winter of 1779-80 (December through June). Various units of the Continental Army had marched to Morristown during the last three weeks of December. Here they built huts, to the specifications provided by Washington himself. And it was well they did, as this winter proved to be the harshest "ever known," the "coldest of the 18th century." Washington, in writing to Lafayette toward the end of this terrible winter (March 18), declared that "The oldest people now living in this Country do not remember so hard a winter as the one we are now emerging from. In a word the severity of the frost exceeded anything of the kind that had ever been experienced in this climate before." And the Baron de Kalb, mentor and good friend of Lafayette, insisted the same. De Kalb had endured Valley Forge too, but about this winter he wrote:

" . . . so cold that the ink freezes on my pen, while I am sitting close to the fire. The roads are piled with snow until, at some places they are elevated twelve feet above their ordinary level." Indeed, historians of the weather register for the 1779-80 winter in this New Jersey region twenty-eight distinctly separate snow storms! It is known that 1072 soldiers deserted the army at this time, and between 100 and 300 perished to the cold or to sickness. At the earlier Valley Forge encampment, for which the winter was only average, some 1000-3000 soldiers perished. Although Morristown suffered a much more extremely harsh winter, the casualties were fewer than at Valley Forge for two good reasons: (1) Washington and his soldiers by this time knew how to build huts, and (2) Most of the soldiers had been inoculated against smallpox.

For this second Morristown encampment Washington established headquarters at the Ford Mansion, which was just at the edge of town, some five miles from the Jockey Hollow, in which the foot soldiers were constructing their huts. And Martha would be with him, as she was for virtually all of the eight winter encampments.

As the army settled in, the General Orders for December 14, 1779, reported that Major General Lord Stirling "is appointed to the command of the division composed of Maxwell's and Hand's brigades," both of which of course had marched on the Sullivan Expedition.[1] It was on this very day, and apparently General Hand was home in Lancaster at the time, that Kitty Hand gave birth to her third child, another girl. Named for her mother Katherine (or Catherine), the poor child was destined for a short life.

Three days later, Friday, December 17, 1779, the Commander-in-Chief provided for his officers the general order of battle. "The following is to be considered as our general order of battle; the army is to form in two lines, the first composed of three divisions, the second of two. Hand's division is in the first line, forming left to right."[2]

On the day before Christmas, Major Thomas Church, previously a captain with Samuel Smith's Company E of the 5th Pennsylvania Regiment, was appointed Brigade Major and Inspector to General Hand's brigade, and the riflemen were by Washington's General Orders told to "respect and obey him as such."

Among the more notable events of this winter encampment was Washington's proclamation declaring Saint Patrick's Day a holiday, "in honor of our many Irish troops." And the Commander-in-Chief had the very good news from Lafayette that France would be sending ships and trained soldiers "soon" to the continent.

But, besides the almost intolerable weather, there are

some petty annoyances. One involved the field officers. A distressing number of officers were absent from camp on leave. And as it was a great number all at the same time, with some tardy in return, the Commander-in-Chief was much perturbed. To him these unwarranted absences suggested a lack of discipline, and did little for the morale of the foot soldier. Among the officers absent is Brigadier General Edward Hand, who of course was determined to see his third child. And once again Washington is becoming most impatient with the general, for he is overstaying his authorized leave, by many days. He gets off a plain-enough letter to Hand on February 6: "Dr Sir: The number of Genl. Officers in Camp is so Small, and of that number, several very anxious for leave to be absent that I am, exceedingly distressed, and put to it to conduct the ordinary business of the Army, with the smallest degree of propriety. I must therefore request, that upon receipt of this Letter you will repair to Camp." [3]

Hand is returned before the end of the month, just in time for the first of a succession of councils, at least one of which seemed always to be on the schedule. Almost immediately the general is complaining to Kitty, "I am not able to describe the Uneasiness I feel at not hearing from you." [4]

Washington called his high-ranking officers together for councils on March 27, April 1, June 6, September 6, and October 31. Brigadier General Edward Hand was present at each one of these sessions. The three big considerations were what to do about the British in New York City; how big an expedition, if any, should be sent to the south to beef up the Continental Army forces there; and what the arrival of the French would mean to the military strategy.

The winter of 1779-80, although Washington's main army saw no major action, was a most memorable period for the Revolution. British activity is evident shortly after Christmas, and a most significant military action occurs with the arrival of the most welcome spring. Washington, made conscious of the threat that was forming, convened a council of his major generals and his brigadiers. The officers were assembled at Morristown on March 27. They were promptly apprised of the meaning of Clinton's long-ago departure from New York City and of imminent danger to Charleston. Amazingly, the generals reached a *unanimous* decision, which was that "no detachment could safely be made from the army at Morristown."

In November of the year 1779 the British command, finally appreciating the need for a major military action, and hopeful of a very meaningful victory, had shifted its focus to the Southern theater. Lord Cornwallis had the impression, rightly so, that the Loyalist influence was much stronger in the south than in the north. Besides, at such port cities as Charleston he could bring his enormous navy into play. He was thinking back to the capture of Savannah some fifteen months ago. Accordingly, in December, having selected his target, Cornwallis proposed to his superior Henry Clinton that the British army be moved south. General Clinton needed no urging. He was very quick to oblige. Leaving the Hessians under the command of the Hessian General Wilhelm von Knyphausen in New York City, he hastened down the coast, setting sail from New York on the day after Christmas, 1779.

The arrival of Clinton in Charleston with his British Regulars meant for Cornwallis an army of 14,000 (!) and a fleet of ninety ships providing an awesome artillery. It was a much more formidable force than that which had been turned away by General Charles Lee and Carlisle's John Armstrong, and most especially by Colonel William Moultrie, in June of 1776, in the earlier British attempt to capture the city.

Cornwallis, after almost three months of preparation, finally laid siege to the city. The date was March 29. Major General Benjamin Lincoln, a most able and fearless officer, was in command of the defense. Incredibly, Lincoln held out through the whole month of April, and only after six weeks of a strangling siege did he surrender the city. At the same time of course, General Lincoln was surrendering the entire army that had been so tenaciously resisting the siege. This was a force of 5000 troops, the largest body of Continental soldiers to surrender during the entire revolution.

The fall of Charleston was a major victory for the British, akin to their capture of New York City. It delivered a devastating blow to the Cause. Flushed with the success, Clinton returned to New York City in June. Both Charleston and New York City would remain in British hands until the very end of the war.

The council held by Washington during the siege of Charleston, April 1 (also at Morristown), was convened to consider what reaction should be made to the news that still another detachment had been dispatched by the British from New York City to further reinforce their army in the south. What to do? The decision arrived at by the nine generals present was that if the report turned out indeed to be true, "about Two Thousand Men should be sent from hence [Morristown] to reinforce the Southern States." All signed the decision except Washington.

Hand in letters to Kitty, May 3 and May 7, reported that "Nothing has happened here worth relating." It is all talk. But he did enclose six thousand dollars! And in his next, posted June 5, while complaining that "Doctor Shippens trial [at which Hand was presiding] continues, and it is likely for what I now know that it will not terminate before the close of the ensuing Campaign," he expresses the deeply-felt hope that his situation in the summer will allow for a visit. [5]

The council held, again at Morristown, on June 6, which included Lafayette (who did not regularly attend the council meetings), took chiefly the form of an update on the relative strength of the two armies.

That was not all for the summer of 1780. Still another major, major victory went to the British in this southern theater. Known as the battle of Camden, it took place on August 16. Arrayed against each other on the field of battle were 2100 British Regulars in the command of Charles Cornwallis, who had marched from Charleston, and 3700 Continentals and militia under the command of Major General Horatio Gates.

The fighting was furious, including as it did several bayonet charges. It was fought in the densely wooded swamps of South Carolina, in the Gum Swamp and at Sanders Creek, a few miles to the north of Camden. Owing largely to confusion and actual errors on the part of Gates, the battle was turned into a rout of the Continentals.

Very costly to the Revolutionary cause was the death of the Continentals' second in command, Major General Johann de Kalb. De Kalb had been placed in charge of the right wing, at the head of one regiment of Delaware troops and two brigades of the Maryland Division. Even though the other divisions of Gates's army had fled the field in panic, General de Kalb's soldiers offered a fierce and very stubborn resistance to the advancing Redcoats, fighting on, even while totally surrounded and enveloped by fire.

The heroic death of General de Kalb, for his close friend Lafayette and for anybody who knew this courageous officer, would always be one of the most memorable and saddest events of the entire revolution. De

Baron Johann de Kalb

Kalb, after his horse had been shot out from under him, continued to fight on foot, shoulder to shoulder with his loyal troops of the Maryland Second Brigade. Finally he fell, mortally wounded, stricken with three musket balls (Some historians say eleven!) and pierced eight times by British bayonets. The general was saved from instant death by his devoted aide Charles du Buysson.[6] As the general was being carried away, a prisoner of war, he could not believe what he was being told, that for the Americans all was lost. Cornwallis, supervising while de Kalb's wounds were being treated by the British surgeons, assured him it was so. The heroic General Johann de Kalb died three days later.

It was a devastating loss and a humiliating defeat for the colonials. Not only did the Continental army lose 2000 troops, it had lost one of its most able officers in Major General de Kalb and, in effect, had lost General Horatio Gates as well. So disgraced was Gates, having terribly mismanaged the action, and having fled the field on "a fast horse," that the hero of Saratoga was never again given a field command. For the Southern Theater General Nathanael Greene would succeed him.

General Hand, when he had the news was much sorrowed, of course, by the defeat and by the loss of so many soldiers, but certainly too by the death of Baron de Kalb. He had never got to know the general well, but he knew enough about him to know that he was one of the most able of all Washington's officers, and certainly among the most courageous. And Hand knew that de Kalb was fiercely loyal to the Commander-in-Chief. He could appreciate what this tragic loss would mean to Washington.

But Washington's main army was not engaged in any major military action during the spring and summer of 1780. What General Hand found himself doing was not all that exciting. Over and over again he was called upon to preside at some court martial proceeding. These trials, although generally unpleasant for him, provided a very different kind of experience, which would be of real benefit to him one day.

One of the trials at which he presided, as noted above, was the very lengthy and notorious court martial of Dr. William Shippen, Jr. [7] It was begun in March at Morristown and continued into the middle of June at Short Hills, and carried on at Springfield. Shippen had been in hot water for some time. It was supposed by those close to his longtime friend and colleague Dr. John Morgan that Shippen had been responsible for some underhanded deals in order to replace Morgan as Director of Hospitals. Unable to cope with these charges, Shippen resigned. This brought on a court martial: "A general Court Martial of the line is to sit tomorrow [March 14, 1780] 10 o'clock at the new store room in Morristown for the trial of Doctor William Shippen junior and such other persons as may be brought before them, Brigadier General Edward Hand is appointed president." [8]

Dr. Shippen was charged on two counts. For one he was accused of misappropriating the supplies which arrived at hospitals for wounded soldiers; in the second place he was charged with not reporting deaths properly, presumably in some way for his own personal gain. Finally after a long drawn-out trial Dr. Shippen was, on some technicality, cleared of both charges. This was in July of 1780.

General Hand complained about this "very troublesome Court

William Shippen, Jr.

Martial," which he found "tedious," but he was never perceived to nod off.

Though there was little to enjoy in most of the cases which came before him, his role he accepted, characteristically, as a duty. And he became quite good at presiding, bringing courts martial expeditiously (except in the case of Dr. Shippen) to conclusion. Besides others, he was president for courts martial (all at Morristown) on April 10, April 29, and May 15. He could not know that he would become before long a member of the Board at the most sensational of all courts martial of the time.

But there was this summer, although it rarely grew into anything more than skirmishing, some actual battlefield action. Two of the last major battles of the Revolution occurred in June of 1780 at the gates to Washington's Morristown encampment in the Watchung Mountains. The first is known as the battle of Connecticut Farms.

With the army in June at the Scotch Plains and Edison region of New Jersey, Washington was notified by Captain Jonathan Dayton (June 7) that the enemy had landed at midnight, moving from Staten Island to Perth Amboy, and were marching inland.

According to his report the British force numbered four to five thousand men [Actually 6000 is a more accurate figure.] carrying twelve field pieces. The British (Hessian troops) were under the command of Hessian General Wilhelm von Knyphausen, of Fort Washington and the Brandywine fame. Having heard that Washington's troops were much depleted by disease and desertion (and in fact Washington had only 3500 able soldiers at Morristown), he had calculated that the chances were good for major damage to the Continental army.

Accordingly, he ordered three divisions to board the available boats, and at midnight crossed over from Staten Island to hit the shores at Elizabethtown Point.

Washington, with the warning, had sprung into action. His Morning Orders, posted at four o'clock a. m., required "The Troops to be held in readiness to march at a moment's warning; Each man to be furnish'd with 40 rounds and two days provisions." At seven o'clock he put the troops into motion. He had them marching in the following order: 2nd Connecticut, 1st Connecticut, Starks's, Hand's, 2nd Pennsylvania and 1st Pennsylvania.

Knyphausen's plan was to advance from Elizabethtown Point the necessary seven miles to the northwest and seize the town of Springfield at sunrise. He was expecting little resistance. He got more than he could handle. At Connecticut Farms (present Union Township) he encountered furious opposition from the New Jersey militia forces, so much, indeed, that he was compelled to halt the advance, and stay out the night right where he was.

What Washington had ordered was harassment. He was satisfied with skirmishing, and, as always for this kind of action, was depending a lot on General Edward Hand. To Lord Stirling on the next day he reported: "My Lord: I am just making a detachment of those battalions under Hand, which are to be employed to-day as actively as the situation will permit in conjunction with the Militia." He felt that the action would be chiefly "in the woods," which of course was very much to the liking of General Edward Hand.

The kind of skirmishing Knyphausen was getting was not to *his* liking. Sensing, certainly accurately, that further advance would result in an even stiffer resistance, the Hessian General, setting fire "to at least a dozen houses," [9] elected to back off toward Springfield. He observed of the harassing scrimmage action (doubtless thinking back to Trenton), that "The Rebels, as they often did, withdrew from house to house and from wood path to wood path, resisting with all means available."

It was at just about this time that Washington himself

appeared, found the houses in flames and sent forward his personal guard, some 153 skilled riflemen under the command of Major Caleb Gibbs. [10] As General Hand was very active in this engagement, his firsthand account is of great interest. From the encampment "near Springfield," on June 19, he reports to "Dearest Kitty" the action: "The night of the 6th the Enemy landed in force at Elizabeth Town & marched out some miles, a Brigade of Continental troops stationed at Springfield and the Militia of the neighborhood gave them much opposition on the 7th. The Army marched to oppose their progress & reached this Place in the evening, that night the Enemy retired to Elizabeth Town point where they yet remain (June 7) in a Position which tho it must be Disagreeable to them prevents our giving them much Disturbance . . . . The Enemy have rendered their communication wth Staten Island easier by a Bridge of Boats over the Sound. On the 8th, in the morning the Gen[l]. Not knowing that the Enemy had retired, ordered out a Detachment of 600 men to relieve the Party which had been Engaged the Day before & maintain a Difficult Post by which the Enemy must enter Springfield. This Command evolved on me. On my entering Springfield I found the Enemy had abandoned the Posts they held the night before. Therefore I proceeded to Elizabeth Town hoping to be able to harass their men as I had reason to think they would immediately drop to Staten Island. Our men advanced with great rapidity & attacked what we thought was their rear guard which soon gave way & discovered their Armt drawn up in order of Battle yet they did not attempt to revenge the Insult offered them but . . . even permitted us to hold the ground from which we had driven their Piquets — our loss in the Skirmish was 2 men kild & three wounded. Capt Leighten commanded my advance Party & behaved gallantly the Jersey Militia [threw themselves?] in with very great Spirit & as far as opertunity served & Distinguished themselves — " [11]

    Some two weeks later occurred another, more

consequential, action. On June 20 Hand had marching orders from Washington, who was now at the Short Hills. Hand was to take the troops for which he was responsible to Pompton Plains, where his men were to halt "til further orders."

It was shortly after Hand got to Pompton, on June 23, that the battle of Springfield occurred. A British force of 5000-6000, under the command of Lt. General Sir Henry Clinton and the Hessian General Knyphausen, attacked a portion of Washington's army. The British had been en route for Morristown, in the hope of capturing stores which they felt were present there. But they were intent on Washington's army too, and had even dispatched Major General Alexander Leslie up the Hudson with an entrapment force designed to cut off Washington's retreat. Clinton was able to burn Springfield, but was repulsed by the 1500 troops under the command of General Nathanael Greene and Colonel Elias Dayton. This army included a brigade in the command of Brigadier General William Maxwell, a brigade under Brigadier General John Stark, a task force of 500 soldiers in the charge of General Hand, and a number of New Jersey militia.

It was not long before Clinton suffered the same discouragement Knyphausen had experienced. Recognizing that any further attempt to advance would be costly and probably in vain, the British generals fell back to Elizabethtown Point and at midnight retired once more over their "bridge of boats" to Staten Island.

For the two battles of Connecticut Farms and Springfield casualties were light. The British lost twenty-five killed, 234 wounded, and forty-eight missing; the rebel forces lost thirteen killed, forty-nine wounded, nine missing. To these battles, though losses were not great on either side, a real significance attaches. Washington's army, greatly outnumbered, was at risk. Success in these engagements was a must for the Continentals.[12]

It was shortly after the Springfield engagement that

General Hand was given the command of a brigade of light infantry that had just been formed. [13]

Washington in the meanwhile was able to get the main army established in an encampment at Whippany, [14] just a little north of Morristown. There he remained for three days, June 23-25.

For three months in the year 1780 (July 1-July 28 and October 8-Nov. 27) Washington made his headquarters at the Dey Mansion, in the region of northern New Jersey known as the Preakness Valley (Washington, and Hand too, always spelled it *Pracaness*.). He was very fond of this site, for its strategic location and for the ready availability of food. And he very much enjoyed the mansion itself, which could accommodate officers and advisors whom he needed to consult. Among his regular visitors were Alexander Hamilton, James McHenry, Tench Tilghman, Lafayette, Anthony Wayne, Lord Stirling, and General Robert Howe.

The Commander-in-Chief was at the Dey Mansion when in July he was notified of the arrival of the French army. Hand, from the encampment at Pracaness, promptly (July 27) sent this great good news to Kitty: "The first Division of the French Auxiliaries consisting of 8 Sail of the Line 3 Frigates 2 Bomb [illegible] & Some Smaller Armed Vessels with land forces have arrived at Rhode Island. The Second Division is Daily expected." As for our army, it "remains quiet." He then describes for Kitty the new uniforms: "By a Genl. Order all the Genl. Officers of Our Army are obliged to Wear Blew Coats with Buff facings, with yellow Buttons & Gold Epaulets . . . & every Officer is obliged to have a Dash of White in his Coattail to represent the Union with the French Troops." [15]

It had been a long time ago, May 5, 1778, that Washington and his army, encamped at Valley Forge, had received the most welcome news of the alliance with France. It surely was the most joyous moment of that long, hard winter. What the soldiers at Valley Forge were learning was that three months ago, on February 6, the Treaty had been concluded in Paris, with Benjamin Franklin signing for the United States. And just yesterday, May 4, Congress had ratified the document. By this announcement the troops were made very nearly delirious. Washington ordered a celebration with the regiments at their finest. Lafayette of course became the center of attention. The young officer stood proudly on parade, together with the Continental Army of General Washington, while, three times, thirteen guns of the Henry Knox artillery boomed their salute. [16]

In the General Orders for this day, Tuesday, May 5, 1778, in which the alliance was proclaimed, an ecstatic Washington noted the need "to set apart a day for gratefully acknowledging the divine Goodness."

Just how much joy was occasioned in the Commander-in-Chief can be realized from the fact that he promptly pardoned two soldiers who had been condemned to execution, and returned them to their companies. And that night he entertained his officers at the Potts House with the kind of elegant dinner he so much enjoyed. And all cheered with every toast, to the French, to Benjamin Franklin, to Lafayette.

This news, that France would now be formally and actively supporting the American cause could not have come at a better time. The prospect of the French naval forces coming into the picture, and perhaps troops as

Comte de Rochambeau

well, heightened considerably the mood of the Valley Forge encampment. [17]

It turned out, however, to be twenty-six months before the French forces reached America, but now, here in July of 1780, the army had the news that it had actually happened. And those who could see clearly the big picture were most confident that the success of the revolution was insured.

Comte de Rochambeau, dispatched from France by King Louis XVI, reached the beaches of Newport, Rhode Island, with almost 6000 regular French army troops, in July of 1780. The army had been conveyed in thirty-six troop transport ships, escorted by seven capital ships and three frigates under command of the Chevalier de Ternay. It was good news for the Continental Army, but, even though Washington had hurried off to meet the French as soon as they landed, it was a long time before the Commander-in-Chief and Rochambeau could get together in a meaningful meeting. Indeed, it was not until September 21 that the French commander and the American Commander-in-Chief were able to come together "to concert the details of a plan of operations," this at Hartford, Connecticut. And nothing was going to happen now until the next year. In fact, it was not until May 21 that the two got together again, this time in Wethersfield, Connecticut.

Meanwhile General Hand's contingent was moved to the Infantry Camp, near Orangetown (Tappan). From this site, on August 20, Hand noticed for Kitty merely "a change of ground," and also conveyed the news that General Nathanael Greene "is ordered to the Southern Department to take command in the place of Gen. Gates." And in just a wee bit more than a week later Hand is writing from another encampment, this in the "English Neighbourhood, just thirteen miles removed from the last station. Except for a forage raid on Bergen Point ("so near the Enemy that their Centinels on Paulus Hook [were?] discovered with ours"), he noted that "nothing much has happened," the British making no movement at all.[18]

The September 6 council called by Washington, composed of the familiar figures, was scheduled for the encampment in Bergen County, at the village of Hackensack, the site of the headquarters of the Commander-in-Chief. Washington delivered detailed reports on a number of important recent events, including the French activity, the loss of Charleston, and the terrible defeat at Camden. From his generals Washington requested a plan, and he wanted it by September 10! The generals did provide one, not really satisfactory to the Commander-in-Chief. It was the opinion of the officers that it would not be prudent to attack New York City before the arrival of the second division of the French, and most voices were raised also against an expedition into the south. This decision was partially in accord with the advice urged by the French commander, who had already attempted to discourage Washington against immediately attacking New York City.

It was just at this time that one of the saddest days of the Revolution occurred. On September 5, after the whole army had marched from Orangetown to encamp at Steenrapie, the Continentals lost one of their most highly respected generals. This was the aforementioned Enoch Poor, who had served the Sullivan Expedition so impressively and who had become a very close friend to Edward Hand. He had become ill during the last days of August, and is presumed to have died of putrid fever (typhus, camp fever). He was sixty-four years old. He was provided a very formal, very solemn military funeral, with all the honors of war.

Orders for September 9 read: "Brigadier General Poor will be interred tomorrow afternoon at Hackensack church; the funeral procession will commence at four o'clock from Brewer's house in front of the infantry."

The procession to the interment site has been described by Dr. James Thacher, who was present: "A regiment of light

Enoch Poor

infantry, in uniform, with arms reversed, four field-pieces; Major [Henry ("Light Horse Harry")]Lee's regiment of light horse, General Hand and his brigade; the major on horseback; two chaplains; the horse of the deceased, with his boots and spurs suspended from the saddle, led by a servant; the corpse borne by four serjeants, and the pall supported by six officers . . . . The corpse was followed by the officers of the New Hampshire brigade; the officers of the brigade of light-infantry, which the deceased had lately commanded. Other officers fell in promiscuously, and were followed by his Excellency General Washington, and other general officers." [19]

On the 15th Washington delivered the sad news to the Congress: "It is with extreme regret, I announce the death of Brigadier General Poor the 9th instant, an officer of distinguished merit, who as a citizen and a Soldier had every claim to the esteem of his Country."

It was nearly a week later, the morning of September 20, that the most of the army decamped from Steenrapie, in order to take up new quarters at Orangetown-Tappan, Washington, with Lafayette and Henry Knox having left for Hartford to meet with Rochambeau.

It was at this time that there occurred "one of the most extraordinary events in modern history." It was the discovery of the treacherous plot of Major-General Benedict Arnold to turn over West Point to the British. This treason was being accomplished through the agency of British Major John André.

Arnold was to receive from the British 20,000 pounds (!) if the plan was successful, and 10,000 if not. Of course a meeting between André and Arnold was required, and was arranged. General Henry Clinton insisted of his major that (1) he not cross into enemy lines, and (2) that he remain always in uniform. On his attempted return to New York from the American territory of the West Point region, now (contrary to orders) attired in civilian clothes and having assumed the identity of John Anderson, he was come upon, near Tarrytown, by three rebel militiamen, who were promptly made suspicious by André's demeanor. Discovering incriminating documents in his boots, the militiamen arrested the major and turned him over to Continental officers at Sands Hill in Armonk, a tiny hamlet in the town of North Castle in Westchester County New York, and ultimately to twenty-nine-year-old Lieutenant Colonel John Jameson, who, mis-reading the situation, notified Arnold, who promptly fled, and then very nearly made possible André's escape as well.

John André

A shocked Washington, once convinced that indeed his trusted General Arnold had betrayed the Cause, committed André over to trial (Arnold having escaped). The Board that he appointed was composed of fourteen high-ranking officers: Major Generals Nathanael Greene (who was asked to preside), Lord Stirling, Arthur St. Clair, Robert Howe, Baron Friedrich von Steuben, and Lafayette; Brigadier Generals Edward Hand, John Paterson, John Glover, Henry Knox, James Clinton, John

Stark, and Jedediah Huntington. The Judge-Advocate was General John Laurance (sometimes Lawrence, or Laurence).

The trial was convened at Tappan. Washington's charge to the Board was dated September 29, 1780. It read as follows: "GENTLEMEN: Major André, adjutant-general to the British Army, will be brought before you, for your examination. He came within our lines in the night, on an interview with Major-General Arnold, and in an assumed character; and was taken within our lines, in a disguised habit, with a pass under a feigned name, and with the inclosed papers concealed on him. After a careful examination, you will be pleased as speedily as possible to report a precise state of his case, together with your opinion of the light in which he ought to be considered, and the punishment that ought to be inflicted. The judge advocate [Laurence] will attend to insist in the examination, who has sundry other papers relative to this matter, which he will lay before the Board." [20] On the day it was given the case, September 29, the Board rendered its verdict. André was found guilty of behavior that declared spying for the enemy. He was sentenced to death by hanging. At the execution, which took place in Tappan, General John Glover served as Officer of the Day. General Edward Hand, with other officers was present on horseback. General Washington, whose hand had trembled so that he could hardly sign the execution order, did not witness the hanging. [21] The date was October 2, 1780.

On the very next day after the execution, Hand expressed his feelings to Jasper Yeates: "Dear Yeates: I have your fav^r of the 23^d August before me. We have had little interesting here since the discovery of the Horrid Plot fabricated by Genl Arnold, the happy & Providential discovery of which has prevented the severest blow to the independence of America — "

Edward Hand, so passionately devoted to the Cause, is much offended: "Gracious Heaven! The very recollection of the little Dirty Villianies perpetrated by that man during his command at W. Point mark his Character better than his Grand design of Betraying his trust into the hands of an Enemy to what he ought to call his country — "

Yet, like Washington, he exhibits some sympathy for the unfortunate André: "Major André Adjt Genl to the British Army, the same you knew [as] a Prisoner of War in Lancaster in 1775 a very accomplished young man, ended his life yesterday on a Gibbett, as victim of the Traitor who possibly one day may meet his [just] desert . . . ." [22]

Washington had been willing to exchange André for Arnold, but the British were not receptive. It was not that they were so happy with Arnold, for they considered the treason not all that beneficial. Indeed, they paid Arnold not the £20,000 he might have enjoyed, but a mere £6315. Of course he was promised an annual pension and was commissioned a brigadier general.

As commander of British troops, Arnold led vicious raids on Virginia and on the Connecticut towns of Groton and New London.

For the last day of October Washington called a very important council, to meet at Prackness in New Jersey. Able to attend were four major generals, including Lafayette, and seven brigadier generals, including Edward Hand and John Glover. Washington, noting that Clinton has left New York City with a detachment of 3000 men [turned out to be 6000!] supposedly to "cooperate with Lord Cornwallis in the South," asked the generals to consider what should be done. And, before answering, they were obliged to consider the site of a winter encampment.

Almost all of the officers registered opinion negative on making a detachment to the southern army. Wayne and Hand were for a detachment, but only on the condition that these troops would be augmented by French forces. Lafayette would detach the duc de Lauzun's legion [23] and 400 men. General

Jedediah Huntington [24] favored providing a substantial detachment to the forces in the south.

As to winter quarters, opinions varied greatly, but the generals were unanimous in the necessity to choose a site that would ensure the safety of West Point. [25]

The French brigades, under the command of Rochembeau, idle for now, prepared an encampment for Newport, and sat out the winter of 1780-81 at the site of their coming ashore. Washington for the winter returned a portion of his army (the Pennsylvania brigades — about 2500 soldiers) to Morristown. The New York and New England regiments he detached to an encampment in the Hudson River Highlands. The Commander-in-Chief himself established headquarters in New Windsor, New York, not far from Newburgh.

While yet in Morristown, November 28, 1780, Washington, writing to the President of Congress, John Hanson, had Brigadier General Edward Hand on his mind. To the Continental Congress he addressed the following: "I have lately had a very pressing application from Colo. Alexander Scammell [responsible for the confusion in Washington's escape plans on Long Island] for liberty to resign the Office of Adjutant General, and resume the Command of his Regiment. Finding him determined upon the measure, I thought it my duty to cast about for a proper person to succeed in so important an Office, before I mentioned his request. The Gentleman I would recommend is Brigadier General Hand, who I have Sounded upon the occasion, and who I find will accept the appointment should Congress think proper to confer it upon him. His Rank, independent of his other qualities, is a circumstance of consequence, besides giving weight and dignity to the Office, it will take off any uneasiness which might have arisen, had an Officer, younger than any of the present Inspectors been appointed, because by the Regulations, the Adjut. General is Assist. Inspector General, and of course commands the others in that Department." [26]

Congress promptly held an election, "and the ballots being taken, Brigadier General Hand was elected." According to General Nathanael Greene, no less a person than Alexander Hamilton had had an eye on the office. [27] Congress, meeting in Philadelphia, made this appointment on January 8, 1781. General Hand was advised of it on January 12: "I have the Pleasure to inform you that Congress have been pleased to appoint you Adjutant General, as you will see by the enclosed Copy of the 8th Instant." [28] And Washington had the news on the 21st. On the 23rd of the month, from his present headquarters at New Windsor, he advised Hand of his new office, and put him promptly into harness: "Dear Sir . . . I have the pleasure to congratulate you on your appointment as Adjutant General of the army." Because Scammell was impatient to return to his old command, Washington promptly issued his first order to the new Adjutant General: "I have to request . . . that you will be pleased to repair to the army as soon as conveniently may be, and enter upon the Duties to which you are appointed." [29]

While all of this was going on, a real crisis occurred. Happily for Hand, he had nothing to do with it.

It was at Pompton Lakes (sometimes Federal Hill),[30] Washington's Headquarters briefly during the relentlessly cold winter of 1780-81, that a mutiny of 300 soldiers of the Continental Army, under the command of Israel Shreve, occurred. The date was January 20.

Washington was always okay with complaints — about the weather, about the food, about shoes, about the prospect of a long march, about faulty muskets or a paucity of ammunition, but mutiny was a little much. Threats of that kind did much damage to his patience. After all, his army was a volunteer army. The soldiers in the beginning pledged service for a year; and later for the duration.

Shreve had had command of this same 2nd New Jersey for the Sullivan Expedition and for the recent battle of

Springfield. He was able enough, but was not regarded as the kind of officer to inspire troops and to keep morale high, and here at Pompton Lakes he was experiencing a big problem.

For tardy pay (even failure of pay), and for some other grievances as well, and following the lead of the mutinous soldiers of the Pennsylvania Line, the men of the New Jersey 2nd acknowledged leaders and organized a rebellion.

Informed by a woman (unknown to history) of what was going on, Colonel Shreve promptly got off a letter to the Commander-in-Chief: "Dear General Washington, It is with pain that I inform your Excellency that the troops at this place revolted this evening and have marched towards Trenton: their behavior and demands are similar to those of the Pennsylvania Line; although no blood has been spilt. I was informed by a woman of their intentions, late this afternoon, and immediately ordered all men off duty to be paroled; with an intention to detach them in different parties for the night; but found but very few that would turn out. I was amongst them for some time but could not prevail upon them to desist. They have lately received a part of the depreciation of their pay, and most of them are much disguised with liquor. Col. [Frederick] Frelinghauyen [Frelinghuysen], [31] one of the Commissioners of the State is now here." [32]

Robert Howe

Washington replied immediately to both Colonel Shreve and to Colonel Frelinghuysen. He informed both that he

~ Yorktown ~ 221

would be sending troops from West Point, under the command of General Robert Howe,[33] to help in restoring order.

On January 22, he ordered General Robert Howe to compel the mutineers to "unconditional submission." The orders were delivered plainly enough: "You are to take the command of the detachment [500 troops!], which has been ordered to march from this post against the mutineers of the Jersey line. You will rendezvous the whole of your command at Ringwood or Pompton. . . . The object of your detachment is to compel the mutineers to unconditional submission, and I am to desire you will grant no terms while they are with arms in their hands in a state of resistance. The manner of executing this I leave to your discretion according to circumstances. If you succeed in compelling the revolted troops to surrender you will instantly execute a few of the most active and most incendiary leaders." [34]

Howe was quick to oblige. On the 27th, he caught up with the mutineers, who were apparently on their way to Trenton. He surrounded the 300 mutineers, who offered no resistance, and (faithful to the orders from Washington) had the ringleaders, Sergeants David Gilmore and John Tuttle, executed. As Howe required that the execution be carried out by a firing squad made up of twelve of the condemned men's fellow mutineers, all were punished. Howe's instructions to the firing squad were precise: Three soldiers were to aim for the heads of the two condemned, and three were to fire at the hearts. The remaining six were to stand ready in order to dispatch either who survived.

It was some time later than this drama, on February 13, that Hand, who had made his way to Philadelphia, delivered his acceptance of the office of Adjutant General. Addressing Congress as "Sir," he writes, "On my arrival in Town [Philadelphia] yesterday evening [February 12] being informed that Congress have been pleased to confer on me the Appointment of Adjutant Genl. to the Armies of the United

States, I beg leave from you . . . to offer my most sincere Thanks to that Honourable body for so distinguished a mark of their confidence.

"Fully convinced that my abilities are by no means equal to the discharge of the duties of this important office, I can't help wishing their choice had fallen on Some person Better qualified, yet as it is the pleasure of Congress & the Commander in Chief, I will not hesitate to attempt it & I shall esteem myself superlatively happy if by asiduity & unwearied Application I can in any degree remove the difficulties that want of method & experience lay me under.

"At the Same time I must beg leave to entreat the Congress may be pleased to give me an assurance that this appointment shall not injure my Rank or be any obstacle to a future command in the Army at large or in the Line of the State I have the Honour particularly to Serve." [35]

With this appointment a new chapter in the military life of Edward Hand begins. He would now be an administrator rather than a field officer. Indeed he would be the administrator of the entire Continental Army. Just a cursory review of the responsibilities of the office would overwhelm the most zealous of the military personnel. From this date forward Adjutant General Edward Hand would be recording and transmitting orders from the Commander-in-Chief to the army. He would be filing military returns, the weekly and monthly reports documenting the numbers and types of commissioned and non-commissioned officers, staff, and "rank and file" members at the brigade and regimental level. He would be reporting to the Commander-in-Chief the number of soldiers fit for duty, the number sick, the number on leave, the number of desertions and the number dead since the last muster, as well as the names of those promoted or transferred. It becomes his responsibility to schedule drills and maneuvers, and to supervise them. He is expected also to see to the inspection and review of the troops (The Adjutant General is by office the

Assistant Inspector General.). The Adjutant General is expected to keep track of enlistment terms; and he has the authority to make arrests and arrangements for trial. He would of course be working closely with the Quartermaster General on provisions, uniforms, muskets and rifles and ammunition. At his fingertips he must have at any given moment the number of troops at the various summer and winter encampments. Upon request he would be expected to provide such services as a plan for improving pay or even advice on military strategy. And besides all of this, the Adjutant General may be, and often was, ordered to the command of a military unit in the field. [36]

The Adjutant General is actually an advisor to the Commander-in-Chief. As he has the figures for the army in all of its units, he is in a favorable position for determining the most desirable assignment for any division or regiment.

What all of this meant for Edward Hand was close company for General Washington. He could not ever be far out of reach. Certainly he would not again be overstaying any leave, and was not even likely to get one. What he would get was his own headquarters and office.

The French army, during the spring of 1781 had marched from Providence to the Hudson. At Philipsburg, near White Plains, where the troops would remain for a month, it began to join with the American forces. On July 6, Washington, with the armies united north of New York City, held a conference, the purpose of which was to determine just where to lodge the attack on the British.

Washington of course had for two years now been concentrating on the Clinton army holed up in New York City, and in fact through the fall and winter of 1779-80 continued to declare New York his top priority. So, not surprisingly, he was proposing an attack on northern York Island (now Manhattan). He noted that the combined French and American force now outnumbered Clinton 3-1.

As early as May 17, 1781, Washington from New

Windsor had notified Colonel Alexander Scammell [37] that the British appeared to be building a Block House at or near the former Fort Lee. Eleven days later he had informed Scammell that he was devising some plans, and in June he had set down some "Thoughts on . . . the Surprise of . . . the North End of York Island," stressing absolute secrecy (no loud talk, no fires). He addressed the matter of boats, their landing and their concealment. He noted that many attacks would be scheduled to occur at the same moment.

On July 2, 1781, Washington placed in the hands of his new Adjutant General an *extremely* long letter of instructions for a surprise attack on York Island and appointed Hand to the command of one unit: "Sir: You will take the Command of the detachment which is intended to Surprise the Enemy's Pos[ts on the] end of York Island."

Then he says he will not restrict Hand by providing instructions, as "I entertain too high an opinion of your diligence abilities and judgement as an Officer." Then he proceeds to provide instructions! These instructions, greatly detailed, he urges Hand simply to consider as hints, which may be improved upon, or departed from, as the circumstances may dictate. [38]

His urging an attack on the city prompted a study of the chances of success. Together Rochambeau and Washington conducted a reconnaissance of the British defenses, only to find them so strong as to make an assault seem a most risky operation. But Washington had worked out a highly detailed plan and he was not about to be dissuaded from it all that easily. From his headquarters near Dobbs Ferry on July 13, he sent out "Instructions for Reconnoitering the Enemy's Posts at the North End of York Island." Washington's marching instructions had all units "ready to march at 8:00 this evening. These included Rochambeau with a detachment of 2000 French soldiers, and 2000 American troops, including Scammell's Light Infantry, and Elisha Sheldon's Legion. Rochambeau was provided the guides he would need. The North River Road and the Saw Mill River Road were designated routes. But, because of the weather all movements were postponed.

Now that his proposal was formalized, still in early July, and it was made clear that Washington is "of the opinion that the Enterprise against New York and its Dependencies should be our primary object," it received a closer scrutiny. His officers shot it down, and Rochambeau, too, was thinking very differently. Washington prepared himself to listen. He first agreed to postpone a final decision until such time as word was received from Admiral Francois de Grasse.

Washington of course had devised a most intricate operation, and he very much hated to see it wasted, but, as one student of it all, has explained, it was not wasted.

Dr. James Thacher of the Massachusetts 16th Regiment was reminded by all of this indecision "of some theatrical exhibition, where the interest and expectation of the spectators are continually increasing, and when curiosity is wrought to the highest point. Our destination has been for some time [a] matter of perplexing doubt and uncertainty; bets have run high on one side that we were to occupy the ground marked out on the Jersey shore, to aid in the siege of New York, and on the other, that we are stealing a march on the enemy, and are actually destined to Virginia, in pursuit of the army under Lord Cornwallis . . . . The great secret respecting our late preparations can now be explained. It was a judiciously

Dr. James Thacher

concerted stratagem, calculated to menace and alarm Sir Henry Clinton for the safety of the garrison of New York, and induce him to recall a part of his troops from Virginia for his own defence . . . .His Excellency General Washington, having succeeded in a masterly piece of generalship has now the satisfaction of leaving his adversary to ruminate on his own mortifying situation and to anticipate the perilous fate which awaits his friend, Lord Cornwallis, in a different quarter." [39]

    The French commander Rochambeau had laid out before Washington and his officers a strategy very different from what was presently being employed. It was Rochambeau's idea to forget Clinton, and instead head south to join with the southern Continental Army, and attack Cornwallis, who, having failed in the Carolinas, had come north to join other British forces at Yorktown. Most of Washington's officers heartily approved this plan, and Washington himself by and by, having been informed that Admiral de Grasse could participate only a little longer, that is, until October 15, was persuaded to it. A conference with Rochambeau in camp at Dobbs Ferry on July 19 sealed the deal.

    And when on August 14, Rochambeau and Washington had the great news from Admiral de Grasse that (1) the admiral was under sail for Virginia, and (2) he would indeed be unable to contribute to the siege beyond October 15, all systems were given a "Go." And Yorktown it was.

    Through July and the first three weeks of August of 1781 Washington has had a large portion of the Continental troops encamped right alongside a large number of the French forces, at Dobbs Ferry on the Hudson.

    On June 29, because Washington at that time had still not given up on his plan to attack York Island, General Hand encouraged him a little. Hand drew up an intricate plan for a review of a sham engagement at Peekskill, simply to test the practicability of an assault on York Island. Of course nothing ever came of this.

It was about a month later that the Adjutant General found himself very hopeful of getting together with Kitty and the girls. On July 28, he writes: "I am very anxious to see you & will if Possible accomplish it." But it won't be easy. "I am obliged to be on the Parade every morning at 6 o'clock & frequently spend the whole day out . . . ." But Kitty and the children have been at Peekskill, and by the time he writes next to her, on August 1 and 11, he has managed a get-together.

Now, on August 19, the Continental Army forces, together with a portion of the French army, broke camp at Dobbs Ferry, stole across the river (hoping the crossing would deceive the British as to their real intent), and began the march to Virginia. As the troops made their first encampment at King's Ferry, still another good opportunity was afforded Hand to meet with Kitty. It is August 22: "I have the pleasure to inform you," writes Hand, " that I am once more on the same side of the Hudson River with you, and expect to see you this Evening or tomorrow . . . . you will have an Opertunity of seeing the French Army past your present Quarters . . . ." [40]

As the combined force marched south, beginning August 19, it snowballed in size all the way.

De Grasse, fresh from his defeat of the British at Tobago, in early September reached the Chesapeake Cape. Within a week he had delivered his troops, 3000 well equipped French soldiers, to Lafayette and returned to pick up more American soldiers.

It was at Head of Elk, the northern tip of the Chesapeake Bay, that Hand, having been in Philadelphia and having sent Kitty back to Lancaster, joined Washington for the march south. And on September 26 here at Head of Elk the army received still more troops and generous supplies. Washington by now had amassed an army of some 20,000 (7000 Frenchmen, 3100 militiamen, and 8000 regular Continental Army soldiers). It was truly a colossal force.

While this was going on, Washington took a moment out from the march to stop at his Mount Vernon home. He and General Hand arrived on September 9, Rochambeau and his staff on the next day. All departed Mount Vernon on September 12. Meanwhile the portion of the French army that had marched overland was arriving at Annapolis (September 17). Here it was joined by those soldiers who had embarked at Head of Elk, and who had arrived on the 13th. All were transported by boats down the Chesapeake to Williamsburg.

On September 14, Washington, together with his Adjutant General and Rochambeau, arrived in Williamsburg. Soon thereafter they were joined by Lafayette.

Hand has been keeping Yeates informed, supplying all details of the assembling of the force. He is very happy to report to him the "universal joy" experienced by all with the news that the British fleet has declined an engagement with the Count de Grasse.

Here, on the 17th General Hand found time to get a letter off to Kitty: "I have the pleasure to tell you that I arrived here Safe & well the evening of the 14th, with the Genl. I met him on my way from Lancaster at the Head of Elk, & at his desire came on with him having only two Shirts in my Portmanteau . . . I hope our stay here will not be long. The French fleets from the W. Indies . . . are both in the Bay . . . enemy busy fortifying York . . . ." [41] At the end of the month this huge army began the short march for Yorktown, the Americans arriving on the 27th, the French on the next day. On the night of the 28th all slept out in the open, and on the next day, with the army moving very close to the fortifications, the first exchange of gunfire occurred. Washington at this time is right at the front, as he was much of the time throughout the engagement.

Cornwallis, who by now has been promised some relief from Henry Clinton, responded to the increasing pressure from the French-American force by pulling back from his outer defenses, to leave only one redoubt on the west side of town, two on the east.

With Washington constantly visiting the front lines, through October 6-9, the assaulting army moves ever and ever closer by means of trenches dug to accept the artillery. With Henry Knox's big guns now in very close position, at five o'clock in the afternoon, and with Washington himself firing the first shot, the closely placed artillery opened up. According to the legend which has come down, the ball touched off by Washington smashed into a table at which British officers were eating.

During the assault on the fortifications "Hand was busy helping to direct the siege by organizing regimental formations, inspecting troops, and apportioning materials to the army." [42] How much he had to do with the overall very effective strategy is not known, but doubtless he had a hand in it.

In any case, for the great success of the siege all credit, as General Edward Hand very well understood, goes to the artillery.

On the 12th he got off an up-date letter to Yeates: "When I wrote you [last] . . . I informed you that we had broken ground within 800 or 900 yards of the enemy. This was no more than erecting redoubts to cover our approaches, and too distant to mount artillery. The sixth [of October] at night, our first parallel was within 600 yards. The 9th [of October] our batteries opened for the first time to the astonishment of the besieged soldiers, who were taught to believe we had no heavy artillery. We now had 52 pieces of heavy ordinance constantly playing on them which affords aweful music, which they very faintly returned . . . ." [43]

Washington, from the beginning had been confident that the artillery would be sufficient to subdue the city. Turned out that he was right. There occurred some up-close fighting as a French column overran redoubt #9 and an American force, under Alexander Hamilton, took redoubt #10, but the artillery was devastating. The British held out for another week as the French guns and those of Knox bombarded the city, but their situation was hopeless.

This huge military power, with the regular Continental Army troops and the Virginia militia at its core, now had the British army of seven thousand at Yorktown under the most effective siege "conceivable."

With this massive force enveloping the garrison, and moving ever closer by way of entrenchments, and the French fleet blockading the rivers and presiding over the sea, and the failure of a number of British efforts to break through, and the defeat by the French navy of the British squadron that had been bringing reinforcements from General Clinton, and supplies running low, and weariness from the incessant and merciless fire of the French artillery and that of Henry Knox, whose heavy cannon were described as "extraordinary," Lord Cornwallis finally requested surrender terms. The date was October 17, 1781. After two days of negotiation, finding the conditions for surrender "acceptable," he agreed to deliver his forces to Washington. But, pleading illness, he did not appear for the surrender ceremony. Adjutant Hand was present, with Washington and Rochambeau. The date was October 19, 1781.

Washington held a victory dinner for his officers, one of whom of course was Brigadier General Edward Hand. The sword of Cornwallis Washington did not accept but asked that it be handed to General Benjamin Lincoln, who had given up his sword to the British with the fall of Charleston. [44]

Casualty figures had the French losing sixty killed, 194 wounded; the Americans twenty-eight killed, 107 wounded; the British 142 (156?) killed, 326 (328?) wounded, and seventy missing. Cornwallis surrendered 7089 officers and enlisted men, besides 840 British sailors.

Like just about everybody else, General Edward Hand assumed that the rebellion had ended in success, and that he would be shortly on his way to Lancaster. On the day of the

British surrender, after the victory dinner, he got off a joyous letter to Yeates: "My dear Yeates, When I last addressed you [one week ago] I expected our Second parallel would make the Garrison Squeak, but did not imagine we should finish the affair so soon as we have done. The 14th at night we carried two [of] the enemy's flank redoubts by assault, with little loss. The French Grenadiers and Chassseurs were employed on one attack and the American Light Infantry on the other. They made themselves masters of the works at the same instant and with equal address.. The 17th in the morning, the enemy beat a parley, and this day marched out with shouldered arms, Collours Cased, and drums beating a British March."

He is *very* happy: "I have not now time to say more than that I hope soon to set my face Lancaster wards and entreat you to present my love to my dearest Kitty, my little children, your family &c^a. At leisure will be more particular." [45] At the same time, Hand knew enough about the British and enough about the frontier to know that he, like everybody else, was engaged more in wishful thinking than in reality.

Washington made his farewells to the French and to the site of the siege on November 4. On his way north from Yorktown, accompanied by Adjutant Hand, [46] he spent a very short time at Mount Vernon, and then, in order to meet with a joyful and most appreciative Congress stayed on in Philadelphia for roughly two months. Hand, too, returned with the army to Philadelphia. He found lodgings on Spruce Street, and promptly sent for Kitty and the three children.

With the surrender of Cornwallis at Yorktown the war appeared to be at an end. This meant, for one thing, that New York City, which had always seemed so critical and which had been fought for so hard, and which Washington had hovered over for five years, and which Clinton continued to occupy, was now totally irrelevant.

But the impression that the war was over, so welcome that it was readily believed, was distant from the fact. The weary war, which had dragged itself along through six long winters and seven long summers, and which had *seemed* to end with Yorktown, was not over. Because there occurred no large-scale fighting after October 19, it might be argued that the capitulation of the British forces in Virginia meant the end of the long war. And most certainly it did. It *meant* the end, but it was not the end. The defeat of the British at Yorktown only implied the end; it defined the ultimate victory and defeat. General Lafayette, after the Cornwallis surrender, observed to his Commander-in-Chief that "The play, sir, is over." And Britain's Prime Minister, Lord Frederick North, when he heard the news, was moved to exclaim, "Oh God, it's all over."

But the war was not over, not by a long shot. Soldiers who had committed "for the duration" were not going home, not for a long, long time yet.

General Hand, who knew a little bit about Indians appreciated the truth of that as well as anybody else. The War of the Revolution was not at an end, not for the frontier settlements. No one had suggested to the Indian allies of the British that they lay down their tomahawks, and give up their lands to the westward-moving settlers. The British, with 28,000 (!) troops occupied New York City, Charleston, and Savannah. Formal hostilities, with rival forces arrayed against each other, would continue for almost two more years! Hundreds of lives would be lost, and the horrible pains that attach to every war would be suffered, by the British serving the King, by the rebellious colonists, by the native American Indians.

One of the many battles that did occur after Yorktown was the battle of Blue Licks, on August 19, 1782. The battle was fought in the wilderness, on the "dark and bloody ground" of Indian warfare, in a region called Kentucky, at that time a county in the state of Virginia. It was fought between two forces very different in their make-up. Pitted against a company of 182 Kentucky militia was the largest army of Indians and

British regulars ever assembled, numbering almost 1000 strong. The infamous Simon Girty, who had been in Pittsburgh at the time General Hand was Head of the Western Department, had organized the British-Indian force, rounding up the warriors of the Ohio nations and the Iroquois, and bringing them together with the Rangers to follow the battle plan he had himself drawn up. At the head of the army was the notorious Tory officer Alexander McKee, who also had been in Pittsburgh during Hand's tenure. At the head of one company of the Kentucky militia was Daniel Boone, at this time nearly forty-eight years old.

The battle site, as determined by the Indians, was an area of some salt springs in a bend of the Licking River known as the Blue Licks, not far north of Boonesborough, the settlement which Boone with a company of thirty men had founded in 1775. The Indians employed their favorite trick, inviting the Kentuckians to follow what was meant to seem a small party of warriors into the ambush prepared by the main force. In spite of cautions expressed along the way by Boone, who could read in the "too obvious" trail signs that the Indians wanted to be followed, that is, desired an engagement, the militia fell into the trap. What followed was an incredibly costly battle for the Americans. The Kentucky militia lost seventy of their riflemen killed or captured, including eighteen officers, more than one-third of their whole force.

Boone's son Israel was mortally wounded. As the militia fell back, Israel, mounted upon a horse his father had found for him, paused for one last shot at the pursuing warriors. It cost him his life, as he was fatally wounded. Daniel, carrying his dying son to a cave, and seizing a riderless horse, led the remnants of the militia force to safety on the far side of the Licking River. The British-Indian army lost only three men killed, some few wounded.

But that was not all. This disaster inspired a revenge mission. General Hand's friend George Rogers Clark, at the head of more than one thousand (!) experienced riflemen drove the Shawnee from their villages on the Ohio River, destroying the town of Chillicothe, as well as a number of lesser towns.

No, the Revolutionary War did not end with the battle of Yorktown.

It did pretty much end at that time for Washington's Continental Army. After the success at Yorktown, and with General Clinton still ensconced in New York with the remainder of the British troops, Washington moved his army, via a winter encampment at Pompton Lakes, to New Windsor, near West Point and just six miles from Newburgh, New York, where it was to remain stationed until the Treaty of Paris was finally concluded, September 3, 1783 (even though not ratified by the Congress until January 14, 1784!).

The French army stayed out the winter of 1781-82 in Williamsburg.

X

Newburgh and New Windsor

The Commander in Chief orders the Cessation of Hostilities between the United States of America and the King of Great Britain . . . .

— George Washington

Washington left some New Jersey regiments at the Morristown winter encampment site, with instructions to keep an eye on their old nemesis, General Clinton.

To the permanent camp site at New Windsor the Commander-in-Chief brought more than 7000 troops and some 500 women and children. As they figured to be here a while, the soldiers promptly built a village. Seven hundred huts were constructed, as well as a hospital, stables, blacksmith shops, and other buildings to meet the needs of a community.

Washington made his headquarters in the home of Jonathan Hasbrouck in nearby Newburgh, a beautiful spot right on the Hudson.

General Hand had been mentioning retirement, and certainly would welcome it, but he did not expect to be pressured, and was certainly not about to abandon Washington, whom he had come to respect the more with every passing day.

At New Windsor he had lots to do. For one thing he

had to keep track of the men belonging to different regiments. For another there was the continuing threat of a mutiny over lack of pay. That had to be quieted, and naturally it fell to the Adjutant General to see to it. But busy, busy as he was, he was able to get several letters off to Kitty during the fall season. He described his responsibilities, expressed some concern over pay, and regularly inquired about his "dear daughters."

There were no battles to be fought at this time by the Continental Army. But there were problems enough, especially for the Adjutant General. Washington had had worrisome communications from the City of Brotherly Love, and became much concerned by what he heard on March 18. It was obvious, in this spring of 1782, that the terrific political tensions in Philadelphia, instead of easing, as one had every right to expect, were actually intensifying. It was here of course, that the Pennsylvania Executive Council held its meetings. Threats on the life of President Joseph Reed had been made known. On this day, March 18, Washington apprised Hand of the touchy situation, and advised him on measures to be taken. It was not long before the Adjutant General had that ugly business quieted.

Hasbrouck House

On April 15, 1782, Washington, in Newburgh, called a council of the General Officers. According to his best information, General Clinton, in New York City still, with

9,000 men, was apparently considering some kind of military action. Up again came the old question: Should we assault the city? Generals Von Steuben, William Heath, and William Patterson were opposed (although Patterson did suggest a siege), Lord Stirling favored an attack. Robert Howe regarded an assault as "difficult if not impossible." General Hand regarded it as a doubtful undertaking. Some opinions were qualified, as a judgment would depend upon the size of the attacking force. No formal action was agreed upon.

And in the very next month, General Henry Clinton, in a somewhat turbulent exchange, was relieved of his command and replaced by the former Lieutenant Governor of Quebec, the fifty-seven-year-old Sir Guy Carleton, who had been dispatched to the "colonies" from England. When the British abandoned Savannah in the succeeding July, it became apparent enough that King George had little interest in continuing the occupation of any part of the United States.

When responsibly informed that King George would honor the independence of the United States, Carleton promptly asked to be relieved of his command. After some consultations with Washington on what to do with Loyalists, he returned, November 28, to England.

It was in the late summer of 1782 that the Congress determined to reorganize the office of the Adjutant General. From what Hand could learn, his commission would be lost in the shuffle. Learning of Hand's perfectly natural threat to resign, Washington, on August 21 got off to the Secretary of War Henry Knox an expression of his concern: "It is with the highest regret that I am brought to part with an Officer of General Hand's Abilities from the Office of the Adjutant General; an office which, so long as he has Sustained it, he has exercised with very great [Accuracy,] Attention and Professional Knowledge. If the Ideas of Congress in this Arrangement are not unalterably fixed, I could wish Measures might be adopted, that would retain Genl Hand in his present office."[1] A response from the Secretary of War, dated December 22, came to Washington too late for him to do any more politicking. But Knox's letter was a hopeful one: "By the late regulation of the department of Adjutant General, all appointments cease on the first day of January next. I hope Congress will immediately fill the office of Adjutant General. I am happy to inform them that General Hand, if reappointed, will continue in office."[2] As the Congress had long ago got in the habit of acting as its Commander-in-Chief suggested, General Hand, in action taken December 31, 1782, was continued as Adjutant General. The notice was posted in the General Orders at headquarters in Newburgh, January 8, 1783: "Resolved, That Brigadier General Hand be, and he is hereby, continued in the Office of adjutant general."

Hand, as Adjutant General, was still at Newburgh July 3, 1783, one of four brigadier generals left in camp.

Hand is in New Windsor on August 19; so his letter to Washington is easily delivered. Recognizing that the subject of this letter is a most disagreeable one for the Commander-in-Chief, he yet turns out an extremely long letter in which he expresses concern for both pay and status under the new regulations. And two months later (!) he is *still* fussing about pay: "Oconomy [Economy?] is Laudable and every Officer ought to encourage & support it, yet when partially applied may become a grievance to Individuals, & I may venture to say that I am the Only Instance where it has had a retrospective operation." He believes he should be recompensed for special expenses of the office of Adjutant-General (like the forage of horses, over which on June 30 he had experienced a dispute with Quartermaster General Timothy Pickering).[3]

For the fall of 1782, Washington had established temporary winter headquarters at Verplanke Point, on the east side of the Hudson across from Stony Point. The Continental Army had crossed the Hudson on the ferry at this point, on its way south to Yorktown. Now, almost a year after Yorktown, on the last day of August, 1782, Washington, coming from New Windsor, conducted an amphibious assault at Verplanke Point, just as a rehearsal. He *still* had in mind an attack on Clinton in New York. The camp was in a very strategic spot, as the King's Ferry made this a major crossing point of the Hudson. This was a very pleasant camp, with wholesome air and good water. Hand, as Adjutant General, conducted a close survey of the approaches to the encampment and the whole extent of the creek. Among other things, he had to determine what pickets would be necessary, and the best manner in which to defend the encampment in the most unlikely event of a detachment arriving from Henry Clinton.

Hand was still with this force at Verplanke Point on September 9; but before much longer the army was entirely returned to the permanent Newburgh encampment.

That Hand had been considering retirement from the service is plain from a letter he addressed to Yeates from New Windsor on March 31, 1783. But he is simply not confident that he can continue to practice medicine: "I have many reasons for declining the reassumption of my civil profession, the injury my sight has suffered would greatly incommode me in the practice of Surgery." [4]

The soldiers were still at Newburgh on Friday, April 18, 1783, which was a great day for the portions of the army still encamped here. Indeed it was a great day for the Continental Army wherever the soldiers were stationed. It was a great day for the new United States of America. It was on this day, April 18, that General George Washington posted his happiest General Orders ever: " . . . the Commander in Chief orders the Cessation of Hostilities between the United States of America and the King of Great Britain to be publickly proclaimed tomorrow at 12 o'clock [the eighth anniversary of Lexington/Concord, to the very day] at the Newbuilding, and that the Proclamation . . . be read tomorrow evening at the head of every regiment and corps of the army. After which the

Chaplains with the several Brigades will render thanks to almighty God for all his mercies, particularly for his over ruling the wrath of man to his own glory, and causing the rage of war to cease amongst the nations."

General Hand was given the pleasure of preparing for a general rejoicing and organizing the celebration. And Washington directed his Adjutant General to see to it that "an extra ration of Liquor . . . be issued to *every* man tomorrow to drink Perpetual Peace, Independence and Happiness to the United States of America."[5]

Of course, joyous as this moment was, every man of the army had to understand that all of this meant only the cessation of hostilities. Actual peace between the nations was not guaranteed. Hand and the main portion of the army would still be at Newburgh through the remainder of the spring and some of the summer of 1783.

It had been eighteen months since the huge victory at Yorktown, but a cessation of hostilities had been proclaimed, and even though a substantial army of the British still occupied New York City, the war between the rebellious colonists and Mother England was over. Somewhat abruptly it began to dawn on Congress that now the new freedoms that were arriving with independence would have to be somehow protected. There would no longer be in the colonies (now states) a British army to provide security from Indians, or from the French, or from whatever hostile force might find reason to assault the infant United States. Congress was now compelled to address the question of peacetime security. And, quite naturally, it turned to the Continental Army and to its Commander-in-Chief George Washington.

All were agreed that a very sound and reliable defense would be necessary if the hard-won freedoms and civil liberties were to be protected. But on how best to provide that security was a matter on which many varied opinions had already been registered. Congress, which had many times, in "strident debate" heard the matter discussed, urged Washington, by means of a Congressional committee (chaired by Hamilton), to consult with his advisors and submit a plan to the Congress. Washington, who had for some time been closeted with Hamilton on this matter, was happy to oblige. It was one of his most pressing concerns.

The question was whether to establish and maintain a professional standing army, as a number of the Old World countries were doing. If instead the country decided to rely upon militia forces, should these companies be organized and maintained by each of the several states, or should the defense be composed of a national militia?

Still another question was that of a military academy. Should the country create and maintain an academy for the training of officers? Washington of course had his own long-studied opinion on these questions. But, dutifully, he turned to his advisors for opinions, in the hope, if not the confidence, that a plan could be agreed upon. He consulted not only Alexander Hamilton, but the major officers whom he most respected, as well as others, like David Ramsay, and George Clinton, Governor of New York. The officers upon whom he was depending were Generals Friedrich Von Steuben, Henry Knox, Timothy Pickering, Rufus Putnam, William Heath, Jedediah Huntington, and of course his Adjutant General Edward Hand. Before the end of this April Washington had in hand quite a flurry of proposals.

As the Commander-in-Chief pored over the recommendations, he perceived that all were agreed on the need to create *some* military establishment that would guarantee the safety of the people, but, as could be expected, he found that these officers did not closely agree on what form it should take. Edward Hand, together with Governor Clinton, and General Putnam, was very sensitive to the nervousness among the citizenry about a standing army during peacetime. Hand's proposal was entitled "On the Peace Establishment."

Pickering was even more adamant than the others inclined this way, declaring that "a standing army would endanger our liberties." With Henry Knox he was strong for the militia, "the palladium of a free people."

Indeed the opinions of the officers seemed to lead toward a conclusion that the militia must remain "the principal instrument of national defense." Henry Knox was most enthusiastic about this, insisting that the European system (of a professional standing army) would be "totally inadmissable."

On the question of the military academy for the training of officers, Washington discovered much less agreement. Steuben, Knox, and Edward Hand were strong for academies (as Hand very well knew Washington was himself). These officers felt that academies which were administered properly could obviate the need for a large standing army. Steuben got very specific. He would like to see officer-training academies well spaced geographically, one in New England, one in the Middle Atlantic States, and one in the South.

Washington, out of all this, with his great capacity for molding varying opinions into one that credited them all, produced a plan. It draws most heavily upon the plans submitted by Knox and Pickering. It has as its premise the "indisputable need" to organize and maintain such a respectable and formidable "Continental Militia" as to discourage any threat to the country. The plan called also for enrolling "all" able-bodied young men (aged eighteen to twenty-five) in this militia. At the same time Washington urged Congress to maintain a small, regular army in the field. This was *not* to be a force sufficient to replace the militia.

Hamilton had Washington's plan early in May, but it was not until September of 1786 (!) that the Congressional Committee that had commissioned the plan gave it a reading.[6]

Because so much of great significance occurred at Newburgh and at the encampment at New Windsor, the region is presently home to a Revolutionary War historical site. There is a Visitors' Center here. It provides an audio-visual show of the Revolution's last chapter, and regularly there are staged re-enactments. Washington's New Windsor encampment is the source of the Purple Heart, today the badge of a wounded veteran. One of the exhibits at the Visitors' Center displays Washington's proclamation: "Headquarters, Newburgh, Aug. 7, 1782. The General, ever desirous to cherish a virtuous ambition in his soldiers, as well as to foster and encourage every species of military merit, directs that "whenever any singularly meritorius action is performed, the author of it shall be permitted to wear on his facings, over his left breast, the figure of a heart in purple cloth, or silk, edged with narrow lace or binding. Not only instances of unusual gallantry, but also of extraordinary fidelity and essential service in any war shall meet with a due reward . . . . The road to glory in a patriot army and a free country is thus open to all." George Washington.

It is not known whether General Edward Hand noticed or made much of one of the houses here. Built by William Edmonston in 1755, it is called the Edmonston House, naturally. It served during the encampment as the headquarters for Generals Horatio Gates and Arthur St. Clair. For a time it served also to provide a kind of headquarters for the medical staff of the encampment. Edmonstone of course was the name of the captain who had led Hand's company to Fort Pitt, and back to Philadelphia a long, long time ago.

While still at New Windsor, Hand was breveted to Major General. The date was September 30, 1783. He served out his commission until November 3 of this year, 1783, then returned to his medical practice in Lancaster.

How much General Edward Hand meant to Washington is apparent from a letter written by the Commander-in-Chief on January 14, 1784, from Mount Vernon. He was addressing a letter to an officer who had meant a great deal to him for over eight years: "Dear Sir: When I left Philadelphia I hoped to have had the pleasure of seeing you at Annapolis before my departure from thence, and to have had an oppertunity (previous to my resignation) of expressing to you personally, amongst the last acts of my Official Life, my entire approbation of your public conduct, particularly in the execution of the important duties of Adjutant General."

And the letter continues with an obviously genuine expression of his great regard for an officer who had served him loyally throughout the entire war: ". . . I . . . have it now in my power, only as a private character, to make known my Sentiments and feelings respecting my Military friends, yet I cannot decline making use of the first occasion after my retirement of informing you, My dear Sir, how much reason I have had to be satisfied with the great zeal, attention, and ability manifested by you in conducting the business of your Department; and how happy I should be in oppertunities of demonstrating my sincere regard and esteem for you; It is unnecessary I hope to add with what pleasure I should see you at this place [Mount Vernon] . . . ." [7]

XI

Lancaster

Good God! The people of Pennsylvania in seven years will be glad to petition the crown of Britain for reconciliation in order to be delivered from the tyranny of their new Constitution.

— John Adams

When William Penn organized the Province of Pennsylvania in 1682, and laid out the City of Philadelphia, only three counties were designated. These original counties were Philadelphia, Bucks (which was named for the Penn family home in England, Buckinghamshire), and Chester. By 1752 five more counties had been defined and established. Lancaster was the first of these five, carved as it was from parts of Chester County in 1729.

This was at a time of immense and incessant growth, chiefly because of the unhappy Scotch-Irish, who found Pennsylvania the most attractive of all the colonies. They were made excited by the prospect of religious freedom and the promise of land, which their forerunners were describing as "free." From a time roughly about 1740 immigration from the Old World into Pennsylvania was very steady for the rest of the century. Lancaster was one of the most attractive of the Pennsylvania communities, for its rich soil, for the Conestoga River, and for its proximity to Philadelphia. So what had been for some years a nondescript backwater village was all of a sudden a thriving community, in fact the largest non-port community in all of British North America. By many it was even considered a city.

Lancaster and Lancaster County were much distinguished during the Revolutionary War. Not only was the region peopled by the Scotch-Irish, who were fiercely patriotic, and by the Germans, it became, after the British occupation of Philadelphia, the capital of the United States, if only for one day.[1]

The Pennsylvania Council of Safety, too, by the first week of October, 1777, had moved its meeting place to Lancaster. Besides, Lancaster had become one of the major holding sites for the British and Hessian captured soldiers, as many as 1400 (not counting accompanying women and children) confined there in June of 1781. Most of these were the Hessians made prisoners at the battles of Trenton and Princeton, but there were as well a few of the Hessians and British Regulars taken at Burgoyne's surrender at Saratoga. Although most of Burgoyne's army of 5800 were detained in Boston, some were conducted to Lancaster and there confined "for the duration." [2]

Indeed it was in Lancaster that Clinton's adjutant Major John André, who had been captured by the soldiers of General Richard Montgomery at St. John, near Lake Champlain, on November 2, 1775, was held as a prisoner-of-war. In Lancaster captured enlisted men were held in barracks, while officers were permitted, at their own expense, to lodge in inns. And some were even permitted to serve their time as guests in private homes.

From the time they arrived in Lancaster, on December 9, until the middle of March of 1776 Lieutenant André (with whom Edward Hand would by and by become closely acquainted) and his very close friend the twenty-four-year-old Lieutenant Edward Marcus Despard were provided lodging at a tavern belonging to Martin Bartgis. This public house was located on Lancaster's South Queen Street, on the west side of what in those days was called Court House Square.

On the 14th of the month the pair were confined for a short time under house arrest in the home of Caleb Cope, before being transported to Carlisle. In Carlisle, during the summer and fall of 1776, the two British officers were kept prisoner in the stone house on General John Armstrong's lot number 161, at the corner of South Hanover Street and Chapel (Locust) Alley. The prisoners here were on a parole of honor, which gave them six miles in which to walk, and from André's own reports it is known that the two very much enjoyed both Lancaster and Carlisle. [3]

At the close of the year 1776, the officers were taken to the nearby Pennsylvania community of York, and very shortly afterwards, as part of a prisoner exchange, were delivered to General William Howe, who at this time was wintering in New York City.

Besides, Lancaster County was the chief source of the munitions on which the Continental Army depended. This was the case for two very good reasons. In the first place, for the war Lancaster was in a most favorable geographical spot, as it was centrally located. In the second place, and even more important, there was the geology of the region. Here were to be found the two chief essentials of gun production, rich iron ore deposits (which inspired the appearance of scores of iron furnaces) and acres of hardwood trees so desirable for the stocks of rifles. Because of these two features, the gunsmiths emigrating from the Old World, most notably from Germany and Switzerland, found this area of southeastern Pennsylvania (York, Carlisle, Shippensburg, Chambersburg,, Hummelstown, and, most notably, Lancaster) quite attractive.

Gunsmithing was a big business for the frontier communities, and it became an even bigger business of course in wartime. Lancaster rapidly became the rifle capital of the early eighteenth-century colonies and of the infant nation to follow. Some historians of the gunsmithing industry even declare that Pennsylvania "probably" produced more rifles during this time than did all of the other colonies combined.

What happened was this: The German and Swiss gunsmiths, upon emigrating to the colonies very naturally, for the reasons above noted, settled in the Lancaster region. And it was not long before they were producing a rifle much improved over the rifle that they had carried across the ocean. This became known as the Pennsylvania Long Rifle, and later, because of Daniel Boone, was provided the appellation of the Kentucky Long Rifle.

It was called "long" because it was. It was an incredible forty inches longer than the rifle that the gunsmiths had been producing. But the other major improvement was in the caliber, which actually resulted in a weapon that was lighter than what the gunsmiths had been turning out. The advantages of this rifle for both distance and accuracy were huge and meant a lot to the Continental army forces when contending with the British still armed with muskets. Some historians insist that the value of the Pennsylvania Long Rifle to the Revolutionary Cause was terrific, and they stress especially the battles of Saratoga and King's Mountain in North Carolina.

Certainly throughout the war, Washington and Henry Knox and the Quartermaster General regarded southeastern Pennsylvania as their chief source of munitions. No one suggests that the rebel cause would have been lost without it, but many will insist that the war may have been extended without this rifle, accurate at 300 yards.

And certainly throughout the entire war Lancaster was an important, perhaps the most important, munitions depot, arms steadily flowing into the city for repair and out of the city ready for instant use.

In the Lancaster County region gun shops (factories even) steadily appeared in ever increasing numbers through the eighteenth century. These shops were a family business, the production of rifles carried on by descendants. The descendants of the brothers John and William Henry, for example, conducted the business right on through five generations.

Indeed it should be noted that even the birthplace of this "most effective weapon in early American history" was Lancaster, Pennsylvania. To be specific, according to credible research, the birthplace was the gun shop of Martin Mylin in Lancaster. Mylin was a German immigrant to the county somewhere around 1700. A rifle of this type which was manufactured as early as 1704 bears the name of Marin Mylin. [4]

During the revolution, as noted, the Courthouse in Lancaster served as the Capital of the United States. It was for one day only, September 27, 1777, while the British were occupying Philadelphia. From that date on until June 2, 1778, the Congress met in York, Pennsylvania. And of course when the British occupation of Philadelphia began, the Supreme Executive Council of Pennsylvania also had to find another place in which to hold its meetings. It chose Lancaster, and met there regularly, October 1, 1777, until June 25, 1778.

Moreover, Lancaster County was up front when it came to supplying distinguished officers (including Edward Hand), militia forces and soldiers for the Continental Army. For the years of the war, 1775-1783, Lancaster County achieved, or exceeded, her quota of soldiers required by the Commander-in-Chief of the Continental Army. Official tallies show that the County produced 7357 militia and 22,198 continentals. In the year 1776 alone, the contribution was 4876 militia and 5519 continentals. [5]

After the Revolution, Hand returned to Lancaster, to

Kitty and their growing family, which included at this time four children: eight-year-old Sarah, six-year-old Dorothy, four-year-old Katherine, and the infant John, born March 2, 1782, on Spruce Street in Philadelphia. This first son, John, Dr. Hand described for Yeates as a "chopping boy." And the physician who had helped introduce him to this world was none other than Dr. William Shippen!

By this time there were a number of physicians practicing in the Lancaster region. Dr. Hans Heinrich Neff had been the first, but now, besides Neff's descendants and Dr. Hand, there were Doctors Thomas Whiteside, Hieronimus Bruback, Samuel Bonde, John Leidy, Robert Thompson, and Albert Dufresne, who lived in the second square of North Duke Street in the borough of Lancaster, and was known as the "Swisser Doctor." There was a Doctor Jacob Reiger too, who had been a surgeon in the regiment commanded by Colonel Samuel Miles. [6]

A later physician is of much interest. This is Dr. Edwin Augustus Atlee. He was born in 1778, the first son of the Honorable William Augustus Atlee, an intense patriot and future Chief Justice of the Supreme Court of Pennsylvania. When the lad was fifteen years old, his father died. He resided then with Dr. Edward Hand, who had been appointed guardian. He read medicine with Dr. Hand, who saw in the boy great promise, and then pursued his studies at Dickinson College in nearby Carlisle, earning a Master's Degree. He was quite exceptional also in music, and in his adult life became one of the most distinguished citizens of Lancaster, and later Philadelphia. [7]

Among these many physicians Dr. Edward Hand was extremely popular. Not only was he exceptionally skillful in diagnosis and in surgery, but he was genuinely concerned about every patient and attentive way beyond the call of duty. For patients who found it difficult to meet the regular physicians' fee he rendered his service pro bono. One historian of the Lancaster community reports of him: "As a citizen he was highly esteemed, and as a physician greatly sought after and beloved, especially by the poor, to whom he was in the habit of rendering his services gratuitously." [8]

Most unfortunately, his vision, damaged at the battles of New York and Trenton, continued steadily to fail, and naturally his practice thus became more and more limited.

The First Continental Congress had convened in Carpenters' Hall in Philadelphia September 5, 1774, and was in session until October 26, 1774. Its principal function during this time was to address the wrongs suffered by the colonists at the hands of Mother England. One of the consequences of this concern was the organization of an economic boycott. Delegates from twelve of the thirteen colonies attended. Georgia did not send a delegate, as the colony was privately negotiating with the crown at the time. Among the fifty-six delegates present were many close friends of Edward Hand, including Patrick Henry, George Washington, John Adams, John Jay, New Hampshire's John Sullivan, Richard Henry Lee, and Pennsylvania's Joseph Galloway. Virginia's Peyton Randolph presided.

The Second Continental Congress convened in Philadelphia on May 10, 1775, after the battle of Lexington/Concord. All thirteen colonies were represented by delegates, although the Georgia delegation did not appear until July. Many of the delegates who had composed the First Continental Congress were present. Elected President was the same Peyton Randolph who had presided over the First Continental Congress. Notable among the new delegates were Benjamin Franklin, John Hancock, and Thomas Jefferson, who shortly replaced Peyton Randolph.

The Revolution was of course already in progress. Congress took charge of the war, authorizing the Continental

Army in June and commissioning a Commander-in-Chief. It approved the Resolution of Independence on July 2, 1776, and the Declaration of Independence on July 4.

On March 1, 1781, after more than three years of consideration, it approved the Articles of Confederation. Virginia was the first of the thirteen states to ratify the Articles and Maryland was the last. This act required of course a new name for the country's governing body. That became the Congress of Confederation. The same delegates as had composed the Second Continental Congress continued as delegates to the Congress of Confederation. The Congress of Confederation continued for eight years and three days, until succeeded, on March 4, 1789, by the United States Congress, which would be operating under a new constitution. For the Constitutional Convention of 1787-88, Pennsylvania, with sixty-eight, sent the most delegates. Of these, six were from Lancaster County: Judge Jasper Yeates, John Whitehill, Robert Coleman, Sebastian Grave, Stephen Chambers, and John Hubley. Two of these six, Coleman and Chambers, like Edward Hand, had been born in Ireland and arrived in America as youngsters. The family of John Whitehill, who was an ardent patriot, had *very* early emigrated from Ireland.

The Congress of Confederation of course saw the country through Yorktown and the cessation of hostilities, the Treaty of Paris (for which it named the delegates), and five post-war years. During this decade, although many of the leading men in the several states preferred to serve their state governments, forty-six different very distinguished and influential citizens of the new country contributed their services. Among them were General John Armstrong of Carlisle and his son John Jr, who would become Secretary of War under Madison, Joseph Galloway, Benjamin Franklin, Thomas Mifflin, Robert Morris, Joseph Reed, General Arthur St. Clair, and James Wilson.

Considering that Dr. Edward Hand continued, in spite

of his impaired vision, a very steady medical practice, it is amazing that he was during these post-war years able also to function in the civic affairs of his community, his state, and his nation. A Federalist, as Washington was inclined, he was elected to or appointed to a great many posts in the government. Shortly after war's end he was elected, on November 12, 1783, to the United States Congress of Confederation and served from November 26 until August 19, 1784. Other delegates from Pennsylvania elected at that time (all acknowledged at a session of the Congress called for Annapolis on December 13) were Thomas Mifflin, Richard Peters, Carlisle's John Montgomery, and Cadwalader Morris.

Hand was not present for that meeting of December 13, when his credentials were read, but he was seated when the Congress convened on the day immediately before Christmas ("Mr. [Edward] Hand, a delegate from Pennsylvania, attended and took his seat."). [9]

It is very apparent from the *Journals of the Continental Congress* and from the *Papers of the Continental Congress* that General Edward Hand was an extremely active member of the Congress through his term. He entered twenty-two motions, he was present for voting on sixty-eight occasions (often in the minority) and he was mentioned in the records 539 times! Besides, he addressed a number of letters to the Congress during the time he was serving. He was constantly placed on committees of course, often on several at the same time. And it was Hand who regularly was called upon to file the committee report. He served during his time with a number of illustrious delegates, including (besides Thomas Mifflin)Thomas Jefferson, James Monroe, and Samuel Osgood.

One of his most important contributions was the schedule he provided for garrisoning the Northwestern frontier. Hand noted that with the British surrender of the Northwest territory, defense of the region from the still hostile Indian tribes had abruptly become the responsibility of the new United

States. Drawing upon his most memorable experiences as Head of the Western Department, as Head of the Northern Department, and as an officer for the Sullivan Expedition, he provided for the Congress a plan for the necessary protection of that vast territory.

Fort Niagara, at the mouth of the Niagara River, had to be acknowledged as a problem. Captured from the French in July of 1759 by a British force under the command of the Ireland-born (County Meath) Sir William Johnson, it had been a big thorn in the side of General Hand for the time he was in command at Fort Pitt. For now, even though the fort had been ceded to the United States by the Treaty of Paris, the British continued in possession of it and would for thirteen years following the treaty!

Hand's notions and recommendations on this subject proved very helpful to the president of the United States, when in October of 1790, November of 1791, and August of 1794, Washington found it necessary to launch campaigns against the Miami, the Shawnee, the Potawatomie, the Wyandots, the Chippewas, the Ottawas, and a number of other tribes which had drawn the line for white settlements at the Ohio River.

Another noteworthy contribution made to the activity of the 1783-84 Congress by Edward Hand had to do with the offices of Inspector General of the Army and Adjutant General. He had very specific recommendations to make on the structure, organization, responsibilities, and operation of these departments. Certainly no member of the Congress was better equipped than was Edward Hand to lay out a plan for these offices. Was his service as Adjutant General not for all of 1781, 1782, and 1783, not the most crucial period of the war? And did he not have Washington's commendation for it?

The first committee to which Edward Hand was appointed was the committee asked to review Major General Chevalier Louis Lebègue de Presle Duportail's recommendation that Captain Peter Castaing be breveted. On this committee also were Jacob Reed of South Carolina and James Monroe of Virginia. The General's request was denied.

One of his most interesting and most challenging committee assignments was the one inspired by a letter from the late John Sullivan, whom of course Hand had known very, very well, and another letter from the New Hampshire legislature. These letters concerned the dispute arising from the capture of the brig *Lusannah* by the brig *McClay*. It was a very complicated case, and therefore a challenge for the committee, which included also Richard Dobbs Spaight, Thomas Jefferson, and Arthur Lee, of Virginia. In fact it turned out to be so difficult that it dragged on and on.

One of the assignments that interested Dr. Hand a great deal was the one that made him a member of a committee to respond to the State of New York, which was making application to Congress to declare the number of troops which are necessary to be kept up by the said state. At war's end, as noted above, General Hand was promptly among those who saw the need to organize a peacetime protection for the liberties so costly won. Washington and Hamilton, and of course Knox, were much concerned. Others serving with Hand on this very important question about state responsibilities for a standing militia and its relationship to the federal army were Thomas Stone of Maryland, Jacob Read of South Carolina, John Francis Mercer of Virginia, and John Beatty of New Jersey.

This committee, after long deliberation, filed, in the handwriting of Stone, a decisive report. It concluded "that the State of New York be permitted to raise men, including non-commissioned Officers, for the purpose of garrisoning such posts within the said State not possessed by the forces of the United States, as the said State shall judge proper; which troops so to be raised by the State of New York shall be discharged whenever the United States in Congress assembled shall so direct." [10]

Edward Hand wrote the report of this committee (Jeremiah Townley Chase, of Maryland, and Jacob Read) in response to a letter from General George Rogers Clark, who had just (March 4, 1784) been appointed Commissioner to the Indians, who had questions about the extent of his authority. General Hand was the right person to consider this matter. [11]

Most interesting is the reception made by Congress, May 15, to General Hand's letter of April 19, 1784. Hand had noted that he had incurred heavy expenses by having separate commands on the frontiers of Virginia, Pennsylvania, and New York, and also while he executed the office of Adjutant General. He was "praying" that the Paymaster General "may be ordered to credit him for the pay and emoluments of a general officer, commanding a separate department during his command at the said posts, and such allowance for extra services and expences as Adjutant General as shall appear just and reasonable."

The committee assigned to this problem was composed of Roger Sherman, of Connecticut, George Partridge of Massachusetts, and William Ellery, of Rhode Island. (Hand was not made a member of this committee!) The congressmen had a delicate matter to handle here, as General Hand was at this very time a legislative colleague with whom they rubbed shoulders constantly. After some diligent research, it handled the problem beautifully.

Its report to the Congress, in the handwriting of Sherman, read as follows: ". . . it does not appear that any general provision has been made by Congress for additional pay or emoluments to a general officer commanding at a separate post, except the resolution of the 16th of June 1775, all owing double pay to a Major General when acting in a separate Department for his pay and expences, but by special resolutions like allowances have been made to brigadiers commanding a separate army . . . and in some cases particular grants have been made to officers for extra services and expences according to the circumstances attending their particular cases. But it does not appear that any such allowance has been made to other officers, who have commanded the aforesaid posts on the frontiers of Virginia and Pennsylvania, and to grant it in this case would open a wide door for other applications — "

Now how can we make an exception in this case? The committee explains: "But as General Hand commanded at Fort Pitt more than a year, and some short time at Wyoming and Albany, whereby he incurred greater expence, than if he had been with the Main Army, and he having also incurred extra expences in the office of Adjutant General by removing with the Main Army from New Jersey to Virginia in the year 1781, your committee are of opinion, that he is equitably entitled to some compensation, and thereupon submit the following resolution: *Resolved,* that General Edward Hand be allowed one thousand dollars in full compensation for his extra expences while he commanded at Fort Pitt and separate posts, and in the office of Adjutant General and the Paymaster General is hereby directed to give him credit for said sum in the settlement of his account with the United States." [12]

Congress met at the Maryland State House in Annapolis for the time November 26, 1783, until August 19, 1784. Hand is of course writing regularly to Kitty, and describing the activity of Congress. But as always he is eager ("Embrace my dear little ones for me.") to get to Lancaster, and more especially now as he has four and then five children with whom to romp. His letter of April 26 is a bit hopeful: "My Dearest Kitty," he writes, "The only news I have to tell you is that Congress have this Day Resolved to Adjourn the 3^d day of June next to Meet at Trenton on the 30th of October following . . . ."

But on May 6 he has even happier news to report: "My Dearest Kitty, When I wrote to you last I told you that Congress was to adjourn on the 3rd. of next month. I now please myself . . . the reflection that the time wherein I may reasonably expect to See you draws Sensibly nearer. Indeed I can't Indulge a more agreeable expectation and it serves to beguile the hours that would otherwise [weigh] . . . very heavily — The Season here as yet is very moderate & the Town healthy. I hope it will continue so — at least as long as I can be a Sojourner in it.

"Farewell my Dearest Life. Caress my Dear little ones for me. Present my duty to our Dear Mother, my love and Compliments to everybody else that deserves them and believe me to be the Unalterably & most affectionately y^{rs}. Edwd. Hand"

Shortly after he addressed this letter he heard from Kitty that she was having trouble making ends meet. He promptly replied (May 11): "I am not surprised that your finances run low, and am only sorry that I cannot render them more efficient . . . . I would have sent you money from Philad^a. if it had been in my power but the issuance of our Allowance as Delegates did not take place during my first Attendance on Congress. I hope to see you about the middle of next month, in the mean time I have no doubt that Mr. Yeates [a *very* wealthy man] will have the Goodness to advance you any Money you want . . . ." [13]

In his two letters of May 16, he reports "nothing extraordinary" and "I am well and one day nearer the 3rd. of June." In his letter of May 25 he writes, "I hope next week Will take me from this place." His letter of June 1 contained a hint of bad news: "When last I wrote you I expected the happiness of seeing you about the Middle of this month as Congress are to adjourn on the 3rd. I am not now altogether so positive as I then was because I have since been Elected to the Committee of the States [In the Confederation Congress, the Committee of the States was composed of one Congressman from each state. It was responsible for the functions of the government during the time the Congress was in recess.] — but I hope that

Congress will direct the Committee to meet at Trenton. If they do, I shall have no doubt of seeing you and my dear family soon — ." And sure enough, Congress did adjourn on June 3, to convene next at Trenton, June 30. And even though the Committee of the States was scheduled to meet at Annapolis on the 26th, Dr. Hand had a window. "Hope soon to be with you," he closed his letter of June 7. [14]

It might seem, from some of his remarks to Kitty, that General Hand as a delegate to Congress was not all that conscientious. Nothing could be more distant from the truth. He accepted every responsibility assigned him, was an earnest and hard-working member of more than his share of committees, and faithful in attendance. He had at home in Lancaster, besides a wife to whom he could not be more devoted, five children, aged nine, seven, five, two, and (little John) just three months old. Impatience to get home from time to time would seem to be quite natural and not out of tune with duty.

He was back in Annapolis on schedule for the meeting of the Committee of the States. His letter to Kitty is dated June 29: "I have the pleasure to acquaint you that I arrived here safe & well on Saturday Morning." He has journeyed by way of Baltimore, but regrets that he made Baltimore just a little too late "to be a spectator of the flight of a large Balloon." In Annapolis "I found my old Landlady so much Indisposed that I was obliged to look out for other Lodgings." [15]

General Edward Hand and his wife Kitty exchanged a good many letters through July of this busy Congressional year. He reports the sporadic arrival of the members, like James Wilson, while Kitty (on the 13th) from Lancaster is reporting a much greater commotion, which was a fire at the courthouse. Hand, having asked about the children, adds that he hopes "your Self was perfectly recovered from your fright. I presume it arose from an hurry [?] of Spirits occasioned by the fire, and that it has left no sad effects. In your next perhaps you can inform me by what accident the Court House took fire." [16]

Hand had a most distinguished courier for his letter of July 25: "Mr Jos. Galloway Sets out for Lancaster tomorrow by the way of Carlisle & as it is likely he will be there before a letter could reach you by post I cant miss the Opertunity — tho I have nothing particular to communicate. . . . I write to [John] Montgomery [of Carlisle] by M^r. Galloway. I expect him to relieve me about the first of Sept^r."

As always, he closes with an expression of affection for both Kitty and the children: "Kiss my Sweet Babies for me." And now, as nine-year-old Sarah is old enough to write letters herself, "Tell Sally I expect her letter Impatiently." [17]

Anticipating the arrival of Montgomery, Hand sets out from Annapolis for Philadelphia at the end of August. From Philadelphia on the 28th he writes to his "Dearest Kitty, I have the pleasure to tell you that I arrived here last night from Annapolis & I hope I shall see you some time next week — if the Committee of the States assembles again before the meeting of Congress it will be at this place or at Trenton — Mr. Montgomery will I expect be here next week to take my place — but should he not come it will not oblige me to remain long."

General Edward Hand, who has come through many a battle without a scar, is now in trouble. "Indeed I shall want a few days to recover [from] a lameness which tho much better prevents my walking altogether at my ease. I strained one of my ankles before I left Annapolis. I would, I am persuaded, have been quite well before now had I continued to indulge myself — as it is, it is much better. I can walk on smooth ground with a Stick without much pain — but it always causes my leg to swell." [18]

Either because he had not yet tired of this kind of work, or because he was simply duty-bound, Dr. Edward Hand, together with his good friends Adam Hubley and Samuel Atlee, agreed to election to the Pennsylvania Assembly in 1785. Hand is in Philadelphia October 30 of this year, serving his term. As we know from his letter to Kitty, he is much concerned about young Jasper (just a year and six months old), whose health has been poor. He is determined to get the three girls and young John fine presents, and has settled on a whip for the boy. He reports that "yesterday Doctor Franklin [Benjamin Franklin, now seventy-six years old] was proclaimed President [of the Pennsylvania Assembly] [19] & Charles Biddle, Esq[r.] Vice President."

The weather has been miserable with lots of dreary rain, but on Friday last he "dined at Mr. [Richard] Peters's [20] in company with Baron Steuben who desired I might present his compliments to you." Peters and the Baron von Steuben were very close friends. This dinner was doubtless at Peters's elegant Belmont mansion in Philadelphia, now a museum in Fairmount Park, Philadelphia. And Hand informed Kitty that "I lodge at M[rs]. Jenkins's Market Street." [21]

Judge Richard Peters

As the year 1785 closes out and Hand's term in the Assembly reaches its end, the general, from Philadelphia, on November 24 alerts Kitty: " . . . hurrying my Departure from this place, you may rely on my being with you next week if it please God I am alive & well . . . . before I leave this [place] I shall resign my Seat in the Assembly which will effectually prevent my being farther importuned on that Score — by this post I send your Ermine . . . . Nancy Craig who bought it tells me it is of the finest quality & newest fashion . . . ." He also has gifts for the youngsters, a few books "for the Childrens amusement and two small pencil Cases for Sally & Dolly [Dorothy, whose seventh birthday is now but two days away] . . . ." [22]

But General Hand would be called upon again for legislation work, and very important work it was.

At pretty much the same time as the new United States was determined to replace the Articles of Confederation, the Supreme Executive Council of Pennsylvania authorized the writing of a new constitution for the state. Pennsylvania's first constitution had been written in 1776, chiefly by Benjamin Franklin, who presided. [23]

The first constitution, known historically as Pennsylvania's Liberal Constitution of 1776, had put an end to the old proprietary government of the colony. The second, known as the Conservative Constitution of 1790, would provide a body of law, by which the Commonwealth would hereafter be governed. The constitution adopted by Pennsylvania in 1776 was hailed as "the most democratic state constitution" in the new United States. And John Adams, when he got to know its text, was heard to exclaim, "Good God! The people of Pennsylvania in seven years will be glad to petition the Crown of Britain for reconciliation in order to be delivered from the tyranny of their new Constitution."

And, indeed, so it turned out to be. As the Revolution wearily struggled to its end, the 1776 Pennsylvania Constitution became steadily more and more unpopular with the citizenry. Benjamin Rush, for example, found it "big with tyranny." And the Republican Society of Philadelphia was existing chiefly to accomplish a revision of the Constitution of 1776. In response to the mounting criticism, The Supreme Executive Council called for a Constitutional Convention.

And on August 9, 1789, sixty-nine delegates from the various counties of the state were put on notice; in November the Assembly, now controlled by the Republicans, urged all to appear at the State House in Philadelphia by November 24, when the convention would be convened. Six of the delegates were residents of Lancaster County.

The delegates from Lancaster County to the State Constitutional Convention in Philadelphia which framed the state constitution of 1790 were (besides Edward Hand) Robert Coleman, Sebastian Grave, William Atlee, John Hubley, and John Breckbill. Thomas Mifflin, who was President of the Supreme Executive Council at the time, presided over the committee of delegates.[24]

Thomas Mifflin

Edward Hand of course knew Thomas Mifflin very, very well from the Revolutionary War experiences, notably at Long Island and in the battles of New York, Trenton, and Princeton. Except for Breckbill, he was well acquainted with his other fellow delegates too.

Robert Coleman, four years younger than Hand, was a most energetic iron-master. Like Hand, he had been born in Ireland. He had lived in a number of Pennsylvania communities before arriving in Lancaster. He had been a member of the General Assembly (1783-84), a delegate to the 1787 Constitutional Convention, and would be a presidential elector in 1792 and again in 1796. He would become an Associate

Judge in Lancaster County and serve for twenty years.

Sebastian Grave was the grandson of Sebastian Graff, who had come to America from Germany. He belonged to the German community of Lancaster, his father having moved there in 1731-32, before the settlement was incorporated into a borough. He was eight months older than Hand, and had been active in the anti-British, pre-Revolutionary expression of Lancaster, serving on the Committee of Observation. Like Coleman, he had been a delegate to the Federal Constitutional Convention of 1787-88. Dr. Hand knew him as the Associate Burgess of Lancaster. He died shortly after the close of the Pennsylvania Constitutional Convention, in July of 1792.

Dr. Hand knew William Atlee's brother Samuel John Atlee (1739-86) better than he did William, having served with him in the battle of Brooklyn, where he was captured by the British and having served with him after the war in the Pennsylvania Assembly.

William Augustus Atlee was eight years older than Dr. Hand. A most intense and fierce patriot, he was known to the residents of Lancaster as "savage Atlee." He served the Lancaster area as Deputy Commissary General during the war years. In 1777 he was named to the Pennsylvania Supreme Court and served for fifteen years. Under the 1790 constitution he became the first President Judge of the Lancaster County Courts and held court in Penn Square.

Edward Hand was well acquainted with the Hubley family. John Hubley, just three years younger than Hand, had been born in Lancaster on Christmas Day, 1747. The son of Michael Hubley, he studied law, and although perhaps not the most brilliant of attorneys, he rapidly became the most popular in Lancaster County. He had served on the Supreme Executive Council in 1777, and would be a presidential elector in 1801.

The delegates, taking note of the harsh criticism of the Constitution written in 1776, and recognizing many real problems with the document, after a lot of discussion, produced in the end a document that has been oft regarded by students of government a "model Constitution."

Providing for a more conservative form of government than did the constitution of 1776, it included a "Declaration of Rights" (composed of twenty-eight sections) and nine Articles. The constitution provided for three branches of government (legislative, judicial, and executive), and designated a single, very powerful, governor elected for a three-year term. This governor, by Article IV, was endowed with "supreme executive power."

This new constitution provided also for an independent judiciary and a Senate, installed by popular election.

Naturally the document totally replaced the constitution of 1776 and abolished the Supreme Executive Council, which had presided over Pennsylvania for so long a time. This new constitution of 1790, like the 1776 constitution, was not submitted to the people for judgment. It was simply adopted by the delegates.

When the convention met on Friday, January 29, it had a statement from its chairman of the committee as a whole, the honorable Thomas McKean, reading "The state of my health renders it inconvenient for me to resume the chair." Hand was promptly elected chairman. The convention closed out on February 6, 1790 (McKean back in place as chairman), but reassembled on September 2, the delegates having been urged to "see how the people feel about it." It was in September that the delegates signed the document. Of the sixty-nine delegates, sixty-three, including Dr. Edward Hand, signed. Lancaster's William Atlee was one who did not.

As the document replaced the Supreme Executive Council with a single governor, a governor needed to be elected. It required no time at all for the delegates to nominate candidates. Not surprisingly the current President of the Supreme Executive Council, Thomas Mifflin, who was also chairing the convention, won out, easily defeating General

Arthur St. Clair. Thus Mifflin became Pennsylvania's last President of the Supreme Executive Council and the first Governor of the Commonwealth of Pennsylvania. [25]

James Wilson, [26] who had been (by General John Armstrong) invited to practice law in Carlisle, in Cumberland County, was among the most active in the framing of the final document. He deserves much of the credit for the agreement that was finally reached. By some he is regarded as "the father of the Pennsylvania Constitution."

Long before the ink was finally dry on the Treaty of Paris, Washington's head of artillery, Major General Henry Knox, who had long been concerned about his fellow officers, had a happy idea. Why not establish a society in which the officers of the Continental Army could perpetuate their fellowship and at the same time promote among the citizenry a greater appreciation of the struggle for independence?

In April of 1783, having turned his notion over and over in his mind, he decided to draw up a constitution (He called it an "institution.") for the organization; and in May he assembled a number of officers to consider his great idea. The officers who were present at this exploratory meeting on May 10 or at the second meeting just three days later, are considered the founders of the Society of

James Wilson

the Cincinnati. Among them were a number from Pennsylvania. Besides Adjutant General Edward Hand, there were present John Armstrong, Jr., Daniel Brodhead, Josiah Harmar, William Irvine, John Paul Jones, Arthur St. Clair, William Thompson, Baron von Steuben, Thomas Mifflin and Anthony Wayne. Other notables present were the Marquis de Lafayette, Nathanael Greene, and John Sullivan.

John Paul Jones

At the very first meeting Knox presented his constitution and explained just what he had in mind for the Society. A number of proposals were voiced by one officer or another, and some amendments were suggested. Those who were most active in the discussion wound up on a committee. This committee of course included Henry Knox. The other members were Brigadier Generals Edward Hand and Jedediah Huntington, and Captain Samuel Shaw. The committee had as its assignment the revision of Knox's document and the preparation of a copy "to be laid before this assembly at their next meeting." As the next meeting of the founders of the society was scheduled for May 13 the committee would have its hands full.

On the 13th the officers of the original meeting, together with some additional ones, assembled for a dinner meeting at Mount Gulian (Verplanck House) at Fishkill-on-Hudson, the home and headquarters of General von Steuben. At this time, of course, General Henry Clinton with a very substantial army of British regulars still occupied New York City. Either von

Steuben or Alexander Hamilton or both presided over the meeting.

Much was accomplished at this formal get-together. The organization, all agreed, should be known as the Society of the Cincinnati, in reverent honor of Lucius Quintius Cincinnatus, one of the heroes of early Rome.[27] As the life of Cincinnatus was one of service to his country, and as he successfully squelched the many threats to the Roman empire and pulled her through one crisis after another, his name seemed right for such a society as the officers had in mind. Besides, even though his successes were so remarkable, Cincinnatus was ever humble and modest. After each crisis had been resolved, he always eagerly returned to his small farm. He is famous for the remark "And now we will pound our swords into plow shares and proceed with peace."

Having agreed on the name, the founding members adopted a motto, with the Roman farmer in mind: "He gave up everything to save the republic." And to explain their name they adopted this premise: "The officers of the American Army having generally been taken from the citizens of America, possess high veneration for the character of that illustrious Roman Lucius Quintius Cincinnatus; and being resolved to follow his example by returning to their citizenship, they think they may with propriety denominate themselves the Society of the Cincinnati."

These officers, all of whom had honorably served the Revolution, next defined their mission: "To promote knowledge and appreciation of the achievement of American independence."

The members heard Knox's constitution, as revised by the Knox-Hand-Huntington-Shaw committee. For this document there was no wrangling. With hardly a suggestion for any change in its wording, the members present approved and accepted the constitution as its governing document. The assembly next established the requirements for membership, insisting first that membership be limited to officers who had served at least three years in the Continental Army or Navy and including officers of the French army or navy.

It determined a schedule for annual meetings, fixing the meeting date for the first Monday in May. [28]

The officers present on this night agreed that another organizational meeting was required. And it very promptly occurred. On June 19, well aware of the concern of the Commander-in-Chief for his officers, the members present elected George Washington as the first president of the Society of the Cincinnati. Although Washington had taken no part in the early meetings or in the plans for the organization, he was of course much flattered, and willingly agreed to serve. In fact, he served from that December of 1783 until his death December 14, 1799, when he was succeeded by Alexander Hamilton.

Henry Knox was elected Secretary General, and Major General Alexander McDougall was elected Treasurer General.

During the succeeding five or six months chapters were organized in each of the thirteen states; and the French Society soon joined. The first general meeting of the whole Society was convened in Philadelphia on May 4, 1784. Here its raison d'être was defined. Its purposes were considered to be six: (1) to perpetuate the memory of the War for Independence; (2) to maintain the fraternal bonds formed in the war; (3) to preserve the liberties for which the officers had fought and to encourage "union and honor" between the respective states; (4) to demonstrate "brotherly kindness" in all things; (5) to distinguish its members as men of honor, whose civic virtue has been clearly demonstrated by their dedication to the cause of American independence at the risk of their lives and the sacrifice of their private interests; (6) to advocate on behalf of the officers to secure the arrears in pay and half-pay for life that had been promised them.

General Lachlan McIntosh, who had relieved Edward

Hand as Head of the Western Department in 1778, from Savannah, on April 20, 1784, put it well: "The greatest glory of the Cincinnati is that they were prime agents in giving freedom to a great portion of the Globe and leading the way for all the rest to obtain it."

    The Pennsylvania chapter of the Society of the Cincinnati was organized in Philadelphia on October 4, 1783, the ninth chapter to be formed. Meeting at the City Tavern in the City of Brotherly Love, the founding members elected Major General Arthur St. Clair as their first president. Other officers elected at this organizational meeting were Brigadier General Anthony Wayne, Vice President; Lt. Colonel Josiah Harmar, Secretary; [29] Carlisle's Brigadier General William Irvine, Treasurer; and Colonel Francis Johnston, Assistant Treasurer. [30] In 1790 Major General Edward Hand of Lancaster was elected President of the State Society of the Cincinnati of Pennsylvania. He was made very happy when the Commonwealth of Pennsylvania incorporated the Society, April 4, 1792.

    But Hand was also keenly Irish. It should surprise no one that he became an enthusiastic member of the Society of the Friendly Sons of Saint Patrick. The Society had been organized in Philadelphia by a number of businessmen who were closely associated, twenty-four in number. Of course it was formed to honor Saint Patrick, and its membership was limited to native-born Irish. The Society held its first annual dinner on Saint Patrick's Day in 1771. Among the founding members were five Irishmen whom Washington would one day make generals: Henry Knox, Edward Hand, Anthony Wayne, William Irvine and Stephen Moylan.

    At a time in the winter after Yorktown, these five officers, together with a great many like-minded members of the society, determined to make George Washington a member of the Society. Of course Washington, although he regularly exhibited much of the character of the Irish, had not been born in Ireland, and his ancestry was far from sufficient to qualify him. But the Irish are nothing if not resourceful. To a dinner given by the Society on January 1, 1782 (at $120 dollars per head), General Washington was invited. He was made an Irishman "by adoption," and was presented a badge which said so. The ever gracious Washington was much pleased and, after all he had seen of the Irish in battle, rather proud to be thought an Irishman. He promptly got off a letter to George Campbell, at that time President of the Society: "I accept with singular pleasure the Ensign so worthy a Fraternity as that of the Sons of St. Patrick in this City, a Society distinguished for the firm adherence of its Members to the glorious cause in which we are embarked. Give me leave to assure you, Sir, that I shall never cast my eyes on the Badge with which I am honoured, but with a grateful remembrance of the polite and affectionate manner in which it was presented." And on Saint Patrick's Day of that same year, the Irish George Washington attended the annual dinner.

For the years after the war, Edward Hand devoted himself, as best he could to the people of Lancaster. For the time September 15, 1787 and into the early years of Washington's first administration, he served as the community's Chief Burgess. One of his first official acts was the presentation of a petition to the new Congress of the United States in which it was urged that Lancaster, Pennsylvania, be made the site of the capital of the United States. Judge Jasper Yeates had drafted the document and Hand had signed it.

On March 17, 1789, acting as Chief Burgess of the community of Lancaster, which had been for one day, September 27, 1777, the capital of the infant nation, General Edward Hand appealed to the Congress: "Gentlemen: The Corporation of the Borough have been instructed by the Inhabitants thereof and the Adjoining Townships to address you. The new Constitution to which we anxiously look . . . as the means of establishing the Empire of America on the most sure and solid basis is here and now in motion, and one of the Objects of Congress will be to fix upon a Permanent Place of Residence . . ." [31]

It was earlier in 1789, February 4, that Edward Hand served his state and his country by casting an electoral college vote for the first president of the United States under the newly ratified constitution. At the time only ten of the thirteen states provided voting delegates. North Carolina and Rhode Island were disqualified for failure to ratify the Constitution; and New York, which had been entitled to eight electors, was able to send none, because of an unfortunate deadlock in its legislature. In only six of the ten states providing voting delegates were the electors chosen by popular vote.

Each elector cast two votes for president. General Edward Hand found it very easy to name George Washington; and Dr. Edward Hand found it very easy to name George Washington. Washington, enormously popular at the time, of course was named on every ballot of the sixty-nine. As the candidate with the second-most votes becomes vice-president, John Adams, named on thirty-four ballots, won that office. John Jay finished a distant third with nine votes. Besides that of George Washington, it is not known just whose name Dr. Hand placed on his ballot.

And General Hand, always keen about economics even got into taxes. Two years into his term as President, Washington put the Secretary of the Treasury in Philadelphia on notice that Pennsylvania would be conducting four surveys. "To each of these surveys there shall be an Inspector, whose compensation shall be in a salary of 450 Dollars and a Commission of one per Cent. It is my wish to appoint for No. 3 Edwd. Hand. But as his acceptance is doubted. . . . " [32]

But Hand did accept, and on March 8, 1792, President Washington appointed General Edward Hand "Inspector of Revenue for Survey # 3 in the District of Pennsylvania." Hand served in this office for a decade, into the last year of his life, spending considerable time in overseeing local tax collectors, and in patiently reviewing complaints.

On May 8, 1792, Congress passed a bill entitled "An act to provide more effectually for the national defence, by establishing an uniform militia throughout the United States, at that time still only fifteen states. Agreeably to the requisition of the President of the United States (Washington of course), contained in a letter from the Secretary of War (Henry Knox), dated the 19th of May, 1794, Pennsylvania responded. For the frontier defence, several brigades were organized to form a pool of 10,768 from which detachments could be formed "to be in readiness to march at a moment's warning." [33]

During the year 1792, Edward Hand was considered for a number of military positions, including the offices of Quartermaster General, Adjutant General, and even Commander-in-Chief. In the "Letter Book," March 7, 1792, appears a press copy of the letter of the Secretary of State, March 7, 1792. It includes the composite expression of opinions of all officers yet living (brigadier and major generals), who might be considered for Commander-in-Chief. Those who were described were Major Generals Lincoln, Baron von Steuben, Moultrie, McIntosh, Wayne, Weedon, Scott, and Huntington; and seven brigadier generals. The opinion registered for General Hand: "A sensible and judicious man; his integrity unimpeached; and was esteemed a pretty good Officer. But, if I recollect rightly, not a very active one [!]. He has never been charged with intemperance to my knowledge; His name has rarely been mentioned under the present difficulty of chusing an Officer to comm'd, but this may, in a great measure, be owing to his being at a distance." [34]

During his first term as President, Washington, for almost a decade the leader of a rebellion, had a modest rebellion of his own to suppress. Alexander Hamilton's programs for raising funds included in 1791 a tax on whiskey.

Not surprisingly whiskey-producing farmers stoutly resisted. By 1794 violence seemed to be unescapable. In May, Washington called for the governors of states to raise militia forces expressly charged with quelling the protest, and himself led a force from Carlisle to Bedford in Pennsylvania. A Pennsylvania militia detachment, composed of 10,768, authorized by Governor Thomas Mifflin, was readied for enforcing the tax. Edward Hand (since September 3, 1783 a Major General of the Pennsylvania State troops) was on April 11 given the command of two brigades of militiamen from the counties of York and Lancaster. Happily, even though Hand did lead troops into the west, no real confrontation ever occurred for his forces.

 For Washington's first administration there were other problems requiring military action. His troubles with the country's native Americans had not vacated with his election to the Presidency. To address these, he may well have called upon General Hand, whose responsibilities for the Sullivan Expedition had been huge. But Hand did not participate as an officer in any of the three expeditions dispatched by President George Washington against the hostile Indians of the Ohio Valley, in 1790, 1791, and 1794. He was, however, much relied upon for help, for not only could he draw upon a rich experience in fighting Indians, he was also an influential figure at the heart of the rifle production country.

 To his long-time friend and military associate Major General Edward Hand, Governor Thomas Mifflin of Pennsylvania dispatched on September 27, 1794, an urgent request. General Anthony Wayne, preparing for a battle against the Shawnee, the Potawatomie, and the Miami (and eight other tribes), the earlier expeditions of Harmar and St. Clair having been wiped out, was much in need of rifles.

 It was now more than a decade beyond the end of the Revolution, but Lancaster, which throughout the Revolution, as noted above, was regarded the primary source for munitions, especially rifles and muskets, was still looked to as the most likely locale in which to secure the weapons needed by the army, as in the area there were still active a number of German gunsmiths, and a very productive secret gun factory in nearby Hummelstown.

Mifflin conveys the request: "Sir: — In a conversation with Mr. Secretary [Alexander] Hamilton, acting on behalf of the Secretary of War [Henry Knox], he informed me that I could obtain from you a supply of Rifles, for a company of one hundred men, being raised by Captain Seely, in Northampton County, for the Western Expedition. Though you should not have received an official instruction for that purpose, I hope you will think yourself justifiable in delivering the rifles upon my application, as it is certainly an object of great importance to the public service. Captain Seely will promise to account for them."

And he added, then, in a postscript, "I have just received from the Brigade Inspector of York County [a message], informing me that he, likewise, is in want of Rifles, and requesting that an order might be given for putting into his possession from fifty to one hundred of those which you have contracted for in York. [35] Hand was quick to oblige on both requests.

Although his life during these years was largely a public one of service, Dr. Hand did have another life. He was a member of the Montgomery Military Lodge number fourteen, earning status as a 32nd degree Freemason. And in 1790 he joined the Hibernian Society of Lancaster, a strictly Irish organization, devoted to the welfare of the Irish in their adopted country. Besides, he was becoming quite a farmer, with horses to breed and fruit to harvest, and plantations to oversee.

By the summer of 1796, by which time the family had moved lock, stock, and barrel, to a new home on the river, the Hand household numbered eight members, including the proud parents. The firstborn, Sarah, was now eighteen. Dorothy was sixteen. John, the first son, was thirteen. Jasper was twelve. Mary was ten. Margaret was seven. Dear little Katharine had died April 14, 1791.

XII

Rock Ford

*The benevolence and humanity he evinced, in
gratuitously giving his professional aid
to the poor and sick, crowned all the distinguished
acts of his life . . . .*

— Lancaster New Era

There stands no equestrian statue of General Edward Hand in the historic Penn Square of South Queen Street in the Lancaster community. And there is no monument to him anywhere in New York City, nor in Pittsburgh, nor in Philadelphia, nor anywhere in the Seneca Indian country of western New York. But he is fondly remembered in his beautiful home called Rock Ford.

Dr. Hand had been a visitor in Washington's impressive Mount Vernon plantation home on the River Potomac. The Washington estate remained vivid in his mind for a decade and more. He had been much taken by its location, so close to the Potomac, and of course by the stables, and the number of farms, and by the vast expanse of grazing land and land for crops. Now in his forties and quite able financially to think in terms of the plantation life, he invested in a tract of arable land very close to the Conestoga River, and not all that far from the borough of Lancaster, some 160 acres. The year was 1785.

Because the river at this point featured a number of picturesque outcroppings, and because it was here that so many travelers forded the stream, the family determined on a most appropriate name for their new home, Rock Ford. The general built at this site a large and very beautiful three-story brick mansion. The home is in the style of the Georgian architecture so popular in colonial Pennsylvania.

It was in 1792 that the last child of the Hands was born. This was the son Edward. He came into the world on January 19. And it was in this year that Dr. Hand determined to enlarge his estate. He now added seventeen acres to the plantation, and over the succeeding years he had builders construct a tenant house, two barns, a number of odd outbuildings, and the very necessary springhouse. By this time he had ventured into real farming. He had planted orchards of fruit trees (and by and by actually had a variety of plum named for him!) and was harvesting apples and peaches. Farmer Hand had also invested in livestock. He was then, as he had always been, most enthusiastic about horses, and he had acquired quite a reputation as a breeder and as a horseman extraordinaire.

By 1795 all members of the Hand family were living at Rock Ford, excepting the dear child Katharine, whose chronic illness had finally carried her off. And of course both General Hand and Kitty died here at Rock Ford, as well as eleven-year-old Margaret. But tragedy came to the home some five years after the death of Dr. Hand and two years after the death of his wife. Twenty-five-year-old John, the first born of the three sons of the Hands, after an apparently very happy afternoon with his fiancée, came home and shot himself. He left no note. There has never been provided a satisfactory answer to everyone's question, "Why?"

John's younger brother Jasper (He was only thirteen at the time.) was made terribly depressed, and never really recovered from the shock. Despite some difference in age, the two boys had been very close.

Before very long the home was closed, and it remained so for twenty-seven years. It even acquired the reputation of "haunted."

But eventually it was lived in, and today it is preserved by the Rock Ford Foundation and can be visited by interested parties. This beautiful home reposes still on the banks of the Conestoga, an enduring monument to one whose life was devoted to his adopted country.

Dr. Edward Hand's home is today on the National Register of Historic Places. It is listed in the Historic American Building Survey. In the entire county of Lancaster the Rock Ford mansion is the most intact building of those built before 1800. The home has been restored in some features and is preserved by the Rock Ford Foundation, a non-profit organization. The Foundation, beginning in 1960, has

Rock Ford

generously made it accessible to the public and provides tours of the estate April through October.

In the home can be viewed General Hand's portable writing desk, with its compartments for ink and wax. Included in it is a portrait of Charles II. There is also the original dinner invitation extended to the Hands by the President of the United States, and General Hand's Society of the Cincinnati membership certificate (signed by George Washington).

A tour of the mansion will include, besides the parlor and the bedrooms and porches, the cellar, with its several kitchens.

And wonder of wonders, General Edward Hand was afforded the opportunity to show off his elegant mansion to his dear friend and his Commander-in-Chief, now the President of the United States. Washington, during his first term as President of the young nation, had determined early on to get to know the several states on an up-close basis. Accordingly he insisted on a tour of the New England states, and having completed that, he embarked on a similar tour of the southern states, this in the spring of 1791. In early July, as he was returning north from this journey, which had occupied him for some three months, he received a warm invitation from the "Inhabitants of Lancaster, Pennsylvania" to visit the community.

Noting that they had already prepared a large celebration in commemoration of the fifteenth anniversary of the signing of the Declaration of Independence, the people of the region were confident that they could provide the president a most memorable day. Washington, appreciating that he had never once set foot in this community, to which the success of the Revolution owed so much, and remembering also that many of his officers and soldiers were of this region of Pennsylvania, was only too happy to accept: "This being the anniversary of American Independence and being kindly requested to do it, I agreed to halt here this day and partake of the entertainment which was prepared for the celebration of it."

He arrived, coming from York, at six o'clock in the evening of Sunday, July 3. Burgess Hand, together with a number of additional prominent citizens of Lancaster, had ridden to Columbia, on the Susquehanna to receive the President. He arrived on schedule, being transported across the wide river by John Wright's animal-drawn ferry. [1]

After the President had been wined and dined, he was escorted the remaining few miles by a huge company of wildly cheering citizens. As they approached the Lancaster city square, the president found the flags flying everywhere, from every nook and cranny of the courthouse, from the lamp posts and from windows of offices and homes.

It is not known just where in Lancaster the President lodged on the night of July 3. He could very well have been accommodated by Kitty and Edward Hand, as General Hand was not only the mayor of the community, but its most prominent and distinguished citizen at this time. Besides, no officer had been closer to Washington in the final two years of the war than Adjutant General Edward Hand.

George Washington

In any case, we know from Washington's diary how he spent the morning of the fifteenth anniversary of the signing of the Declaration of Independence: "In the forenoon I walked about town." Of course in observance of the 4th of July, Mayor Hand had the cannon fired; and the bells were ringing and drums were beating constantly.

Mayor Hand and his associates escorted the President to the courthouse in Penn Square, where they discovered the local company of light infantry on parade.

As the president's party approached the building, the infantry fired three celebratory volleys, and Washington in a salute acknowledged the honor. All were treated, then, to a most "elegant dinner," which, however, had to wait until Washington had been most formally received by the citizenry of Lancaster.

This welcoming address, which had been prepared by the officials of the community, was, presumably, delivered by Burgess Hand: "On behalf of the Inhabitants of the Borough of *Lancaster*, the Members of the Corporation beg leave to congratulate you on your Arrival at this place. On this joyful Occasion, they approach the first Magistrate of the Union, with hearts impressed with no less grateful Respect than their fellow Citizens of the East and of the South. With them they have achieved those Talents, and that firm Prudence in the field, which finally ensured Success to the American Arms. But, at this time, Reverence forbids the language which would naturally flow from the Recapitulation of the Events of the late glorious Revolution. The faithful page of History will record your illustrious Action for Posterity. Yet we cannot forbear to mention what we, in our Day, have beheld & witnessed. We have seen you, at the awful Period when the Storm of War was bursting around us, and our fertile plains were deluged with the richest blood of *America*, rising above Adversity, and exerting all the Talents of the Patriot & the Hero, to save our Country from the threatened Ruin: And when by the Will of Heaven, those Exertions had restored peace and prosperity to the *United States* and the great Object for which you drew the Sword was accomplished, we have beheld you, adorned with every private social Virtue, mingling with your fellow Citizens. Yet that transcendent Love of Country, by which you have always been actuated, did not suffer you to rest here; but when the united voice of Freemen (your fellow Citizens) called you, from the repose of domestic life, actuated solely by the principles of true Glory, not seeking your own Aggrandizement, but sacrificing the sweets of retired Life to the Wishes and happiness of your Country, we have beheld you, possessed of the Confidence of a great people, presiding over their Councils, and, by your happy Administration, uniting them together by the great political Bond of one common Interest. It is therefore the Inhabitants of this Borough seize with joy the only Opportunity which has offered to them to testify their Approbation of, and their Gratitude for, your Services. Long, very long, Sir, may you enjoy the Affection of your Fellow-Citizens. We pray for a long Continuance of your Health & Happiness, and the choicest Blessings of Heaven on our *beloved Country*, and on You, its *Father* & its *Friend*." [2]

  The address is then signed "on behalf of themselves & the Inhabitants of the Borough of Lancaster" by Burgesses Edward Hand and Paul Zantzinger, and assistants John Hubley, Jacob Krug, Casper Shaffner, and Jacob Frey.

  To this sincere and heartfelt address, which adds up to a big THANK YOU, Washington promptly replied, in his characteristically gracious manner: "Gentlemen, Your congratulations on my arrival in Lancaster are received with pleasure, and the flattering expressions of your esteem are replied to with sincere regard. While I confess my gratitude for the distinguished estimation in which you are pleased to hold my public services, a sense of justice to my fellow-citizens ascribes to other causes the peace and prosperity of our highly favored country — her freedom and happiness are founded in their patriotic exertions, and will, I trust, be transmitted to distant ages through the same medium of wisdom and virtue. With sincere wishes for your social, I offer an earnest prayer for your individual welfare."

It was now three o'clock in the afternoon, and after Washington had been further welcomed in the many compliments of the clergy of different denominations, all sat down to an elegant dinner. The last entry in Washington's diary for this day, the 4th of July, 1791, reads: "At half passed 2 oclock I received, and answered an address from the Corporation [of Lancaster] and the complim[en]ts of the Clergy of different denominations." [3]

At some time on this memorable occasion, Dr. Edward Hand and his wife Kitty had the Chief Executive for tea. As the family at this time was not yet permanently established in Rock Ford, it is not known whether the tea was enjoyed in the Lancaster borough home of Dr. Hand or at Rock Ford on the river. Nor is there any record of the conversation. But as Washington was at that time President of the Society of the Cincinnati and Hand was President of the Pennsylvania chapter of the Society, it is likely that the tea-time chatter wandered into that a little. And doubtless it must have included some flattering observations about the Rock Ford plantation from Washington and probably something like "I owe it all to Mount Vernon" from Dr. Hand.

Some five years later Dr. and Mrs. Hand, together with their oldest daughter, Sarah, now twenty-one years old, received a very happy invitation: "The President of the United States and Mrs. Washington, Request the Pleasure of Genl. & Mrs. Hand's and Miss Hand's Company to Dine, on Wednesday next, at 4 o'clock 25 Jany 1796. An answer is requested."

This dinner occasion, which must have been a very happy get-together, provided the last opportunity for General Edward Hand and his Commander-in-Chief (after a close association lasting two decades) to enjoy each other's company.

The Hand family had taken up a permanent residence at Rock Ford in 1794-95. All of the family were able to enjoy some very happy years at the estate, all except dear little Katherine, who, as above noted, had died at age eleven, April 14, 1791.

After Washington's retirement from his second term as President and during the administration of John Adams serious trouble occurred between the nations of France and the new United States. Noting the strong possibility of an outright war, Adams appointed George Washington Commander-in-Chief "of all armies to be raised." He was given the rank of Lieutenant General. In accepting, Washington laid out plans for the organization of the army. In this his choice for Adjutant General was Edward Hand. In 1798, with the threat of war with France still very real, Washington recommended to the Congress that General Hand be commissioned Adjutant General. But it did not happen; and Washington was much disappointed.

Hand was, however, in this year (1798) commissioned a Major General in the United States Provisional army.

In a letter to the Secretary of State Timothy Pickering, dated September 8, Washington complains that he did not know until a letter from the Secretary of State, Sept. 1, 1798, that Colonel William North had been commissioned Adjutant General on July 19. He has a comment to make: "Mr. [Jonathan] Dayton would, I believe, have filled it [the office of Adjutant General] with ability; and he or Genl. Hand (the latter from experience in it) commanded my wishes." [4]

Of course nothing like a war with France ever occurred. Except for a few skirmishes at sea, the differences between the nations vacated without military action.

But very sad news was received by the people of Lancaster on Thursday, December 19, 1799. It was the report of the death of the Father of the Country, the first President of the United States. Washington, who had been come for by the Grim Reaper a thousand times, who had suffered almost every disease known to the eighteenth century, including the three big killers, smallpox, malaria, and tuberculosis, who had experienced many frightening death-threatening accidents, who had braved the perils of the wilderness, and who had escaped thousands of bullets and cannon balls on many a battlefield, was dead.

The nation's first president had died at 10:20 Saturday night, December 14. As the sad news reached out to all corners of the sixteen states, thousands grieved privately and thousands more grieved in congregations. No one who knew the Revolution or anything of Washington as President was unmoved. When the news reached Europe, Napoleon ordered ten days of mourning. Notice of his death reached the capital city of Philadelphia on the 18th; and on the 19th, almost five days after his passing, the nation's loss was entered into the records of Congress.

Washington had been interred in the family vault, a red brick structure tucked into the hillside overlooking the Potomac. At three o'clock in the afternoon of the 18th the funeral procession had moved out from the estate house at Mount Vernon for the services conducted at the tomb.

The honor of making the formal announcement to the assembled Congress went to Washington's good friend Representative John Marshall of Virginia. A State Funeral was held in Philadelphia, with 4000 mourners in attendance at the Zion Lutheran Church. The honor of delivering the eulogy went to Henry Lee, III, the ninth governor of Virginia, beloved by Washington.

Washington's birthday, February 22, 1800, was proclaimed by Congress the official national day of mourning. But in communities all across the country services were held all through December and January. Some communities scheduled and organized very formal services. Lancaster, Pennsylvania, which town had been visited by the President just eight years ago, was one of those. Tuesday, January 7, was the day set apart by the citizenry of the borough of Lancaster as "a day of mourning, tribulation and respect for the memory of the illustrious Washington, whose beloved and renowned fame shall perish only with the last vestige of human recollection."

The *Lancaster Journal* for the next day, January 8, reported on the procession and the ceremony: "On Tuesday, January 7, 1800, at a little before one o'clock, in conformity with the orders of Major General Edward Hand, a military procession was formed, in honor of the memory of the late General Washington. It was joined by a number of the members of our state legislature, some clergymen from the neighborhood, the brethren of the Lodge of Freemasons, and a number of private citizens."

Following a troop of cavalry were thirty militia officers, marching two by two, and then followed Major General Edward Hand. The first governor of Pennsylvania, General Thomas Mifflin, who had not long ago removed from his home city of Philadelphia to Lancaster, came next. A great many elements of the procession followed after.

The *Lancaster Journal* reported of the solemn procession that "The concourse of people was very great. It could not be less than five thousand." The paper noted that "All the stores were shut and all business suspended. It was indeed a day of mourning. The feelings expressed by the countenance of every good man was a sure pledge of the gratitude of Americans, and a confirmation that we have suffered a great national loss." [5]

Washington's General Hand followed not long after. Dr. Edward Hand died at his plantation home of Rock Ford, September 3, 1802, [6] after a brief illness. The cause of death was first determined to be cholera, although there was no epidemic in the Lancaster area at the time, and his illness was short. It is now supposed that he died of a stroke.[7]

During the week of September 8, 1802, his obituary appeared in the Lancaster *New Era*: "DIED, after a few hours of sickness of a *cholera morbus* on the 4th Inst. At his Seat on the Conestogoe, in the vicinity of this Borough, Gen. Edward Hand, in the 58th year of his age, and his remains were interred the following day in the Episcopal Burial-ground in the Borough of Lancaster, attended by his weeping relatives, and a crowd of sympathizing Friends.

"This gentleman was a native of Ireland; he arrived in this country before the revolution; and, during that period, entered the continental army, and rose to the rank of adjutant-general. In this character, he rendered important service to the country. After the war, he retired to the practice of physic, a profession in which he had been brought up. In the year of '93, he was appointed a major-general in the professional army of the United States.

"As a physician, he was eminently useful, ever ready to the calls of necessity and distress; neither poverty nor condition were consulted in his visits. The benevolence and humanity he evinced, in gratuitously giving his professional aid to the poor and sick, crown all the distinguished acts of his life; and will cause his name to be long revered and long lamented, by those who have experienced his influence and who may stand in need of medical aid. Affectionate as a husband, tender as a parent, and useful as a citizen and physician, he has left a disconsolate widow, and his children (with a numerous circle of friends and acquaintances) to bewail his death."[8]

He is buried at the church that he loved, that he had served for a long time as vestryman, in the St. James's Episcopal Churchyard in Lancaster, under an obelisk with the inscription "Edward Hand, M D. A General Officer of the Revolution. The Friend and Companion in Arms of Washington . . . His public services are part of his country's history."

Mrs. Hand died at Rock Ford June 21(sometimes given as June 28), 1805, and is buried with her husband. They rest in peace in the churchyard near their family church, "a serene and beautiful place."

Afterword

Edward Hand of Lancaster, Pennsylvania, will long be remembered as a fervent patriot and as a distinguished, heroic, high-level officer of the American Revolution, whose contribution to the birth of the country was immense. And he will be remembered as a most prominent citizen of the city of Lancaster, Pennsylvania, a very popular and highly celebrated physician, who pioneered in the quarantine hospital and in the smallpox inoculation. His name refers all to both the United States Congress and to the Pennsylvania State Assembly. Many will revere him as a Pennsylvania farmer, devoted to the health of the soil. His concern for others and his devotion to his immediate family and to his larger family is most impressive to all, and it would tax the resources of the keenest students of character to register a negative for Dr. Edward Hand.

On November 24, 1899, there was organized an Edward Hand Chapter of the Daughters of the American Revolution. It did not appear in Lancaster, Pennsylvania, but in Ottawa, Kansas! It was the fourth chapter of the D.A.R. to be organized in the state of Kansas. It was given the name of Edward Hand for a very good reason. Remarkably, two of the chapter's charter members, Mrs. Alexina Davis and Mrs. Jane Gilley, were direct descendants of General Hand.

As it was thought by some that Colonel Hand is one of the figures in the boat in the famous "Crossing the Delaware" painting, Mrs. Davis, so the story goes, had at some time commissioned the artist of the original, Emanuel Leutze, to do a rendering. He promptly obliged. Upon the death of Mrs. Davis, her family presented the painting to the chapter. The presentation was made on October 17, 1930: "We are glad to present this painting to Edward Hand Chapter — D. A. R. in memory of our Mother Alexina St. Clair Williamson Davis, who was a charter and active member until her death, 1928. Gen. Edward Hand was her ancestor and his portrait is in the painting."

And the letter is signed by the five children of Mrs. Davis (Frank E. Davis, Jepitha D. Davis, John B. Davis, Edwin C. Davis, and Earl A. Davis). The painting is large, 57.5 x 42.5 inches. It now hangs in the Ottawa Library.

Ottawa, Kansas, a community of some 13,000, is on the Marais des Cygnes River. It has grown up on the site of the Ottawa Indian settlements, and of course it takes its name from those Native Americans. At the present time about one of every 100 citizens is of Ottawa Indian heritage.

Those responsible for the chapter's charter probably did not know that General Edward Hand, while at Fort Pitt, had experienced some dealings with the larger tribe of Ottawa Indians. Of his councils with their chiefs he reported "fruitful mediations."

Edward Hand enjoys still another monument to his memory, one that is in tribute to his professional skills and character as a physician.

In 1982, a group of physicians of the Medical Society of the Lancaster area founded the Edward Hand Medical College. It has a vision: "To preserve and make accessible the rich heritage of the healing arts, with special attention given to Lancaster County." In addition to the founding physicians of the medical society the organization includes members of Lancaster's citizenry from a wide spectrum of other medical and non-medical professions.

The Society has assembled a huge collection of items of local medical interest. In the Collection (as it is called) can be discovered more than 10,000 artifacts, "including books, photographs, and medical instruments, which taken together

~ *Afterword* ~

provide a well documented medical history of the Lancaster County region."

All of this can and should be respected as a token of regard for those early physicians who with their "home remedies," like castor oil and alum, attempted to fight off the devastating diseases that in the eighteenth century took the lives of four of every ten children before they matured.

In Lancaster, Pennsylvania, Dr. Hand (General Hand) is remembered in the name of the Edward Hand Middle School, a public junior high school. Located on South Ann Street within the borough, it accommodates 500-600 students. It programs lots of activities, sponsors field trips, competes in both boys' and girls' sports, and schedules educational excursions. The school is providing a fine education for its youngsters, but, like most public schools in the present day, it has problems. One likes to think that General Hand could put an end to them.

And one of Lancaster's most prominent institutions also owes a lot to Dr. Edward Hand. This is the Lancaster County Almshouse and Hospital, also known as the Lancaster County Poor and House of Employment. The general was one of the principal movers in its birth in 1799, and promptly became a trustee. It was primarily intended to accommodate the poor, and, more specifically was designed for the care of dependent or delinquent or impoverished children.

It was built in the Gothic Revival Style, construction beginning in 1799 and continuing through 1801, at what is currently 900 East King Street. Now closed, it is protected by the Historic Preservation Trust. The "facade easement" which was granted to the Trust guarantees that the building, now 214 years old, can never be demolished nor even see its exterior altered. The structure has been listed since April 17, 1980, on the National Register of Historic Places.

Just how much Edward Hand had to do with Lancaster's most prestigious institution of education, the very highly regarded Franklin and Marshall College is not perfectly clear, but it is known definitely that he was a supporter.

And there is yet another monument to the memory of Edward Hand. It is not of marble or even granite, nor is it a tablet cast in bronze. No, this most distinguished, heroic, high-level officer of the American Revolution, this very popular, and highly celebrated physician, this very influential member of both the Pennsylvania and the United States Congress has been remembered for 220 years for — well, for a plum! Long before the plaster had dried on the wall of the Rock Ford mansion, General Hand and Doctor Hand had become Horticulturist Hand. He loved horses of course, and he loved sheep, too, and the various breeds of cattle and swine. But he absolutely delighted in the fruits of the soil, the grains and the berries, and the soil itself.

Perhaps the greatest of his many delights at Rock Ford were his orchards. He doted on fruit trees, and tenderly babied the apple trees and the peach trees. But he was most especially fond of the plum, and very keen about the possibilities in the many varieties. He had had no real training in pomology, but somehow he had learned enough to know about grafting, and he determined to produce a plum that was even more luscious to the taste than those varieties that were on the market now. And he did it. The plum that Dr. Hand eventually produced is a striped, greenish-colored fruit. It has been described as featuring a "moderately juicy" flesh, yellowish in color and somewhat coarse. Those who have tasted the Edward Hand plum have found it mild and very pleasant, just plain "good."

Dr. Hand was very generous with grafts for his farmer friends and very happy to have cultivated quite an interest. He would be happy to know that the birthplace of the Edward Hand plum has been authoritatively identified as Lancaster, Pennsylvania.[1]

Lancaster County, from the time of its first settlers, including the native Americans, has earned a well deserved reputation for "the garden spot of the world." For its rich soil it

~ *Afterword* ~

has over the centuries steadily attracted those who love farming. The attitude of these settlers has been most impressively one of respect for the land. And the farms have been passed on from generation to generation. It would much please Farmer Hand to know that 212 years beyond his own time his Lancaster County has become the first county in the entire nation to put into preservation 100,000 acres of farmland, which means that this land cannot be developed for commercial, or even residential, use! It is there for fruit trees. [2]

Appendix A

The Hanging of John André

General Edward Hand served on the court that condemned John André and was present for the execution. Here follows an eye-witness account of the execution of Major John André in Tappan, New York. This account was recorded in the *Military Journal* of Dr. James Thacher, a surgeon in the Massachusetts 16th Regiment, and at the time of this event twenty-six years old. The date is October 2, 1780.

"Major André is no more among the living. I have just witnessed his exit. It was a tragical scene of the deepest interest. During his confinement and trial, he exhibited those proud and elevated sensibilities which designate greatness and dignity of mind. Not a murmur or a sigh ever escaped him, and the civilities and attention bestowed on him were politely acknowledged. Having left a mother and two sisters in England, he was heard to mention them in terms of the tenderest affection, and in his letter to Sir Henry Clinton, he recommended them to his particular attention. The principal guard officer, who was constantly in the room with the prisoner, relates that when the hour of execution was announced to him in the morning, he received it without emotion, and while all present were affected with silent gloom, he retained a firm countenance, with calmness and composure of mind. Observing his servant enter the room in tears, he exclaimed, 'Leave me till you can show yourself more manly!' His breakfast being sent to him from the table of General

Washington, which had been done every day of his confinement, he partook of it as usual, and having shaved and dressed himself, he placed his hat upon the table, and cheerfully said to the guard officers, 'I am ready at any moment, gentlemen, to wait on you.' The fatal hour having arrived, a large detachment of troops was paraded, and an immense concourse of people assembled; almost all our general and field officers, excepting his excellency and staff, were present on horseback, melancholy and gloom pervaded all ranks, and the scene was affectingly awful. I was so near during the solemn march to the fatal spot, as to observe every movement, and participate in every emotion which the melancholy scene was calculated to produce.

"Major André walked from the stone house, in which he had been confined, between two of our subaltern officers, arm in arm; the eyes of the immense multitude were fixed on him, who, rising superior to the fears of death, appeared as if conscious of the dignified deportment which he displayed. He betrayed no want of fortitude, but retained a complacent smile on his countenance, and politely bowed to several gentlemen whom he knew, which was respectfully returned. It was his earnest desire to be shot, as being the mode of death most comfortable to the feelings of a military man, and he had indulged the hope that his request would be granted. At the moment, therefore, when he suddenly came in view of the gallows, he involuntarily started backward, and made a pause. 'Why this emotion, sir?' said an officer by his side. Instantly recovering his composure, he said, 'I am reconciled to my death, but I detest the mode.' While waiting and standing near the gallows, I observed some degree of trepidation; placing his foot on a stone, and rolling it over and choking in his throat, as if attempting to swallow. So soon, however, as he perceived that things were in readiness, he stepped quickly into the wagon, and at this moment he appeared to shrink, but instantly elevating his head with firmness he said, 'It will be but a momentary pang,' and taking from his pocket two white handkerchiefs, the provost-marshal, with one, loosely pinioned his arms, and with the other, the victim, after taking off his hat and stock, bandaged his own eyes with perfect firmness, which melted the hearts and moistened the cheeks, not only of his servant, but of the throng of spectators. The rope being appended to the gallows, he slipped the noose over his head and adjusted it to his neck, without the assistance of the awkward executioner. Colonel Scammell now informed him that he had an opportunity to speak, if he desired it; he raised the handkerchief from his eyes, and said, 'I pray you to bear me witness that I meet my fate like a brave man.' The wagon being now removed from under him, he was suspended, and instantly expired; it proved indeed 'but a momentary pang.' He was dressed in his royal regimentals and boots, and his remains, in the same dress, were placed in an ordinary coffin, and interred at the foot of the gallows; and the spot was consecrated by the tears of thousands.

"Thus died, in the bloom of life, the accomplished Major André, the pride of the royal army, and the valued friend of Sir Henry Clinton. He was about twenty-nine years of age, in his person well proportioned, tall, genteel and graceful. His mien respectable and dignified . . . . General Washington was called to discharge a duty from which his soul revolted; and it is asserted that his hand could scarcely command his pen, when signing the warrant for the execution of Major André."[1]

Appendix B

The Edward Hand Plum

Here, by Alfred A. Hoffy and Dr. Eli Parry, is the story of the General Hand plum:

"The General Hand Plum is believed to be a native of Pennsylvania. Dr. Eli Parry, of Lancaster, Pennsylvania, has published in the 1st Vol. of *The Pennsylvania Farm Journal* the following historical notice of this variety. 'As my object in this communication is to endeavor to establish beyond a doubt, that the plum called the General Hand Plum, first received that name in the County of Lancaster, and not in Maryland. I called on Mrs. Brien, of our city, a daughter of the late Gen. Edward Hand [This is Dorothy, who in 1805, at age twenty-eight, married Edward Brien, a native of Ireland, County Tyrone.], from whom I learned that he took great pains in collecting and cultivating choice fruit trees. She remembers his planting a number of small plum trees, but she cannot tell where he got them. Plums were very scarce in this variety at that time. She also suggested that I might learn something further relative to the matter, by calling on Mr. Benedict, an aged and respectable citizen of our place, who informed me that in the autumn of 1791, he assisted in plastering the mansion house of the late General Hand, on the Conestoga, about one mile south-east of Lancaster, and he remembers that the plum trees were planted before that time; but that they were still quite small, and had not borne any fruit — he said that George Wein procured some grafts from the tree on General Hand's place, and gave Mr. George Miller, the present clerk of the Lancaster market, some of them. I called on Mr. Miller and he told me that in 1810 or 1811 [This is a mistake, as Hand died in 1802.], Mr. George Wein procured about a dozen grafts from General Hand, (who was always very liberal to his neighbors in such matters,) and gave him two of them at his request; one, a young shoot, the other a year old piece with one lateral bud on it — and that one grew, but threw out no lateral branches that season — Mr. Wein not so fortunate — none of his grew; and the following spring he applied to Mr. Miller for grafts, which he declined, giving as a reason the fact, that he could not cut off any grafts without spoiling his tree. During the second summer, there had been some lateral branches thrown out, and Mr. Miller furnished Mr. Wein with a few of them; but he was equally unfortunate in his second attempt to propagate them. That summer the *parent tree* died to the ground, so that in 1812 or 1813 we find all that beautiful variety of fruit concentrated in one little stalk, grown from the lateral bud on one of the grafts given to Mr. George Miller by Mr. Wein. From that circumstance, they were for a time called the 'Miller Plum,' until Mr. Miller objected to that name, and said that it was General Hand's Plum. From that time to the present day they have been so called. Some years afterwards, Mr. Emanuel Carpenter procured some cuttings from Mr. Miller, and succeeded in propagating them, and as he told me, sent them to his brother in Ohio, to Mr. Sinclair, in Baltimore, and others. Thus it appears to me that some pomologists have improperly given Baltimore the credit of the nativity of this superb plum, which properly belongs to Lancaster County, Pennsylvania." [1]

Image Credits

Cover   Edward Hand. Author: Baron Friedrich Wilhelm von Egloffstein, steel engraving portrait from the nineteenth-century work by Henry P. Johnston, *The Campaign of 1776 and New York and Brooklyn* (1878). See also *Pennsylvania Archives*, Second Series, Vol. X. In this year, 1878, Hand's portrait was in the possession of his granddaughter Mrs. S. B. Rogers, of Lancaster, Pa.

Page 3   Arms of the King.

Page 25   Edward Burd. Portrait by Charles Willson Peale, from life, 1820. Oil on canvas. Burd is sixty-nine.

Page 26   Judge Jasper Yeates home, 24 South Queen Street in central Lancaster. On National Register of Historic Places since September 23, 1982. Photo by Smallbones. House built by a blacksmith named John Miller, in 1765.

Page 28   James Wilkinson. Portrait by Charles Willson Peale, 1797. Courtesy National Historical Park Collection, Philadelphia.

Page 36   Standard of First Pennsylvania Regiment.

Page 41   Israel Putnam. Medium: Graphic lithograph by Dominque C. Fabronius, May 12, 1864. Library of Congress.

Page 47   James Grant. Author unknown. Ca. 1770. State Archives of Florida.

Page 49   William Alexander, Lord Stirling. Engraving. Author: Harper & Brothers. Source: *Harper's Encyclopedia of United States History*, Vol. I (1905), p. 95.

Page 53   Alexander Scammel. Source: *The Granite Monthly*, XIV, No. 9 (Sept., 1892), following page 272.

Page 64   The Capture of Nathaniel Woodhull. Author unknown. Date unknown.

Page 69 Washington Crossing the Delaware. Painting, oil on canvas, by Emanuel Gottlieb Leutze, 1849-51. Metropolitan Museum of Art. Colonel Edward Hand is thought to be the officer seated at the rear of the boat and holding his hat. The officer standing next to Washington is thought to be eighteen-year-old James Monroe.

Page 70 Thomas Forrest. Portrait by Charles Willson Peale, 1820. Independence National Historical Park.

Page 71 Charles Cornwallis. Portrait by John Singleton Copley, ca. 1785. Source: His Majesty's First Regiment of Foot Guards in America, 1776-1783.

Page 72 Surrender of the Hessians at Trenton, December 26, 1776. Painting by John Trumbull, oil on canvas, 1786. Depicts the mortally wounded Colonel Rall and the badly wounded Lieutenant James Monroe. Yale University Art Gallery, Trumbull Collection.

Page 79 The Death of General Hugh Mercer at the Battle of Princeton, January 3, 1777. Painted by John Trumbull, oil on canvas, ca. 1791. Encore Editions. Yale University Art Gallery.

Page 81 Washington Rallying the Rebel Forces at the Battle of Princeton, by William T. Ranney, 1848. Oil on canvas. Courtesy of the Princeton University Museum of Art.

Page 107 Daniel Brodhead. portrait (artist unknown) from the New York Public Library, Thomas Addis Emmett Collection of Illustrations Relating to the American Revolution. Dated 1886.

Page 117 William Crawford cabin, Connellsville, Pa. Author photo, 2005.

Page 122 Captain Pipe. Statue in New Portage Park, Barberton, Ohio, 1911.

~ *Image Credits* ~ 305

Page 125   George Rogers Clark. Painting by John Wesley Jarvis, 1820? Engraved by Thomas B. Welch after a copy of the original by James Barton Longacre. Courtesy of Filson Historical Society Collection, Louisville, Ky.

Page 126   George Clymer. By Edward Marchant, after Charles Willson Peale, 1807-09. Pennsylvania Academy of Fine Arts.

Page 131   Edward Hand letter to Kitty, August 6, 1778.

Page 132   General Lachlan McIntosh. Photographic print of original (October 19, 1789) portrait. McIntosh is sixty-four years old. Rollins College Archives.

Page 142   Cornplanter. Portrait by Frederick Bartoli, 1796, from life. Collection of New York Historical Society.

Page 144   Joseph Brant. Portrait by Charles Willson Peale, from life, 1797. Independence National Historical Park.

Page 154   Philip Schuyler. By Jacob H. Lazarus, 1881. Mirror-image copy of a portrait copied from the John Trumbull miniature (oil on wood), which is with the New York Historical Society. The Lazarus painting is on exhibit at the Schuyler Mansion State Historic Site, Albany.

Page 163   John Sullivan. Portrait by A. Tenney, after portrait by Ulysses Dow Tenney, developed from 1790 pencil sketch by John Trumbull. Collections of the State of New Hampshire Division of Historical Resources.

Page 169   William Irvine. Portrait from an oil painting by B. Otis, after one by Robert Edge Pine, an eminent English artist who came to America in 1784. The original was taken in New York City, when Irvine (at age 48) was a member of Congress. Courtesy of Archives and Special Collections. Dickinson College, Carlisle, Pennsylvania.

Page 203   Baron Johann de Kalb. Charles Willson Peale, 1781-82, a replica of the original, painted for the Philadelphia Museum. Oil on canvas. Independence National Historical Park.

Page 205   Dr. William Shippen, Jr. From the portrait by Gilbert Stuart, which has been in the possession of the Shippen family. Etched by H. Wright Smith, date unknown. Source: *The Surgeon Generals of the Army of the United States of America*, by James Pilcher (Carlisle, Pa.: The Association of Military Surgeons, 1905), page 12.

Page 211   Jean-Baptiste Donatien de Vimeur, Comte de Rochambeau. Artist: Charles Philippe Lariviere. Oil on canvas, 1834. Painting is at Chateau de Versailles. Washington County (Md.) Historical Society Collection.

Page 214   Enoch Poor. Portrait by Ulysses Dow Tenney, 1873, after an earlier portrait by Tadeudz Kosciusko. New Hampshire Division of Historical Resources.

Page 215   John Andrė. Line and stipple engraving, by John Scoles, probably after Hopwood after John Andrė. Source: Frontispiece in Joshua Hett Smith's *An Authentic Narrative of the Causes Which Led to the Death of Major Andrė, Adjutant-General of His Majesty's Forces in North America* (New York: Evert Duyckinck, 1809). Courtesy American Antiquarian Society, Worcester, Massachusetts.

Page 220   Robert Howe. Portrait is English, but artist and date are unknown. Source: Charles Lukens Davis, *A Brief History of the North Carolina Troops on the Continental Establishment in the War of the Revolution* (Philadelphia: npbl., 1896), page 80.

Page 225   Dr. James Thacher. Lithographic print of original. Date unknown (1825-1836?). Lithography by John Pendleton.

Page 236   Hasbrouck House. Photographer Rolf Müller, May 21, 2005.

Page 261   Judge Richard Peters. Scan of frontispiece from 1904 biography by Nellie Peters Black: *Richard Peters, His Ancestors and Descendants* (Atlanta: Foote and Davies Company, 1904).

~ Image Credits ~

Page 263 Thomas Mifflin. By Charles Willson Peale, portrait in oil, 1783-84. Independence National Historical Park.

Page 266 James Wilson. By Ole Erekson, engraver, ca. 1878-79. Graphic portrait. Official portrait of Supreme Court Justice James Wilson. Courtesy of National Portrait Gallery, Smithsonian Institution.

Page 267 John Paul Jones. Charles Willson Peale, oil on canvas. 1781 or 1783 or 1784. The City of Philadelphia. Independence National Historical Park.

Page 279 Rock Ford. Author photograph, Sept. 26, 2013.

Page 281 George Washington. George Washington in 1795. Portrait by the Swedish artist Adolf Ulric Wertmüller. Oil on canvas, 1795. Courtesy of Philadelphia Museum of Art. Bequest by Allen Munn, 1924.

Works Consulted

Manuscript Collections

Manuscripts having to do with Edward Hand are located in eleven different repositories:

(1) Peter Force Transcripts, Library of Congress, Manuscript Division, Washington, D. C. 150,000 items. In the Miscellaneous Manuscript Collection, 1777-1801 are to be found eight items concerning Edward Hand. Two maps concerning topography for the Sullivan Campaign.
(2) The Historical Society of Pennsylvania, Philadelphia. The Society is the custodian of the Edward Hand Papers (Collection ID 0261). The collection, covering the years 1771-1807, is housed in two boxes, and in three bound volumes. Box 1 contains Hand's 109 letters to his wife, as well as many to various officials (much of it military correspondence). It also includes the Valley Forge Orderly Book for the month of January, 1778 – not the work of Edward Hand. Box 2 contains much material reflecting his business interests (receipts, revenue accounts, etc.).The three bound volumes accommodate a great many miscellaneous documents. The collection can be made available on microfilm.
(3) Library of Congress, Washington, D. C. Here are the Peter Force materials, including "Documentary History of the American Revolution." Among his transcripts are a few items, including letters and maps, which have to do with Edward Hand for the years 1774-76.
(4) The Morgan Library, Department of Literary and Historical Manuscripts, New York City (One item, letter from Hand to General Philip Schuyler), written on March 8, 1779, Hand requesting information about the Indian country).
(5) The New York Public Library, Rare Books, and Manuscript Division, New York City. Hand papers, 1775-1801(chiefly correspondence). Letters composed and received while Hand was stationed at Fort Pitt; Hand diary or journal for Sullivan Campaign; lots on Sullivan Campaign; lots of letters to Jasper Yeates.
(6) Pennsylvania Historical and Museum Commission, Division of Archives and MSS, Harrisburg, Pa.. Hand's personal letters to military associates. Available on microfilm.
(7) University of Pittsburgh, University Library System, Darlington Library, Pittsburgh, Pa. Twenty-six items, dating 1777-1785 (letters from Fort Pitt and to Hand from other frontier forts (letters written from Fort Pitt, 1777-78). Index to the papers is available.
(8) Bowden, Alfred James, cat., *The Unpublished Revolutionary Papers of*

Major General Hand of Pennsylvania, 1777-1784 (New York: George H. Richmond, 1907). Contains 61 items, dating 1775-1785. Among these items are a copy of a petition for redress of grievances, addressed to Patrick Henry, then Governor of Virginia; a number of letters expressing concern over militia forces in the Fort Pitt region; Washington's reply to Hand's letter reporting on the Cherry Valley massacre; a number of letters on the Sullivan expedition; letters on the outrages perpetrated in the Wyoming Valley; petition of the inhabitants of Port Royal on the need for ammunition and protection; extracts from the Resolves of Congress; letter to Joseph Reed, Governor of Pennsylvania; marching orders for various units in the Yorktown campaign (1780-81); Hand's plan for the establishment of the office of Inspector General (13 pages!); Hand's plan for a standing army for the United States (12 pages); manuscript prepared while Hand was a member of Congress (relates to the number of troops required for the occupation of the western forts after their evacuation by the British; Hand's plan for the establishment of an Adjutant General's Department (12 folio pages); 17 miscellaneous military and political papers of historic value (much on the history of the U. S. Army).

(9) The Draper Manuscripts. The Lyman Copeland Draper Manuscript Collection is housed by the Wisconsin Historical Society. It is organized into 491 volumes, divided into fifty series. A microfilm edition is available (F 586 D7 1980), and it is also available online at FamilySearch.org. It contains a good bit of material from the time of Edward Hand's service at Fort Pitt (1777-78), including a number of letters. Much of this material has been of use to Reuben Gold Thwaites and Louise Phelps Kellogg for their edition of *Frontier Defense in the Upper Ohio.*

(10) Lancaster County Historical Society. A few items, including a genealogy of the Hand family, in a booklet *Commemoration of Lancaster County in the Revolution, at Indian Rock, Williamson Park, near Rock Ford, Sept. 20, 1912;* also a chronology of Lancaster County in the Revolution, with particular reference to the service of Edward Hand, Folders 2 and 3 in Edward Hand Reunion and Genealogy Collection, 1805-1984 (call no.: MG-116, Lancaster County Historical Society).

(11) University of Pennsylvania, Special Collections, Van Pelt Library, Philadelphia. Two items: letters from Hand to Samuel Powel concerning the cultivation of oats.

~ *Works Consulted* ~ 311

Abbot, W. W., Dorothy Twohig, and Philander D. Chase, eds. *The Papers of George Washington: Colonial Series* (Charlottesville: University of Virginia Press, 1983-95). 10 vols.

Abbot, W. W., and Dorothy Twohig, eds. *The Papers of George Washington: Confederation Series* (Charlottesville: University of Virginia Press, 1992-97). 6 vols.

Abbott, W. W., and Dorothy Twohig, eds. *The Papers of George Washington: Presidential Series* (Charlottesville: University of Virginia Press, 1987-2010). 11 vols.

Abbott, W. W., Dorothy Twohig, and Philander D. Chase, eds. *The Papers of George Washington: Revolutionary War Series* (Charlottesville: University of Virginia Press, 1985-2010). 12 vols.

Abbot, W. W., ed. *The Papers of George Washington: Retirement Series* (Charlottesville: University of Virginia Press 1998-99). 4 vols.

Adams, Abigail, and John Adams, *The Letters of John and Abigail Adams*, ed. Frank Shuffleton (New York: Penguin Books, 2004).

Albert, George Dallas, ed. *History of the County of Westmoreland, Pennsylvania, with Biographical Sketches of Many of Its Pioneers and Prominent Men* (Philadelphia: L. H. Everts and Co., 1882).

American Archives, Produced by Northern Illinois Libraries.

Anderson, Dale, *The Battle of Yorktown* (Milwaukee, Wisc.: Gareth Stevens Publishing, 2004).

Arthur, Robert, *The Sieges of Yorktown, 1781, and 1862* (Fort Monroe, Va.: Coast Artillery School, 1927).

Baule, Steven M., Protecting the Empire's Frontier, Officers of the 18th (Royal Irish) Regiment of Foot during Its North American Service, 1767-1776 (Athens, Ohio: Ohio University Press,

Baule, Steven M.., "The 18th (Royal Irish) Regiment of Foot," internet blog, August 24, 2013.

Bell, Herbert C., *History of Northumberland County, Pennsylvania* (Chicago: Brown, Runk and Co., 1891).

Bell, Whitfield Jenks, *The Court Martial of Dr. William Shippen, Jr.*, (S.I.: s.n., 1964).

Berg, Fred Anderson, *Encyclopedia of Continental Army Units* (Harrisburg: Stackpole Books, 1972).

Betts, William W., Jr., *Bombardier John Harris and the Rivers of the Revolution* (Westminster, Md.: Heritage Books, 2006).

Betts, William W., Jr., *Rank and Gravity, The Life of General John Armstrong of Carlisle* (Westminster, Md.: Heritage Books, 2011).

Betts, William W., Jr., *The Nine Lives of George Washington* (Bloomington, Indiana: iUniverse, 2013).

Billias, George Athan, "Pelham Bay: a Forgotten Battle," *New York Historical Society Quarterly*, XLII (January, 1958), 20-38.
Black, Nellie Peters, ed. *Richard Peters, His Ancestors and+ Descendants* (Atlanta: Foote and Davies Company, 1904).
Bliven, Bruce, Jr., *Battle for Manhattan* (New York: Henry Holt, 1955).
Boatner, Mark Mayo, III, *Encyclopedia of the American Revolution* (New York: D. McKay Co., 1974).
Bonk, David, and Graham Turner, *Trenton and Princeton,1776-1777* (Oxford: Osprey Publishing, 2009).
Branning, Rosalind L., *Pennsylvania's Constitutional Development* (Pittsburgh: University of Pittsburgh Press, 2004).
Brunhouse, Robert L., *The Counter-Revolution in Pennsylvania,1776-1790* (Harrisburg: Pennsylvania Historical Commission,1942).
Buck, Solon J., and Elizabeth Hawthorne Buck, *The Planting of Civilization* (Pittsburgh: University of Pittsburgh Press, 1939).
Burd, Edward, and Thomas Lynch, "Letters of Edward Burd, *The Pennsylvania Magazine of History and Biography*, XLII, No. 1 (1918), 62-68.
Butterfield, Consul Willshire, *History of the Girtys: Being a Concise Account of the Girty Brothers— Thomas, Simon, James and George, and of Their Half-brother, John Turner . . .* (Cincinnati: Robert Clarke & Co., 1890).
Butterfield, Consul Willshire, ed. *The Washington-Crawford Letters, Being the Correspondence between George Washington and William Crawford, from 1767 to 1781,Concerning Western Lands* (Cincinnati: Robert Clarke & Co., 1877).
Calendar of the Correspondence of George Washington, Commander in Chief of the Continental Army, with the Officers (Washington, D. C.: Government Printing Office,1915). 4 vols.
Canby, Henry Seidel, *The Brandywine* (New York and Toronto: Farrar and Rinehart, 1941).
Cannon, Richard, *Historical Record of the Eighteenth, or the Royal Irish Regiment of Foot: containing an account of the formation of the regiment in 1684, and of its subsequent services to 1848* (London, England: Parker, Furnivall and Parker, 1848).
Carrington, Henry Beebe, *Battles of the American Revolution* (New York: A. S. Barnes and Co., 1876).
Cave, Alfred A., "George Croghan and the Emergence of British Influence on the Ohio Frontier," in *Builders of Ohio, A Biographical History* (Athens, Ohio: Ohio State University Press, 2002).

~ *Works Consulted* ~ 313

Clare, Israel Smith, *A Brief History of Lancaster County* (Lancaster, Pa.: Argus Publishing Co., 1892).
Colonial Records of Pennsylvania (Harrisburg: Theodore Fenn, 1852-1853). 16 vols.
Conrad, W. P., *From Terror to Freedom in the Cumberland Valley* (Greencastle, Pa.: Lilian S. Besore Memorial Library, 1976).
Cook, Frederick, *Journals of the Military Expedition of Major General John Sullivan Against the Six Nations of Indians in 1779, with Records of the Centennial Celebrations* (Auburn, N. Y.: Knapp, Peck & Thomson, 1887).
"Correspondence of General Edward Hand, of the Continental Line, 1779-1781," *Pennsylvania Magazine of History and Biography*, XXXIII, No. 3 (1909), 353-360.
Crackel, Theodore J., ed. *The Papers of George Washington Digital Edition* (Charlottesville: University of Virginia Press, Rotunda, 2008).
Craft, David, *The Sullivan Expedition, An Address, Delivered at the Seneca County Centennial Celebration in Waterloo, New York, Sept. 3rd, 1879* (Waterloo, New York: Observer Book and Job Printing House, 1880).
Craig, Michel Williams, *General Edward Hand:Winter's Doctor* (Lancaster, Pa.: Rock Ford Foundation, 1984).
Craig, Neville, B., ed. *The Olden Time* (Cincinnati: Rptd. By R. Clarke and Co., 1787-1863).
Cress, Lawrence Delbert, "Republican Liberty and National Security, American Military Policy as an Ideological Problem, 1783-1789," *William and Mary Quarterly*, XXXVIII, Third Series (January, 1981), 73-96.
Crumrine, Boyd, Franklin Ellis, and Austin N. Hungerford, *History of Washington County, Pennsylvania: with biographical sketches of many of its pioneers and prominent men* (Phila.: H. L. Everts and Co., 1882).
Darlington, Mary C., *Fort Pitt and Letters from the Frontier* (New York: Arno Press, 1892; 1971).
Davis, Andrew McFarland, "Account of the Wyoming Massacre of 1778," *Proceedings of the Massachusetts Historical Society*, XXIII (October, 1887), 340-347.
Davis, Burke, *The Campaign That Won America* (New York: Harper Collins, 2007).
Davis, Charles Lukens, and Henry Hobart Bellas, *A Brief History of the North Carolina Troops on the Continental Establishment in the*

War of the Revolution (Philadelphia: n. pbl., 1896).
De Haas, Willis, *History of the Early Settlement and Indian Wars of Western Virginia; embracing an account of the various expeditions in the West, previous to 1795* (Phila.: King & Baird, 1851).
Dillon, John Grace Wolfe, *The Kentucky Rifle* (York, Pa.: George Shamway, 1967).
Dunaway, Wayland Fuller, *The Scotch-Irish of Colonial Pennsylvania* (Chapel Hill, N. C.: University of North Carolina Press, 1944).
Dyke, Samuel E., *The Pennsylvania Rifle* (Lancaster, Pa.: Sutter House, 1974).
Egle, William Henry, *Pennsylvania in the War of the Revolution, Battalions and Line, 1775-1783,* ed. John Blair Linn and William Henry Egle (Harrisburg: Lane S. Hart, 1880). 2 vols.
Egle, William Henry, "The Federal Constitution of 1787,"*The Pennsylvania Magazine of History and Biography*, X, No. 4 (Jan., 1, 1887), 446-460; VII, No. 1 (April, 1887), 69-79; VII, No. 2 (July. 1887), 213-222; VII, No. 3 (Oct., 1887), 249-275.
Egle, William Henry, *The First Indian Massacre in the Valley of Wyoming, Fifteenth of October, 1763. An Address Delivered at the Wyoming Monument on July 3, 1889* (Harrisburg: Harrisburg Publishing Co., 1890).
Ellis, Franklin, and Samuel Evans, *History of Lancaster County, Pennsylvania, with Biographical Sketches of Many of the Pioneers and Prominent Men* (Phila.: Everts and Peck, 1883).
Ferling, John E., *Almost a Miracle: The American Victory in the War of Independence* (New York: Oxford University Press, 2007).
Field, Thomas W., *The Battle of Long Island* (Brooklyn, N. Y.: Long Island Historical Society, 1869).
Fischer, David Hackett, *Washington's Crossing* (Oxford, England: Oxford University Press, 2004).
Fischer, Joseph, *A Well Executed Failure: The Sullivan Campaign against the Iroquois, July-September, 1779* (Columbia, S. C.: University of South Carolina Press, 1997).
Fish, Sidney M., *Barnard and Michael Gratz: Their Lives and Times* (Landam, Md.: University Press of America, 1994).
Fitzpatrick, John C., ed. *The Diaries of George Washington* (Boston: Mt. Vernon Ladies' Association, 1925).
Fitzpatrick, John C., ed. *The Writings of George Washington,1744-1799* (Washington, D. C.: United States Government Printing Office, 1931-1944; rptd. New York: Greenwood Press, 1970). 39 vols.
Fleming, Thomas, *Forgotten Victory: The Battle for New Jersey — 1780*

~ *Works Consulted* ~

(New York: Reader's Digest Press, 1973).
Ford, Worthington Chauncey, et al., eds. *Journals of the Continental Congress,1774-1789* (Washington, D. C.: Library of Congress, Government Printing Office, 1904-37). 34 vols.
Ford, Worthington Chauncey, ed. *The Writings of George Washington* (New York: G. P. Putnam's Sons, 1889-1893). 14 vols.
Gabel, Ronald G., *Early Pennsylvania Gunsmithing* (S.l.: s.n., 2008).
Gibson, John, ed. *History of York County* (Chicago: F. A. Battey Printing Co., 1886).
Godcharles, Frederic Antes, "The First Expedition against the Indians of the Six Nations," in Charles F. Snyder, ed. *Northumberland County in the American Revolution* (Sunbury, Pa.: Northumberland County Historical Society, 1976), pp. 103-128.
Grainger, John D., *The Battle of Yorktown,1781: A Reassessment* (Woodbridge, Suffolk: Boydell Press, 2005).
Graydon, Alexander, *Memoirs of His Own Time, with Reminiscences of the Men and Events of the Revolution.* Ed. Jon Stockton Littell (Philadelphia: Lindsay & Blakiston, 1846).
Graydon, Alexander, *Memories of a Life Chiefly Passed in Pennsylvania within the Last Sixty Years; with occasional remarks upon the general occurrences, character and spirit of that eventful period* (Harrisburg, Pa.: published anonymously, 1811; republished in Philadelphia in 1846 under title of *Graydon's Memories of His Own Time. With Reminiscences of the Men and Events of the Revolution.* Rptd. twice, once in 1900 and again in1969).
Graymont, Barbara, *The Iroquois in the American Revolution* (Syracuse, New York: Syracuse University Press, 1972).
Greene, Jerome A., *The Guns of Independence: The Siege of Yorktown, 1781* (New York: Savas Beatie, 2005).
Hamilton, Alexander, *The Papers of Alexander Hamilton*, volume II, 1779-1781, ed. Harold C. Syrett (New York: Columbia University Press, 1961.
Hamilton, Otis G., ed. *The Letters and Papers of Major General John Sullivan* (Concord, N. H.: New Hampshire Historical Society Collections, 1930-1939). 3 vols.
Hand, Edward, Alfred Jones Bowden, and George H. Richmond, *The Unpublished Revolutionary Papers of Major General Edward Hand of Pennsylvania, 1777-1784* (New York: George H. Richmond, 1907).
Hand Papers, "Military," in 1880 in the office of the Secretary of War, at Washington. For a time in the possession of his granddaughter,

Mrs. S. B. Rogers of Lancaster. Cover his military career during the 1770s and 1780s. Available for research at the Historical Society of Pa., Lancaster, Pa.

Hanko, Charles W., *The Life of John Gibson: Soldier, Patriot, Statesman* (Daytona Beach, Fl.: College Publishing Co., 1955).

Harris, Alex, *A Biographical History of Lancaster County: Being a History of Early Settlers and Eminent Men of the County* .... (Lancaster, Pa.: Elias Barr & Co., 1872).

Hassler, Edgar W., *Old Westmoreland, A History of Western Pennsylvania During the Revolution* (Pittsburgh: J. R. Weldon & Co., 1900).

Hayden, Horace Edwin, "Echoes of the Massacre of Wyoming," *Proceedings and Collections of the Wyoming Historical and Genealogical Society*, VII (1902), 78-105; XII (1911-1912), 69-104).

Headley, Joel Tyler, *Washington and His Generals* (New York: Scribner, Armstrong & Co., 1875). 2 vols. in one.

Heath, William, *Memoirs of Major-General William Heath*, ed. William Abbatt (New York: New York Times and Arno Press, 1968).

Henry, John Joseph, *A Narrative* (Lancaster, n. pbl.,1812).

Heuvel, Sean, "Washington's Adjutant: General Edward Hand," *Patriots of the American Revolution* (March-April, 2011), 18-27.

Hoffy, Alfred A., *North American Pomologist: Containing Numerous Finely Colored Drawings, Accompanied by Letter Press Descriptions, &C., of Fruits of American Origin* (Ithaca, N. Y.: Cornell University Library print collections, 2009).

Hufeland, Otto, *Westchester County During the American Revolution, 1775-1783* (Harrison, N. Y.: Harbor Hill Books, 1974).

Hunter, William A., "First Line of Defense, 1755-1756," *Pennsylvania History*, XXII, No. 3 (July, 1955), 229-255).

Hunter, William A., *Forts on the Pennsylvania Frontier, 1753-1758* (Harrisburg: Pennsylvania Historical and Museum Commission; Wennawoods reprint, 1999).

Hurt, R. Douglas, *The Ohio Frontier: Crucible of the Old Northwest, 1720-1830* (Bloomington, Indiana: Indiana University Press, 1996).

Irwin, Benjamin H., *Clothed in Robes of Sovereignty* (New York: Oxford University Press, 2011).

Jackson, Donald, and Dorothy Twohig, eds.*The Diaries of George Washington* (Charlottesville, Va.: University Press of Virginia, 1976-79). 6 vols.

Jensen, Merrill, *New Nation: A History of the United States During the*

Confederation,1781-1789 (New York: Knopf, 1950).

Johnston, Henry Phelps,*The Campaign of 1776 around New York and Brooklyn* (Brooklyn, New York: Long Island Historical Society,1878; republished in New York: Da Capo Press, 1971).

Jordan, John W., ed. "Adam Hubley, Jr., Lt. Colo. Comdt 11th Penna. Regt., His Journal, Commencing at Wyoming, July 30th, 1779," *Pennsylvania Magazine of History and Biography*, XXXIII (1909), 129-146; 279-302; 409-422.

Kauffman, Henry J., *The Pennsylvania-Kentucky Rifle* (New York, Bonanza Books, 1960).

Kellogg, Louise Phelps, *Frontier Retreat on the Upper Ohio, 1779-1781* (Madison: Publications of the State Historical Society of Wisconsin, 1917).

Ketchum, Richard M., *The Winter Soldiers: The Battles for Trenton and Princeton* (New York: Holt Paperbacks, 1999).

Ketchum, Richard M.,*Victory at Yorktown: The Campaign That Won the Revolution* (New York: Henry Holt, 2004).

Kilmeade, Brian, and Don Yeager, *George Washington's Secret Six,The Spy Ring That Saved the American Revolution* (New York: Sentinel, 2013).

Kindig, Joe, and Mary Ann Cresswell, *Thoughts on the Kentucky Rifle in Its Golden Age* (York Pa.: Trimmer Printing, 1960; Wilmington, Del.: G. N. Hyatt, 1960).

Kirkpatrick, T. Percy C., *History of the Medical Teaching in Trinity College Dublin and the School of Physic in Ireland* (Dublin: Hanna and Neale, 1912).

Klett, Guy Soulliard, *The Scotch-Irish in Pennsylvania* (Gettysburg: Pennsylvania History Association, 1948).

Knouff, Gregory T., *The Soldiers' Revolution, Pennsylvanians in Arms and the Forging of Early American Identity* (University Park, Pa.: The Pennsylvania State University Press, 2004).

Landers, Howard Lee, *The Battle of Camden, South Carolina, August 16, 1780* (Washington, D. C.: U. S. Government Printing Office, 1931).

Landis, Charles J., *Major John André's German Letter* (read before the Lancaster County Historical Society, Friday, June 5, 1914) (Lancaster, Pa.: Lancaster County Historical Society, 1914).

Lengel, Edward J., *General George Washington* (New York: Random House, 2005).

Linn, John Blair, and William Henry Egle, *Pennsylvania in the War of the Revolution: Battalions and Line, 1775-1783* (Harrisburg: Lane S. Hart, State Printer, 1880). 2 vols.

Lossing, Benson John, *The Pictorial Field-Book of the Revolution* (New York: Harper Bros., 1860). 3 vols.

Lowell, Edward J.,*The Hessians and the Other German Auxiliaries of Great Britain in the Revolutionary War* (New York: Harper Brothers, 1884).

Ludlum, David McWilliams, *Early American Winters, 1604-1820* (Boston: American Meteorological Society, 1966).

Mann, Alison V., "What Really Caused the Death of General Edward Hand?" Lancaster, Pa.: Edward Hand Medical Heritage Foundation website.

Mapes, George E., "Two Famous Military Roads of Pennsylvania," *Kittochtinny Papers*, VI (1920), 93-104.

Martin, Betsy, *The Story of Crafton*, 1740-1992 (Crafton, Pa.: Crafton Historical Society, 1992).

McCullough, David, *1776* (New York: Simon and Schuster, 2006).

McGuire, Thomas J., *The Philadelphia Campaign* (Mechanicsburg, Pa.: Stackpole Books, 2006-07). 2 vols.

McMaster, John Bach, and Frederick Dawson Stone, eds. *Pennsylvania and the Federal Constitution,1787-1788* (Harrisburg: Historical Society of Pennsylvania, 1888; New York: Da Capo Press, 1970).

Meginess, John F., *Biographical Annals of Lancaster County, Pennsylvania, containing biographical and genealogical sketches of prominent and representative citizens and of many of the early settlers . . . .*(Chicago: J. H. Beers & Co., 1903).

Miner, William Penn, *History of Wyoming* (Philadelphia: J. Crissy, 1845).

Montgomery, Thomas L., ed. "Report of the Commission to Locate the Site of the Frontier Forts of Pennsylvania," *Frontier Forts of Pennsylvania* (Harrisburg: State Printing Office, 1st edn., 1896; 2nd edn., 1916).

Morgan, George, *Letter Book*, in Carnegie Library, Pittsburgh, Pa.

Morris, Charles, *Historical Tales: The Romance of Reality* (Phila.: J. B. Lippincott, 1897).

Morrissey, Brendan, *Yorktown 1781:The World Turned Upside Down* (London: Osprey, 1997).

Murray, Elsie, "Hartley's and Sullivan's Expeditions against the Iroquois," in Charles F. Snyder, ed. *Northumberland County in the American Revolution* (Sunbury, Pa.: Northumberland County Historical Society, 1976), pp. 129 and ff.

Neumann, George C., "American-made Muskets in the Revolutionary War," *Journal of the National Rifle Association*.

Norris, Major, "Journal of Sullivan's Expedition," *Buffalo Historical*

Society Publications, I (1879), 217-252.

Norton, A. Tiffany, *History of Sullivan's Campaign against the Iroquois* (Lima, N. Y.: privately published, 1879).

Olmstead, Earl P., *David Zeisberger: A Life among the Indians* (Kent, Ohio: Kent State University Press, 1997).

Papers read before the Lancaster County Historical Society, Lancaster County Historical Society, Lancaster, Pa.

Peck, George, *Wyoming: Its History, Stirring Incidents, and Romantic Adventures* (New York: Harper & Bros., 1858).

Peckham, Howard H., *The Toll of Independence: Engagements and Battle Casualties of the American Revolution* (Chicago: University of Chicago Press, 1974).

Pennlines, XLIX, No. 1 (January, 2014), 4.

Pennsylvania Archives, Second Series, ed. John B. Linn and William Henry Egle (Harrisburg: Lane S. Hart, State Printer, 1874-1890). 19 vols.

Pennsylvania Archives, Third Series, ed. (first 26 vols.) by William Henry Egle; (four index vols.) by George Edward Reed (Harrisburg: State Printer, 1894-1899. 30 vols.

Pennsylvania Farm Journal, Vol. I (1851-1852).

Pilcher, James Evelyn, *The Surgeon Generals of the Army of the United States of America* (Carlisle, Pa.: The Association of Military Surgeons, 1905).

Prowell, George Reeser, *History of York County, Pennsylvania* (Chicago: J. H. Beers and Co., 1907).

Ragsdale, Bruce, and Kathryn A. Jacob, *Biographical Dictionary of the United States Congress, 1774-1989* (Washington, D. C.: National Government Publication, 1989).

Read, William B., copied from the original, "Orderly Book of General Edward Hand, Valley Forge, January, 1778," *Pennsylvania Magazine of History and Biography*, XLI, No. 2, pp. 198-223; No. 3, pp.253-273; 458-467).

Reed, William B., *Life and Correspondence of Joseph Reed* (Philadelphia: Lindsay and Blakiston, 1847). 2 vols.

Rupp, Israel Daniel, *History of Lancaster County: to which is prefixed a Brief Sketch of the Early History of Pennsylvania* (Lancaster, Pa.: Gilbert Hills, 1844).

Schecter, Barnet, *The Battle for New York: The City at the Heart of the Revolution* (New York: Walker & Co., 2002).

Scheer, George F., and Hugh F. Rankin, *Rebels and Redcoats: The American Revolution Through the Eyes of Those Who Fought and*

Lived It (New York: D Capo Press, 1987).
Siebert, Wilbur H., "The Loyalists of Pennsylvania," *The Ohio State University Bulletin*, XXIV, No. 23 (April 1, 1920), 1-109.
Sipe, Chester Hale, "General Sullivan's Expedition against the Six Nations," in Charles F. Snyder, ed. *Northumberland County in the American Revolution* (Sunbury, Pa.: Northumberland County Historical Society, 1976), pp. 191-199.
Smith, Joshua Hett, *An Authentic Narrative of the Causes Which Led to the Death of Major André, Adjutant-General of His Majesty's Forces in North America* (New York: Evert Duyckinck, 1809).
Smith Samuel Robert, *The Story of Wyoming Valley* (Kingston, Pa.: S. R. Smith, 1906).
Smith, Samuel Stelle, *The Battle of Princeton* (Monmouth Beach, N. J.: Philip Freneau Press, 1967).
Smith, Samuel Stelle, *The Battle of Trenton* (Monmouth Beach, N. J.: Philip Freneau Press, 1965).
Sparks, Jared, ed. *Correspondence of the American Revolution: Being Letters of Eminent Men to George Washington* (Boston: Little, Brown and Co., 1853). 4 vols.
Sparks, Jared, ed. *The Writings of George Washington, with a Life of the Author* (Boston: American Stationers Co., 1834-1837). 12 vols.
Stark, Caleb, and John Stark, Memoirana, *Official Correspondence of Gen. John Stark, with notices of several other officers of the Revolution* (Boston: Gregg Press, 1972).
Stone, William Leete, *The Poetry and History of Wyoming* (Albany: T. Marshall, 1864).
Stryker, William S., *The Battles of Trenton and Princeton* (Boston: Houghton, Mifflin and Co., 1898).
Thacher, James, *A Military Journal during the American Revolutionary War from 1775 to 1783* (Boston: Richardson & Lord, 1823).
Thacher, James, *The American Revolution: From the Commencement to the Disbanding of the American Army Given in the Form of a Daily Journal, with the Exact Dates of all the Important Events* (Hartford, Ct.: Hurlbut, Kellogg & Company, 1862).
"The Frontier Forts of Western Pennsylvania, Fort Pitt," in Vol. II of the *Report of the Commission to Locate the Sites of the Frontier Forts of Pennsylvania*, pp. 99-159 (Harrisburg: Clarence M. Barsh, State Printer of Pennsylvania, 1846).
"The Haunted History of Rock Ford," *Entertainment Lancaster*, September 27, 2013.
The Herald, Sharon, Pa., Tuesday, June 29, 1976.

The New York Times, July 5, 1931.

The Sullivan-Clinton Campaign in 1779 (prepared by the Division of Archives and History) (Albany: The University of the State of New York, 1929).

Thompson, Benjamin F., *History of Long Island, From Its Discovery and Settlement to the Present Times* (Port Washington, N. Y.: I. J. Friedman, 1962; first published 1918).

Thwaites, Reuben Gold, and Louise Phelps Kellogg, eds. *Frontier Defense in the Upper Ohio, 1777-1778* (Madison, Wisc.: Wisconsin Historical Society, 1912).

Thwaites, Reuben Gold, and Louise Phelps Kellogg, *Revolution on the Upper Ohio* (Madison: Publications of the State Historical Society of Wisconsin, 1908).

Todd, Charles Burr, *Guide to Putnam Memorial Camp: with a complete history of the encampments, incidents, organization of the brigades, itinerary, etc.* (Washington, D. C.: Byron S. Adams, 1890).

Trussell, John B. B., Jr., *The Battle of Brandywine* (Harrisburg: Pennsylvania Historical and Museum Commission, 1974).

Trussell, John B. B., Jr., *The Battle of Germantown* (Harrisburg: Pennsylvania Historical and Museum Commission, 1974).

Trussell, John B. B., Jr., *The Pennsylvania Line. Regimental Organizations and Operations,1776-1783* (Harrisburg: Pennsylvania Historical and Museum Commission, 1977).

Trussell, Timothy, and Joel Dworsky, *The Mylin Gun Shop Survey Project* (Millersville, Pa.: Millersville University, Department of Archaeology, 2009).

Volwiler, Albert T., *George Croghan and the Westward Movement, 1741-1782* (Cleveland: The Arthur H. Clark Company, 1926).

Wainwright, Nicholas B., *George Croghan: Wilderness Diplomat* (Chapel Hill: University of North Carolina Press, 1959).

Walsh, John Evangelist, *The Execution of Major André* (New York: Palgrave Macmillan 2001).

Ward, Christopher, *The Delaware Continentals, 1776-1783* (Wilmington, Del.: Historical Society of Delaware, 1941).

Wertenbaker, Thomas J., "The Battle of Princeton," *Proceedings of the New Jersey Historical Society*, New Series, XIV, No. 1(January, 1929), 1-14.

Wilkinson, *James, Memoirs of General Wilkinson* (Washington City: printed for the author, 1811). 3 vols.

Wood, Jerome H., Jr., *Conestoga Crossroads: Lancaster, Pennsylvania, 1730-1790* (Harrisburg: Pennsylvania Historical and Museum

Commission, 1979).
Wormer, William Frederic, "Washington's First Visit to Lancaster and the Observance of his Death," *Papers Read Before the Lancaster County Historical Society*, Vol. XXI, No. 10 (December 1, 1922). monograph.
Wright, Albert H., *The Sullivan Expedition of 1779* (Ithaca, N. Y.: A. H. Wright, 1943).

Notes

I: The New World

1. Philadelphia of course would seem "huge" to Hand, but actually at this time, one could walk completely around the city in less than a day.
2. King's County is now, since 1922, the County Offaly. Some reference works have Edward Hand's birthplace simply in what is known as the Midlands. Today's Leinster Province is the easternmost province of Ireland, and includes, besides Offaly, eleven others, one of which is Dublin.
3. Trinity College, founded 1592 (!), with the School of Medicine, dating from 1711, is the oldest medical school in Ireland. It proudly claims such distinguished teachers as James Macartney, Robert Graves, and William Stokes.
4. The regiment served King George III during the Revolution. It was active at Lexington/Concord and at Bunker Hill. It returned to Gibralter in 1783.
5. *The Dublin Journal*, Cork, May 21, 1767. Craig, p. 3.
6. Wainwright, p. 250.
7. Captain Edmonstone, who had been promoted to his present rank in 1758 (and later to major), did a lot of land speculation in the region of Fort Pitt during his years there, actually selling off Fort Pitt! He would return to his native Ireland a much more wealthy man than he was on his arrival in the New World.
8. Bullock Pens is today known as Churchill.
9. Betts, *Bombardier John Harris*, p. 222.
10. As there is no account of Edward Hand's march to Fort Pitt, or of the return trip, the description provided here is imagined. Yet it must be very close to what actually did occur.
11. Craig, p. 4.
12. For Edward Hand's participation in this sale see copies of two letters held by the Lancaster County Historical Society. See Craig, p. 6.
13. "Report of Committee on Petition of Alexander Ross and William Thompson, of Pittsburgh," *American Archives*, Series 4, Vol. 4, page 0112. See also *The Olden Time*, II, No. 2 (February, 1817), 96.
14. Craig, p. 5.

II: The Gathering Storm

1. Lancaster County, originally a part of Chester County, on May 10, 1729, became Pennsylvania's fourth county. Although the population was largely German, there were here to be found some English, some Welsh, and lots of Scots-Irish, all attracted by the rich soil, the mild climate, and the easy availability of William Penn's land.
2. Craig, p. 7.

3. Reverend Thomas Barton was the first minister of the Saint James Episcopal Church in Lancaster, and had been in the pulpit fifteen years before Hand's introduction to him. He had served the Forbes Expedition of 1758 as Chaplain, and in Lancaster was much beloved because of his great energy, his gracious manner, and his most engaging personality. But he was devoted to King George III, and when the war came his Loyalist sympathies so much alienated him from the Lancaster populace that he had to seek refuge in New York City. He died during the war, and is buried in the St. James churchyard.
4. For the pre-war activity of Lancaster see Clare, pp. 151-156.
5. Clare, p. 156.
6. Colonel George Ross of Lancaster was a close friend to Edward Hand. He served the Pennsylvania militia and was later among those who signed the Declaration of Independence. See Craig, p. 11.
7. Hand's brother-in-law Jasper Ewing.
8. For this letter see Peter Force Transcripts, Hand to Yeates, June 23, 1775. Quoted by Heuvel, p. 19.
9. Ellis, pp. 38-39.
10. Clare, pp. 156-157.
11. There were several men by the name of Hubley in Lancaster at this time. One was Captain George Hubley, who commanded a company in the German regiment. Another was captain Bernard Hubley. And still another was the shoemaker John Hubley. Hand was closest to Adam Hubley, who would for the Sullivan expedition command a regiment in Hand's brigade, and after the war would be elected to the Pennsylvania state senate.

III: Cambridge and Boston

1. Thacher, in Ellis, p. 39.
2. Judge Henry, in Ellis, p. 39n.
3. Thacher, in Ellis, p. 39.
4. Ellis, p. 39.
5. Edward Burd (1749-1833), who was for years a close friend of the Hand family, was married (during the third year of the war) to Elizabeth Shippen, the daughter of Chief Justice Edward Shippen, under whom Burd studied law. He rose to the rank of major in a battalion of the Flying Camp. For the initial stages of the battle of Long Island, Burd was given the command of the picquets stationed at the Red Lion Inn. As Edward Hand had supposed, Burd was made a prisoner, together with sixteen soldiers under his command. He was released not long after, but as he was much too ill to continue in the military, he returned, at age twenty-seven to his law offices in Reading, Pennsylvania. Of interest is the portrait painted by Charles Willson Peale, for which attorney Burd sat at age seventy-one. This portrait, given as a gift to the bride of Peale's son Rubens Peale, who was

~ *Notes* ~

Burd's niece, has quite a history. In 1822, two years after the wedding the portrait was placed on exhibit at the Pennsylvania Academy of Fine Arts. It also was exhibited at Peale's Museum in New York City. Judge Jasper Yeates was married to Sarah Burd, eldest daughter of Colonel James Burd, who was married to Elizabeth Shippen.

6. Hand Papers, item # 208.
7. Walker, p. 74.
8. Before it was made famous by the Revolution, Prospect Hill lay in the midst of a dairy farm, just a little out of Boston. The thing about it is that it commands a great view of Boston and the harbor, and, of course, the countryside. At the time of the Revolution, because of its impressive fortifications it became known as the Citadel. The British gave it another name, Mount Pisgah, in reference to Moses, who from the heights of Pisgah hoped to view the Promised Land.
9. Edward Hand to Jasper Yeates, June 29, 1775, Lancaster County Historical Society. Quoted by Heuvel, p. 19.
10. Wilkinson (1757-1825) was a soldier and an adventurer, and, like Hand, was a physician. He was commissioned a captain in 1775, and breveted a major general, November, 1777.
11. Wilkinson, *Memoirs*, I, 16.
12. *Pennsylvania Archives*, Second Series, X, 6.
13. Knouff, p. 90.
14. *Pennsylvania Archives*, Second Series, X, 8.
15. James Ross, who was promoted to Lt. Colonel, was the son of the very prominent and highly distinguished Lancasterite George Ross (a very good friend of Edward Hand), who served in the Continental Congress, 1774-1777, and was a signer of the Declaration of Independence. George Ross's home was at the site of the present courthouse in Lancaster. The highly regarded Philadelphia attorney, John Ross, was elder brother to George. And there was a William Ross, too, who was a captain in Thomas Porter's battalion.
16. Jasper Yeates was a very good friend of Doctor and Mrs. Hand. The son of John and Elizabeth (Sidbotham) Yeates, he was one year younger than Edward Hand. He was admitted to the bar in 1765 at the age of twenty, and became a most distinguished attorney, earning, in 1791, a place on Pennsylvania's Supreme Court, a position that he held until his death in 1817. He contributed much to the Revolution, serving through 1776 as Chairman of the Committee of Correspondence of Lancaster County. Asked by Washington at the time of the Whiskey Rebellion to go west and "quiet those people who are upset by this tax," he did so, and as he was a most prominent and influential person he was able to help out a good bit. Judge Yeates and his devoted wife Elizabeth had ten children, all born in Lancaster. Yeates died March 14, 1817, at the age of seventy-two, and is buried, as are Edward and Katherine Hand, in the St. James Episcopal churchyard.
17. *Pennsylvania Archives*, Second Series X, 8, 10; Ellis, pp. 40-41. For a

portrait, see Ellis, p. 227

18. These companies of riflemen were among those who advanced farthest into the town of Quebec. Captain Hendricks was killed, and his lieutenant Archibald Steele (who was the brother of the Captain John Steele of the 10th Pennsylvania Regiment who was wounded at the Brandywine) was wounded, losing three fingers to a musket ball.
19. Ellis, p. 41.
20. Hand Papers, item # 215.
21. Note: British Captain Henry Mowatt, under orders from Admiral Samuel Graves to burn all seaports from Boston to Halifax, on October 18 did fire the town of Falmouth, which, ironically, was a stronghold for Loyalists. Mowatt had warned the people and had given them time to withdraw from the town, but their pleas to spare the town went unheeded.
22. Hand Papers, item # 216.
23. See Moore's *Diary of the American Revolution*, Vol. I. See also the *Philadelphia Evening Post,* 1775, the letters of Abigail Adams, p. 61, and *Pennsylvania Archives*, Second Series, X, 11-12.
24. *Pennsylvania Archives*, Second Series, X, 11; and Ellis & Evans, p.44.
25. Brunhouse, p. 87; Hand Papers, item # 221.
26. Hand Papers, items # 221 and 222.
27. Fitzpatrick, *Writings*, IV, 393.
28. Note: Brunhouse, p. 87. This standard has been in the possession of the Commonwealth of Pennsylvania.
29. Hand Papers, items # 225, 226.
30. Ibid., item # 226.

IV: New York City

1. Hand Papers, item # 227.
2. *Pennsylvania Archives*, Second Series, X, 12.
3. Hand Papers, item # 228.
4. *Pennsylvania Archives*, Second Series, X, 13 and 305; Ellis and Evans, p. 44.
5. Hand Papers, items 229 and 230.
6. Ibid., item # 231.
7. *Pennsylvania Archives*, Second Series, X, 305.
8. *Pennsylvania Archives*, Second Series, X, 13; Ellis and Evans, p. 44.
9. Idem.
10. Hand Papers, item # 232.
11. Ibid., item # 234.
12. Ibid., item # 247.
13. Field, Part I, p. 160. Quoted by Schecter, p. 123.
14. Johnston, II, 48. The original (in 1878) was in the possession of Mrs. S. B. Rogers, Lancaster, Pa.
15. Fitzpatrick, Writigs, V, 465.

~ *Notes* ~

16. Walker, p. 90; Johnston, II, 48.
17. Walker, p. 91.
18. Sullivan, who was dispatched by Howe to the Continental Congress to deliver peace terms was rudely received by Adams and other members of the Congress who were not ready after one battle to capitulate. Sullivan was later, like Major Burd, paroled, actually in time to get in on the fighting at Trenton.
19. Fort Greene was named for General Nathanael Greene of course, and likewise Fort Green Park. The fort was at the time of the Battle of Long Island, the largest fort on the island. It was an earthenworks, star-shaped and designed for six eight-pound cannon. After the withdrawal of the American army it was allowed to deteriorate.
20. For the fighting between Hand's riflemen and the Hessians August 26 along the Gowanus Road and in the neighborhood of the Red Lion Tavern, see Craig, pp. 27-29.
21. Samuel J. Atlee (1739-1786), his family having moved from Trenton to Lancaster, when he was seven years old, made his home in Lancaster. He served the 1758 Forbes Expedition and was promoted to captain in 1759. On March 21, 1776, as Washington prepared to defend New York, he was promoted to Colonel and placed in command of the Pennsylvania Musketry Battalion. In the battle of Long Island, he led the defense of the Old Stone House in Brooklyn, and helped to cover the withdrawal of the army. He was captured by the British, but not until after he had exhibited incredible courage, inspiring Washington to remark, "Good God, what brave men must I lose this day." Atlee, after long confinement on a prison ship, was exchanged in October of 1778, in time to become a delegate to the Continental Congress from Pennsylvania, which he served four years. In 1790 he served Pennsylvania as a delegate to the state's Constitutional Convention.
22. Edward Burd's father was Colonel James Burd, a battalion commander.
23. General Grant was Howe's planning officer. He was responsible for the strategy worked out for the battle of Long Island. In the fighting he headed up Howe's left wing to address the right wing of the Continental Army. In 1758 he had been an officer for General John Forbes on the expedition to capture Fort Duquesne. It was Grant who was in command of the forces who were ambushed and destroyed by the French at the costly battle of Grant's Hill, in the shadows of Fort Duquesne. Grant was captured by the French in this action, and later paroled. He became Governor of East Florida during the time of the British colonies, serving from 1764 to 1771.
24. *Pennsylvania Archives*, Second Series, X, 308; Ellis, pp. 46-47.
25. Ellis, p. 47; Johnston, II, 50.
26. *Pennsylvania Archives*, Second Series, X, 306-307.
27. Thomas Mifflin was a very important figure in the life of Edward Hand, both during the Revolution and afterwards. He was reared in Philadelphia as a Quaker, but of course on joining the military was

promptly expelled from that faith. He was Washington's first aide-de-camp and served the Commander-in-Chief as Quartermaster General, but much preferred to be in the fighting. He commanded troops in the battles of Long Island, Trenton and Princeton, and was commissioned Major General in 1777. He served Pennsylvania as President of the Supreme Executive Council and befriended the Seneca war-chief Cornplanter by approving for him a grant of land on the Allegheny River. As President of the Supreme Executive Council he presided at the Pennsylvania Constitutional Convention in 1790, and was promptly elected, under the new constitution, the first Governor of the Commonwealth. He was thus the last President of Pennsylvania and its first Governor. He died at age fifty-six, not in Philadelphia, from which city he had removed in 1799, but in his adopted community of Lancaster. His grave site, in front of the Trinity Lutheran Church on Duke Street in Lancaster, is identified by an historical marker.

28. *Pennsylvania Archives*, Second Series, X, 308-309. See also Schecter, p. 164, and Scheer and Rankin, pp. 170-171.
29. Jasper Ewing was promoted to brigade major to General Hand at Fort Pitt. After the war he became prothonotary of Northumberland County. He died at Sunbury in 1800.
30. *Pennsylvania Archives*, Second Series, X, 310. For another account of the Long Island retreat, see Linn and Egle, I, 308.
31. Hand Papers, item # 241.
32. Weedon had been commissioned Lt. Colonel of the Third Virginia Regiment under Hugh Mercer in 1725. He was made Colonel August 13, 1776, while at Long Island. Besides at Long Island, he commanded troops at Trenton, the Brandywine, Germantown, and Yorktown. He died a decade after war's end, in 1793.
33. Fitzpatrick, *Writings*, VI, 198-199.
34. Ibid., VI, 84, 160, 208.
35. Hand Papers, item # 241.
36. Powles Hook (or Paulus Hook) in the Hudson River (present-day Jersey City) was a very strategic military position.
37. Hand Papers, item # 243.
38. Orders, Sept. 20, 1776, Orderly Book of Hand's Rifle Regiment. Quoted by Knouff, p. 90.
39. Throg's Neck was the fitting name given to the very narrow strip of land reaching out between the East River and Long Island Sound. At high tide it was little better than some grassy spots showing here and there.
40. William Duer, as quoted in Johnston, Part I, pp. 265-266, note 1.
41. Heath, pp. 59-60.
42. Hufeland, p. 112.
43. David Fischer, p. 109.
44. Quoted in Billias, p. 23.
45. David Fischer, p. 109; Heuvel, p. 21; Craig, p. 35.
46. Wilkinson, *Memoirs*, I, 135-136.

47. Craig, p. 36. Quoted by David Fischer, p. 109. Hand Papers, item # 246.
48. John Haslet (1727-1777), a Presbyterian minister, had marched as a militia captain with General Forbes to capture Fort Duquesne. During the early years of the Revolution he very ably commanded Delaware's only regiment, fighting in the Battle of Brooklyn and at Trenton and at Princeton. He was a very good friend of General Hugh Mercer, and died with him at Princeton.
49. Letter of Robert Hanson Harrison to Congress, October 25. See Fitzpatrick, *Writings*, VI, 228n.
50. For a very fine, readable impression of the battle for New York, see David McCullough's *1776*, pp. 115-251.
51. Woodhull, a native of Long Island, who had fought for the British during the French and Indian wars was at the time of the British landings on Long Island at the head of militia forces determined upon the removal of livestock that might have been useful to Howe. He was captured near Jamaica and committed to a British prison ship. His capture and subsequent treatment constitute one of the many ugly moments of the Revolution. Lieutenant Jabez Finch, of General Huntington's regiment, has the story: "On ye 6th [of September] General Woodhull, of ye Long Island militia, was sent home from ye Mentor to ye Hospital at Newatrect [New Utrecht]; he was an aged Gentleman [in his 55th year], & was taken by a party of ye Enemy's light Horse at Jameca [Jamaica], altho he was not taken in arms, yet those Bloodthirsty Savages [because he would not say "God save the King"] cut & wounded him in ye head and other parts of ye body, with their Swords, in a most Inhuman manner of which wounds he Died at ye Hospital; and altho ye Director of their affairs took but little care to preserve his Life yet they were so generous to his lady, as to endulge her with liberty to carry home ye General's corpse and bury it with Deacence." (See Thompson, I, 199, 206.).

V: The New Jersey Campaign

1. Fitzpatrick, *Writings*, VI, 294.
2. Kirkbride's Ferry is at Bellevue, opposite Bordentown, which is at the confluence of the Delaware River, Black's Creek and Crosswicks Creek. At the time of the Revolution it was operated by Joseph Kirkbride, who the British supposed had facilitated the escape of Washington's army. In revenge they burned down the home of Joseph Kirkbride.
3. Hand Papers, item # 253.
4. Ibid., item # 254.
5. David Fischer, p. 237.
6. Whether it was the painter's intent to include Edward Hand on the boat that carried the Commander-in-Chief is not definitely known. But there

is good reason to believe it was so. When the Edward Hand Chapter of the Daughters of the American Revolution was formed in Ottawa, Kansas, one of the two charter members who were descendants of Edward Hand, with the understanding that her ancestor was one of the figures in the now famous painting, requested of the painter a rendering of the painting. As Leutze did oblige, with no denial of the officer's assumed identity, it is reasonable to suppose that his intent was indeed to portray Colonel Edward Hand. The painting now hangs in the Ottawa Library. (See Afterword).

After fifty-three years in the Metropolitan Museum of Art in New York City and exhibit periods at the Art Museum in Dallas, Texas, and at the Washington Crossing State Park, the original painting (twelve feet by twenty feet!) has been, since 1970, returned to the Metropolitan Museum. For a very good account of Leutze's famous painting, see *Washington's Crossing*, pp. 1-6.

As for Lieutenant James Monroe, who had dropped out of the College of William Mary in order to participate in the revolution, and was not yet nineteen by the time of the crossing, the same is true. And he is also the principal figure in another famous painting, John Trumbull's depiction of "The Capture of the Hessians at the Battle of Trenton." Monroe, who indeed was wounded at the battle, having taken a musket ball in the shoulder, may be seen lying wounded at left center of the painting.

7. Forrest was promoted to major shortly after the battle of Trenton, on March 3, and to Lt. Colonel Dec. 2, 1778. He resigned from the Continental Army just before the siege of Yorktown, on October 7, 1781. As a Federalist, he represented Pennsylvania in the United States House of Representatives, 1819-1823.

8. Fermoy, seven years older than Hand, was a Frenchman. But he was not Lafayette. He resigned his commission in January of 1779, having disgraced himself, not only at Assunpink, but in the surrender of Fort Ticonderoga in July of 1777, and having been rejected for promotion to Major General. He returned to the French West Indies.

9. Scott had taken command of the 5th Virginia Regiment in February of 1776 at the Richmond County Courthouse. There were Lancaster men in it.

10. David Fischer, p. 281; Wilkinson, *Memoirs*, I, 135; Samuel Stelle Smith, *The Battle of Princeton*, p. 11.

11. Fitzpatrick, *Writings*, VI, 442-443 and 443n. See also Wilkinson, *Memoirs of My Own Time*, I, 131.

12. David Fischer, p. 251; see also Samuel Stelle Smith, *The Battle of Trenton*, p. 23.

13. Ketchum, p. 286.

14. Ketchum, p. 288. Whether de Fermoy was drunk at the time of his flight back down the road to Trenton, or became so afterwards is not known.

15. Wilkinson, *Memoirs*, I, 137. Quoted by David Fischer, p. 296.

16. Wilkinson, *Memoirs*, I, 135-136; Craig, pp. 47-49; David Fischer, p. 296.

17. Wilkinson, *Memoirs*, I, 137.

~ *Notes* ~ 331

18. Ketchum, p. 289.
19. Ibid., p. 288.
20. Henry Knox to Lucy Knox, Jan. 7, 1777; quoted by Stryker, p. 451.
21. Stryker, pp. 263-264; David Fischer, p. 297.
22. Graydon (1752-1818), an attorney, was a delegate to the 1790 Pennsylvania Constitutional Convention.
23. Graydon, *Memories of His Own Time.* Quoted by Stryker, pp. 263-264. Certainly there was lots of evidence to suggest, if not to prove, that Hausegger was communicating with the British during the war. And, indeed, in 1782 he was declared a traitor and his property, which was in Lancaster County, forfeited. He died shortly after, in 1786.
24. Lengel, p. 201; David Fischer, pp. 297-298; Wilkinson, *Memoirs*, I, 138.
25. Note: Peckham, p. 293.
26. Stryker, pp. 263-264. Winthrop Sargent commanded troops also at Trenton, the Brandywine, Germantown, and Monmouth. He was commissioned by Congress the first Secretary of the Northwest Territory.
27. Ketchum, p. 290.
28. Ibid., p. 291.
29. Idem.
30. Hugh Mercer was a longtime good friend of George Washington. A nineteen-year-old survivor of the grisly 1746 battle of Culloden, he had come to America in March of 1747 as a fugitive from his turbulent homeland. He was in Philadelphia in May. He was the first physician to practice medicine in what is today Franklin County, Pennsylvania. He was with Washington at the battle of Fort Necessity. As the captain of a company of Pennsylvania militiamen he marched to the Allegheny as a member of Colonel John Armstrong's expedition which destroyed the Delaware Indian village of Kittanning. He suffered a wound to his right arm in this battle. He rose to the rank of colonel and was with Washington and Armstrong in the army of General John Forbes, which in 1758 captured Fort Duquesne. At one time or another Mercer was in command of the garrisons at Forts Pitt, Venango, and Augusta. During the years 1761-1775 he practiced medicine in Fredericksburg, Va., in the region of Washington's boyhood home. He bought Washington's childhood farm, the Ferry Farm, in 1774, but never had a chance to live there. One of his patients at this time was Washington's mother, Mary Ball Washington.

    Mercer had the command of the Third Virginia Regiment of the Continental Line from the time of its formation (December, 1775) until the time of his promotion to Brigadier General in June of 1776. He had been commissioned by Washington as Surgeon General of the Continental Army. He was in the middle of the action at Trenton. His tragic death at Princeton was one of the most costly losses suffered by the Continental Army.

    The oak tree under which the mortally wounded general is thought to have rested was for a long time known as the Mercer Oak, a living memorial to the courageous martyrdom of General Hugh Mercer until it was felled by high winds on March 3, 2000. The Clarke House, to which the wounded general was borne, is to this day preserved as a museum on the grounds of the Princeton Battlefield. And the general's sword is today one of the most precious of historical items belonging to the Saint Andrew's Society of Philadelphia. It is carried always in the procession of the Society's Annual Dinner.

The British poet Alfred Noyes wrote a poem for the battle site, and at Stockton and Bayard Streets in Princeton (on the Battlefield Park property) there has been erected a monument commemorating the battle. It was designed by sculptor Frederick MacMonniat and was dedicated by President Warren Harding.

Four states, besides New Jersey, have honored General Mercer by giving his name to a county. The community of Mercersburg in Pennsylvania, which is the birthplace of the country's fifteenth president, James Buchanan, bears his name. And so, of course, does the Mercersburg Academy, a private, secondary, co-educational boarding school. In Fredericksburg, Virginia, there was erected to Mercer's memory, in 1906, a bronze statue. It stands on Washington Avenue, at Fauquier Street. Two streets in that town are named for Mercer, as well as the apothecary shop and an elementary school. A second memorial statue, on October 25, 1970, was erected at Red Bank, New Jersey, on the Delaware River, south of Camden, and very near to the site of the Revolutionary War fort that was named for the general.

31. Cadwalader, although he had declined promotion to brigadier general already and would again, was considered a general.
32. Graydon, *Memoirs of His Own Time,* as published by *The New York Times,* p. 73.
33. Ketchum, p. 307; see also McCullough, p. 289.
34. Ibid., p. 309.
35. Idem.
36. Quoted by McCullough, p. 291.

VI: Fort Pitt

1. Fitzpatrick, *Writings,* VII, 29, 241.
2. Ibid., VII, 289.
3. Ibid., VII, 314, 326-327.
4. Ford, VII, 252.
5. Although in the literature there exists some confusion in dates, James Chambers was born on April 5, 1736, in the Pennsylvania settlement which was founded by his father, Benjamin Chambers, and is today's Chambersburg, Pennsylvania. He had been an officer, under the provincial law, in the British service, but resigned his commission when the rebellion seemed imminent. In accord with the resolution passed by the Continental Congress, he raised a company of 125

riflemen and with the First Pennsylvania Regiment marched to Cambridge. In April of 1775, at the age of thirty-nine, he was commissioned Captain of a company. In July of 1776, he was commissioned Lieutenant Colonel, and on March 12, 1777, was made Colonel Commandant of what was now being called the 10th Pennsylvania Regiment. He served throughout the war, at Long Island, through the New Jersey campaign, at Piscataway, Somerset Court House, New Brunswick, in the Neshaminy encampment, at the Brandywine (where he was severely wounded), Paoli, Germantown, Whitemarsh, Valley Forge, Monmouth, Bergen Heights, and West Point. After his retirement in 1781, he served for four years as Justice of the Peace in Franklin County, Pa.; and for his last twenty years he was Associate Judge, Court of Common Pleas, in Franklin County. He died on April 25, 1805.

6. Hand Papers, items # 256, 257, 258, 260.
7. "This Indenture made the fifteenth day of March in the year of our Lord one thousand four Hundred and Seventy Seven Between George Payne of Fawn Township in the County of York Yeoman in the Province of Pennsylvania . . . and Rachel his Wife of the one part and Edward Hand of the Borough of Lancaster in the County of Lancaster Practitioner of Physic of the other part [land that Payne had secured in April of 1751 and April of 1757] in consideration of the Sum of nine Hundred and Eighty-five pounds and Ten Shillings *lawful* money of Pennsylvania's *lawful money of Pennsylvania* to them [George and Rachel Payne] in Hand well and truly paid by the said Edward Hand." (Jasper Yeates a witness)

"This Indenture made the tenth day of April in the year of our Lord one thousand, seven hundred and seventy-seven Between Robert Haislet of Fawn Township in the County of York Yeoman & Hannah his wife of the one Part and Edward Hand of the Borough of Lancaster in the County of Lancaster Practitioner of Physic of the Other Part, whereas in pursuance of a warrant from the Proprietary Land office bearing Date the thirtieth day of March 1763 granted unto Robert Stevenson for fifty acres of land . . . the following described Tract of Land situate in Fawn Township . . . . Now the Indenture Witnesseth that the said Robert Haislet and Hannah his wife for and in Consideration of one hundred and ninety-five Pounds lawful Money of Pennsylvania to them in Hand well and truly paid by the said Edward Hand." (Jasper Yeates a witness)

Hand "by deed dated 9th February 1779 conveyed the same to the said Levin Bill Hopkins, who dying Intestate the said Gerrard [Hopkins] was appointed his Administrator." The document is signed with the governor's seal by Thomas Mifflin, President of the Supreme Executive Council.

8. Ibid., item # 261. It has been theorized that "Sancho" is perhaps the name of a farm animal (a mule maybe or a hog) named for Don Quixote's

squire Sancho Panza because of his prodigious appetite.
9. Bowden, item # 1.
10. Hand's brother-in-law Jasper Ewing was nine years younger than the general. Apparently named for his mother's uncle, Judge Jasper Yeates, under whom he studied law, he served General Edward Hand as Brigadier Major and as Adjutant for most of the time Hand was in command of the Western Department. Hand generally referred to him as Jessy, Jesse, Jefry, or Jeffy.
11. Hand Papers, item # 262.
12. Thwaites & Kellogg, *Frontier Defense*, pp. 1-3.
13. *Pennsylvania Archives*, First Series, XII, 371.
14. Letter of Thomas Scott to Timothy Matlack, Aug. 1, 1778, *Pennsylvania Archives*, First Series, VI, 673.
15. McClelland was later captured by the hostile Delawares during the anti-Indian Crawford expedition and tortured to death (Kellogg, *Frontier Retreat*, p. 408).
16. For a sketch of Fort Hand see Thwaites and Kellogg, *Frontier Defense*, p. 41, note 83. Some feel that they know the exact location of Fort Hand. Upon a corner of what they take to be the remains of the fort's foundation a huge boulder, weighing some four tons, and including a bronze tablet, has been installed by the Fort Hand Chapter of the Daughters of the American Revolution. The information that we have has been provided courtesy of the Leechburg Museum, Leechburg, Pa. See *Patriots of the American Revolution,* November 20, 2010.
17. Thwaites & Kellogg, *Frontier Defense*, pp. 5-6.
18. Ibid., p.16.
19. After the death of Chief White Eyes from smallpox in 1778 (which put an end to the chances for an American-Lenape alliance), Morgan cared for his son, George Morgan White Eyes, for several years. The lad graduated from the College of New Jersey (now Princeton University).
20. Gibson was Irish, his father having been born in Antrim, Ireland, and on coming to America (in 1730), to Lancaster, he became a trader and was very active among the Conestoga Indians in the Lancaster area. Born in 1740, he served the Forbes Expedition at age seventeen, and continued active in the military, participating in Lord Dunmore's War as a Britisher and in the Revolution as a patriot. During the Pontiac Wars he was captured by the Delaware Indians and was saved from being burned at the stake when an Indian woman who had just lost her son suddenly adopted him. He lived among the Indians for a time but was set free at Logstown thanks to the Henri Bouquet expedition. But he built a house here and married a Mingo, who was, not long after (May, 1774), murdered by settlers.

Gibson was second in command to Colonel Daniel Brodhead for the anti-Indian expedition up the Allegheny in 1779; and when Brodhead was removed as Head of the Western Department in May of 1781, Gibson assumed command at Fort Pitt. Later he fought in the Tecumseh Wars,

~ *Notes* ~ 335

and became very active in the Indiana Territory. He served as Secretary to Governor William Henry Harrison, and in Harrison's absence twice served as Acting Governor of the Indiana Territory.
21. For an account of the Gratz brothers, who were orphaned in their childhood, see the Sidney Fish biography, *Barnard and Michael Gratz: Their Lives and Times.*
22. This George Chroghan should not be confused with the later George Croghan, who fought in the war of 1812 and was the "hero of Fort Stephenson." For the story of George Croghan see Nicholas Wainwright's biography, *George Croghan: Wilderness Diplomat.*
23. Hand Papers, items # 262, 263.
24. Ibid., item # 272.
25. It has been noted that Hand's hospital was the first federal hospital erected in the country and that for sixty-nine years it was "the only medical facility west of the Alleghenies." See "Peters Township," pp. 877-899 in *History of Washington County, Pennsylvania*. Edward Hand's name appears, together with those of a number of military men on the assessment listings for Peters Township for the year 1788. In this year his property was assessed at 1300 acres.
26. Draper MSS 3 E 1. A. L. S. See also Kellogg, *Frontier Retreat*, pp. 224-227.
27. Knouff, p. 179.
28. Knouff, p. 179. See also the *General Hand Correspondence*, Darlington Memorial Library, Pittsburgh.
29. Thwaites and Kellogg, *Frontier Defense*, p. 86.
30. Idem.
31. Edward Hand to Jasper Yeates, July 12, 1777. Quoted by Thwaites and Kellogg, *Frontier Defense*, p. 190.
32. Knouff, p. 192.
33. Timothy Pickering to George Washington, May 19, 1778. See *Washington Papers*, Revolutionary War Series. See also Thwaites and Kellogg, *Frontier Defense*, p. 192.
34. *Pennsylvania Archives*, First Series, VI, 601-602.
35. *Pennsylvania Archives*, First Series, V, 443-444.
36. Colonel William Fleming (1729-1795), was, like Hand, a physician. In Lord Dunmore's War, he led the Botetourt County Militia in the climactic battle of Point Pleasant, and was most heroic in doing so. For a time he acted as Governor of Virginia.
37. Thwaites & Kellogg, *Frontier Defense*, pp. 30-33.
38. *Pennsylvania Archives*, First Series V, 443.
39. *Colonial Records*, XI, 261.
40. *Pennsylvania Archives*, First Series, V, 528. See also Ford, VIII, 148-149.
41. *Pennsylvania Archives*, First Series, V, 540-541.
42. Thwaites & Kellogg, *Frontier Defense*, pp. 48-49.
43. Thwaites & Kellogg, *Frontier Defense*, pp. 49-50; Hand Papers, item #

270.
44. Fitzpatrick, *Writings*, IX, 175.
45. Ibid., IX, 361-362.
46. Thwaites & Kellogg, *Frontier Defense*, p. 74.
47. See "Foreman's Defeat," pp. 106-112 in Thwaites & Kellogg, *Frontier Defense*. *Frontier Defense* provides a list of the names of those killed.
48. Thwaites & Kellogg, *Frontier Defense*, pp. 113-118.
49. Manuscript in New York Public Library. Thwaites & Kellogg, *Frontier Defense*, pp. 118-120. See also Knouff, p. 179.
50. Hand Papers, item # 273.
51. Colonel William Russell, of southwest Virginia, was nine years older than General Hand. He had fought in the battle of Point Pleasant, and at Yorktown. Educated at the College of William and Mary, he served Virginia in the Commonwealth's House of Delegates. He assisted in the drafting of the Declaration of Independence. His second wife, Elizabeth Henry, was a sister to Patrick Henry. She outlived her husband by many years, and proved a most important figure in the history of the Methodist Church in the United States.
52. Thwaites & Kellogg, *Frontier Defense*, pp. 120-122; 133-134.
53. Ibid., pp. 138-139.
54. Thwaites & Kellogg, *Frontier Defense*, p. 146; Hand Papers, item # 275.
55. Thwaites & Kellogg, *Frontier Defense*, pp. 154-156.
56. Thwaites & Kellogg, *Frontier Defense*, p. 156; Hand Papers, item # 276.
57. Chief Cornstalk was buried at Fort Randolph, but in 1840 his remains were removed to the Mason County Courthouse grounds. Later they were moved again, this time back to Point Pleasant, where the rivers he loved so much come together. He was one of the most distinguished of Native Americans, an orator nonpareil, some insisting that he spoke with more passion and a greater eloquence than did those celebrated Virginians Patrick Henry and Richard Henry Lee.
58. Letter of Roberdeau to Wharton, Nov. 19, 1777, *Pennsylvania Archives*, First Series, VI, 18.
59. Ford, IX (1777), 943.
60. Lochry's anti-Indian expeditionary force on a mission down the Ohio River, during the time Daniel Brodhead was Head of the Western Department, was wiped out in July of 1781 (every man killed or captured) by George Girty (brother to the infamous Simon Girty) and the Mohawk Chief Joseph Brant.
61. *Pennsylvania Archives*, First Series, VI, 69.
62. *Pennsylvania Archives*, First Series, V, 741; VI, 68; *Frontier Forts*, II, 236 and passim.
63. *The Papers of George Washington*, Revolutionary War Series, XII, 562-563.
64. Crawford, a surveyor whose home was on the Youghiogheny (present Connellsville), had done, over the past decade a lot of land acquisition

for Washington. With Washington he had served the Forbes expedition and was a very close friend to both Washington and General John Armstrong of Carlisle, also a surveyor.

65. Thwaites & Kellogg, *Frontier Defense*, pp. 201-202.
66. Draper MSS 3 S 28-32. "Recollections of Samuel Murphy," quoted by Thwaites & Kellogg, *Frontier Defense*, 215-216, 219-220. Knouff, pp. 164-165. Buck and Buck, pp. 188-189. See also *Pennsylvania Archives*, Sixth Series, II, 272.
67. Edward Hand to Jasper Yeates, March 7, 1778. MS in New York Public Library. See also Hand Papers. Quoted by Knouff, pp. 164-165. Thwaites & Kellogg, *Frontier Defense*, pp. 215-216.
68. Hand Papers, item # 278.
69. *The Herald* (Sharon, Pa.), June 29, 1976.
70. George Morgan's Letter Book.
71. Captain John Killbuck was, together with Pipe and White Eyes, one of the three principal Delaware chiefs at this time. Captain Pipe had succeeded his uncle Chief Custaloga in 1774.
72. *The Herald* (Sharon, Pa.), June 29, 1976. See also Thwaites & Kellogg, *Frontier Defense*.
73. *The Herald* (Sharon, Pa.), June 29, 1976.
74. Remarkably, a later Head of the Western Department, his fellow officer and a fellow physician, Brigadier General William Irvine, had an even worse "incident" to stomach. On March 6-7, while General Irvine was at home in Carlisle, on leave from Fort Pitt, there occurred the massacre of Gnadenhuetten. In retaliation for Indian raids on the settlements, a militia force from what is now Washington County, south of Fort Pitt, determined to destroy three settlements of Moravian Indians. Ninety horsemen, organized and led by Colonel David Williamson, set out for the villages. Finding no warriors, they pretended friendship and rounded up the women and children and old men from two of the villages. They took a vote on what to do. Seventy-two of the ninety voted for murder! The Indians, absolutely innocent of any crime, and certainly helpless, and friendly and Christianized, were herded into the chapel, and were murdered, one at a time, by one after another of the militiamen, with a cooper's mallet, that was very effective in crushing a skull.

The Commandant of the Western Department, when he had news of the "mallet murders," was thunderstruck. He was on horseback at once, and in a remarkably short time was back at Fort Pitt. As the details poured into him, he became more and more horrified. In a letter to his wife, he declared that those responsible for the murders "must be hanged."

He was able to identify the leaders of the militia easily enough. Everybody knew who they were. But Irvine, in conducting interviews, discovered, incredibly, that the people of Pittsburgh and the settlements of the region, while not actually applauding the heinous deed, were not disturbed by it! In the end, nobody was punished. Except by the Indians. Their turn would come. The Gnaddenhuetten massacre has been described in many places. One is Betts, *Bombardier John Harris*, pp. 246-258.

75. The Secretary of War at this time was composed of five parties. These were Quartermaster General Thomas Mifflin, Adjutant General Timothy Pickering, Richard Peters (permanent secretary), General Horatio Gates, and Commissary General Joseph Trumbull.
76. Thwaites & Kellogg, *Frontier Defense*, pp. 188-189.
77. Ibid., pp. 189-192.
78. Ibid., pp. 196-197.
79. See letter of Patrick Henry to Hand, Jan. 15, 1778, and letter of Captain James Willing to Hand, January 7. (Thwaites & Kellogg, *Frontier Defense*, pp. 198-199). On the expedition of David Rogers to New Orleans see Morris, "The Fatal Expedition of Colonel Rogers," in *Historical Tales*, pp. 145-152.
80. Some accounts identify the third commissioner as Samuel Washington, George Washington's brother (rather than McDowell).
81. Hand Papers, item # 280.
82. Thwaites & Kellogg, *Frontier Defense*, pp. 238-240.
83. Ibid., pp. 221-222.
84. Ibid., p. 245.
85. Ibid., pp. 246-248.
86. Ibid., pp. 249-250.
87. Siebert, p. 15.
88. Thwaites & Kellogg, *Frontier Defense*, p. 252.
89. The Holston is a major river system in southwest Virginia. It is named after Stephen Holstein, who, as early as 1746, built a log cabin on the upper reaches of one fork.
90. Thwaites & Kellogg, *Frontier Defense*, pp. 271-272.
91. Boatner, pp. 484-485.
92. Hand Papers, items # 284, 286.
93. Ibid., item # 287.
94. Ibid., item 288.
95. *Pennsylvania Archives*, Second Series, X, 312-313.
96. Ibid., X, 314.
97. Ibid., X, 314-315.
98. Lieutenant Colonel Robert Monckton was the younger half-brother of the more distinguished General Henry Monckton. Edward Hand had experienced some dealings with him, particularly at Assunpink Creek in the second battle of Trenton, where Monckton had had the command of a hastily formed brigade of grenadiers. Monckton had fought also at the battle of Long Island (where he was wounded), and had led battalions of grenadiers at both the Brandywine and Germantown.
99. Ibid., X, 317-318.
100. Thwaites & Kellogg, *Frontier Defense*, pp. 293-294.

~ Notes ~ 339

101. Ibid., pp. 297-298.
102. Fitzpatrick, *Writings*, XI, 461.
103. Fitzpatrick, *Writings*, XIII, 85n. Most of the opinions that were returned to Washington by October 20 may be read in the *Washington Papers*.

VII: Wyoming

1. Besides being named to the important offices under President Washington, Pickering was made Commissioner to the Iroquois and negotiated the very important Treaty of Canandaigua in 1794. He was elected to the U. S. Senate from Massachusetts in 1803, and to the House of Representatives for the years 1812-1817.
2. Myers p. 13.
3. Idem.
4. Graymont, pp. 169-171.
5. Samuel Robert Smith, *The Story of Wyoming Valley*, p. 40.
6. Ibid., p. 40.
7. Ibid., p. 41.
8. Ibid., p. 45.
9. Abler, p. 101.
10. Quoted by Samuel Robert Smith, p. 45.
11. For this account of the Wyoming massacre, see Betts, *The Hatchet and the Plow,* pp. 66-74.

VIII: The Sullivan Expedition

1. *Correspondence of John Stark*, pp. 193-194.
2. For Thomas Hartley's letter to Congress of October 8, see Henry Laurens to George Washington, 13 October, and note 4 to that document, *The Papers of George Washington*, Revolutionary War Series.
3. Washington had given these orders to Colonel Philip Van Cortlandt's 2nd New York Regiment (See Washington's letters of October 17 to George Clinton, James Clinton, and Van Cortlandt, *The Papers of George Washington*, Revolutionary War Series.).
4. Letter from Washington to Henry Laurens, October 22-23, 1778. For the report on the proposed Chemung expedition that George Clinton, Philip Schuyler and Edward Hand composed on October 22, see George Washington to Laurens, October 26-27, and note 6 to that document. See also George Clinton's plan of October 20 for an expedition to Chemung (letter to George Washington, October 21, note 2. *The Papers of George Washington*, Revolutionary War Series.
5. Ichabod Alden was the great grandson of the Mayflower pilgrim John Alden. In 1775 he was appointed Lieutenant Colonel of the Plymouth militia. He saw action in the siege of Boston. He had been promoted to Colonel in November of 1776 and given the command of the

Massachusetts Regiment (sixteen soldiers only) which was in the fall of 1778 garrisoned at Cherry Valley, New York.
6. *The Sullivan-Clinton Campaign*, p. 20.
7. Fitzpatrick, *Writings*, XIII, 110-112.
8. Stark, a native of New Hampshire, was sixteen years older than Hand. He was something of a hero during the siege of Boston. He commanded troops at Trenton, at Princeton and during the defeat of Burgoyne. He was made a brigadier general October 4, 1777. He would have the command of the Northern Department three times during the years 1778-1781. He is famous for the motto "Live Free or Die," which was adopted as a slogan by his native state of New Hampshire in 1945.
9. Washington to Hand, Oct. 21, 1778. *The Papers of George Washington* Digital Edition, ed. Theodore J. Crackel (Charlottesville, Va.: University of Virginia Press, Rotunda 2008). Hereinafter cited as Crackel.
10. Fitzpatrick, *Writings*, IV, 315n.
11. Crackel, Washington letter to Hand, 16 Nov., 1778.
12. Crackel, Washington letter to Hand, 20 Nov., 1778; Fitzpatrick, *Writings*, XIII, 292-293, 306.
13. Pulaski was a Polish cavalry officer, who came to this country (arriving at Marblehead, Massachusetts) July 23, 1777. Known as the "father of American cavalry," he was something of a hero at the Brandywine, and has been given credit for averting a total disaster. He fought also at Germantown and had been ordered to serve the Sullivan Campaign, but requested and was given assignment to the southern front. At the siege of Savannah, where again his conduct was described as heroic, he was mortally wounded.
14. Fitzpatrick, *Writings*, XIII, 338-339.
15. Crackel, Hand letter to Washington, 28th Nov., 1778.
16. Crackel, letter of Washington to Hand, Jan. 1, 1779; Fitzpatrick, *Writings*, XIII, 475.
17. Crackel, Washington to Hand, 7th Feb., 1779; Fitzpatrick, *Writings*, XIV, 74-76.
18. Fitzpatrick, *Writings*, XIV, 163-164.
19. Answers to Washington's nineteen questions, not only from Hand but from Colonels John Cox, William Patterson, Charles Stewart, and Zebulon Butler, are summarized in the *Washington Papers* as a document "Queries Concerning the Indian Country," March '79.
20. Crackel, Hand to Washington, 20 March and Washington to Hand 24 March, 1779; Fitzpatrick, *Writings*, XIV, 286-289.
21. Fitzpatrick, *Writings*, XIV, 198-201.
22. Craft, p. 10.
23. Ibid., p. 9.
24. Crackel, Washington to Hand, April 30, 1779.
25. Bowden, item 15. See also "Correspondence of General Edward Hand of the Continental Line," *Pennsylvania Magazine of History and*

Biography, XXXIII, No. 3 (1908), 356.
26. Fitzpatrick, *Writings*, XIV, 355.
27. *Pennsylvania Archives*, Second Series, XI, 73; Linn and Egle, II, 73.
28. *Pennsylvania Archives*, First Series, VII, 321.
29. Ibid., p. 342.
30. Ibid., p. 344.
31. Fitzpatrick, *Writings*, XIV, 492-493.
32. General Poor was born in Massachusetts, but was living in New Hampshire at the time of Lexington/Concord. He was given the command of one of the three New Hampshire regiments which were contributed to Washington's army at Cambridge. He built a considerable reputation for courage at the battles of Stillwater and Saratoga. He died of a fever (possibly malaria, but more likely typhus or "camp fever"), before the end of the war, at Hackensack, New Jersey, September 9, 1780. His death, like that of Hugh Mercer at Princeton and that of Baron de Kalb at Camden, just a month before, came as a terrible blow to the Continental Army. Lafayette, who was extremely fond of all three of these officers, on his second visit to the United States after the war, at a public entertainment, proposed a toast to "The memory of Light Infantry Poor and Yorktown Scammel."

Washington, who was much moved by the loss of General Poor, declared the general to be "an officer of distinguished merit, who as a citizen and a soldier, had every claim to the esteem of his country." (*Seneca County Centennial of Sullivan's Expedition*, p. 12)
33. Remarkably similar are the lives lived by Generals Hand and Irvine. Both officers were born in Ireland, both studied medicine at Dublin, both served the British in their early years as surgeon mates, both came at an early age to America, and both settled in southeastern Pennsylvania. Both married women much younger than themselves. And both had many children, Hand eight and Irvine eleven. Both were active in the pre-war meetings to consider independence. Both were officers in William Thompson's rifle regiment. Both served as Head of the Western Department, headquartered at Fort Pitt. Both had to suffer the shame of atrocities committed by the militia forces of the Pittsburgh area. Both served the Continental Army for the entire war, not resigning their commissions until after the signing of the Treaty of Paris in September of 1783. Both resumed the practice of medicine in Lancaster-Carlisle. Both represented Pennsylvania in the U. S. House of Representatives.
34. Crackel, letter of Hand to Washington, 12 May, 1779; Fitzpatrick, *Writings*, XIV, 65 and XV, 124-126, 197. For a discussion of the ongoing rank dispute between the two generals, see The Board of War to Washington, May, n.d.
35. Washington had had the problem as early as January of this year. Because of its complexity he had kept Hand "upon a detached command." (See Washington's memorandum of January, n.d., Fitzpatrick, *Writings*,

XIV, 65). Washington's May 22 letter to the Board of War reads as follows: "Besides the absence of General Hand and the want of a State of his claim, the Resolution of the 4th of February only authorises me to settle the rank of officers under the degree of a Brigadier, and therefore at any rate, the case between him and General Irvine could not be taken up without special authority for the purpose; which has been customary where General Officers had disputes, who derive their appointments as well as their Commissions, not from any particular State, but immediately from Congress themselves. But these are not the only difficulties, and it appears to me if General Irvine's claim is to be taken up, that Congress should determine it themselves. It is not a mere personal dispute between him and General Hand, but from its nature and his Letter it is to involve many embarrassing and important consequences and at best is to supersede sundry other Brigadiers, by obtaining a Commission anterior to General Hand's in point of date. This would affect the interests of so many Officers immediately and ultimately that it would not be easy to form a Court to decide it. I cannot tell, nor do I mean to enter upon a consideration of the merits of the question between the two Gentlemen, or to intimate which of them ought to have been promoted first; but to establish the claim General Irvine makes, would be to violate and exclude the principle which has been adopted by Congress and which has generally prevailed, that of appointing Brigadiers from the Officers of the *line of each state*, in proportion to their Quota's [sic] of Troops, without regard to their seniority *in the line of the army*; and which has made the dates of their appointments the only and absolute criterion to fix their precedence. The idea of relative rank in such cases never existed in our service, and were it to obtain, it might nearly unhinge the whole System of the Army. Priority of appointment, where *a single person* has been promoted, and in the order of appointment, *where several* have been elected together, have constantly decided their precedence unless there were special directions to the contrary; and to introduce a different principle, would be to set a float ten thousand difficulties, and perhaps to dissolve the Army. If it were, as I have observed a mere question between General Hand and General Irvine on an appointment made at the same time, or if there were no intermediate promotions between theirs as they were both in the same line, the case might admit an investigation and decision without involving such great difficulties, but as matters are otherwise, it is hardly within the compass of human foresight to prescribe boundaries to the mischiefs to which the claim leads in all its extent." (Fitzpatrick, XV, 124-126)

36. Fitzpatrick, *Writings*, XV, 196-197; XIX, 112; XIX, 138.
37. Ibid., XV, 189-190.
38. Ibid., XV, 196-200; XVI, 141-142.
39. Rogers in the year previous had been made Brigade Chaplain in the Pennsylvania Line. Born at Newport, Rhode Island, July 22, 1751, he

became Pastor of the Baptist Church in Philadelphia. When the war broke out he was appointed Chaplain of the Pennsylvania Rifle Regiment, Colonel Samuel Miles commanding. He held the position of Brigade Chaplain until 1781, when he retired from military service. In 1789 he was appointed a Professor of English and Belles Lettres at the University of Pennsylvania. In 1816-17 he served in the Pennsylvania Legislature. He died in Philadelphia, April 7, 1824. The journal which he kept for a portion of the Sullivan Expedition, was published, with notes and biography, as No. 7 of the *Rhode Island Historical Tracts*, by Sidney B. Rider, Providence, Rhode Island, 1879. It was reprinted in the *Pennsylvania Archives*, Second Series XV, 257-288; and in Cook, pp. 247 ff. Some portions were printed in Vols. I and II of the *Universal Magazine*, 1797. (See Cook, p. 246)

40. *Pennsylvania Archives*, Second Series XV, 257-258.
41. Idem.
42. *Pennsylvania Archives*, Second Series, XV, 258-259.
43. Ibid., p. 260.
44. Israel Shreve, with the rank of Colonel in the 2nd New Jersey Regiment would later fight at the battle of Springfield. General Sullivan on the way north left Shreve and his brother John at Tioga's newly built Fort Sullivan. Israel Shreve died on the very same day as did his General Washington.
45. *Pennsylvania Archives*, Second Series XV, 264-265.
46. Ibid., pp. 265-266.
47. Snowden was wounded at the battle of Guilford Court House in March of 1781.
48. Cook, p. 252.
49. *Pennsylvania Archives*, Second Series, XV, 272.
50. Cook, p. 255.
51. Idem.
52. Cook, p. 260.
53. Hand diary of the Sullivan Campaign, New York Public Library, Ref. # 4813. Quoted by Craig, p. 66.
54. Ibid., p. 261.
55. Ibid., p. 262.
56. Rogers journal, in Cook, p. 263, and the journal of Headley, in Cook, p.194.
57. Cook, p. 94; Joseph Fischer, p. 89.
58. Joseph Fischer, p. 89.
59. *The Sullivan-Clinton Campaign*, p. 38. For a good short account of the battle see, pp. 38-39.
60. Cook, p. 474. For Sullivan's report to Washington, see Cook, pp. 473-476.
61. *Pennsylvania Archives*, Second Series, XV, 755-756; quoted by Joseph Fischer, pp. 90-91. For a full account of the battle, see Fischer, pp. 89-95. See also the account supplied by General John S. Clark, in Craft, pp. 29-40.

62. *Pennsylvania Archives*, Second Series, XV, 756.
63. Trussell, *The Pennslvania Line*, p. 228.
64. Ibid., p. 208 and 208n.
65. Cook, p. 199.
66. Ibid., p. 197.
67. Ibid., p. 476.
68. Ibid., p. 382.
69. In the fall of 1778, in response to Wyoming, the Eleventh Pennsylvania, together with other troops of the militia, was called into action. Hartley's expedition, though modest when compared to that of the later Sullivan campaign, has to be counted a success. His forces (200 soldiers), operating out of Fort Muncy, were able to negotiate the deep gorge of Lycoming Creek and make their way to Tioga. Although he did not catch up with Butler and his Royal Greens, for they had just fled the region, he did set fire to Queen Esther's town and eight other towns he came upon, including one, which was, unfortunately, completely innocent. Hand had asked permission of Washington (Dec. 17, 1778) to join Colonel Hartley at Wyoming in an attempt to reduce "the Indian and Tory Settlements remaining on the East Branch of the Susquehanna and Delaware.
70. Cook, p. 130.
71. The Reverend John Breckenridge, as quoted by Stone, in *The Life and Times of Red Jacket*, p. 22.
72. See Graymont, p.216.
73. Ibid., p. 217.
74. Seaver, p.73.
75. *Pennsylvania Archives*, First Series, VII, 715.
76. *Colonial Records*, XII, 138.
77. Cook, p. 205.
78. Graymont, p. 192; Joseph Fischer, p. 7.
79. Anthony Wallace, p. 144.
80. Ellis, p. 59.
81. Anthony Wallace, pp. 145-146.

IX: Yorktown

1. Fitzpatrick.,*Writings*, XVII, 265.
2. Ibid., p. 281.
3. Ibid., p. 499.
4. Hand Papers, item # 292.
5. Ibid., items # 283, 294, and 295.
6. De Kalb was the highest ranking officer of the Continental Army to be killed in action during the Revolutionary War. Washington, who had come to know the general well at Valley Forge, and had always much respected him, said of him: "The manner in which he died fully justified the opinion which I ever entertained of him, and will endear

his memory to the country." Congress promptly passed a resolution, October 14, 1780: "*Resolved,* That a monument be erected to the memory of the late Major General the Baron De Kalb, in the city of Annapolis." More than a century later, on February 19, 1883, Congress *finally* appropriated the necessary funds, and on August 16, 1886, a statue of the General, fashioned in Rome by the sculptor Ephraim Keyser, was dedicated in Annapolis, Maryland. It stands before the courthouse in the state's capital. Long before that, in 1825, a monument was erected at Camden by the citizens of the community. The cornerstone was laid by de Kalb's student and dear friend Lafayette, when he visited the United States that same year. The silver trowel which Lafayette used is now in the possession of the Grand Lodge of Masons of South Carolina. On one side of the marker is carved: "His love of liberty induced him to leave the old world to aid the citizens of the new in their struggle for independence." Six counties in the United States are named for the much revered general. Betts, *Bombardier*, pp. 80-83, 90-92, 225-226. For an account of the action at Camden, see H. L. Landers, *The Battle of Camden.*

7. Dr. William Shippen, Jr., of the most distinguished Shippen family of Shippensburg, Lancaster, and Philadelphia (1736-1808), followed his father into medicine. He studied medicine with his father and at the College of New Jersey (now Princeton University) and earned a medical degree from Edinburgh Medical School in Scotland (Benjamin Rush's alma mater). With his friend Dr. John Morgan, he founded (in 1765) the country's first medical school, known at first as The College of Philadelphia and now as the University of Pennsylvania. He is considered responsible for the first maternity hospital in America, and is regarded as the first physician in this country to teach in a systematic way anatomy, and obstetrics. During the Revolution he served (1776) as Chief Physician and Director General of the Hospital of the Continental Army in New Jersey. He also for that same year (1776) held the office of Director General of the Hospitals West of the Hudson River. For the succeeding five years of the war he was Director of Hospitals for the Continental Army, a post which later would have the title Surgeon General of the U. S. Army. For this trial, and Hand's role in it, see Whitfield Bell, The Court Martial of Dr. William Shippen, Jr.

8. Fitzpatrick, *Writings*, XVIII, 109.
9. Fleming, p. 166.
10. Ibid., pp. 168-169.
11. Hand Papers, items # 296, 297.
12. For a full account of these battles, see Thomas Fleming, *The Battle for New Jersey.*
13. See Boatner, p. 485.
14. Whippany, "the place where the willow trees grow," was later an encampment site for Rochambeau and his French army of 5000 on their march south, August 27-28, 1781.

15. Hand Papers, item # 298.
16. Trussell, *Epic on the Schuylkill*, p.43.
17. Betts, *Bombardier John Harris*, pp. 111-112.
18. Hand Papers, item # 302.
19. Thacher, *Journal*, September 10, 1780. There is another theory (not popular) on the death of Enoch Poor. The theory is that his death was occasioned by wounds suffered in an illegal duel with a subordinate officer, the whole affair having been discreetly covered up.
20. Ibid., September 26, 1780.
21. For an eye-witness account of the execution, see Appendix A.
22. Hand to Yeates, October 3, 1780, New York Public Library.
23. The legion commanded by Armand Louis de Gontaut, duc de Lauzun, was a French regiment, the original French Foreign Legion. It was most active at White Plains and at Yorktown.
24. Huntington, a year older than Edward Hand, was a native of Connecticut. He raised a regiment and as its captain marched it the short distance to Cambridge on April 26, 1775. Because of the great courage he exhibited at Bunker Hill, he was made Colonel; and on May 12, 1777, he was promoted to Brigadier General. He was a member of the court martial of General Charles Lee, and also of that which condemned John André.
25. On these council meetings, see Fitzpatrick, *Writings*, XVIII, 164n, 195n, 482, 482n; XX, 5n, 9n, 272n.
26. Ibid., XX, 419, 471.
27. Ibid., XX, 470-471.
28. Hand Papers, items # 381, 382.
29. Fitzpatrick, *Writings*, XXI, 131-132.
30. The Continental Army, or most often just a portion of it, often camped at Pompton Lakes, which was in the mountains on the main route north. Washington himself was here in July of 1777 and again in March of 1782.
31. The twenty-eight-year-old Colonel Frederick Frelinghuysen served at Trenton and at Monmouth as an artillery captain. He was elected by New Jersey to the Second Continental Congress, 1779. He was made a brigadier general for Washington's ill-fated 1790 campaign against the Ohio Indians. He served in the United States Senate 1793-96. He was on "ready" for the Whiskey Rebellion. He died on his birthday, April 13, 1804.
32. George Washington to Colonel Israel Shreve, 21 January, 1781, Founders Online, National Archives. Source: The papers of Alexander Hamilton, II, 1779-1781, ed. Harold C. Syrett (New York: Columbia University Press, 1961, p. 541.
33. General Robert Howe, born the same year as Washington, and, like Washington a veteran of the French and Indian Wars, was a somewhat contentious and very controversial figure during the Revolution. He was very active in the Southern Department, assisting General Charles Lee

at the first siege of Charleston and assuming command (until close to the surrender of the city, when he was replaced by General Benjamin Lincoln) of the Continental forces defending Savannah in the winter of 1778-79. He was asked by Washington to serve as president of the court-martial board for the trial of Benedict Arnold for Arnold's conduct during his time in Philadelphia. He was named Commandant of West Point on February 21, 1780, and he held that post during the time immediately before the Arnold conspiracy. And he served on the court-martial board which sentenced John André to execution. The mutiny at Pompton Lakes was but one of several (including the Pennsylvania Mutiny of 1783) that he was asked to squelch. Of interest, too, is the fact that Robert Howe participated in the founding of the Society of the Cincinnati, and was the second officer to sign the national charter.

34. George Washington letter to Major General Robert Howe, January 22, 1781. Jared Sparks, The Writings of george Washington, VII, 380-381.
35. Hand Papers, item # 336.
36. Fitzpatrick, *Writings*, XXIII, 413; XXIV, 192.
37. Alexander Scammell was a Harvard educated attorney. He studied law with John Sullivan. He fought for Washington at Trenton, Princeton, Saratoga, and Monmouth. While at Valley Forge he was appointed Adjutant General, in which office he served January 5, 1778, until January 1, 1781, when he resigned and was succeeded by Edward Hand. He had been appointed executioner to Major John André. For the Yorktown campaign he commanded Scammell's Light Infantry at the battle of King's Bridge, and provided the vanguard for the army's march south to Yorktown. After his capture by the British at Yorktown, he may have been murdered. He died of wounds received either before or after his capture. George Washington thought him one of the funniest men in the army.
38. Fitzpatrick, *Writings*, XXII, 312-320. The instructions to Hand, incredibly detailed, are entitled "Thoughts on . . . the Surprise of . . . the North End of York Island."
39. Thacher, *Military Journal*, August 31, 1781.
40. Hand Papers, items # 306, 307, 308.
41. Ibid., item # 309.
42. Heuvel, p. 24. See also Greene, pp. 163, 183.
43. Hand to Yeates, October 12, 1781, Peter Force Transcripts.
44. Some accounts have Washington selecting General Richard Butler to receive the surrender sword. Washington at the dinner toasted "The Butlers and their five sons." Richard Butler, who as Major General was later second in command at the terrible defeat of General Arthur St. Clair by Little Turtle and the Ohio Indians, was killed in this battle on the Little Wabash, with two of his brothers, in the fall of 1791. See Betts, *Rank and Gravity*, p. 614.
45. Hand to Yeates, October 19, 1781, Peter Force Transcripts.

46. Craig, p. 95; Heuvel, p. 25.

X: Newburgh and New Windsor

1. Fitzpatrick, *Writings*, XXV, 48-49.
2. Ford, XXIII (1782), 836. See also *Papers of the Continental Congress*, No. 149, II, folio 209.
3. Hand Papers, items # 338, 340.
4. Hand to Yeates, March 31, 1783, New York Public Library.
5. Fitzpatrick, *Writings*, XXVI, 334, 336, 337. See also Thacher, *The American Revolution*, p. 341.
6. On the matter of national defense during peacetime, see Irwin; also Cress.
7. Fitzpatrick, *Writings*, XXVII, 302; Ellis, p.45.

XI: Lancaster

1. The meeting place of the Continental Congress (and thus the capital of the country) was changed a number of times during the Revolution, chiefly because of the British threat to Philadelphia and then the city's actual occupation. The meeting places of the Continental Congress: September 5, 1774, Philadelphia; May 11, 1775, Philadelphia; December 20, 1776, Baltimore; March 4, 1777, Philadelphia; September 27, 1777, the old Lancaster County Courthouse in Penn Square, Lancaster; September 30, 1777, York, Pa.; July 2, 1778, Philadelphia; June 30, 1783, Princeton, N. J.; November 26, 1783, Annapolis.
2. Some of the Hessian prisoners were confined in nearby Lebanon. Many of those held in Lancaster were employed as farmhands.
3. In Lancaster André had made many friends, especially with the German residents, whose language the young officer spoke fluently. While in Carlisle he corresponded with his Lancaster friends. One letter, April 10, 1776, was directed to Eberhart Michael, his "highly respected friend," who had been born in Germany forty years ago. The letter was composed in German. Unaware that his friend's expected letter has miscarried André opens with a lament. The English translation reads: "Highly respected friend: After you made me so kind a promise when I left Lancaster, I expected to receive a few lines from you. We become easily impatient by waiting upon news we expect to be gratifying."
And then he speaks graciously of the German language: "I will therefore write the first letter, and although my language may be bad, it is German, because I am happy to express myself in a language in which I have enjoyed intercourse with so many honest and sensible men."
He declares that he would much prefer to be with Michael back in Lancaster, but "I must say this [Carlisle] is a fine country and the inhabitants show considerable respect towards me." That perception is followed by something of a contradiction: "We [André and Despard]

~ *Notes* ~

very seldom have conversation with them, because, generally, no good results from it; nothing but uncivil and hostile answers."

That they are making the best of what could be a bad time there is no question: "We pass our time in making music, reading books, and await humbly our liberation, and upon more peaceable times. Myself and Mr. Despard are much engaged in playing duetts; he sends his best respects." André wants to be remembered to his German friends: "If you see Mr. [Major Christian] Wirtz, and Rev. Mr. [Justus Heinrich Christian] Hellemuth, and H[ans] Graff, please give my respects to them,– from the last mentioned, I have received the maps and thank him."

The letter closes: "I am with great respect, dear sir, your obedient servant. JohnAndré."

Eberhart Michael responded to it, with obvious affection and respect, on April 26.

For John André in Lancaster and Carlisle, see Landis, *Major John André's Geman Letter*.

4. For trustworthy accounts of the Pennsylvania Long Rifle, see Neuman; and Dillin.
5. Rupp, p. 410.
6. Ellis, pp. 247-248.
7. Ibid., pp. 226-227.
8. Harris, 269.
9. Ford, XXV, 839.
10. Ford, XXVII, 487; *Papers of the Continental Congress*, No. 20, I, folio 401.
11. For Hand's letter to Clark, see Ford, XXVII (1784), 581; and *Papers of the Continental Congress*, No. 32, folio 39.
12. This report, in the hand of Roger Sherman, is in the *Papers of the Continental Congress*, No.1 9, III, folio 25. Hand's letter is in No. 41, IV, folios 238 and 250. Ford XXVII (1784), 3387-388.
13. Hand papers, items # 310, 312, 314, 315.
14. Ibid., items # 317, 318, 319, 322.
15. Ibid., item # 320.
16. Ibid., item # 324.
17. Ibid., item # 325.
18. Ibid., item # 326.
19. It was by special balloting conducted October 18 of that fall (1785) that Franklin was elected the sixth President of the Supreme Executive Council, succeeding John Dickinson. He held the office (equivalent of the Governor of Pennsylvania) for a little more than three years.
20. Richard Peters was a very able Philadelphia attorney. The same age as General Hand, he served Congress as a delegate from Pennsylvania. In 1786 he was elected to the Pennsylvania House of Representatives and served as Speaker of the Assembly, 1788-1790.
21. Hand papers, item # 329.

22. Ibid., item #334.
23. Pennsylvania has had five constitutions (1776, 1790, 1838, 1874, and 1968). The third merely made some amendments to the second; the fourth addressed the very real need for social legislation and attended to problems that had arisen because of the Civil War.
24. Clare, p. 161.
25. Mifflin at this time was not a party member, but had pretty much adopted the Federalist line. For a good account of the convention, see Branning's Chapter 2, "Pennsylvania's Conservative Constitution of 1790," pp. 17-20.
26. James Wilson, two years older than Edward Hand, and, like Hand, born in the Old World, in Scotland, has long, and properly, been regarded as a Founding Father of the United States. He studied law under John Dickinson, and from his later practice in Reading, Pa., was invited by General John Armstrong of Carlisle to help meet attorney needs in Cumberland County. Much impressed by what he found, he became a resident of Cumberland County, eventually owning a small farm close to Carlisle. With the war he served in the Pennsylvania militia forces, reaching the rank of brigadier general. He was twice elected to the Continental Congress, and was a major figure in the drafting of both the United States Constitution (as a delegate from Pennsylvania) and the Pennsylvania Constitution of 1790. By historians he is regarded as "the most learned of the framers of the Constitution." Nominated by President George Washington, James Wilson became one of the six original judges of the Supreme Court of the United States.
27. Cincinnati, Ohio, is not named for Lucius Quinctius Cincinnatus, but actually for the Society.
28. The date of this meeting, May 13, 1783, has long been recognized as the day upon which the Society was created.
29. Harmar was promoted to brigadier general in 1787. From 1784 to 1791 he was senior officer in the United States Army. His troops were badly defeated by Little Turtle in 1790 at the Battle of the Maumee. Harmar was later court-martialed but acquitted. He served as Adjutant General of Pennsylvania 1795-1799. Fort Harmar, on the Ohio, is named for him.
30. Johnston commanded the 2nd Pennsylvania Brigade at Monmouth (Hand's close friend Colonel James Chambers had the command of the 1st Pennsylvania Brigade at Monmouth.); and Johnston had the command of the 5th Pennsylvania Regiment at the battle of the Brandywine.
31. Holograph document of Yeates letter, Lancaster County Historical Society. Quoted by Craig, p. 108.
32. Fitzpatrick, *Writings*, XXXI, 236.
33. *Pennsylvania Archives*, Second Series, IV, 642.
34. Fitzpatrick, *Writings*, XXXI, 510. Copy in *The Papers of George Washington*, Presidential Series.
35. *Pennsylvania Archives*, Second Series, III, 379.

XII: Rock Ford

1. The region of Wright's Ferry, once the site of a Susquehannock Indian Village was early on considered as a site for the nation's capital. In fact, it was favored by Washington himself, and fell only one vote short when Congress polled its members in 1790.
2. Founders Online, National Archives. Source: *The Papers of George Washington,* Presidential Series, VIII, March 22, 1791, ed. Mark A. A. Mastromarino. Charlottesville, Va.: Univ. of Va, 1999, pp. 317-318.
3. Jackson, *Diaries,* VI, 169.
4. Fitzpatrick, *Writings,* XXXVI, 43.
5. *Lancaster Journal,* January 8, 1800; and Saturday, March 1, 1800.
6. Hand's death date has been reported as September 2, September 3, and September 4. But 11:30 a.m. appears to be the right time of day.
7. *The Dictionary of American Biography* has him dying of an apoplectic stroke.
8. *Lancaster Era,* September 11, 1802; Hand Papers, no item #.

Afterword

1. See Appendix B for the story of the Edward Hand plum.
2. *Pennlines,* Vol. XLIX, No. 1 (January, 2014), 4.

Appendix A

1. Thacher, *The American Revolution*, pp. 226-229.

Appendix B

1. Hoffy, *North American Pomologist,* Book # 1, no page no. In Darborn, Michigan, there may exist a graft of the tree.

Index

Adams, John, 39, 163, 251, 261, 271, 284, 327
adjutant general, 24, 213-218, 216-222, 231-238, 248-256, 285
Adventure, 175
Agnew, General James, 46
Albany, 24, 103, 142, 153, 157-156, 167, 256
Albany Road, 62
Alden, Ichabod, 153-153, 329
Alden, John, 333
Allegheny Mountains, 329
Allegheny River, 5, 92, 94, 100, 102, 114-115, 142, 162, 193, 331, 334
Almshouse (See Lancaster County Almshouse and Hospital.)
Anaquaga, 153
Anderson, John, 214
André, John, 214-212, 246-241, 297-299, 346, 347, 348-349
Anglican, 4
Annapolis, 226, 243, 246, 257-260, 344
Anne (See Cape Ann.)
Appalachian Mountains, 8, 97
Appletown (See Kendaia.)
Arch Street, 4
Armonk, 214
Armstrong, Colonel John, 6, 201, 241, 246, 259, 331, 336, 350
Armstrong, John, Jr., 246, 259
Arnold, Benedict, 214-212, 347
Articles of Confederation, 251, 261
Art Museum, Dallas, Texas, 317
Associators, 18
Assunpink Creek, (second battle of Trenton), battle of, 69-71, 74-76, 79, 330
Athens, Pa., 148, 177
Atlee, Edwin Augustus, 244
Atlee, Samuel John, 45, 48, 260, 327
Atlee, William Augustus, 244, 256-264

B

Ball, Mary, 326
Baltimore, 73, 85, 252, 302
Barr, Alexander, 116
Bartgis, Martin, 241
Barton, Thomas, 16, 324
Batt, Major, 46
Bayard Street, Princeton, 332
Beatty, Charles Clinton, 11
Beatty, Erkuries, 192
Beatty, John, 11, 255
Beaver Run (Creek), 106, 110, 117, 121
Bedford, 6, 8, 88, 272
Bedford County, 103, 105, 109, 112, 115
Bellevue, 329
Belmont Mansion, 260
Benedict, Mr. 301
Bergen County, 208
Bergen Neck (Point) (Heights), 136, 208, 333
Biddle, Charles, 260
Big Sewickley Creek, 92
Black's Creek, 324
Blacksnake, 147, 184, 187, 188
Blairsville, Pa., 44
Blake, Thomas, 192
Blue Licks, battle of, 231-228
Blue Mountains, 169
Board of War, 110, 167, 170, 187
Boatner, Mark, 75
Bonde, Samuel, 244
Boone, Daniel, 231, 228, 248
Boone, Israel, 228
Boonesborough, 231
Booth, James, 104
Bordentown, 68, 329
Boston, 16, 18, 23-36, 39-40, 76, 138, 163, 246, 325, 339
Boston Port Bill, 17
Boston Tea Party, 17
Bottecourt County, 103
Bouquet, Henri, 7, 10, 334

Bowyer, John, 103
Boyd, Robert, 21
Boyd, Thomas, 188-192
Braddock, Edward, 7
Braddock Road, 116
Brady, William, 118
Brandywine, battle of, 134, 163, 202, 326, 328, 331, 340
Brant, Joseph, 143-144 150, 154-153, 157, 181, 188, 336
Breckbill, John, 256
Breed's Hill, 32, 39, 154
Brenton, Major, 118
Brien, Dorothy, 301
Brien, Edward, 301
British Parliament, 17, 193
Brodhead, Daniel, 92, 106, 162, 188, 193, 259, 334, 336
Brodhead-Fording Road, 98-99
Brooklyn, 44, 78
Brooklyn, battle of, 45, 52, 55, 263, 327, 329
Brooklyn Church, 53
Brooklyn Heights, battle of, 45, 52
Brown, Christian, 144
Brown, Enoch, 7
Brown, Thomas, 103
Bruback, Hieronimus, 244
Brunswick, 118, 119, 122, 132, 135
Buckinghamshire, 245
Bucks County, 245
Bullock Pens, 10-11, 323
Bunker(s) Hill, 27, 28, 32-33, 154, 323
Burchardt, Daniel, 166, 174
Burd, Billy, 34
Burd, Edward, 26, 28, 30, 45, 46, 48, 50, 51, 56, 324, 327
Burd, James, 26, 327
Burd, Sarah Shippen, 26, 325
Burgess of Lancaster, 263, 264, 273-282
Burgoyne, John, 111, 246, 340
Burke, 33
Bush, George, 165
Bushy Run, 7, 10

Butler, Henry, 127
Butler, John, 128-130, 142-143, 143-147, 154, 157, 181, 187, 188, 344
Butler, Richard, 133, 347
Butler, Walter, 154-153
Butler, William, 150, 153, 153-154, 173, 174
Butler, Zebulon, 144-147, 147, 160, 166, 173, 340
Buttermilk Run, 178
Buttricks, George, 4
Buysson, Charles du, 203

C

Cadwalader, John, 71, 72, 73, 76-79, 332
Cahokia, 129
Cambridge, Massachusetts, 19, 23-36, 40, 55, 332, 341
Cambridge River, 31
Camden, 203, 332, 341
Camden, battle of, 198-200, 208
Campbell, George, 263
Campbell, Thomas, 139
Camp Fatigue, 169
camp fever, 213, 341
Canada, 30, 39
Canandaigua, 339
Cannon (Canon), John, 121
Cape Anne, 26
Captain Davis, 172
Captain Pipe, 108-111, 120, 122, 337
Captain Pipe's brother, 110, 118, 121
Captain Pipe's mother, 118-119
Captain Pipe's wife, 118
Carleton, Guy, 231
Carlisle, 2, 6, 8, 9, 11, 16, 20, 34, 61, 86, 87, 168, 241, 244, 253, 259, 272, 337, 348, 350
Carnahan's Blockhouse, 91-92
Carpenter, Emanuel, 302
Carpenters' Hall, 251
Carrell's Ferry, 120, 133
Castaing, Peter, 248,

~ Index ~

Catfish Camp, 94, 109
Catherine's Town, 187
Cayuga Indians, 150
Cessation of Hostilities, 239-234, 246
Chambers, Benjamin, 332
Chambersburg, 241, 332
Chambers, James, 33, 35-36, 39, 46, 55, 83-85, 117-118, 119-122, 131-135, 332-333
Chambers, James (Western Department), 104
Chambers, Stephen, 246
Chapel (Locust) Alley, 241
Charleston, S. C., siege of, 31, 201, 198, 208, 225, 231, 347
Charles II, 280
Charlestown Peninsula, 28, 33
Chartiers Creek, 98-99
Chase, Jeremiah Townley, 255
Chatterton Hill, 62
Che,cheas, 121
Chemung River, 177, 184
Chemung Valley, 177, 181, 184
Chemung village, 153, 153, 154, 157, 161, 162, 165, 177, 180, 181, 184, 187
Cherry Tree, 142, 154
Cherry Valley massacre, 150, 154, 154-157, 162, 184, 181, 340
Chesapeake Bay, 142, 226
Chesapeake Cape, 226
Chester, 132
Chester County, 245, 323
Chew, James, 109, 110
Chillicothe, 228
Chippewa Indians, 94, 106, 248
cholera, 279
Christ Episcopal Church, 4, 8
Churchill, 311
Church, Thomas, 193
Cincinnati, 350
Cincinnatus, Lucius Quintius, 260-267
Citadel, 325
City Tavern, 268
Clark, George Rogers, 124, 128, 129, 228, 255
Clarke House, 78, 332
Clarke, Thomas, 78
Cleveland, 115
Clinton, George, 153, 153, 241
Clinton, Henry, 97, 134, 151, 193-192, 201, 208, 205, 214, 212, 222, 224, 221, 223, 228, 230, 228, 229, 231, 239, 260, 297, 299
Clinton, James, 143, 150, 154, 157, 156, 162, 170, 181, 181, 192, 188, 215
Clove, the, 132
Cluggage, Robert, 33, 36, 42
Clydruff (Clyduff), 2
Clymer, George, 125
Cobb, 3
Cobleskill massacre, 144, 147
Cochockon (Coshocton), 101
Coleman, Robert, 246, 256, 263
Colesqua (See Cornstalk)
College of New Jersey (Princeton University), 334, 349
College of Philadelphia (University of Pennsylvania), 349
Columbia, Pa., 273
Columbia University, 143
Committee of Correspondence (Carlisle), 17
Committee of Correspondence (Lancaster), 17, 18, 325
Committee of Observation, 18, 263
Committee of Safety (Pittsburgh), 96-97
Committee of the States, 252, 253
Conemaugh River, 92, 246
Conestoga, 279
Conestoga Indians, 7, 100, 334
Conestoga River, 278, 279, 301
Congress of Confederation, 251, 256
Congress of the United States, 264
Connecticut Farms (present Union Township), battle of, 202-205
Connellsville, 336
Connell, Zach, 119

Conservative Constitution, 261, 350
Constitutional Convention of 1807-88, 246-248
Continental Congress, 18-19, 20, 24, 25, 42, 56-57, 59, 68, 70, 85, 90, 94, 105, 108, 113, 120, 125, 129, 136, 153, 163, 167, 210, 213-218, 216-221, 230, 231-238, 234-241, 243, 278, 327, 348, 350
"Cooch," 6-10
Coochachunk (Coshocton) (Cooshackung), 108, 122
Cope, Caleb, 241
Copp's Hills, 32
Cork, Ireland, 3
Cornplanter, Chief, 142-143, 184, 188, 192, 193, 328
Cornplanter Tract, 100, 328
Cornstalk, Chief, 111-112, 123, 128, 188, 336
Cornwallis, Charles, 63, 65, 67, 68, 71, 73, 74-78, 193, 201, 198, 200, 212, 224, 221, 223-225, 230
Cortlandt, Philip Van, 333
Coughnawaga, 154
County Meath, Ireland 253
County Offaly, Ireland, 323
County Tyrone, Ireland, 301
Court House Square, Lancaster, 241
Cox, John, 340
Crafton High School, 98
Craig, Charles, 42, 57
Craig, Nancy, 261
Craig, Robert, 134
Crawford, William, 106, 113-116, 118, 123, 128, 336-337
Creighton, Alexander, 33
Croghan, George, the earlier, 4-5, 96-97, 335
Croghan, George, the later, 335
Croghan Hall, 97
Crosswick's Creek, 329
Culloden, battle of, 331
Cumberland County, 259, 350
Cunningham, Robert, 42
Custaloga, Chief, 337
Cuyahoga River, 115, 117

D

Daughters of the American Revolution, 281-290, 330, 334
Davis, Alexina, 281-290
Davis, Captain, 172
Davis, Earl A., 290
Davis, Edwin C., 290
Davis, Frank E., 290
Davis, Jepitha D., 290
Davis, John B., 290
Dayton, Elias, 208
Dayton, Jonathan, 202, 285
Dearborn, Henry, 192
Declaration of Independence, 251, 280, 273, 324, 336
Delancey's Mills, 41, 46, 58, 132
Delaware Blues, 62
Delaware Indians, 88-119, 334
Delaware River, 68, 74, 133, 332
Delaware River, the crossing, 23, 68
Denison, Nathan, 144
Despard, Edward Marcus, 348-349
Dey Mansion, 205-210
Diary of the American Revolution, 32-33, 326
Dickinson College, 244
Dickinson, John, 349
Dick, John, 42
Divine Providence, 49
Dobbs Ferry, 219, 221-226
Donegal, Ireland, 86
Don Quixote, 333
Dorchester, 36
Douglass, Alexander, 77
Dublin, 1, 2, 4, 15, 323, 341
Dublin Castle, 3
Dublin Journal, 3, 323
Dufresne, Albert, 244
Duke Street, Lancaster, 244, 328
Duportail, Chevalier Louis Lebègue de Presle, 248

~ Index ~

Dutch, 1, 119

E

Earl of Granard, 3
Eastchester, 44
East Florida, 327
East King Street, Lancaster, 293
Easton, Pa., 57, 165, 168, 170-169, 187
East River, 52, 58, 78, 328
Edge Hill, 10
Edison, N.J., 202
Edmonstone, Charles, 5, 9, 10-13, 323
Edmonstone House, 243
Edmonstone, William, 243
Edward Hand Chapter of the D.A.R., 281-290
Edward Hand Medical College, 290
Edward Hand Middle School, 291
Edward Hand plum (See General Hand plum.)
Edwards, Major, 180
Eighteenth Royal Irish Regiment, 2-14, 31, 85, 99, 315
Eighth Pennsylvania Regiment, 114
Eight-Mile Run (See Shipetaukin Creek.)
Eliot, Matthew, 95-96, 113, 127
Elizabethtown Point, 51, 202, 208, 205
Elinipsico, 111
Ellery, William, 256
Elmira, 184
Englishtown, 134
Erskine, Sir William, 76
Ewing, Jasper, 19, 45, 46, 49, 51, 55-56, 86, 88-89, 98, 109, 111, 120, 123, 124, 127, 131, 132, 134, 328, 334
Ewing, John, 16, 45, 49, 51-52, 54
Ewing, Katherine, 16,
Ewing, Mrs. John, 36
eye infection, 41

F

Fahen County, Ireland, 86
Fairmount Park, 260
Falmouth, 31, 326
Fauquier Street, Mercersburg, 332
Fawn Township, 86-87, 333
Federal Hill (See Pompton Lakes.)
Fermoy, Matthias Alexis Roche de, 72-73, 330
Ferry Farm, 331
Fifth Pennsylvania Regiment, 193
Finch, Jabez, 329
finger lakes, 150, 162, 187
First Continental Congress, 251-253
First Continental Regiment of Foot, 20
First New Hampshire Regiment, 192
First Pennsylvania Regiment, 20, 29, 34, 40-42, 43, 46, 50, 52-53, 62, 68, 83-85, 131, 202, 332
Fischer, David, 79
Fish Carrier, 188
Fishkill-on-Hudson, 260
Fitzpatrick, John, 160
Five-Mile Run, 75
Flatbush, 45, 48, 49
Fleming, William, 103, 107, 128
Flying Camp, 48, 51, 324
Fogg, Jeremiah, 184
Forbes Expedition, 78-79, 324, 327, 336
Forbes, John, 7, 8, 11, 12-13, 327, 329, 331
Forbes Road, 6, 88
Ford Mansion, 193
Foreman, William, 108-109
Forrest, Thomas, 69-70, 73-75, 330
Fort Green Park, 327
Forts: Augusta, 331; Beacon, 33; Bedford, 9; Brown, 47-48; Chartres, 99; Constitution, 63; Crawford, 92; Detroit, 9, 13, 78, 90, 94, 95, 100, 101, 108, 113, 114, 115, 127; Duquesne, 7, 8, 73, 327, 329, 331; Forty,

144, 173; Greene, 48, 327; Hand, 92-93, 334; Harmar, 350; Henry, 91, 97, 100, 101-104, 106, 109, 110, 114; Jenkins, 144, 165, 165; Knyphausen, 63; Laurens, 121; Lee, 23, 63, 222; Ligonier, 8; McIntosh, 137; Michilimackinack, 13; Muncy, 165, 344; Necessity, 326, 335; Niagara, 9, 13, 101, 192, 193, 253; Ontario, 103-104; Oswego, 13, 103, 142-142; Penn, 166; Pitt, 4-14, 23, 85-130, 133, 142, 154, 160, 175, 174, 243, 253, 256, 295, 334, 337, 341, 323; Randolph, 91, 107, 111, 112, 123, 126, 336; Redstone Old Fort, 103, 128, 129; Stephenson, 335; Sullivan, 177, 187, 343; Ticonderoga, 72, 330; Venango, 331; Vincennes, 13; Wallace, 114; Washington, 23, 58, 63-64, 74, 202; Wintermoot, 144, 173

Foster, Isaac, 31
Fourth Continental Artillery, 174
Fourth Pennsylvania Regiment, 150, 153, 192
Fowler, Alexander, 99
Franklin, Benjamin, 18, 100, 210, 251, 246, 260, 261, 349
Franklin and Marshall College, 293
Franklin County, 331, 333
Franklin, John, 147, 174
Fredericksburg, N.Y., 157
Fredericksburg, Va., 138, 331, 332
Freehold Church, 135
Frelinghuysen, Frederick, 215, 346
French Alliance, 137, 210
French and Indian Wars, 7, 11, 329, 346
French Creek, 128
French Foreign Legion, 346
French Society (of the Cincinnati), 268
French West Indies, 330
Frey, Jacob, 283
Frogs Neck, 44, 58-60
Front Street, Philadelphia, 44

G

Gage, Thomas, 39
Galloway, Joseph, 251, 246, 253
garden spot of America, 15
Gates, Horatio, 85, 114, 115, 117, 123, 127, 131, 138, 160-163, 198-203, 200, 208, 243, 338
Gathsegwarohare, 188
General Hand plum, 284, 302-304
Genesee Castle, 188, 192
Genesee Valley, 142, 187, 193
Geneva, 188
Genishau, 192
George III (See King George, III.)
George Morgan White Eyes (See White Eyes, George Morgan.)
German Flats, 142, 154
German people, 1, 246, 241-248, 243, 263, 323, 348
Germantown, 133
Germantown, battle of, 134, 163, 328, 331, 333
German troops, 20, 70-71, 74
"Gertrude of Wyoming," 139
Gettysburg, 11
Gibbs, Caleb, 203
Gibralter, 34, 323
Gibson, John, 95, 99-100, 104, 106, 110, 114, 334
Gilley, Jane, 281
Gilmore, David, 216
Girty, George, 336
Girty, James, 127
Girty, Simon, 95-96, 115, 118, 119, 127, 231, 336
Gist, Christopher, 10
Glover, John, 55, 215
Gnadenhuetten, 337-338
Gontaut, Armand Louis de, duc de

~ *Index* ~

Lauzun, 346
Gowanus Road, 45, 327
Graff,Sebastian, 260
Grand Retreat, 53-57
Grant, James, 47, 327
Grant's Hill, 327
Grasse, Admiral Francois Joseph Paul comte de, 224, 221-223
Gratz, Barnard, 96, 335
Gratz, Michael,96, 335
Gravesend Bay, 44-45
Grave, Sebastian, 246, 256, 263
Graves, Robert, 323
Graves, Samuel, 326
Graydon, Alexander, 74, 330, 331
Graymont, Barbara, 144-147
Great Island, 3
Great Kanawha River, 94, 107, 111, 112
Great Swamp, 169
Great Tree, 188
Green, John, 62
Greene, Nathanael, 47, 61, 64, 75, 80, 84, 167, 170, 200, 208, 208, 212, 218, 260, 327
Greensburg, 88
Grier, James, 42, 134
Griffin, Edmund, 143
Groton, Ct., 212
Guilford Court House, 343
Gum Swamp, 203
gunsmithing, 241-243
Guyasuta (Kyashota), 115

H

Hackensack, N. J., 67, 208, 341
Hackett's, 132
Haislet, Hannah L., 333
Haislet, Robert, 333
Halifax, 43, 44, 326
Hamilton, Alexander, 80, 205, 218, 228, 241, 255, 260, 268, 272, 267
Hamilton, Henry, 95, 101, 127
Hamilton, James, 42, 48

Hamilton, John, 118
Hamilton, William, 34
Hampshire County, Va., 108
Hancock, John, 40, 65, 67, 251
Hand, Dorothy, the elder, 2
Hand, Dorothy, the younger, 113, 117, 125, 131, 243, 261, 274
Hand, Edward, in Philadelphia, with 18th Regiment, 1-4; settles in Lancaster, 15-17; marriage, 16, 27; Pennsylvania Rifle Battalion, 18-20; at Cambridge-Boston, 23-36; battle of New York, 39-62; White Plains, 23, 59; Trenton, 63-66; Assunpinck, 68-74; Princeton, 72-74; Morristown, 75, 77-78; Fort Pitt (Western Department), 77-138; Albany (Northern Department), 151-160; Sullivan expedition, 160-196; Yorktown Campaign, 193-230; trial of John André, 214-213; Newburgh and New Windsor, 229-244; First Continental Congress and the Congress of Confederation, 251-253; the Pennsylvania Assembly, 260-256; Pennsylvania Constitutional Convention of 1810, 256-259; Society of the Cincinnati, 259-263; Friendly Sons of Saint Patrick, 263-264; Lancaster, Rock Ford, and the United States provisional Army, 271-280; Hand entertains George Washington in Lancaster, 280-284; Lancaster observes death of President Washington, 285-279; death of General Edward Hand, 279-288
Hand, Edward, Jr., 278
Hand, Jasper, 260, 274, 278
Hand, John, the elder, 2
Hand, John (General Hand's child),

243-244, 252, 260, 274, 278
Hand, Katherine (Kitty), 16, 19, 25, 26, 28, 30-36, 40-41, 43, 44, 45-47, 56, 57, 62, 68, 86, 87, 89, 94, 97-98. 106, 109, 110, 113, 120, 125, 129, 130, 131, 137, 161, 193, 200, 198, 203, 210, 208, 221-223, 225, 230, 230, 243, 257-253, 260, 261, 278, 273, 284, 288, 325
Hand, Katherine, 199, 243, 274, 278, 285
Hand, Margaret, 274, 278
Hand, Mary, 274
Hand, Sarah ("Sally"), 34, 36, 37, 40, 41, 43-44, 58, 61, 68, 86, 87, 113, 117, 125, 131, 243, 253, 261, 274, 285
Hannastown (Hannah's Town), 88, 92
Hanneyaye, 188
Hanover Street, Carlisle, 241
Hanson, John, 213
Harding, Warren, 332
Harlem Heights, 23, 56, 57, 61, 74
Harmer, Josiah, 259, 263, 267, 350
Harris, David, 42, 44, 131, 133-134
Harrison, William Henry, 335
Harris's Ferry, 174
Hartford, Ct., 36, 40, 207, 213,
Hartley, Thomas, 150, 153, 156, 187, 344
Hasbrouck House, 230
Hasbrouck, Jonathan, 230
Haslet, John, 49, 62, 67, 78, 80, 329
Hatfield Hill, 62
Hausegger, Nicholas, 69-71, 73-76, 323
Head of Elk, 226, 223
Heath, William, 45, 58-59, 231, 241
Heister, Captain, 45-46
Hendricks, William, 30, 326
Henry, Elizabeth, 336
Henry, John, 243
Henry, Patrick, 104, 110, 112, 124, 251, 336
Henry, William, 243

Herbert, Captain, 45
Heron (?), 80
Hessians, 44-48, 56-64, 64-78, 132, 151, 201, 202, 203, 208, 246, 330, 348
Hibernian Society of Lancaster, 274
Higgins, John, 127
Highlanders, 133
Hiokatoo, 191
Historic American Building Survey, 279
Historic Preservation Trust, 291
Hoar, Charles, 15
Hoffy, Alfred A., 299
Hokoleskwa (See Cornstalk.)
Holliday, John, 134
Holstein, Stephen, 338
Holston River, 128, 338
Holston, Stephen, 338
Hopkins, Gerrard, 333
Hopkins, Levin, 333
Hopocan (See Captain Pipe.)
Hough, 87
Howell's Ferry, 120, 132
Howe, Robert, 205, 215, 215-216, 231, 346-347
Howe, William, 39, 40, 44, 50, 54, 56-58, 59, 62, 64, 65, 97, 119, 133, 134, 241, 329
Hubley, Adam, 58, 174, 174, 177, 260, 324
Hubley, Bernard, 324
Hubley, Frederick, 21
Hubley, George, 324
Hubley, John, 246, 256, 263, 283, 324
Hubley, Michael, 263
Hudson River, 24, 58, 59, 63, 208, 222, 221, 226, 230, 239, 320
Hudson River Highlands, 213
Hudson, Thomas (Telenemut), 187
Hughes, John, 106
Hummelstown, 241, 267
Hunter, Samuel, 105
Huntington, Jedediah, 215-213, 241, 260, 267, 272, 346

~ Index ~ 361

I

Illinois, 4, 12, 13, 126
Ingram, 98
Ireland, 6, 8
Irish, 2, 16, 18, 21
Iroquois Federation, 139, 142
Iroqouis Indians, 122, 143-147, 150, 162, 193, 231, 324
Inspector of Revenue, 271
Irvine, William, 168-170, 259, 263, 337, 341

J

Jacob Arnold's Tavern, 192
Jamaica, 329
Jameson, John, 214
Jay, John, 251, 271
Jefferson, Thomas, 251, 253, 248
Jemison, Mary, 191
Jenkins, John, 161-160
Jersey City, 320
Jockey Hollow, 199
Johnston, Francis, 263
Johnston, Sir John, 196
Johnston, Sir William, 143, 253
Jones, John, 101
Jones, John Paul, 259
Jones, Lieutenant, 172
Journals of the Continental Congress, 323

K

Kalb, Baron Johannes de, 138, 192, 203-200, 341, 344
Kanadaseaga, 187-188
Kanadaseaga Creek, 187-188
Kanaghsaws, 188
Kananddaigua (See. Canandaigua.)
Kanawha (See Great Kanawha.)
Kanawaluhaly, 192
Kaskaskia, 129
Kayahsotha (Guyasuta), 142-143
Kendaia (Appletown), 187

Kennedy, William, 174
Kentucky, 231
Kentucky Long Rifle, 248
Keyser, Ephraim, 334
Kickapoo Indians, 108
Killbuck, John, 101, 122, 337
King George III, 3, 16, 17, 65, 139, 174, 184, 193, 231, 231, 239, 323, 324
King and Queen's Streets, Trenton, 69
King Louis, XVI, 207
Kingsbridge (King's Bridge), 46, 50, 52, 56, 61, 347
King's County, Ireland, 2, 323
King's Ferry, 226, 239
King's Mountain, battle of, 248
Kips (Kip's) Bay, 57
Kirkbride's Ferry, 68, 329
Kirkland, Joseph, 329
Kiskiminetas River, 92
Kittanning, 91, 331
Knouff, Gregory, 29
Knox, Henry, 74, 75, 76, 80, 138, 167, 210, 213-214, 215, 223, 228, 231-238, 241-236, 248, 255, 259, 260, 267, 268, 263, 271, 267
Knox, Lucy, 74
Knyphausen, Wilhelm, 63, 193, 201, 202, 203, 208
Konieschquanoheel (See Captain Pipe.)
Krug, Jacob, 283
Kuskuski, 121

L

Lafayette, Marquis de, 135, 137, 167, 193-199, 198, 203, 205, 210, 213-214, 215, 212, 226, 230, 243, 260, 330, 341, 344
Lake Champlain, 246
Lake Oswego, 126
Lancaster, 2, 6, 7, 15-21, 26, 28, 30, 58, 86, 88, 95, 97, 102, 111,

113, 123, 124, 134, 137, 156, 161, 165, 174, 177, 226, 227, 225, 245-248, 257, 252-253, 263, 267, 269, 278, 280, 283, 278, 328, 333, 334
Lancaster County, 20, 246, 256, 263, 272, 279, 290, 284-293, 301-302, 323
Lancaster County Almshouse and Hospital, 293
Lancaster Journal, 278, 287
Lancaster New Era, 277, 287
Laurel Hill, 88
Laurence, John, 215
Laurens, Henry, 153, 153
Lauzon, duc de, 212, 346
Lechmere's Point, 32-34
Lee, Arthur, 248
Lee, Charles, 26, 62, 65, 160, 201, 346-347
Lee, Henry, 213, 251, 278, 336
Leidy, John, 244
Leighten, Captain, 208
Leinster Province, 323
Lemot, Robert, 102
Lenape (See Delaware Indians.)
Lengel, Edward, 75
Leslie, Alexander, 46, 208
Lexington/Concord, 21, 139, 193, 239, 251, 323, 341
Leutze, Emanuel, 68-69, 281, 330
Licking River, 231-228
Ligonier, 115
Ligonier Valley, 114
Lincoln, Benjamin, 201-198, 225, 272, 347
Linn, William, 109, 129
Little Beard, 188-191, 192
Little, Moses, 43
Little Shabbakunk Creek, 73
Little Turtle, 350
Little Wabash, 348
Lochry, Archibald, 88, 95, 96, 100, 103, 104-105, 110, 112, 114, 336
Lochry, Jeremiah, 88

Logstown, 104, 110, 334
Long Island, battle of, 23, 40-53, 56, 57, 63, 71, 163, 256, 324, 327, 328, 333
Long Island Sound, 56, 58, 328
longhouse, 142
Lodge of Freemasons, 278
Lord Dunmore's War, 111, 334
Loudon, John, 33, 36
Loughry, William, 110
Loyalhanna River, 8, 92
Lusannah, 248
Lycoming Creek, 344

M

Macartney, James, 323
MacMonniat, Frederick, 332
Madeira, 4
Madison, James, 246
Magaw, Robert, 20, 26, 33-35, 51, 61, 64
Mahoning River, 117, 119
Maidenhead, 78
malaria, 347
Marais des Cygnes River, 292
Market Street, 4
Marshall, John, 278
Maryland State House, 257
Manaroneck, battle of, 62
Manhattan, 23, 59
Maryland Second Brigade, 203
Mason, Samuel, 104
Matthews, Sampson, 125
Mason County Courthouse, 335
Matlack, Timothy, 324
Mawhood, Charles, 78-79
Massy-Harbinson-Fort Hand Chapter of the DAR, 92, 93
Maxwell, William, 168, 167, 170, 169, 173, 175, 181, 199, 208
McClay, 248
McClellan, John, 92
McDonald, Angus, 106
McDougall, Alexander, 138, 268
Mclure, David, 103

~ Index ~

McDowell, Samuel, 125, 335
McHenry, James, 205
M'chewamisipu, 142
McKean, Thomas, 264
McKee, Alexander, 89, 95-96, 115, 127, 231
McKee, William, 126
McKibben, John, 91-92
McNeill, Samuel, 184
McIntosh, Lachlan, 129-131, 137, 268, 272
Mercer, Hugh, 7, 71, 73, 76, 78, 80, 329, 331, 341
Mercer, John Francis, 255
Mercer Oak, 331-332
Mercersburg, 332
Mercersburg Academy, 332
Merritt Hill, 62
Metuchen Meeting House (Short Hills), battle of, 132
Metropolitan Museum of Art, 330
Miami Indians, 95, 108, 111, 123, 248, 267
Michaels, 68
Michael, Eberhart, 348
Middlebrook, 118, 119, 151-150, 157, 157, 161, 162, 165, 170
Midlands, 323
Miller, George, 302
Mifflin, Thomas, 32, 52-55, 77, 78, 246, 253, 256, 264-259, 260, 272, 267, 287, 327-328, 333, 338, 350
Miles, Samuel, 48, 244, 342
Military Journal, 297
Miller, Henry, 33, 43, 48, 53, 68, 73, 133
Miller Hill, 62
Miller, Samuel, 92, 106, 114
Milligan, 44
Mingo Indians, 94, 100, 111, 121, 334
Minisink, 157-161, 166
Mohawk Indians, 143-142, 144, 184
Mohawk River, 156, 161, 162
Mohawk Valley, 142, 194

Monckton, Robert, 135, 338
Monckton, Henry, 338
Monmouth, battle of, 134, 135, 137, 143, 331, 346, 347
Monongahela River, 5, 116, 128, 129
Monongahela County, Va., 89
Monroe, James, 69, 248, 330
Montgomery, John, 87, 246, 253
Montgomery Military Lodge, 274
Montgomery, Richard, 30, 246
Montour, Catherine, 187
Montour, John, 121
Moore, Frank, 32-33
Moorhead, Samuel, 103-104
Moorhead, William, 93
Moravian Indians, 338
Morgan, Daniel, 30, 156
Morgan, George, 89, 94-99, 100, 108, 121, 122, 129, 137, 335
Morgan, John, 200-205, 344
Morgan, Zackwell, 103
Morris, Cadwalader, 246
Morris House, 59
Morris, Robert, 246
Morristown encampment, 80, 83-84, 131, 132, 193-198, 200-202, 208-205, 213, 229
Morristown mutiny, 136
Moses, 325
Moultrie, William, 201, 272
Mount Gulian (Verplanck House), 260
Mount Pisgah, 325
Mount Pleasant Tract, 98
Mount Prospect camp, 132, 133
Mount Vernon, 226, 230, 243-244, 277, 284, 278
Mount Washington, 63, 64
Mounts Creek, 118
Mounts, Providence, 118
Mowatt, Henry, 326
Moylan, Stephen, 263
Muncy Indians, 117, 120
Murphy, Samuel, 118
musket, 25
mutiny, 218-216, 230, 347

Mylin, Martin, 243

N

Nagel, George, 33
Napoleon, 278
Nassau Hall, 80
National Register of Historic Places, 279, 291
Neff, Hans Heinrich, 244
Neshaminy encampment, 333
Neshanek River, 118
Neville, John, 85, 86, 95
New Brunswick, 80, 333
New York City, battle of, 23, 36, 39-60
New Windsor, 132, 213, 218, 222, 228-243
New Castle, 117
New Jersey Campaign, 61-74, 333
New London, Ct., 212
New Orleans, 124
New Utrecht, 41-42, 43, 46-48, 329
New Rochelle, 44, 62
New York State, 24, 255
Newbuilding, 234
Newburgh, 213, 228-243
Newport, R.I., 207, 213, 342
Newtown, battle of, 184-187
Newtown, 180, 181
Nicholas, Thomas, 101
Nixon, John, 43, 138
North, William, 285
North Branch (of the Susquehanna), 142, 150, 154, 344
North Castle, 62, 214
North River Road, 219
North, Lord Frederick, 230
Northampton County, 273
Northern Department, 24, 156, 253, 340
Northumberland County, 31, 105, 319
Northumberland, 142, 165
Northwest Territory, 142, 253, 333
Noyes, Alfred, 67, 332

O

O'Leary, Patrick, 6
Offaly County (See County Offaly)
Ohio Valley, 94, 101, 122, 142, 273
Ohio River, 4, 12, 94, 111, 114, 115, 117, 228, 248, 340
Ohio County, Va., 89, 90
Old Stone House, 327
Old Smoke, 143, 181, 188
Onaquaga, 150
Oneida Indians, 150, 162
Onondaga Indians, 181
Orangetown (Tappan), N. J., 208-213
Oriskany, battle of, 143-144, 147, 181
Osgood, Samuel, 253
Oswego Council, 143, 143
Oswego Lake, 143
Otsego Lake, 181
Ottawa, Kansas, 281, 290, 330
Ottawa, Kansas, Library, 290, 330
Ottawa Indians, 94, 248, 292

P

Page, John, 108
Palisades, 60
Paoli, 134, 333
Papers of the Continental Congress, 253
Parker, Michael, 188, 191
Parker, Robert, 187, 184, 191-187
Parr, James, 31, 42, 117, 120, 131, 133, 174, 181
Parry, Eli, 301
Parsons, Samuel Holden, 138
Partridge, George, 256
Passyunk Township, 97
Paterson, John, 138, 215
Patrick, William, 144
Patterson, William, 231, 340
Paulus Hook, 208
Paxton Boys, 7
Paxton, 28
Payne, George, 333
Payne, Rachel, 333

~ Index ~

Peale, Rubens, 324
Peale, Charles Willson, 324
peatlands, 2
Peebles, John, 48
Peekskill, 221
Pelham Road, 59
Penn, William, 323
Penn Square, 263, 277, 273, 282
Pennsylvania Assembly. 19, 20, 260, 261, 263
Pennsylvania Council of Safety, 246
Pennsylvania Farm Journal, 301
Pennsylvania long rifle, 248
Pennsylvania Rifle Regiment, 19, 42, 43, 45, 53
Pennsylvania State Assembly, 260-263, 267, 289, 291, 363
Pennsylvania Rifle Regiment, 19, 42, 43, 45, 53
Pennsylvania's Liberal Constitution of 1776, 261, 263
Pennsylvania's Conservative Constitution of 1810, 261, 263-264, 315, 350
Perth Amboy, 202
Peters Township, 334
Peters, Richard, 110, 112, 246, 260,338, 349
Philadelphia, 1-5, 6, 8, 14, 15, 17, 18, 41, 43, 44, 46, 50, 86, 94, 96-97, 102, 108, 134, 136, 177, 187, 192, 218, 216, 226, 230, 230, 243, 245, 246, 243-251, 268, 263, 277, 278, 287, 323, 327, 331, 348
Philadelphia County, 245
Philipsburg, 222
Phillips Ford, 71, 76
Pickering, Timothy, 100, 143, 238, 241-236, 285, 337
Pipe, Chief (See Captain Pipe.)
Piper, James, 49
Piper, John, 105, 109
Piscataway, 333
Pitt, William, 7
Pittsburgh, 4, 8, 11, 48, 88-123, 191, 231, 277, 343
Ploughed Hill, 27, 28
Pluggystown Gang, 94, 102, 106
Pocono Mountains, 169
Point Pleasant, 91, 111, 335, 336
pomology, 302
Pompton Plains, 208
Pompton Lakes (Federal Hill), 193, 218-216, 228, 346, 347
Pontiac, 8-9
Pontiac Wars, 1, 78, 334
Poo,ques,an,geech,ca, 121
Poor, Enoch, 143-142, 168, 170, 169, 181, 181-184, 208, 213, 341, 346
Port Jervis, 157
Porter, Thomas,175
Portland, 31
Portsmouth, 31
Posey, Thomas, 156
Post Road, 79
Postmaster General, 143
Potawatomie Indians, 248, 273
Potomac River, 277, 278
Potts House, 210
Powles Hook, 58, 329
Pracaness (Preakness), 167, 205-210, 212
Preakness Valley, 205
Presbyterianism, 11
Prescott, William, 43, 128
Preston, William, 115
Princeton Road, 70-71, 73
Princeton, 43, 71
Princeton, battle of, 23, 43, 70, 77-81, 163, 193, 246, 262, 328, 329, 331, 340, 347
Proctor, Thomas, 168, 169, 172, 173, 175, 174, 178, 181, 184, 185, 327
Promised Land, 325
Prospect Park, 45
Prospect Camp, 132
Prospect Hill, 27, 28, 31-34, 325
Providence, 40, 222
Pulaski, Count Casimir, 156, 340

Purdy Hill, 62
Purple Heart, 243
Putnam, Rufus, 241
Putnam, Israel, 26, 41, 160
putrid fever, 208

Q

Quaker, 52, 78, 100, 327
Quaker Meeting House, 78
quarantine hospital, 97-98, 104, 289, 335
Quartermaster General, 221, 238, 248, 272, 328, 337
Quebec, 30, 95, 115, 127, 237, 326
Queen Esther, 148-147, 172-173, 187
Queen Esther's Flats, 148, 330
Queen's Rangers, 62
Queen Street, Lancaster, 241, 277
Queen Street, Trenton, 74

R

"Reliance," 86
"Roslin Castle," 172
Rall, Johannes Gottlieb, 69-71
Ramsay, David, 241
Randolph, Peyton, 251
Ravenscroft, Thomas, 118
Read, Jacob, 248, 255
Reading, Pennsylvania, 26, 47, 324
Red Lion Inn, 45, 46, 324
Red Bank, New Jersey, 332
Red Jacket, 188
Reed, Joseph, 165, 166, 165, 192-187, 230, 246
Reiger, Jacob, 244
Republican Society of Philadelphia, 262
Resolution of Independence, 251
Rhode Island Continentals, 79
Rice, Samuel, 175
Richardson, Richard, 106
Ringwood, 220
Roberdeau, Daniel, 113
Robert, 43, 44, 68

Rochambeau, Comte de, 207, 214, 213, 219, 224, 221, 226, 225, 345
Rock Ford, 277-280
Rock Ford Foundation, 279, 280
Rogers, Robert, 62
Rogers, Reverend William, 169, 172, 174, 174, 177, 180, 181, 342
Rogers, Mrs. S. B., 316, 326
Rogers, David, 124, 125, 126, 338
Roman Empire, 267
Ross, Alexander, 13
Ross, George, 19, 166, 324, 325
Ross, James, 21, 29-30, 33-34, 40, 43, 325
Ross, John, 325
Ross, William, 325
Royal Navy, 58
Royal Greens, 335
rum, 143
Rush Meadow Creek, 177
Rush, Benjamin, 354
Russell, William, 109, 336

S

"Shades of Death," 171
Sagwarithra, 188
Saint James Episcopal Church, Lancaster, 16, 324
Saint Patrick's Day, 199
Saint Andrew's Society of Philadelphia, 332
Saint John, 246
Saint James Episcopal Churchyard, 324, 325
Salem, N.J., 16
Salt Lick(s), 119, 122
Saltonstall, Gurdon, 57
Sancho (?), 87, 333
Sancho Panza, 333
Sanders Creek, 203
Sands Hill, 214
Sandusky, 117
Sandy Hook, 43, 44, 135
Saratoga, battle of, 103, 111, 117,

131, 156, 200, 246, 248, 341, 347
Saratoga Campaign, 101
Sargent, Paul Dudley, 57
Sargent, Winthrop, 76, 331
Savannah, 201, 231, 237, 268, 347
Saw Mill River Road, 78, 219
Sayengueraghta, 147
Scammell, Alexander, 53-55, 213, 218, 222, 219, 299, 341, 347
Schenectady, 194
Schoharie Valley, 143-146, 150-153, 194
Schott's Rifle Corps, 176
Schuyler, Philip, 153-156, 160, 162
Schuylkill Falls, 133
Sciota River, 112
Scotch Plains, 132, 202
Scotch-Irish, 16, 20, 245-246, 323
Scott, Captain, 118, 192
Scott, Charles, 76, 272, 330
Scott, Thomas, 334
Scovell, Elisha, 146
Second New Jersey, 218-215
Second Street, Philadelphia, 4
Second Continental Congress, 251-246
Second Street Barracks, 3-4
Second Pennsylvania, 202
Secretary of State, 145
Secretary of War, 338
Seely, Captain, 273
Selin, Anthony, 176
Seneca Indians,24, 115, 142-147, 150-194, 277
Seneca Lake, 187
Sergeant, 55
Sewickley, 92
Shaffner, Casper, 283
Shannon River, 2
Shaw, Samuel, 260, 267
Shawnee (Shawanese) Indians, 89, 101, 102, 111-113, 122, 123, 128, 191, 228-248, 273
Shee, John, 49, 74
Sheldon, Elisha, 219

Shenango River, 117, 118
Shepherd, David, 90-91, 103, 104, 106, 109, 114, 126
Sherman, Roger, 256
Shipetauken Creek, 73
Shippen, Chief Justice Edward, 26, 324
Shippen, Elizabeth, 26, 30, 324, 325
Shippen, William, Jr., 202, 200-205, 243, 344
Shippensburg, 2, 241, 344
Short Hills (Metuchen Meeting House), battle of, 132
Short Hills, 204, 208
Shreve, Israel, 173, 218-215, 343
Shreve, John, 343
Sidbotham, Elizabeth, 326
Sidbotham, John, 326
Silesia, Germany, 96
Simpson, William, 28
Sinclair, Mr., 302
Sixth Virginia Regiment, 95
Smallman, Thomas, 96
smallpox, 43-44, 56, 61, 97-98, 114, 192-199, 289, 334
Smallwood, William, 138
Smith, William Bailey, 128
Smith, Devereux, 106
Smith, Samuel, 199
Smith, Matthew, 30, 42
Snowden, Jonathan, 174, 176, 337
Society of the Cincinnati, 259-263, 280, 284, 347
Society of the Friendly Sons of Saint Patrick, 263
Somerset Court House, 80, 333
Somerset, 118, 132
Somerville, 151
South Ann Street, 291
Southern Department, 208
Spaight, Richard Dobbs, 248
Spalding, Simon, 176
Spencer, 170
Springfield, battle of, 202-205, 218, 343
Sprout, William, 176

Spruce Street, 230, 243
Squaw Campaign, 114-120, 121-122
St. Leger, Barrimore, 103
St. Clair, Arthur, 72, 76, 215, 243, 246, 264, 266, 273, 347
Standing Stone Flats, 177
Stark, John, 150, 153, 156, 202, 208-205, 215, 340
State House (Philadelphia), 262
Staten Island, 44, 163, 202, 208, 205
Staten Island Ferry, 41
Staunton, Va., 111, 123
Steel(e), Archibald, 109, 326
Steel(e), John, 47, 326
Steenrapie, 208
Steuben, Baron Friedrich von, 138, 215, 237, 241-242, 260, 266, 272
Steuben Street, 98
Stevenson, John, 118
Stevenson, Robert, 333
Stewart, Charles, 340
Stillbrook Hill, 2
Stillwater, battle of, 341
Stirling, Lord, 48, 49-51, 56, 61, 64, 71, 132, 167, 199, 207, 205, 215, 237
Stockton Hollow, 74, 75
Stockton Street, 332
Stokes, William, 323
Stone, Thomas, 255
Stony Point, 135, 239
Stony Brook, 78
Stoops, Jane, 99
Stoops, James, 99
Stroud, Jacob, 166
Stryker, William, 74
Stump, Frederick, 7
Sufferance, 132
Sullivan, John, 24, 36, 40, 43, 46, 56, 57, 64, 70, 78-80, 143, 151, 163-194, 193, 251, 248, 266, 327, 347
Sullivan Expedition, 24, 151-194, 199, 208, 218, 253, 272, 310, 324, 333

Sullivan, Daniel, 121
Sunbury, 165-165, 173, 174, 187, 328
Supreme Executive Council, 93, 102, 104, 105, 165, 165, 192-187, 236, 243, 261-259, 328, 349
Surgeon's Mate, 2, 3, 5
Surphlitt, Robin, 127
Susquehanna River Valley, 144, 187
Susquehanna(h) River, 103, 141, 152, 156, 160, 161, 164-166, 168, 170, 175, 177, 281
Susquehannock Indians, 351
Sussex Court House, 132
Switzerland, 241-248

T

Tappan, 215, 297
Tarrytown, 214
Taylor, Henry, 103
Tecumseh wars, 334
Telenemut (See Thomas Hudson), 187
Ten Broeck, Abraham, 156
Tenth Pennsylvania Regiment, 333
Ternay, Chevalier de, 207
Thacher, James, 23, 213, 224, 297
Thaosagwat, 188
Thirteenth Virginia Regiment, 93, 111, 114
Thirty-fourth Regiment of Foot, 5
Thomasson, Thomas, 12
Thompson, William, land speculator, 13
Thompson, Robert, 244
Thompson, William, 19, 20-21, 26, 27, 32, 34, 35, 87, 266, 341
Thornsburg Bridge, 98
Throg's Neck, 62, 328
Tilghman, Tench, 205
Tioga River, 192, 344
Tioga Point, 148, 153, 164, 168, 177, 180, 181, 187, 192, 344
Tobago, 226
torture tree, 189-190
Tory, 126, 143, 152, 159, 179, 231,

344
Towanda *Republican*, 147
Town Destroyer, 192
Treaty of Paris, 24, 97, 228, 246, 253, 259, 341
Treaty of Canandaigua, 338
Trenton Falls, 68
Trenton, 67-71, 75, 118, 119, 132, 215, 220, 257, 252, 259
Trenton, battle of, 23, 68-70, 79, 191, 207, 246, 244, 262, 327, 328, 329, 331, 340, 346, 347
Trevelyan, Sir George Otto, 81
Trinity College, 2, 323
Trinity Lutheran Church, 328
Trumbull, Joseph, 329, 339
Tunkhannock Creek, 178
Tuttle, John, 220
Twigtwee (Miami) Indians, 108
typhus, 212, 341

U

Unadilla, 152
Unadilla River, 152
Union Township, 206
United States Congress, 246, 289, 291, 294
United States Provincial Army, 284-285

V

Valentine's Tavern, 60
Valley Forge, 120, 123, 134, 137, 192, 210, 333, 334
Van Anglen, John, 176
Vanderlip, Frederick, 178
Varnum, James, 43
Verplank(e) Point, 239
Virginia House of delegates, 322
Virginians, 7
Virginia State Senate, 125
Virgin, Reason, 118
Von Block, 74
Von Lingsingen, 74

W

Wait, Jason, 184
Wallace House, 151
Walnut Street, Philadelphia, 44
Warner, Seth, 153
Washington Avenue, 332
Washington County, 329, 337
Washington Crossing State Park, 330
Washington: George, 21; at Cambridge, 23-36; battle of New York, 39-64; White Plains, 62-64; retreat through New Jersey, and New Jersey Campaign (Trenton, Assunpinck, and Princeton), 67-81; while General Hand is at Fort Pitt, 82-138; the Sullivan campaign, 151-194, Yorktown campaign, 191-230; at Newburgh, 235-244; 251, 255, 277, 280-283; as President, 270-285; Society of the Cincinnati, 259-263; Friends of Saint Patrick, 263-270;Whiskey Rebellion, 272-273; entertained in Lancaster, 277-285; death of George Washington, 285-287; 295, 300, 327, 331, 338, 352; Martha, 199; Mary Ball Washington, 331; Samuel Washington, 336
Washington, Pa., 87, 94
Washington Township, 91
Watchung Mountains, 119, 132, 198, 206
Watertown, 33
Watts, Frederick, 49
Wayne, Anthony, 83, 117, 131, 134, 135, 138, 169, 209, 212, 266, 263, 272, 273
Weedon, George, 56, 272, 328
Wein, George, 301-302
Wendaughaland, Chief, 108
West Branch of the Susquehanna,

127, 144
Westchester County, 46, 60, 61, 214
West End (Pittsburgh), 98
Western Department, 23, 85, 86, 87, 89, 92, 99, 100, 102, 104, 111, 123, 129, 134, 136-138, 156, 162, 231, 253, 268, 334, 336, 337, 341
West Indian Islands, 102, 227, 330
Westmoreland County, 88-89, 92-94, 103, 106, 109, 112, 114, 115
West Point, 186, 214, 212, 217, 219, 232, 333, 347
West Steuben Street, 98
Wethersfield, Ct., 211
Wharton, Thomas, 102-105, 113, 114
Wheeling, Va., 91, 98, 109, 112, 114, 126, 128
Whippany, 209, 345
Whiskey Rebellion, 272-273, 325, 346
White Eyes, Chief, 95, 99-100, 101, 108, 115, 122, 334
White Eyes, George Morgan, 334
Whitehill, John, 252
Whitemarsh, 134, 333
Whiteside, Thomas, 250
White Pine Run, 92
White Plains, 60, 61, 222
White Plains, battle of, 23, 62, 76, 346
Widow Meyers' Wayside Inn, 10
Wilkins, John, 4, 12
Wilkinson, James, 28, 70, 72, 325
William and Mary College, 325, 330, 3336
Williamsburg, Va., 96, 104, 226, 232
Williamson, David, 337
Williamsport, Pa., 144
Willing, James, 337
Wilmington, Delaware, 106
Wilson, James, 252, 259, 265, 350
Winchester, 128
Windsor, N. Y., 152
Winter Hill, 27
Wise, Jacob, 134

Wolf Clan, 117-118
Wolftrap Mountain, 2
Woodhull, Nathaniel, 63-64, 329
Worthington, 31
Wright, John, 281
Wright's Ferry, 281, 351
Wyachtanas Indians, 108
Wyalusing, 178, 179
Wyandot Indians, 94, 95, 100-102, 106, 121, 122, 254
Wyoming, 141-149, 152, 154, 155, 158, 161, 162, 164-167, 171-175, 184, 183, 191, 256, 344
Wyoming Military, 176

Y

Yeates, Elizabeth, 325
Yeates, John, 19, 325
Yeates, Judge Jasper, 15, 19, 25-27, 30, 37, 45, 46, 49, 51, 55, 88-89, 93-94, 100, 106, 108, 119-120, 123, 125, 127, 215-216, 227-225, 239, 249, 252, 257-258, 270, 325, 333
Yeates, Sarah, 16
York County, 86, 272, 273, 333
York (Manhattan) Island, 41, 44, 50, 54, 58, 59, 222, 223, 225
York, Pennsylvania, 2, 20, 113, 247, 249, 273, 281
Yorktown, 123, 136, 137, 197, 225, 230, 239, 240
Yorktown campaign, 122, 346
Yorktown, siege of, 24, 64, 227-229, 231-232, 252, 269 328, 335, 347
Youghiogheny River, 116, 118, 336

Z

Zanck, Jacob, 42
Zantzinger, Paul, 283
Zeigler, David, 21, 33
Zeisberger, David, 108
Zion Lutheran Church, 286

ABOUT THE AUTHOR

William ("Bill") Betts is Professor Emeritus of English, Indiana University of Pennsylvania. He is the author of fourteen books including: *Lincoln and the Poets*; *The Evergreen Farm*; *The Hatchet and the Plow: The Life and Times of Chief Cornplanter*; *Rank and Gravity: The Life of General John Armstrong of Carlisle*; *Bombardier John Harris and the Rivers of the Revolution*; and *The Nine Lives of George Washington*. *Sword and Scalpel* is his fifth book on the American Revolution.

Betts is at home, with his wife Jane, in Indiana, Pennsylvania, and Boynton Beach, Florida.

ABOUT THE AUTHOR

William W. ("Bill") Betts is Professor Emeritus of English, Indiana University of Pennsylvania. Among his books are *Lincoln and the Poets*; *The Evergreen Farm*; *Slips That Pass in the Night*; *Bombardier John Harris and the Rivers of the Revolution*; and *The Hatchet and the Plow: The Life and Times of Chief Cornplanter*. With his wife Jane, he is at home in Indiana, Pennsylvania; Nobel, Ontario; and Boynton Beach, Florida.

www.ingramcontent.com/pod-product-compliance
Lightning Source LLC
Chambersburg PA
CBHW051626230426
43669CB00013B/2191